BARRON'S

CORRECTION OFFICER EXAM

5TH EDITION

Donald J. Schroeder, Ph.D.

Adjunct Professor
John Jay College of Criminal Justice

Senior Instructor
REMS Tutorial, Exam Preparation Specialists

Former Commanding Officer
81st Police Precinct, New York City Police Department

Frank A. Lombardo

Deputy Inspector (retired)
New York City Police Department

Adjunct Professor
John Jay College of Criminal Justice

Former Commanding Officer
30th Police Precinct, New York City Police Department

BARRON'S

Published by Kaplan, Inc., d/b/a Barron's Educational Series
750 Third Avenue
New York, NY 10017
www.barronseduc.com

ISBN: 978-1-4380-1293-3

10 9 8 7 6 5 4 3 2 1

Kaplan, Inc., d/b/a Barron's Educational Series print books are available at special quantity discounts to use for sales promotions, employee premiums, or educational purposes. For more information or to purchase books, please call the Simon & Schuster special sales department at 866-506-1949.

CONTENTS

CORRECT YOUR WEAKNESSES

A FINAL WORD

Preface

This book has been written to assist men and women who are seeking careers in those corrections agencies at the local, state and federal levels that select entry level personnel via a written examination. As the courts exert more and more pressure on public agencies to hire in the strict rank order produced by competitive exams, the importance of passing such examinations with the highest possible mark becomes obvious.

That is what this book can do for you. It can assist you in obtaining the highest possible mark by familiarizing you with the kinds of questions that typically find their way onto entry level correctional examinations. More important, it will acquaint you with different strategies to use while answering these various types of questions. By following our recommended test-taking strategies, you will be able to arrive at the correct answers quickly.

New to this edition are explanations of three new question types: Sentence Ordering Questions, Find the Next Step Questions, and Spatial Orientation Questions. Also included are recommended strategies for answering each question type quickly and accurately, examples of each question type, and practice questions with explained answers. In addition, the overall strategies for taking multiple-choice questions have been updated to reflect feedback we have received from students concerning these strategies in connection with recent exams.

Through this book we offer you many tips and helpful hints we have taught students in our many years of coaching candidates to successfully pass civil service examinations. There is one basic rule that cannot be disputed: SUCCESS IN TAKING CIVIL SERVICE TESTS REQUIRES DEDICATION AND HARD WORK. If you are willing to do that, then this book can help you be as successful as possible in your efforts to become a correction officer. Good Luck!

Donald J. Schroeder
Frank A. Lombardo

ACKNOWLEDGMENTS

We would like to thank the many men and women working as correction officers throughout the country for their help, counsel, and guidance in making this book reflect what correction officers actually do. In addition, we would like to formally acknowledge the fine job they do in their very difficult task of maintaining our correctional system.

CORRECTIONAL OFFICERS CREED

Bob Barrington

International Association of Correctional Officers (IACO)

To speak sparingly ... to act, not to argue ... to be in authority through personal presence ... to correct without nagging ... to speak with the calm voice of certainty ... to see everything, know what is significant and what not to notice ... to be neither insensitive to distress nor so distracted by pity as to miss what must elsewhere be seen ...

To do that which is neither unkind nor self-indulgent in its misplaced charity ... never to obey the impulse to tongue lash that silent insolence which in times past could receive the lash ... to be both firm and fair ... to know I cannot be fair simply by being firm, nor firm simply by being fair ....

To support the reputation of associates and confront them without anger, should they stand short of professional conduct ... to reach for knowledge of the continuing mysteries of human motivation ... to think, always to think ... to be dependable ... to be dependable first to my charges and associates, and thereafter to my duty as employee and citizen ... to keep fit ... to keep forever alert ... to listen to what is meant as well as what is said with words and with silence ...

To expect respect from my charges and my superiors yet never to abuse the one for abuses from the other ... for eight hours each working day to be an example of the person I could be at all times ... to acquiesce in no dishonest act ... to cultivate patience under boredom and calm during confusion ... to understand the why of every order I take or give ...

To hold freedom among the highest values though I deny it to those I guard ... to deny it with dignity that in my example they find no reason to lose their dignity ... to be prompt ... to be honest with all who practice deceit that they not find in me excuse for themselves ... to privately face down my fear that I not signal it ... to privately cool my anger that I not displace it on others ... to hold in confidence what I see and hear, which by the telling could harm or humiliate to no good purpose ... to keep my outside problems outside ... to leave inside that which should stay inside ... to do my duty.

Introduction

About the Correction Officer Exam

→ **OVERVIEW OF THE JOB**

→ **BENEFITS OF A CAREER AS A CORRECTION OFFICER**

→ **GENERAL JOB REQUIREMENTS**

→ **SAMPLE TEST ANNOUNCEMENT**

→ **STEPS TO BECOMING A CORRECTION OFFICER**

WHAT YOU SHOULD KNOW ABOUT THE ENTRANCE TEST

The type of correction officer examination that is administered throughout the country to select qualified men and women for careers in the correctional field has been modified greatly over the past decade. As a result of a Supreme Court decision a number of years ago, test writers are not permitted to use certain kinds of questions. For example, it is against the law to ask questions that require prior knowledge of the law, correctional procedures, or the specific duties and responsibilities of a correction officer. As a candidate, you are not required to know what procedure a correction officer should follow under certain circumstances, such as when he or she witnesses an escape attempt. That is the kind of knowledge you acquire after you become a correction officer and are trained by the correction agency. Therefore, it is a waste of time to prepare for the correction officer examination by learning the law or by memorizing correctional procedures.

The material presented in this book, including the hundreds and hundreds of practice questions, was written after a careful analysis of recent major correction officer examinations and court decisions relating to entrance level testing procedures. And, all the questions in the book are related to the job of the correction officer. This is important because you will see these kinds of questions when you take the official correction officer examination. Therefore, we are confident that using this book will help you achieve your goal of becoming a correction officer.

WHAT A CORRECTION OFFICER DOES

Because you are planning to take the correction officer examination, it seems fitting to provide you with an overall view of the job of a correction officer.

First, however, it is important to recognize the correction officer duties performed by many of the Sheriff's Departments throughout the United States. In such agencies, Sheriff's Department personnel often perform correction officer duties similar to those described below in such settings as large county prisons and local jails. Therefore, throughout this text, when reference is made to the role of correction officers, it includes the roles of many of the sheriffs and deputy sheriffs under their command.

Correction officers are responsible for the safekeeping of incarcerated persons, who are confined in institutions that are called by many names including jails, prisons, and detention centers. A correction officer's responsibility includes providing for the safety and well-being of the population of the entire institution, not just the inmate population. Correction officers must work closely at various times with such other professionals as social workers, probation or parole officers, police officers, psychiatrists, psychologists, and lawyers. After proper training, correction officers also become involved in the counseling of inmates.

The following tasks are commonly performed by correction officers as part of their everyday duties.

SECURITY-RELATED TASKS. Correction officers ensure the physical security of the institution. They do this by patrolling a wall post or engaging in access control on a gate post. Wall posts guard the perimeter of the institution, whereas access control posts regulate movement in and out of the facility through points of entry and exit such as gates. In addition, correction officers must constantly check on the security of doors, windows, and locks of all kinds.

SCREENING TASKS. Correction officers must constantly guard against allowing any and all contraband, especially weapons and drugs, into the facility. Naturally this screening function includes making sure that only authorized persons are allowed into the institution.

ORDER CONTROL. Maintaining order is essential to a well-run correctional institution. Correction officers must be constantly alert to the possibility of disorder. At times they must use physical force to maintain this much needed order, such as breaking up a fight among inmates.

TRANSPORTATION. Every day inmates must travel from their place of detention to various public destinations such as local or state courtrooms. At no time is the potential for escape higher. During these times, correction officers must be extra vigilant to prevent escape.

REPORTING. The essence of a correction officer's job is reporting. Officers act as the eyes and the ears of the rest of the institutional staff.

INMATE CLASSIFICATION. Inmates are housed in prisons according to their behavior and their potential for either engaging in violence or escaping. Correction officers play a key role in this process. They interview inmates and observe and report their behavior.

FIRST AID. In many prison systems, correction officers administer first aid in emergencies.

EMERGENCY SITUATION CONTROL. During instances of widespread riotous behavior or escapes, correction officers might be required to use weapons, such as chemical agents, water cannons, and firearms. These situations could also require some officers to engage in hostage negotiations.

Where a Correction Officer Works

Wherever prisoners are detained after they leave the custody of the police, you will find correction officers. They work in local holding pens where prisoners await arraignment, in jails where prisoners wait for disposition of their cases or where they serve sentences of less than one year, in hospitals where they receive medical treatment, or in prisons where inmates serve sentences of more than one year. These prisons can be either maximum-, medium-, or minimum-security facilities depending on the actual or perceived risk posed by the inmate population.

> **THE JOB IN A NUTSHELL**
>
> Security
> Screening
> Order Control
> Transportation
> Reporting
> Inmate Classification
> First Aid
> Emergency Control

As one might expect, these facilities could be located in urban, suburban, or rural areas. Therefore, we can safely say that interested persons can find employment as correction officers almost anywhere in the country.

Special Working Conditions

Correction officers are required to work on weekends, nights, and holidays. In addition, they often have to work rotating shifts, and they must work overtime when ordered. Furthermore, they may be required to walk or stand in an assigned area for up to 17 hours continuously. Some other physical activities performed and environmental conditions experienced by correction officers include the following: possibly physically restraining an inmate; working outdoors in all possible weather conditions; coming into close contact with inmates; dealing with various inmate categories, such as minors and those with mental problems; lifting heavy objects; and utilizing heavy equipment.

Job Opportunities

The prison population in the United States is at an all-time high and is expected to increase as society continues to wage its war against career criminals. All over the country we are seeing construction of new correctional facilities. Not only is employment of correction officers at an all-time high, but it is also increasing at a rate much higher than almost any other occupation.

The Benefits of a Career as a Correction Officer

The many material benefits typically associated with the position of correction officer follow.

JOB SECURITY. Correction officers, like police and fire officers, are civil servants. Their employment is regulated by Civil Service Law. They have the same job security as all other civil servants.

SALARY. While salary rates for correction officers vary from one jurisdiction to another, it is safe to say that correction officers all over the nation are always among some of the highest paid entry-level civil servants.

INSURANCE BENEFITS. Most correction officers are, as part of their compensation, covered by health, dental, prescription drug, optical, and life insurance.

LEAVE BENEFITS. Correction officers have very liberal leave benefits, which include time off at full pay for annual leave, personal leave, bereavement leave, workers' compensation leave, and sick leave.

> **CAREER BENEFITS**
>
> Job Security
> Salary
> Insurance Benefits
> Leave Benefits
> Retirement Benefits
> Promotional Opportunities

RETIREMENT BENEFITS. Most correction officers are part of the civil employee's retirement system in the state where they are employed. Normal retirement age in many state systems is 62 years old. However, in most cases, correction officers are allowed to retire after 20 or 25 years of service regardless of their age. This means that early retirement is the norm for correction officers.

PROMOTIONAL OPPORTUNITIES. Civil service promotion examinations are very seldom open to the general public. Promotion is from within the employing agency. For this reason, promotional opportunity is one of the most attractive features of the correction officer's job with examinations leading to assistant warden and even warden.

OTHER BENEFITS. Correction officers, depending on where they work, often receive such other benefits as credit union membership, consumer buying power, uniform allowances, education and training incentives, and disability insurance.

GENERAL JOB REQUIREMENTS

Because an overwhelming number of correction officer jobs are civil service positions, the minimum requirements for such jobs are established by the Civil Service Law in the jurisdiction involved. This, of course, makes it impossible to list one definitive set of job requirements. To get the specific information for the job you are seeking, you must contact the civil service agency that is offering the job. However, we have compiled the following set of typical job requirements to give you a general idea of the most commonly accepted standards of employment in the correctional field. If you believe you may have a problem meeting any of these standards, you should be especially alert for them and specifically inquire about any such standard when you apply for the position of correction officer. Such questions should be resolved before you spend a lot of time and effort attempting to become a correction officer.

These standards follow.

> **JOB REQUIREMENTS**
>
> Age Requirements
> Good Character
> Education
> Citizenship
> Medical/Psychological
>   Standards
> Height/Weight
>   Requirements
> Drug Screening
> Probationary Period
> Residency
> Language
> Physical Fitness
> Driver's License

AGE REQUIREMENTS. As is true for many civil service jobs, age requirements for federal, state, and local correction officer positions are in a state of flux. This is especially true for maximum age requirements. Therefore, we strongly suggest that candidates check age requirements for the agency they are interested in joining to receive definitive information. As a general rule, though, candidates must be at least 17½ years of age on the date they take the civil service entrance test. However, they usually must be 18 years of age to be appointed as a correction officer, although in many jurisdictions the minimum age requirement is 21 years of age. Candidates who are too young for appointment when they otherwise become eligible are usually put on a special list. These individuals are then offered employment when they reach the minimum age unless the entire list is terminated prior to that time. Concerning maximum age requirements, the growing trend is to eliminate them. However, many agencies still have a maximum age requirement, which is usually 35 years of age. Note, however, that former military personnel generally have a tolerance equal to the amount of time they spent in the military. For example, if the maximum age for a nonmilitary applicant is 35, then the maximum age for an applicant with five years military service would be 40. However, to be sure of the specific age requirements, check with the agency you are interested in joining.

CHARACTER. Proof of good character is an absolute must for all correction officer positions. However, what is considered to be "good character" varies from jurisdiction to jurisdiction once again determined by the Civil Service Law in effect in that jurisdiction. As a general rule, however, any of the following circumstances would typically be cause for disqualification:

- A criminal conviction for a felony
- A series of criminal convictions regardless of the seriousness of the underlying charges
- Evidence that indicates a propensity for violence
- A history of repeated firings from jobs or long periods of unexplained unemployment
- Dishonorable discharge from the Armed Services

The background investigation that is conducted to determine if candidates meet the character requirements is usually quite thorough and somewhat time-consuming, and it always includes the taking of the candidate's fingerprints. Candidates who are preparing to undergo a background investigation can speed up the process by having ready for the investigator originals or certified copies of such documents as birth certificates, diplomas, military discharge papers, driver's licenses, and naturalization papers if appropriate. If a candidate has one or more arrests, then complete documentation of the details involved is essential. Candidates who are awaiting such an investigation should also prepare a chronological listing of employment from the day they finished attending school on a full-time basis to the present time.

THE PRISON RAPE ELIMINATION ACT (PREA). An appointment as a correction officer is subject to the mandates of the federal regulations of the Prison Rape Elimination Act (PREA). In accordance with these regulations, correction agencies will not hire or promote anyone who may have contact with the prison population and who has engaged in sexual abuse in a prison, jail, lockup, community confinement facility, juvenile facility, or other institution (as defined in 42 U.S.C. 1997) or who has been convicted or civilly or administratively adjudicated to have engaged or attempted to engage in sexual activity in the community facilitated by force, overt or implied threats of force, or coercion, or if the victim did not consent or was unable to consent.

EDUCATION. A minimum of a high school diploma or its equivalent, which usually must be obtained by the date of appointment, is the most prevalent educational requirement. Some jurisdictions, such as New York City, require 60 college credits or two years of military service. These jurisdictions usually permit candidates who do not meet these requirements to take the entrance examination, but they must obtain the college credits or complete military service to be appointed.

CITIZENSHIP. United States citizenship at the time of appointment is an almost universal standard for employment as a correction officer.

MEDICAL AND PSYCHOLOGICAL STANDARDS. Prior to appointment, eligible candidates must meet the medical and psychological standards set by the hiring agency. Any candidate who has a medical or psychological problem that would impair his or her ability to carry out the duties of a correction officer will be disqualified. Candidates are required to reveal their medical history to the doctors who perform the medical examination. It is strongly suggested that those candidates who have had a medical problem that resulted in hospitalization obtain, if possible, a letter from their personal physicians stating that they are now fit to do the job of a correction officer. This letter should then be shown to the doctors from the employing agency along with the other pertinent information about the specific medical problem.

Another important consideration concerning the medical and psychological component of the entry process is the appeals process. The Civil Service Law in almost every jurisdiction allows candidates to appeal the findings of the medical and psychological board of the hiring agency. However, such appeals always have to be made on a timely basis. If you must appeal, make sure that you do so in accordance with the time frames set forth in the law.

Here is one final word in this area. Most civil service hiring rules require correction officer eligibles to pass an eyesight examination, including a color vision test, but they usually allow such eligibles to wear corrective lenses to do so. If you have poor unaided vision, however, you should investigate the eyesight requirement before you make a significant commitment of time and effort to determine if you will be able to meet the standards for the job you are seeking.

HEIGHT AND WEIGHT REQUIREMENTS. In the great majority of cases, there is no minimum height requirement prescribed as a requisite for employment as a correction officer. But, there are usually weight requirements. Such weight requirements are determined by a candidate's height and body frame. In other words, to be eligible for appointment, a candidate's weight must be proportionate to the candidate's height and frame. Body frame is usually categorized into small frame, medium frame, and large frame. The examining doctor from the hiring agency determines the applicable frame size of a candidate. Exceptions are generally made in those cases where excess weight is deemed by the examining doctor to be lean body mass and not fat. For those of you who think you might be overweight, we recommend that you seek a doctor's opinion and then, if necessary, initiate a weight reduction program under medical supervision.

DRUG SCREENING TEST. Eligibles for the position of correction officer are subject to drug screening tests. One of the major responsibilities of a correction officer is to guard against the introduction of illegal drugs into correctional institutions. It follows that those with drug problems of their own are not well suited to perform this important task. Such persons might be inappropriately sympathetic with other drug users, and/or they might be tempted to violate their trust to obtain illegal drugs for their own use. The important point is that candidates who use illegal drugs will not be accepted as correction officers and will be disqualified because of their drug habits.

PROBATIONARY PERIOD. Almost every correctional agency requires newly hired officers to successfully complete a probationary period before they become fully tenured civil service employees with all the rights and privileges that accompany such tenure. The average length of such probationary periods is about 18 months. During this time, probationary correction officers are required to successfully complete a training course that has academic and physical fitness components and, in many cases, a firearms component. Many agencies also require probationary officers to pass another full medical examination at the end of the probationary period. Candidates must understand that during this probationary period they can be dismissed by an agency and such dismissals are not subject to court review. It is a term of employment. Therefore, the conduct of candidates who are serving probationary periods must be exemplary both on and off duty. Serious off-duty indiscretions are cause for dismissals. Although this is also true for tenured employees (those who are not on probation), tenured employees usually have many avenues of appeal to such decisions. This is not true for those who are on probation.

RESIDENCY REQUIREMENTS. Civil Service Law typically imposes residency requirements on correction officers. Usually, such requirements must be met on the date of appointment, not on test day. As such, you can take the test even if you do not reside in the appropriate jurisdictions, but you would have to change your residence prior to appointment if you are offered the position.

LANGUAGE REQUIREMENT. The essence of a correction officer's job is communication. In recognition of this fact, candidates are usually required to demonstrate an ability to understand and be understood in the English language. In many cases, if there is doubt about a candidate's ability to do so, the hiring agency administers an oral test. It should also be noted that, in some cases, candidates who can demonstrate an ability to understand and be understood in a second language, such as Spanish, are given special consideration, most often in the form of additional points added to their written test scores.

PHYSICAL FITNESS TEST. Prior to becoming a tenured correction officer, candidates generally must pass a physical fitness test. This is done in two ways. In some cases the test is administered prior to appointment as part of the hiring process. In other cases, the physical fitness test is administered after hiring as part of the probationary process. Of all the components of the hiring and probationary processes, none is more varied from jurisdiction to jurisdiction than the physical fitness components. However, successful completion of some sort of obstacle course, during which candidates must demonstrate an ability to run, push weighted objects, jump over hurdles, and lift and carry weighted dummies, all within a certain time period, is a very common requirement. Our experience with the physical fitness test has convinced us that, with proper preparation, most candidates can successfully pass it. The key phrase is "with proper preparation." When the test is administered as part of the probationary period, this proper preparation is built into the physical fitness component of the official training curriculum. The physical fitness component is more of a problem when it is administered as part of the hiring process. When this is the case, we always strongly advise candidates to find out the specifics of the physical fitness test and to prepare for it. In many cases, the hiring agencies offer interested candidates the opportunity to prepare for the physical fitness test at no cost. If this is the case in your jurisdiction, we strongly urge you to take advantage of the opportunity.

DRIVER'S LICENSE. Most correctional agencies require candidates to possess a valid driver's license at the date of appointment. We are often asked by candidates whether a history of traffic or parking violations would have an impact on their eligibility to become correction officers. We tell them that the major consideration in this area is whether or not there are any outstanding violations that they have neglected to respond to. Ignoring official citations would definitely have a negative impact on your character investigation. Therefore, should you have any outstanding traffic or parking citations, you should clear them up before your background investigation.

SAMPLE TEST ANNOUNCEMENT

As you can see, there is not just one standard set of requirements for the position of correction officer. Your task is to find out the specific requirements for the position you are seeking. The first step toward obtaining this information is to obtain the "Test Announcement" for that position. This announcement will supply you with general information about that job, the requirements for that job, and the steps to follow to obtain that job. To assist you, we have included a sample test announcement, also referred to as a job announcement or a notice of examination, so that you can read and become familiar with what typically appears on such announcements. You must understand, however, that the information included on our sample announcement is general information, not specific information. Once again, you must get the test announcement to learn the specific information about the job you are seeking. We also remind you that the specifics listed on a test announcement very often change from test to test so it is a mistake to believe that the requirements for the last examination will definitely be the same as the requirements for an upcoming examination.

SAMPLE TEST ANNOUNCEMENT
FOR CORRECTION OFFICER

EXAMINATION NUMBER 007

APPLICATION INFORMATION

APPLICATION FEE: There is a nonrefundable application fee of $35.00, payable by money order only. Money orders must be made payable to the Commissioner of the Department of Personnel. The name and number of the test as well as the applicant's social security number must be included on the money order. This application fee will be waived for applicants receiving welfare assistance who submit proof of their welfare status along with their application.

APPLICATION PERIOD: From May 3rd through June 30th. Completed applications may be submitted by mail or in person to the Hiring Unit of the Department of Personnel, 300 Broadway, Metropolis, zip code 00000. Applications must be postmarked no later than midnight on June 30th, 20xx.

SALARY: Annual salary of $80,000.00 after 5 years of service. In addition there is paid health insurance, holiday pay, an annuity plan, 21-days paid vacation, unlimited sick leave, life insurance, a uniform allowance, tuition reimbursement for higher education, and participation in the Metropolis Retirement System.

LIFE OF THE LIST: The eligible list established as a result of Correction Officer Examination Number 007 shall be at least 1 year but not more than 4 years. However, the list shall be automatically terminated upon the promulgation of a subsequent list for the position of Correction Officer.

REQUIREMENTS TO QUALIFY

AGE REQUIREMENTS: Applicants must have reached their 21st birthday before they are appointed. Those who are too young when they are called for appointment shall go on a special list and become eligible for appointment upon attaining the age of 21 unless the entire list is terminated prior to that time. There is no maximum age requirement.

EDUCATION STANDARDS: By the time you are appointed to this position you must have:

■ earned 39 semester credits at an accredited college or university. In addition, you must complete an additional 21 semester credits, which may be satisfied by successful completion of Academy training, to total 60 semester credits by the end of Academy training; or,

■ a four year high school diploma or its equivalent, and have completed two years of honorable full-time U.S. military service.

DRIVER'S LICENSE: By the date of appointment, possession of a valid driver's license is required.

RESIDENCY STANDARDS: There are no residence requirements for participation in the examination. By the date of appointment, applicants must reside within the boundaries of Metropolis.

CITIZENSHIP: By the date of appointment, United States citizenship is required.

MEDICAL STANDARDS: Eligibles will be refused employment should they have a medical condition that significantly limits their ability to perform the tasks required of a correction officer. Details on medical requirements, including eyesight requirements, are posted at the Medical Unit of the Department of Personnel and are available upon request.

PSYCHOLOGICAL STANDARDS: Candidates are required to pass a battery of standard psychological tests and may also be required to appear for personal psychological evaluation.

PHYSICAL FITNESS STANDARDS: Candidates are required to pass a job-related physical agility test at a yet undetermined date after the written test. Details of this physical fitness test are posted at the Medical Unit of the Department of Personnel and are available upon request. Prior to the administration of this test, all eligibles will be offered an opportunity to train for the physical agility test at a site yet to be selected. Details concerning this no-cost training and the actual physical agility test will be sent to all eligibles via United States mail.

BACKGROUND STANDARDS: Prior to hiring, each eligible will be fingerprinted and subject to an intensive background investigation and a criminal history search which is to be conducted by the Metropolis Police Department Applicant Investigation Unit. Conviction of any felony will be an absolute bar to appointment. All other convictions will be considered on a case by case basis. As part of the background investigation, all eligibles will be required to participate in substance abuse testing prior to appointment and thereafter at any time during the probationary period. Candidates whose overall background is not deemed suitable as determined by the appointing authority shall be rejected. Candidates who fail to cooperate fully with their assigned investigators or who fail to present required documents are also subject to rejection.

LANGUAGE STANDARDS: All candidates must be proficient in the English language so as to be able to communicate orally and in writing at a level established by the Metropolis Department of Corrections. Candidates may be required to pass a communications test at any time prior to the completion of their probationary period.

JOB INFORMATION

PROBATIONARY PERIOD: Each appointed eligible will be required to successfully complete an 18-month probationary period during which they shall have the title of Probationary Correction Officer. Candidates must understand that the probationary period is an extension of the selection process and that they are subject to continuous evaluation during their entire period of probation. Those who do not successfully complete the probationary period shall be rejected with no right to appeal.

TRAINING REQUIREMENTS: Upon appointment and prior to assignment, each probationary correction officer must successfully complete a 12-week training program at the Metropolis Correction Academy. Those who do successfully complete this training will be granted peace officer status.

CORRECTION OFFICER DUTIES AND RESPONSIBILITIES: Correction officers may be required to supervise inmates of either sex. Their responsibilities include protecting life and property and maintaining order and security in a correctional facility. To carry out these responsibilities, correction officers may be given a wide variety of assignments, such as

- Transporting prisoners
- Visiting room supervision
- Perimeter patrol
- Yard patrol
- Gate security
- Fixed wall posts
- Hospital posts
- Canine patrol
- Cell block security
- Mess hall patrol

To meet their responsibilities, correction officers may be required to work rotating tours and shifts that include nights, weekends, and holidays. And, under certain circumstances, correction officers are prohibited from refusing overtime assignments.

WRITTEN TEST INFORMATION

TEST DATE: To be announced. All candidates will receive notification via the United States mail as to the date and time of the examination. Such notification will be given at least 2 weeks in advance of the test date.

ADMISSION CARD: Applicants will not be admitted to the test site without an admission card. Such cards will be sent to candidates via United States mail. Those candidates who do not receive an admission card at least 5 days prior to the announced test date must appear personally at the Admissions Unit of the Department of Personnel between 9:00 A.M. and 5:00 P.M. on one of the 5 days preceding the test to obtain their admission card.

TEST DESCRIPTION: The written test will be of the multiple-choice type and will consist of 100 questions to be answered in a 3½ hour period. It will contain questions to test your memory; your verbal and mathematical ability; your ability to comprehend written material; your ability to complete and interpret forms, charts, and tables; your ability to apply procedures; your reasoning ability; and your ability to understand legal definitions.

PASSING SCORE: The passing score will be determined and announced after statistical analysis of the results of the test.

APPEALS: Within 60 days after the administration of the test, a tentative scoring key will be published. Candidates who petition the Department of Personnel to do so will be allowed to appeal this tentative key providing they do so within 30 days of the publication of the tentative scoring key.

NOTIFICATION OF RESULTS: All applicants who actually took the test will receive notification via the mail of their final test score and, if appropriate, their place on the eligible list within 60 days of the end of the appeals period.

THE STEPS TO BECOMING A CORRECTION OFFICER

1. Determine the date of the next test. This can be done by watching the civil service newspaper that services the area where you are seeking employment. Or, you can contact the civil service agency that administers the test. A third option is to call the training unit of the correction agency you are interested in joining. The bottom line is—do not be afraid to ask. Correction departments want good people. You are taking the time to prepare yourself for the examination and, therefore, have begun to qualify as one of the candidates that correction departments would want.

2. Obtain a test announcement.

3. File an application.

4. Prepare for and pass the written test.

5. Prepare for and take the physical agility test, if required, before appointment.

6. Take the medical examination.

7. Take the psychological examination.

8. Prepare for and undergo the background investigation. (Note that steps 5–8 may occur in a different sequence.)

9. Get appointed.

10. Attend and successfully complete a training school.

11. Successfully complete your probationary period.

A NOTE FROM YOUR AUTHORS

Don't be discouraged by the apparent complexity of the required steps you must take to become a correction officer. Such a job is both rewarding and satisfying. It offers financial security and promotional opportunities plus a liberal retirement benefit. Pursue the job. Make it your goal. Use this book to help you. Remember, all correction officers were once in the position you are in right now. They did it, and you can too!

How to Maximize
Your Test Score

→ **GOOD STUDY HABITS**

→ **TEN STUDY RULES**

→ **STRATEGIES FOR COMPUTER BASED EXAMS**

→ **MULTIPLE-CHOICE QUESTION STRATEGIES**

→ **A TIME-MANAGEMENT PLAN**

→ **TESTS ON VIDEO**

→ **HOW TO USE THIS BOOK**

This section contains information you need to get the best return from your test preparation efforts so that you can achieve the highest possible score on your official correction officer examination. Too many students approach test preparation in a slipshod manner. Consequently, they waste time and do not achieve their potential. The guidelines presented in this chapter are designed to help you avoid such wasted effort.

The first part of this section provides guidelines to help you develop good study habits. Until you are quite familiar with the rules for effective studying contained in this section, you should review them before each study session.

The second part of this section provides specific strategies for dealing with multiple-choice questions. These strategies have been updated to reflect the recent trend in correction officer examinations to use computer-based testing. The era of paper-and-pencil testing is coming to a close. In multiple-choice, computer-based testing, the candidate views the test on a computer monitor and uses a mouse to click on his or her selected answer choices. Although the types of questions being asked remain the same, it is imperative that the candidate use a test-taking strategy geared for computer-based tests. Unfortunately, an unsophisticated test taker can do poorly on such an examination simply because of a lack of familiarity with the computer-based program. Don't let this happen to you. The whole matter is complicated by the fact that the traditional paper-and-pencil examination is still used in some jurisdictions. You must find out which testing method is used for the examination you are taking—paper-and-pencil or computer-based—and then use the appropriate test-taking strategy.

Also included in the second part of this section are specific strategies for dealing with material distributed in advance of the test and with tests that contain a video component. If the test you are taking includes material distributed in advance and/or a video component, understanding and mastering these strategies is vitally important.

Make sure that you review the strategies appearing later in this text dealing with the handling of multiple-choice questions before taking each of the full-length examinations included in this book. Finally, be sure to practice these strategies while taking these examinations. In time, the strategies will become second nature and your organized approach to answering multiple-choice questions will serve you well.

TIP

If you don't know how to use a computer, learn!

Please note that some of the practice questions in this book are based on laws, rules, policies, and procedures that are similar to those that might be found in a typical correctional agency. Do not assume, however, that they are the exact laws, rules, policies, and procedures that are actually in use in any specific correctional agency.

Also note that the difficulty level of the practice questions appearing in this book is, in most cases, higher than what you may encounter on your official examination. *This is a very important point for you to understand.*

If you can learn to master the questions in this book, you should have great success on your official examination. We caution you again, however, that if you are taking a computer-based multiple-choice question test, you must understand the specific strategy required to do well on such an examination. Also, remember not to get discouraged if you miss some questions when tackling the questions in this book. Instead, study the explained answers provided for every question to learn why you got them wrong, and avoid such errors in the future.

GOOD STUDY HABITS—THE KEY TO SUCCESS

Many students incorrectly believe that the amount of time spent studying is the most important factor in test preparation. Of course, all else being equal, the amount of time you devote to your studies is a critical factor. But spending time reading is not necessarily studying. If you want to learn what you read, you must develop a system. For example, a student who devotes 60 minutes a day to uninterrupted study in a quiet, private setting will generally learn more than someone who puts in twice that time by studying five or six times a day for shorter intervals of time.

TEN RULES FOR STUDYING MORE EFFECTIVELY

We have listed a number of rules for you to follow to increase study-time efficiency. If you abide by these rules, you will get the most out of this book.

TIP

Make friends with your dictionary.

1. **MAKE SURE YOU UNDERSTAND THE MEANING OF EVERY WORD YOU READ.** Your ability to understand what you read is the most important skill needed to pass the correction officer examination. Therefore, starting immediately, every time you see a word that you don't fully understand, make certain that you write it down and make note of where you saw it. Then, when you have a chance, look up the meaning of the word in the dictionary. When you think you know what the word means, go back and apply the meaning of the word to the written material that contained the word. Make certain that you fully understand its meaning as well as the written material that contained the word.

   Keep a list of all words you don't know and periodically review them. Also, try to use these words whenever you can in conversation. If you do this faithfully, you will quickly build an extensive vocabulary that will help you not only when you take the correction officer examination, but for the rest of your life.

2. **STUDY UNINTERRUPTED FOR AT LEAST 30 MINUTES.** Unless you can study for at least an uninterrupted period of 30 minutes, you should not bother to study at all. It is essential that you learn to concentrate for extended periods of time. Remember that the actual examination takes anywhere from 3 to 5 hours to complete. You must be prepared to concentrate just as hard in the final hour of the test as you did in the first hour. Therefore, as the examination date approaches, study for more extended periods

of time without interruption. And, when you take the full-length practice examinations in this book, do a complete examination in one sitting, just as you must do at the actual examination. Remember that not being prepared to concentrate effectively throughout the entire examination is a major reason why many candidates fail! Don't let that happen to you.

3. **SIMULATE EXAMINATION CONDITIONS WHEN STUDYING.** Study alone under the same conditions as those of the examination, as much as possible. Eliminate as many outside interferences as you can. If you are a smoker, refrain from smoking when you study because you will not be allowed to smoke in the classroom on the day of your examination.

4. **STUDY ALONE.** People learn original material best when studying alone. In other words, your first attempt to learn original material should be a solitary endeavor. However, after studying the material, if possible form a study group of from three to five serious students and meet with them for 2 to 3 hours periodically, perhaps every other week. Before each meeting, the members of the group should prepare to discuss one area that will probably appear on the examination. In addition, everyone in the group should keep a list of items they are confused about; these items should be discussed at the study group meetings. Items that no one is certain of should be referred to an outside source, such as a teacher, an active-duty correction officer, a librarian, and so on. Arguing in a study group defeats the purpose of the group and must be avoided at all costs.

5. **MAKE SURE THAT YOU UNDERSTAND THE ANSWERS TO EVERY QUESTION IN THIS BOOK.** Every answer is accompanied by an explanation. Whenever you get a question wrong, be sure to understand why you missed it so you won't make the same mistake again. However, it is equally important to make certain that you have answered a question correctly for the right reason. Therefore, study the answer explanation to every multiple-choice question in this book as carefully as you study the question itself.

6. **ALWAYS FOLLOW OUR RECOMMENDED TECHNIQUE FOR ANSWERING MULTIPLE-CHOICE QUESTIONS.** Before the advent of computer-based testing, this was a relatively easy rule to follow. There was only one strategy to learn and follow. In the next section of this chapter, we provide strategies for those of you who will be taking a computer-based multiple-choice examination. Following that we include general strategies for handling multiple-choice questions. These strategies are written to apply to both the traditional paper-and-pencil examination and the computer-based examination. The strategies you use on the test you take, therefore, depend on which of the two types of tests you will be taking. Remember, you must not assume you will be taking the traditional paper-and-pencil examination. You must make it your business to find out which of the two types of examinations you will be taking.

Use a timer.

7. **ALWAYS TIME YOURSELF WHEN DOING PRACTICE QUESTIONS.** Running out of time on a multiple-choice examination is a tragic error that is easily avoided. Learn, through practice, to move to the next question after you spend a reasonable period of time on any one question. When you are doing practice questions, always time yourself and always try to stay within recommended time limits. The correct use of time during the actual examination is an integral part of the technique that will be explained later in this section.

8. **CONCENTRATE YOUR STUDY TIME IN THE AREAS OF YOUR GREATEST WEAKNESS.** The diagnostic examination will give you an idea of the most difficult question types for you. Even though you should spend most of your study time improving yourself in these areas, do not ignore the other types of questions.

9. **EXERCISE REGULARLY AND STAY IN GOOD PHYSICAL CONDITION.** Students who are in good physical condition have an advantage over those who are not. It is a well-established principle that good physical health improves the ability of the mind to function smoothly and efficiently, especially when taking examinations of extended duration, such as the correction officer examination.

10. **ESTABLISH A SCHEDULE FOR STUDYING AND STICK TO IT.** Do not put off studying to those times when you have nothing else to do. Schedule your study time and try not to let anything interfere with that schedule. If you feel yourself weakening, review the beginning of the introduction and remind yourself of why you would like to become a correction officer.

STRATEGIES FOR TAKING COMPUTER-BASED MULTIPLE-CHOICE EXAMINATIONS

1. **PLAN TO BE FLEXIBLE.** Because computer-based multiple-choice testing is in its infancy, there is no one standard method of structuring these examinations. It is a mistake to believe that all you have to do is learn how one such test was administered. Approach each computer-based test you take with a flexible attitude. As time goes by, standardization will probably occur. For now, however, candidates must understand that an essential element of preparing for every computer-based test they take is to learn as much about the computer process that will be used for that particular examination.

2. **DEVELOP BASIC COMPUTER SKILLS.** Today, most candidates for the correction officer examination will probably be comfortable working with a computer. However, if you do not feel comfortable performing basic computer functions, such as using a mouse and navigating around a computer screen, you probably should avoid computer-based testing. A better alternative, however, would be to develop these basic computer skills.

3. **SAMPLE THE FIELD.** Many of the most widely used computer-based multiple-choice examinations, like the GMAT, have tutorials to familiarize the candidate with the specific test interface used for each such examination. Without regard for the test content, correction officer candidates scheduled to take a computer-based multiple-choice examination should seek out these tutorials and learn from them. As much as possible, become familiar with the various formats employed in computer-based multiple-choice tests. This will go a long way toward your being able to focus on seeking out the correct answers while taking a computer-based correction officer test rather than having to focus on familiarizing yourself with the format of the test.

Pay attention!

4. **ASK IN ADVANCE ABOUT THE TEST FORMAT.** Contact the testing agency administering the exam you will be taking, and ask about the test format. Find out if you can view a tutorial for the examination you are taking before exam day. Another recommended step is to seek out people who have already taken the examination you will be

taking. Ask them about the format of the test. Following are some of the details of the computer-based test format that you should ask about.

- Are the written directions/rules outlining the test taker's responsibilities during the test available to the candidate before the day of the test? If so, obtain them and study them.
- Is there a computer-based method to make notes during the test? If not, are candidates supplied with a notepad to take notes? If not, can the candidate bring his or her own notepad into the test room? Later on in this section we will present a specific strategy for handling multiple-choice questions. This strategy includes note taking. It is imperative that candidates taking a computer-based multiple-choice question test understand how to make notes during the test. Such an understanding would include knowing the answers to the following questions:
- How do you navigate from one question to another?
- Does the computer screen show one question at a time?
- Does every question fit on the computer screen or will you need to scroll?
- Must you answer the questions in the order they are presented or can you skip questions? Can you return to questions you have already answered?
- How do you bookmark certain questions to return quickly to them?
- How do you select your answers? Is there a separate answer sheet?
- How do you change an answer already selected?
- Is there one time frame for completing the entire examination or are there several different timed sections?
- Does the computer keep track of time for you?
- What is the procedure to follow in the event of a computer malfunction during the test, such as a frozen screen?

5. **PAY STRICT ATTENTION TO THE EXAM DAY TUTORIAL.** Virtually every computer-based multiple-choice examination begins with a tutorial before the timed examination starts. Do not assume you know the instructions being discussed in the tutorial no matter how much advance preparation you have made. Keep in mind that test formats are continuously evolving. Remain flexible.

6. **CLEAR UP UNRESOLVED ISSUES BEFORE THE START OF THE TEST.** When viewing the exam tutorial, be vigilant and seek out the answers to the questions posed in strategy 4. If, after the tutorial, you are not sure of the answers to these questions or any other questions you may have, make inquiries to the test room monitor before the test begins.

7. **FOLLOW THE SPECIFIC TEST-TAKING STRATEGIES THAT FOLLOW FOR HANDLING MULTIPLE-CHOICE QUESTIONS.** Although these strategies seem complex, with practice they become second nature. And they will serve you well on any multiple-choice test you ever take.

STRATEGIES FOR HANDLING MULTIPLE-CHOICE QUESTIONS

Specific test-taking strategies that are valuable for a multiple-choice examination follow. These strategies will serve you well not only on the correction officer examination but also on any multiple-choice exam you may take. Study the strategies and practice them; then study them again until you have mastered them. Please note that these strategies are written to apply to both the traditional paper-and-pencil examination and the computer-based examination. Also note that at first glance some of the strategies seem overly complex. You will find, however, that if you put in the required effort to master them and use them, you will in all likelihood find yourself at or near the top of the hiring list when it is published.

1. **READ THE INSTRUCTIONS.** Do not assume that you know what the instructions are without reading them. Make sure you read and understand them. There are test instructions and question instructions. *Test instructions* are a set of general instructions that govern the entire examination and are to be read before the exam starts. Question instructions appear throughout the test before each series of questions. They govern the taking of each such series of questions appearing on the exam. On the day of your official examination, if you are unsure about the instructions, ask questions when given the opportunity. If you are taking a computer-based multiple-choice question test, don't forget to pay special attention to instructions regarding the format of the examination.

2. **MAKE SURE THAT YOU HAVE THE COMPLETE EXAMINATION.** If you are taking a traditional paper-and-pencil examination, as soon as your examination officially starts, check the test booklet page by page. Because these booklets have numbered pages, simply count the pages. If you do not have a complete examination, inform a test monitor immediately.

3. **UNDERSTAND HOW TO RECORD ANSWERS PROPERLY.** If you are taking a traditional paper-and-pencil examination, keep in mind that some answer sheets number the questions vertically while other answer sheets number the questions horizontally. This numbering system is used to discourage cheating. The answer sheets used in this book for the practice examination are typical of what you will see on a traditional paper-and-pencil examination. Do not take anything for granted, however. Review the instructions on the answer sheet carefully and familiarize yourself with its format.

   If you are taking a computer-based multiple-choice test, make sure you know the answers to the following questions:

   - Is there a separate answer sheet?
   - How do you select your answers?
   - How do you change an answer already selected?

4. **BE EXTREMELY CAREFUL WHEN MARKING YOUR ANSWERS.** If you are taking a traditional paper-and-pencil examination, sure to mark your answers in accordance with the official instructions. Be absolutely certain that

   - you mark only one answer for each question, unless the instructions specifically indicate the possibility of multiple answers;
   - you do not make extraneous markings on your answer sheet;
   - you completely darken the allotted space for the answer you choose;
   - you erase completely any answer that you wish to change.

   Please note that there is a difference between making extraneous markings on your answer sheet and making notes in your test booklet, which is the booklet that contains the test questions. As you will see, good test-taking strategy demands that you make certain notations in your test booklet. The only exception would be in the very rare instance where the test instructions prohibit writing in the test booklet. If you are taking a computer-based multiple-choice test, this is not as important an issue as it is for those taking traditional paper-and-pencil tests. Most computer-based formats provide for automatic marking of the answer sheet upon selecting the answer for a particular question. To be on the safe side, however, make sure this is the case on the test you are taking. In fact, never assume anything about the format of the examination. Remain flexible and confirm everything.

5. **MAKE ABSOLUTELY CERTAIN THAT YOU ARE MARKING THE ANSWER TO THE RIGHT QUESTION.** Many people have failed traditional paper-and-pencil multiple-choice tests because of carelessness in this area. All it takes is one mistake. If you put down one answer in the wrong space, you will probably continue the mistake for a number of questions until you realize your error. We recommend that you use the following procedure when marking your answer sheet:

- Select the choice you believe is the answer, circle that choice on the test booklet, and remind yourself what question number you are working on.
- If you, for example, select choice C as the answer for question 11, circle choice C on the test booklet, and say to yourself, "C is the answer to question 11."
- Then find the space on your answer sheet for question 11, and again say "C is the answer to question 11" as you mark the answer.

Even though this procedure may seem rather elementary and repetitive, after awhile it becomes automatic. If followed properly, it guarantees that you will not fail the examination because of a careless mistake.

6. **MAKE CERTAIN THAT YOU UNDERSTAND WHAT THE QUESTION IS ASKING.** Test takers often choose wrong answers because they fail to read the question carefully enough. Read the stem of the question (the part before the choices) very carefully to make certain that you know what the examiner is asking. If necessary, read it twice. Be certain to read every word in the question. If you do not, you could select a wrong answer to a very simple question.

7. **ALWAYS READ ALL THE CHOICES BEFORE YOU SELECT AN ANSWER.** Distractors are what test writers call incorrect choices. Every multiple-choice question usually has one best distractor, which is very close to being correct. Many times this best distractor comes before the correct choice. Therefore, don't select the first choice that looks good. Read all the choices.

8. **BE AWARE OF KEY WORDS THAT OFTEN TIP OFF THE CORRECT AND INCORRECT ANSWERS.** When you are stuck on a question and have to guess at the answer, you can often select the correct choice by understanding that absolute words tend to appear more often in incorrect choices, and that limiting words tend to appear more often in correct choices. *Absolute words* are very broad and do not allow for any exceptions. *Limiting words* are not all inclusive and allow for exceptions.

Absolute Words—*Usually a Wrong Choice when making an educated guess.* (They often are too broad and difficult to defend.)

never	always	only	none
none	all	nothing	any
every	everyone	everything	

Limiting Words—*Usually a Correct Choice when making an educated guess.*

usually	sometimes	generally	many
occasionally	possible	some	often

9. **NEVER MAKE A CHOICE BASED ON FREQUENCY OF PREVIOUS ANSWERS.** Some students inappropriately pay attention to the pattern of answers when taking an exam. Multiple-choice exams are not designed to have an equal number of *A, B, C,* and *D* choices as the answers. Always answer the question without regard to what the letter designations of the previous choices have been.

TIP

Develop a system.

10. **MAKE A DECISION ON EACH ANSWER CHOICE AND RECORD IT.** This strategy is designed to enable the test taker to save time and mental energy by recording his or her decisions on each choice for every question in the entire test the first time through the test. The concept is simple. Recording your thoughts on each choice as you review it facilitates speedy review of the question as the need arises.

There are three possible decisions you can make for each answer choice you review. You know *for sure* that a certain choice either (1) is not the answer, (2) is the answer, or (3) may or may not be the answer. The time saving tip for you is to record your decision for each choice you review, as described below in our three-step process.

THE THREE-STEP PROCESS

1. Use process of elimination to arrive at the correct answer.
2. Reread answer choices you were not able to eliminate.
3. If it applies, reread the question stem.

(STEP 1) If you are taking a traditional paper-and-pencil examination, as you consider the various answer choices to each question, put an **X** in the test booklet to cross out the letter designation of any choice you know for sure is *not* the answer. If you cross out all but one of the choices, the remaining choice should be your answer. Read that choice one more time to satisfy yourself, put a circle around its letter designation (if you still feel it is the correct answer) and transfer it to your answer sheet using strategy 5. Spend no more time on this question.

If you are taking a computer-based multiple-choice test, use the note taking function of the computer to record those answer choices you know for sure are not the answer. If you eliminate all but one answer choice, then record that choice as your answer. Spend no more time on this question.

(STEP 2) If, after your initial review of the choices, you are left with more than one possible answer, you need to reread only those choices that you did not eliminate the first time by putting an **X** through them. Often, the second time you read the remaining choices, the answer is clear. If that happens, cross out the wrong choice by putting an **X** through it, and circle the correct one. Then transfer the answer to the answer sheet if you are taking a traditional paper-and-pencil test. If you are taking a computer-based multiple-choice test, use the computer to perform these tasks.

(STEP 3) If, after the second reading of the choices, you still not have selected an answer, reread the stem of the question and make certain that you understand the question. Then review those choices that you did not initially eliminate by putting an **X** through them. Keep in mind the absolute words and limiting words mentioned in strategy 8, which may give you a hint of the correct answer. If you still haven't decided which answer choice to select, guess at the answer and record your guess on the answer sheet. When guessing, be guided by the strategy outlined here in strategies 8, 11, 12, and 16.

11. **GUESS AT THE ANSWERS TO TROUBLESOME QUESTIONS YOU DO NOT KNOW THE ANSWERS TO.** The first time through the examination, do not dwell too long on any one troublesome question. Spending too much time on a troublesome question is an error you must avoid because it is a common cause of running out of time. You can avoid this error by doing the following:

- If you are taking a traditional paper-and-pencil exam and are faced with a question you cannot answer, make an educated guess and record it on your answer sheet. Be sure to put a circle around the question number in the test booklet. Then go on to the next question. The circle around the question number in the test booklet will help you find these troublesome questions the second time through the examination, as explained below in strategy 12. Keep in mind that these questions are the first category of questions you should return to after recording answers for every question on the test.

- If you are taking a computer-based test and are faced with a question you cannot answer, make an educated guess and record it on the computer as required. But, be sure to bookmark the question so you can quickly return to it after you have recorded answers for all of the questions on the test as explained below in strategy 12. Keep in mind that these questions are the first category of questions you should return to after recording answers for every question on the test.

- If you decide on the answer to a question that is troublesome to you without dwelling on it too long, record your answer as required and put a star in the margin in your test booklet or otherwise bookmark it for speedy return. Time permitting, these are the second category of questions you should return to after recording answers for every question on the test in accordance with strategy 12.

12. **RETURN TO THE QUESTIONS YOU GUESSED AT AFTER YOU FINISH THE ENTIRE EXAMINATION.** After you have recorded an answer for all of the questions on the exam, check the time remaining. If time permits (which it should if you follow the time management recommendations), return first to each question where you made an educated guess. Reread the stem of each of these questions and any of the answer choices that you did not eliminate during your initial reading. It should be easy to find these questions if you followed the recommendations outlined in strategy 11. Many times the correct answer will now be easy to determine. Otherwise, time constraints demand that you stick with your best educated guess as discussed below in strategy 15. Then move on.

If you still have time after you have reviewed every question where you originally made an educated guess, you should now review the questions you had trouble answering previously. These questions should also be easy to find if you have followed the recommendation either to put a star in the margin of the test booklet or to bookmark them as outlined in strategy 11.

13. **NEVER LEAVE QUESTIONS UNANSWERED UNLESS THE INSTRUCTIONS INDICATE A PENALTY FOR WRONG ANSWERS.** In most correction officer exams, you do not have extra points subtracted from your final score for choosing wrong answers. In other words, there is no penalty for guessing. If this is the case on your examination, make an educated guess at any question where you are not sure of the answer as discussed in strategy 11.

In rare instances, an extra penalty is assessed for choosing wrong answers on multiple-choice examinations. This would have to be explained in the test instructions. So be sure, as already recommended, to read all of your instructions very carefully. If there is an extra penalty for choosing wrong answers on your examination, decide how certain you are about the answer you have selected for each question. Note, again, that subtracting extra points for wrong answers rarely happens on entry-level examinations such as the one you are planning to take.

TIP

Learn how to make an educated guess.

14. **DEVELOP A TIME MANAGEMENT PLAN.** It is extremely important for you to have a time management plan when you take your examination. Not to systematically monitor the passage of time on an examination is similar to inviting failure. The mechanics of developing a time management plan are presented later in this chapter.

15. **FOLLOW THE RULES FOR MAKING AN EDUCATED GUESS.** Your chances of selecting the correct answers to questions you are not sure of will be significantly increased if you use the following rules:

- Never consider answer choices you have already positively eliminated.
- Be aware of key words that give you clues as to which answer might be right or wrong.
- Always eliminate choices that are very close in meaning to each other.

EXAMPLE

Alicia's complaint about the weather was that

(A) it was too hot.
(B) it was too cold.
(C) it varied too much.
(D) it was unpredictable.

In this example, choices C and D are so close together in meaning that neither is likely to be the correct answer. Choices A and B, on the other hand, are quite opposite each other, and one of them is most likely the correct answer.

- If two choices are worded so that combined they encompass all of the possibilities, one of them must be the correct choice.

EXAMPLE

How old is John?

(A) John is 7 years old or less.
(B) John is 6 years old.
(C) John is over 7 years old.
(D) John is 14 years old.

In this example, it should be clear to you that the correct answer has to be either A or C, because if John is not 7 years old or less (choice A), then he must be over 7 years old (choice C). Please note that even if he is 14 years old (choice D), choice C is still correct. His age must fit into either choice A or choice C.

- An answer choice that has significantly more or significantly fewer words in it is very often the correct choice.

16. **BE VERY RELUCTANT TO CHANGE ANSWERS.** Unless you have a very good reason, do not change an answer once you have chosen it. Experience has shown us that all too often people change their answer from the right one to the wrong one. This doesn't mean that you should never change an answer. If you discover an obvious mistake, for example, you should most certainly change your answer.

17. **UNDERSTAND THAT THERE ARE DIFFERENT STRATEGIES FOR DEALING WITH DIFFERENT QUESTION TYPES.** On every entry-level examination, you will encounter different question types. For example, some questions might test your ability to understand what you read, others might test your verbal or mathematical ability, and still others might test your memory or your ability to interpret graphs, charts or tables, and so forth. If you are to maximize your test score, you must understand that it is wrong to answer all question types on the test using the same strategy. Instead, you should change your strategy or approach based on the question type you are answering at any given time. Included in this book is a discussion of each of the most common question types used on most correction officer examinations throughout the country. Included in each discussion is an explanation of a strategy to follow for the question type being considered. Learn to recognize the various question types and learn the specific strategies for answering each one of them. Then, when you take the practice examinations, use these strategies.

TIP

Learn the different question types.

DEDUCTIVE AND INDUCTIVE REASONING

Some recent notices of examination for correctional titles have specifically listed "deductive and inductive reasoning" as abilities that may be tested on the correction officer entrance test. This has proven to be confusing to some students. For this reason, we will explain the distinction between deductive and inductive reasoning and also explain how exam writers test for these two abilities.

For test-taking purposes, deductive reasoning is used when you apply general rules to specific problems to arrive at logical answers. Conversely, inductive reasoning takes place when you use specific or particular pieces of information to arrive at general conclusions. Years ago we learned that when you go from the **P**articular to the **G**eneral, you are employing **I**nductive reasoning. From that day on we used the code word **PIG** to teach our students the meaning of inductive reasoning.

Examiners use certain question types to test for deductive and inductive reasoning. The question type that is probably used most often, though, involves understanding and applying correctional directives as described in Chapter 6. The most important point is that you do not have to know what ability any particular question is designed to test. What you do have to know, however, is how to recognize the various question types as well as the recommended strategy to answer each question type accurately and quickly. Remember, that every question type has its own answering strategy, and each such strategy is covered in this text.

DEVELOPING AND USING A TIME MANAGEMENT PLAN

The time management plan presented in this section applies to both traditional multiple-choice examinations and computer-based multiple-choice examinations. The primary goal of a time management plan is to determine the average number of minutes you should spend on each multiple-choice question on the test and then to use that information throughout the test to guard against running out of time. In order to develop a time management plan you must know (1) the number of questions on the exam and (2) the amount of time allowed to complete the test. Many times you will not have this information until the day of the test. But, because it is a relatively simple task, you can easily develop your time management plan on test day before you begin to answer any questions.

The following step-by-step explanation details how a time management plan is developed. For the purposes of this explanation, assume that you are taking an examination that has 100 questions and has a time limit of 4 hours.

1. **CONVERT THE TIME ALLOWED TO MINUTES AND PUT 30 MINUTES ASIDE OR, AS WE SAY, IN THE BANK.** This 30 minutes is to be used when you have finished the examination to go back to the questions you have skipped, then to the ones you found difficult, and to otherwise review your exam. Using our example, convert 4 hours to 240 minutes and subtract 30 minutes, which leaves you with 210 minutes to answer 100 questions. Remember that this also leaves you with 30 minutes in the bank to use at the end of the test.

2. **DIVIDE THE TIME ALLOWED TO ANSWER THE QUESTIONS BY THE NUMBER OF QUESTIONS TO DETERMINE THE AVERAGE AMOUNT OF TIME YOU SHOULD SPEND ON EACH QUESTION.** In our example, this means that you would divide 210 minutes by 100 questions and thus determine that you could comfortably spend approximately 2 minutes per question.

TIP

Make sure you have a time management plan.

3. **NOW USE YOUR TIME MANAGEMENT PLAN.** Knowing that you should spend approximately 2 minutes per question is of little value unless you then proceed to monitor your time usage from the start of the exam. On a 100-question test, we recommend that you specifically check your time every 10 questions. Using our example, at the end of the first 10 questions no more than 20 minutes should have passed (2 minutes per question); after completing 20 questions no more than 40 minutes should have passed, and so forth.

By developing and using a time management plan, you will find out early in the test if you are falling behind. This information is quite beneficial because you will still be able to do something about it. Contrast that situation with one in which you realize much too late that you have been using too much time. Clearly the former is the preferable situation.

TEST MATERIAL DISTRIBUTED IN ADVANCE

In some jurisdictions, material about entrance examinations is distributed in advance of the test. This material typically takes the form of a test preparation and orientation booklet. Included in this advance material may be general information about the examination, a description of the types of questions that will appear on the examination, specific suggestions or hints for you to follow when taking the examination, and sample questions. In addition, you might also be given reference material containing information that you should study to prepare for the examination.

The rule to follow when dealing with advance material is both simple and obvious. You should read the material carefully and use it to prepare for the examination. Your score on the examination will, in all probability, be in direct proportion to your understanding of the advance material.

Special Considerations for Reference Materials Distributed in Advance

By reference material we mean material on which actual test questions might be based. Concerning reference material distributed in advance, there are generally three possibilities. The way you deal with this reference material is predicated on which of the three possibilities apply to your particular examination, if indeed your examination involves the use of advance reference material.

The first possibility is that the advance reference material may be similar but not identical to the reference material you will be using on the day of the test. In that case, you should familiarize yourself with the format and structure of the material, but you do not have to memorize it.

The second possibility is that the advance reference material may be identical to the actual reference material to be distributed on the day of the test. In that case you should become very familiar with the advance material since the questions you will be asked will be based on that material, but it is not necessary to memorize the material since you will have it at your disposal on test day.

The third possibility is that the advance reference material will be used on the day of the test but you will not be able to refer to it even though the questions will test your knowledge of it. In that case, you must commit the information involved to memory prior to test day. Failure to do so will result in almost certain failure.

DEALING WITH TESTS PRESENTED ON VIDEO

Another practice occasionally used in entrance-level examinations is the use of video simulations. Should a video be used on your official examination, you can expect the following. On the day of the test, you will be shown a video presentation and then asked questions about what you have heard and seen on the video tape. In some cases the questions you are asked are designed to measure your ability to understand by observing and listening. Other questions are designed to test your ability to apply written material to the situations shown in each scenario.

In many tests that include a video component, candidates are shown a sample video tape prior to the day of the examination. If your test is structured in that way, it is absolutely essential that you view the sample video.

Strategies for Taking a Video Test

1. **MAKE CERTAIN YOU UNDERSTAND WHAT THE QUESTION IS ASKING.** The general rule about the importance of reading and understanding test instructions and directions must be followed if you are to be successful on a video test. If, after reading the instructions, you are unsure about their exact meaning, ask questions when given the opportunity. Make sure that you know what to expect before the video begins because most video tests prohibit the asking of questions once the video begins.

2. **TAKE NOTES AS THE VIDEO PRESENTATION UNFOLDS, UNLESS SPECIFICALLY PROHIBITED BY THE TEST INSTRUCTIONS.** You should not try to record the scene verbatim. Make your notes as brief as possible. Use key words and phrases and not complete sentences. Use abbreviations whenever possible, keeping in mind that your notes are useless if you cannot interpret them later. Also keep in mind that candidates who get overly engrossed in taking notes often miss critical information.

3. **CONCENTRATE.** You must not let your mind wander. You must pay strict attention to what you are seeing and what you are hearing. Completely ignore the actions of those around you. Please note that you can hone your note-taking skills and concentration ability through practice. Simply watch a news show on television (record it, if possible). Make notes of what you hear and see. After the show, see how many of the important points you have captured.

4. **PAY PARTICULAR ATTENTION TO ERRORS AS YOU SEE THEM OCCUR.** Note what appear to be inappropriate actions on the part of the actors in the video. Such actions will often become the basis for questions.

5. **NOTE TIMES, DATES, AND LOCATIONS, WHEN GIVEN.** Understand that the time frames and locations involved are often the subject of questions.

HOW TO USE THIS BOOK EFFECTIVELY

To obtain maximum benefit from the use of this book, we recommend the following approach.

1. Learn the "Strategies for Handling Multiple-Choice Questions," which appear earlier in this chapter.
2. Take the Diagnostic Test in one sitting. After completing this examination, fill out the diagnostic chart that follows the answer key. This will indicate your strengths and weaknesses. You should then devote most of your study time to correcting your weaknesses.
3. As mentioned previously, concentrate your study efforts in your weak areas, but make certain to cover each question type in the Correct Your Weaknesses section of the book. Be sure to follow the "Ten Rules for Studying More Effectively," which appear earlier in this section. Also, make sure to apply the test-taking strategies presented earlier when doing the practice exercises at the end of each review chapter.
4. Take Practice Test 1. When you have finished this examination and have reviewed the explained answers, complete the diagnostic chart that follows the answer key. Then restudy the appropriate chapters in accordance with the directions on the bottom of the diagnostic chart.
5. Take Practice Tests 2 through 5. After you have finished each examination, follow the same procedure that you followed after finishing Practice Test 1.
6. When your actual examination is one week away, read "The Final Countdown." Be sure to follow the recommended strategy for the 7 days immediately preceding the examination.

Diagnose Your Problem

A Diagnostic Test

There are 115 questions on this diagnostic test, and you should finish the entire examination in 4 hours. For maximum benefit, it is strongly recommended that you take this examination in one sitting as if it were the actual test.

The answers to this examination, their explanations, and a diagnostic chart are included in this chapter after the last test question. By completing the diagnostic chart, you can get an idea of which question types give you the most difficulty. You can then devote most of your time to studying those areas.

BEFORE YOU TAKE THE TEST

Before taking this exam, you should have read the introduction. Be certain that you employ the recommended test-taking strategies outlined while taking the examination.

Remember to read each question and related material carefully before choosing your answers. Select the choice you believe to be the answer and mark your answers on the appropriate answer sheet. This answer sheet is similar to the one used on the actual examination. The answer key, diagnostic chart, and answer explanations appear at the end of this test.

ANSWER SHEET
Diagnostic Test

Follow the instructions given in the test. Mark only your answers in the circles below.

WARNING: Be sure that the circle you fill is in the same row as the question you are answering. Use a No. 2 pencil (soft pencil).

BE SURE YOUR PENCIL MARKS ARE HEAVY AND BLACK. ERASE COMPLETELY ANY ANSWER YOU WISH TO CHANGE.

DO NOT make stray pencil dots, dashes, or marks.

1. Ⓐ Ⓑ Ⓒ Ⓓ   30. Ⓐ Ⓑ Ⓒ Ⓓ   59. Ⓐ Ⓑ Ⓒ Ⓓ   88. Ⓐ Ⓑ Ⓒ Ⓓ
2. Ⓐ Ⓑ Ⓒ Ⓓ   31. Ⓐ Ⓑ Ⓒ Ⓓ   60. Ⓐ Ⓑ Ⓒ Ⓓ   39. Ⓐ Ⓑ Ⓒ Ⓓ
3. Ⓐ Ⓑ Ⓒ Ⓓ   32. Ⓐ Ⓑ Ⓒ Ⓓ   61. Ⓐ Ⓑ Ⓒ Ⓓ   90. Ⓐ Ⓑ Ⓒ Ⓓ
4. Ⓐ Ⓑ Ⓒ Ⓓ   33. Ⓐ Ⓑ Ⓒ Ⓓ   62. Ⓐ Ⓑ Ⓒ Ⓓ   91. Ⓐ Ⓑ Ⓒ Ⓓ
5. Ⓐ Ⓑ Ⓒ Ⓓ   34. Ⓐ Ⓑ Ⓒ Ⓓ   63. Ⓐ Ⓑ Ⓒ Ⓓ   92. Ⓐ Ⓑ Ⓒ Ⓓ
6. Ⓐ Ⓑ Ⓒ Ⓓ   35. Ⓐ Ⓑ Ⓒ Ⓓ   64. Ⓐ Ⓑ Ⓒ Ⓓ   93. Ⓐ Ⓑ Ⓒ Ⓓ
7. Ⓐ Ⓑ Ⓒ Ⓓ   36. Ⓐ Ⓑ Ⓒ Ⓓ   65. Ⓐ Ⓑ Ⓒ Ⓓ   94. Ⓐ Ⓑ Ⓒ Ⓓ
8. Ⓐ Ⓑ Ⓒ Ⓓ   37. Ⓐ Ⓑ Ⓒ Ⓓ   66. Ⓐ Ⓑ Ⓒ Ⓓ   95. Ⓐ Ⓑ Ⓒ Ⓓ
9. Ⓐ Ⓑ Ⓒ Ⓓ   38. Ⓐ Ⓑ Ⓒ Ⓓ   67. Ⓐ Ⓑ Ⓒ Ⓓ   96. Ⓐ Ⓑ Ⓒ Ⓓ
10. Ⓐ Ⓑ Ⓒ Ⓓ   39. Ⓐ Ⓑ Ⓒ Ⓓ   68. Ⓐ Ⓑ Ⓒ Ⓓ   97. Ⓐ Ⓑ Ⓒ Ⓓ
11. Ⓐ Ⓑ Ⓒ Ⓓ   40. Ⓐ Ⓑ Ⓒ Ⓓ   69. Ⓐ Ⓑ Ⓒ Ⓓ   98. Ⓐ Ⓑ Ⓒ Ⓓ
12. Ⓐ Ⓑ Ⓒ Ⓓ   41. Ⓐ Ⓑ Ⓒ Ⓓ   70. Ⓐ Ⓑ Ⓒ Ⓓ   99. Ⓐ Ⓑ Ⓒ Ⓓ
13. Ⓐ Ⓑ Ⓒ Ⓓ   42. Ⓐ Ⓑ Ⓒ Ⓓ   71. Ⓐ Ⓑ Ⓒ Ⓓ   100. Ⓐ Ⓑ Ⓒ Ⓓ
14. Ⓐ Ⓑ Ⓒ Ⓓ   43. Ⓐ Ⓑ Ⓒ Ⓓ   72. Ⓐ Ⓑ Ⓒ Ⓓ   101. Ⓐ Ⓑ Ⓒ Ⓓ
15. Ⓐ Ⓑ Ⓒ Ⓓ   44. Ⓐ Ⓑ Ⓒ Ⓓ   73. Ⓐ Ⓑ Ⓒ Ⓓ   102. Ⓐ Ⓑ Ⓒ Ⓓ
16. Ⓐ Ⓑ Ⓒ Ⓓ   45. Ⓐ Ⓑ Ⓒ Ⓓ   74. Ⓐ Ⓑ Ⓒ Ⓓ   103. Ⓐ Ⓑ Ⓒ Ⓓ
17. Ⓐ Ⓑ Ⓒ Ⓓ   46. Ⓐ Ⓑ Ⓒ Ⓓ   75. Ⓐ Ⓑ Ⓒ Ⓓ   104. Ⓐ Ⓑ Ⓒ Ⓓ
18. Ⓐ Ⓑ Ⓒ Ⓓ   47. Ⓐ Ⓑ Ⓒ Ⓓ   76. Ⓐ Ⓑ Ⓒ Ⓓ   105. Ⓐ Ⓑ Ⓒ Ⓓ
19. Ⓐ Ⓑ Ⓒ Ⓓ   48. Ⓐ Ⓑ Ⓒ Ⓓ   77. Ⓐ Ⓑ Ⓒ Ⓓ   106. Ⓐ Ⓑ Ⓒ Ⓓ
20. Ⓐ Ⓑ Ⓒ Ⓓ   49. Ⓐ Ⓑ Ⓒ Ⓓ   78. Ⓐ Ⓑ Ⓒ Ⓓ   107. Ⓐ Ⓑ Ⓒ Ⓓ
21. Ⓐ Ⓑ Ⓒ Ⓓ   50. Ⓐ Ⓑ Ⓒ Ⓓ   79. Ⓐ Ⓑ Ⓒ Ⓓ   108. Ⓐ Ⓑ Ⓒ Ⓓ
22. Ⓐ Ⓑ Ⓒ Ⓓ   51. Ⓐ Ⓑ Ⓒ Ⓓ   80. Ⓐ Ⓑ Ⓒ Ⓓ   109. Ⓐ Ⓑ Ⓒ Ⓓ
23. Ⓐ Ⓑ Ⓒ Ⓓ   52. Ⓐ Ⓑ Ⓒ Ⓓ   81. Ⓐ Ⓑ Ⓒ Ⓓ   110. Ⓐ Ⓑ Ⓒ Ⓓ
24. Ⓐ Ⓑ Ⓒ Ⓓ   53. Ⓐ Ⓑ Ⓒ Ⓓ   82. Ⓐ Ⓑ Ⓒ Ⓓ   111. Ⓐ Ⓑ Ⓒ Ⓓ
25. Ⓐ Ⓑ Ⓒ Ⓓ   54. Ⓐ Ⓑ Ⓒ Ⓓ   83. Ⓐ Ⓑ Ⓒ Ⓓ   112. Ⓐ Ⓑ Ⓒ Ⓓ
26. Ⓐ Ⓑ Ⓒ Ⓓ   55. Ⓐ Ⓑ Ⓒ Ⓓ   84. Ⓐ Ⓑ Ⓒ Ⓓ   113. Ⓐ Ⓑ Ⓒ Ⓓ
27. Ⓐ Ⓑ Ⓒ Ⓓ   56. Ⓐ Ⓑ Ⓒ Ⓓ   85. Ⓐ Ⓑ Ⓒ Ⓓ   114. Ⓐ Ⓑ Ⓒ Ⓓ
28. Ⓐ Ⓑ Ⓒ Ⓓ   57. Ⓐ Ⓑ Ⓒ Ⓓ   86. Ⓐ Ⓑ Ⓒ Ⓓ   115. Ⓐ Ⓑ Ⓒ Ⓓ
29. Ⓐ Ⓑ Ⓒ Ⓓ   58. Ⓐ Ⓑ Ⓒ Ⓓ   87. Ⓐ Ⓑ Ⓒ Ⓓ

SECTION 1—MEMORY

> **Directions:** Answer questions 1–8 based on the following illustration, which depicts items taken from two inmates immediately after they were arrested. You are permitted 5 minutes to study the illustration. Try to remember as many details as possible. Do not make written notes of any kind during this 5-minute period.
>
> At the end of 5 minutes, stop studying the illustration, turn the page, and answer questions 1–8 *without* referring back to the illustration.

DO NOT PROCEED UNTIL 5 MINUTES HAVE PASSED.

Directions: Answer questions 1–8 solely on the basis of the illustration on the preceding page. Do not refer back to the scene when answering these questions.

1. What is the total amount of money possessed by the two inmates?

   (A) $10.30
   (B) Thirty cents
   (C) $10.25
   (D) Five cents

2. Which of the inmates is more likely to have traveled on the subway?

   (A) Charles Adams
   (B) Alicia Smart
   (C) Both Charles Adams and Alicia Smart
   (D) Neither Charles Adams nor Alicia Smart

3. Which of the inmates carried a defensive weapon?

   (A) Charles Adams
   (B) Alicia Smart
   (C) both Charles Adams and Alicia Smart
   (D) neither Charles Adams nor Alicia Smart

4. Which of the inmates lives in Whitestone?

   (A) Charles Adams
   (B) Alicia Smart
   (C) both Charles Adams and Alicia Smart
   (D) neither Charles Adams nor Alicia Smart

5. What is Alicia Smart's address?

   (A) 1632 64th Road
   (B) 618 24th Street
   (C) 618 24th Road
   (D) 1632 24th Street

6. Cathy is most probably

   (A) the daughter of Charles Adams.
   (B) the daughter of Alicia Smart.
   (C) the sister of Charles Adams.
   (D) the sister of Alicia Smart.

7. How many keys did Charles Adams possess?

   (A) one
   (B) two
   (C) three
   (D) four

8. License plate number CA 221 belongs to a

   (A) 1996 Buick.
   (B) 1996 Honda.
   (C) 1996 Chevrolet.
   (D) 1996 Lincoln.

> **Directions:** Answer questions 9–14 solely on the basis of the following passage.

At 12:55 P.M. Correction Officer Smith was on foot patrol on Prison Street between 2nd and 4th Avenue, which is located on the grounds of the Cook County Detention Facility. While standing on the southeast corner of Prison Street and 3rd Avenue, the officer heard a scream coming from the direction of the Administration Building on the opposite side of the street. When he looked in that direction he saw a young white male running on Prison Street toward 2nd Avenue, followed by a woman yelling, "Stop that man." Correction Officer Smith joined in the pursuit, but by the time he caught up with the woman she had fallen over some debris on the sidewalk. The woman was quite upset and appeared to have injured her head. Correction Officer Smith decided that because the young white male had disappeared from sight, he should stay with the injured woman and call for an ambulance. While awaiting the arrival of the ambulance, the injured woman, Ms. Cramdom, told Correction Officer Smith that she was the manager of the Administration Building and that the young white male had taken approximately $35 from the petty cash drawer while she was trying to find a job application for him. She also mentioned that the Administration Building was unattended at the time since her two helpers had not come to work that day.

Correction Officer Smith called for backup assistance at 1:20 P.M. and asked the radio dispatcher to send a correction officer to the Administration Building located at 4241 Prison Street. Correction Officers Jones and Brown arrived at the Administration Building at 1:35 P.M. and saw that the premises were unattended. When Correction Officer Smith arrived at the Administration Building at 1:55 P.M., Correction Officer Brown told him that it would be impossible to determine what items had been taken from the building since there was no listing of the building's equipment readily available.

At 2:10 P.M. a young woman entered the building and identified herself as Ms. Martin, a part-time helper at the building whose shift started at 2:00 P.M. On seeing the situation in the building, she asked the officers what had occurred. After telling her, they asked her where the equipment list for the building was kept. She stated that Administrative Assistant Connors kept that information. She was told to call the dispatcher and notify them when the list was available.

9. Where was Correction Officer Smith when he heard a scream?

   (A) on Prison Street and 4th Avenue
   (B) at 4241 Prison Street
   (C) at the intersection of Prison Street and 3rd Avenue
   (D) in front of the Administration Building

10. At which one of the following addresses is the Administration Building located?

   (A) 4241 3rd Avenue
   (B) 3rd Avenue and Prison Street
   (C) 4241 Prison Street
   (D) Prison Street and 4th Avenue

11. At what time did Correction Officer Smith meet Officers Jones and Brown at the Administration Building?

   (A) 12:55 P.M.
   (B) 1:20 P.M.
   (C) 1:35 P.M.
   (D) 1:55 P.M.

12. Which one of the following people manages the Administration Building?

   (A) Ms. Cramdom
   (B) Ms. Martin
   (C) Mr. Connors
   (D) Ms. Smith

13. What is Ms. Martin's scheduled starting time at the Administration Building?

   (A) 1:35 P.M.
   (B) 1:55 P.M.
   (C) 2:00 P.M.
   (D) 2:10 P.M.

14. Keeping the equipment list is the responsibility of

   (A) Ms. Martin.
   (B) Administrative Assistant Connors.
   (C) Ms. Cramdom.
   (D) the radio dispatcher.

On May 31st Correction Officer Ginty was on duty at the Municipal Jail located in the downtown area of a large urban city. The jail is a 32 floor complex that includes court rooms and a hospital ward.

The third floor of the facility is occupied by social workers who deal mostly with the family and friends of inmates. At 5:00 P.M. Correction Officer Ginty was dispatched to respond to room 314 on the third floor of the complex. Upon his arrival at room 314 at 5:05 P.M., the correction officer was met by Mrs. Ann Bancroft, a black female, age 44, and her daughter Mary. The Bancrofts live at 32-38 Crescent Boulevard, apartment 5C.

Mrs. Bancroft informed the correction officer that her daughter had been robbed. The correction officer questioned the victim, Mary Bancroft, a black female, age 16, date of birth 3/6/79, who stated that she was coming to the Municipal Jail after a day of attending school to meet her mom in room 314. At 4:45 P.M., as she got on the elevator to go to the third floor, an unknown male black entered the elevator with her and pressed the button for the second floor. When the elevator door closed, the man pulled a knife from under his coat and told the victim not to scream. The robber then took the young girl's pocketbook containing about $20 in U.S. currency.

Ms. Bancroft described the suspect as an unknown male black, 6 feet tall, 180 pounds, 25–30 years old, medium complexion, missing right front tooth, who was wearing a black leather bomber jacket, brown pants, and dark shoes. He spoke with an accent.

When asked if she was injured, Mary said, "No." Correction Officer Ginty then transmitted an alarm for the suspect and asked for and received permission from Ann's supervisor for her to leave her job at the facility early. The correction officer stayed with the victim and her mother until they were safely out of the building at about 6:00 P.M. At 6:15 P.M. Correction Officer Ginty filed an official report on the incident.

15. Of the following, it is most likely that Mary Bancroft is a(n)

    (A) student.
    (B) secretary.
    (C) waitress.
    (D) actress.

16. The robbery took place

    (A) in room 314.
    (B) on the second floor.
    (C) on the elevator.
    (D) on the third floor.

17. The robber was

    (A) a foreigner.
    (B) a stranger to the victim.
    (C) an inmate.
    (D) an ex-convict.

18. Which one of the following is Miss Bancroft's correct home address?

    (A) 32-83 Crescent Boulevard, apartment 5C
    (B) 32-38 Crescent Boulevard, apartment 3C
    (C) 34-38 Crescent Boulevard, apartment 3C
    (D) 32-38 Crescent Boulevard, apartment 5C

19. The robber

    (A) stabbed the victim.
    (B) was unarmed.
    (C) was armed with a knife.
    (D) carried a gun.

20. The official report of the robbery was made at

    (A) 4:45 P.M.
    (B) 5:00 P.M.
    (C) 6:00 P.M.
    (D) 6:15 P.M.

Directions: Answer questions 21–26 solely on the basis of the information contained in the following passage.

Officer Richie Fox is the correction officer assigned to maintaining order in the prison kitchen. It is Saturday, June 1st, and the time is 11:30 A.M.

Officer Fox is approached by Inmate Saly, Inmate Number 420123, who asks him, "Why do I have to work in the kitchen? After all, the steam and the heat in here suffocate me. As soon as I walk in here, I start to get pains in my chest." The officer explains to Inmate Saly that the prison doctor can authorize a work detail change if the doctor feels it is medically required.

A little while later, at about 12:10 P.M., Officer Fox is approached by Inmate Cash, Inmate Number 420132, who says that his religion prohibits him from eating the kinds of food that are usually served. The officer tells Inmate Cash that the only person who can authorize a special menu for religious reasons is the prison chaplain.

At 12:30 P.M. Officer Fox has a discussion with Inmate Agresani, Inmate Number 421123, who complains about his current cellmate, Inmate Terri, Inmate Number 422213. Agresani explains to the officer that Terri refuses to keep their cell clean and that the two of them are constantly arguing. The officer tells Inmate Agresani to lodge a complaint with the Inmate's Grievance Board since they have the authority to approve cell changes.

At 12:45 P.M. an argument breaks out in the dining area. It seems that one inmate accused another of intentionally spilling a glass of water on him. The accused inmate, whose Inmate Number is 422213, insisted that what happened was an accident and apologized for his carelessness. That settled the argument.

At 1:00 P.M. Officer Fox was relieved of kitchen duty and went on a meal break.

21. The inmate whose complaint can be resolved by the prison chaplain is Inmate Number

(A) 420123.
(B) 422213.
(C) 422123.
(D) 420132.

22. The inmate who had water spilled on him is

(A) Inmate Number 420123.
(B) Inmate Saly.
(C) Inmate Agresani.
(D) not identified in the passage.

23. The inmate who claimed he accidentally spilled water on another inmate is

(A) Inmate Terri.
(B) Inmate Agresani.
(C) Inmate Saly.
(D) not identified.

24. The authority to approve cell changes belongs to

(A) the prison chaplain.
(B) the warden.
(C) the prison doctor.
(D) the Inmate's Grievance Board.

25. Work detail changes can be made

(A) for any reason.
(B) when a security officer feels they are medically required.
(C) when an inmate makes a claim that the work involved is dangerous.
(D) when the prison doctor feels they are medically required.

26. The complaint that was resolved on June 1st occurred at

(A) 11:30 A.M.
(B) 12:10 P.M.
(C) 12:30 P.M.
(D) 12:45 P.M.

Directions: Answer questions 27–29 solely on the basis of the information contained in the following passage.

Correction Officer Ginty is off-duty. She is shopping in a local mall. At about 1:35 P.M. she observes two males she believes might be escapees from the Municipal Detention Center where she works. The two males are sitting on a bench watching shoppers as they pass. Correction Officer Ginty knows that she is authorized to make off-duty arrests. She also knows that, when she makes an off-duty arrest, she is required to notify her commanding officer by telephone within 1 hour of the arrest. In this case, Correction Officer Ginty does not make immediate arrests since she is not really sure if the two males are indeed escaped prisoners.

At 1:40 P.M. the two males get up from the bench and start walking away. Officer Ginty decides to follow the two males because they are acting suspiciously. The first suspect is a male white, about 35–40 years old, wearing black pants and a black jacket. The second is a male black, about 25–30 years old, wearing brown pants and a white coat. The two suspects stop in front of a bank, which is located right next to an exit from the mall into a parking lot. Correction Officer Ginty observes the two men as they watch people enter and leave the bank. At about 1:50 P.M. an elderly woman carrying her pocketbook in her hand leaves the bank. The two men follow her out of the mall into the parking lot. Thinking that the men were about to steal the woman's pocketbook, Correction Officer Ginty follows them out of the mall.

Sure enough, when the officer spots the two men in the parking lot, they are holding up the old lady. The male with the black jacket has a gun, and the other male is removing cash from the lady's pocketbook. Fearing for the victim's safety, the correction officer waits for the two robbers to finish their crime before she takes any action. At 1:55 P.M. when the robbers are fleeing the scene of the crime, the correction officer, with gun drawn for her own safety, catches them by surprise and arrests them.

Correction Officer Ginty then notifies the local police about her arrests. When the police sergeant arrives on the scene and hears the story, he tells Correction Officer Ginty that she should have notified the police sooner and that it was a mistake for her to take police action against armed perpetrators without sufficient backup.

27. Correction Officer Ginty did not arrest the two males at 1:35 P.M. because

(A) she is not authorized to make off-duty arrests.
(B) she is required to obtain the permission of her commanding officer before making off-duty arrests.
(C) she wasn't sure if they were escaped prisoners.
(D) she wanted to wait to get backup assistance.

28. Why did Correction Officer Ginty decide to follow the two males at 1:40 P.M.?

    (A) They were escaped prisoners.
    (B) They were acting suspiciously.
    (C) They were going to steal an old lady's pocketbook.
    (D) They were armed.

29. The suspect who had the gun was

    (A) a white male.
    (B) about 25–30 years old.
    (C) a black male.
    (D) wearing brown pants.

Directions: The paragraph below contains questions 30–32 in the form of three numbered blanks. Immediately following the paragraph are lists of four word choices that correspond to these numbered blanks. Select the word choice that would MOST appropriately fit the numbered blank in each question.

Correction officers are often assigned to fixed posts. A fixed post is an assignment that involves a __(Q 30)__ or extremely sensitive problem. Such assignments are often tedious, and correction officers assigned to them consistently find themselves combating boredom. Fixed posts require the __(Q 31)__ assigned to stay in a very restricted area. The area may be restricted for a variety of reasons. The __(Q 32)__ for the existence of such restrictions include everything from previous prisoner escape attempts to concern for prisoner safety. Fixed posts are created only after much intuitive thinking and deliberation on the part of the correction facility administrative staff.

30. (A) routine
    (B) serious
    (C) complicated
    (D) fundamental

31. (A) visitor
    (B) medical personnel
    (C) correction officer
    (D) inmate

32. (A) reasons
    (B) rules
    (C) budget
    (D) opposition

SECTION 3—VERBAL AND MATH

Directions: Answer questions 33–35 based solely on the following information.

RECORDS OF INMATES SERVING SENTENCES IN HARPER CORRECTIONAL FACILITY FOR MEN

Inmate	Years Served in Harper	Years Left to Serve
Jay	9	3
Short	6	1
Bellows	8	2
Kites	14	26
Sparks	3	1
Cross	17	13
Hall	6	12
Walls	1	6

33. The average number of years already served in the institution by all the inmates indicated in the table is

   (A) 7.
   (B) 8.
   (C) 9.
   (D) not able to be determined based on the information given.

34. The percentage of inmates with over 10 years left to serve is

   (A) 37½%.
   (B) 40%.
   (C) 62½%.
   (D) not able to be determined based on the information given.

35. Of the following inmates, the inmate who has served the greatest percentage of his sentence is

   (A) Jay.
   (B) Bellows.
   (C) Kites.
   (D) Sparks.

36. Officer Alexa Reyes can typically conduct a maximum of 2 intelligence-gathering interviews each hour during a typical 8-hour tour of duty. She is also, however, required to spend 1 hour each tour patrolling the tiers under her supervision. In addition, she spends typically 1 hour each tour for meals and personal necessities. During a typical month, she works 20 tours. If the time required spent patrolling the tiers under her supervision during a typical tour is represented by V and the time set aside for meals and personal necessities during a typical tour is P, which of the following most closely represents the total number of intelligence-gathering interviews Officer Reyes can typically make each month?

(A) $2 \times 20 \times 8 - V + P$

(B) $2 \times (8 - V - P) \times 20$

(C) $P + V \times (20 + 2)$

(D) $8 \times 2 \times 20 - V - P$

Directions: In each of questions 37–40 you will be given four choices. Each of the choices, A, B, and C, contains a written statement. You are to evaluate the statement in each choice and select the statement that is most accurately and clearly written. If all or none of the three written statements is accurately and clearly written, you are to select choice D.

37. According to the directions, evaluate the following statements.

(A) It is impossible to reach you and I.

(B) Put your gun in the holster.

(C) It's a shame she was convicted.

(D) All or none of the choices are accurate.

38. According to the directions, evaluate the following statements.

(A) Yesterday, all the inmates lay their weapons down and surrendered.

(B) Last night all the inmates laid down in front of the dining room to protest the quality of the food.

(C) We should learn the inmates a lesson.

(D) All or none of the choices are accurate.

39. According to the instructions, evaluate the following statements.

(A) After being searched, the correction officer put the inmate into the cell.

(B) After the inmate was searched, he went in the cell.

(C) The facility's basketball team has good morale.

(D) All or none of the choices are accurate.

40. According to the instructions, evaluate the following statements.

(A) The warden praised Jim and me.

(B) That is too dangerous for the officers.

(C) There is no way out of the prison other than the front gate.

(D) All or none of the choices are accurate.

Directions: Answer questions 41–50 based solely on the information recorded on the following chart.

OVERTIME REPORT

RANK	+	SOCIAL SECURITY NO.	FACILITY
Correction Officer	+		Beacon

SHIELD NO.	+	SURNAME	FIRST
10986	+	Walker	Frank

DATE OF PRESENT RANK	+	DATE ENTERED DEPT.
09/05/11	+	09/05/11

SCHEDULED TO WORK	+	ACTUALLY WORKED
FROM – TO	+	FROM – TO
DATE DATE	+	DATE DATE
5/1/13 5/1/13	+	5/1/13 5/1/13
TIME TIME	+	TIME TIME
0900 Hrs. 1700 Hrs.	+	0900 Hrs. 2100 Hrs.
TOTAL	+	TOTAL
8 Hrs	+	12 Hrs

(Time actually worked [-minus] Time scheduled) = OT

$$12 \quad - \quad 8 \quad = 4$$

CHECK ONE - I opt to take the overtime (OT) in

(x) Cash   ( ) Compensatory Time

FACILITY WHERE OT WAS PERFORMED:

( ) Houston   ( ) Barclay   (x) Carter   ( ) Beacon

REASON FOR OVERTIME

The undersigned was temporarily assigned on May 1, 2013, to Carter Detention Facility to perform residential cell block duty in connection with disturbance occurring there on April 30, 2013.

I certify to accuracy of information:

DATE   RANK and SIGNATURE OF REQUESTING OFFICER
05/02/13   C.O.   *Frank Walker*

OVERTIME RECORDED IN FACILITY LOG   YES (x) NO ( )
(FACILITY)-Carter   (DATE) 05/02/13   (PAGE NUMBER)-407

DATE RANK and SIGNATURE OF SUPERVISOR FACILITY
05/01/13   CAPTAIN   *Don Homes*   CARTER

41. Who worked overtime and made the request?

    (A) Captain Frank Walker
    (B) Don Walker
    (C) Correction Officer Frank Walker
    (D) Correction Officer Don Homes

42. The reason for the overtime was

    (A) an injury to an inmate.
    (B) an injury to a correction officer.
    (C) a disturbance at the Beacon Detention Facility.
    (D) a disturbance at the Carter Detention Facility.

43. What are the last four digits of the social security number of the officer requesting the overtime?

    (A) 4532
    (B) 4352
    (C) 4235
    (D) not able to be determined

44. In the log of which of the following facilities was the overtime recorded?

    (A) Houston
    (B) Barclay
    (C) Carter
    (D) Beacon

45. How many hours did the officer requesting the overtime actually work?

    (A) 8
    (B) 12
    (C) 4
    (D) 14

46. How did the officer request the overtime be compensated?

    (A) in time
    (B) in cash
    (C) in both time and cash
    (D) in time or cash

47. The officer who is requesting the overtime assumed the present rank the officer holds

    (A) 5 years after entering into the department.
    (B) 2 years after entering into the department.
    (C) 1 year after entering into the department.
    (D) at the same time the officer entered the department.

48. According to the form, the supervisor and the correction officer making the overtime request signed the form

    (A) on the same day.
    (B) 1 day apart with the supervisor signing the form first.
    (C) 1 day apart with the correction officer making the request signing the form first.
    (D) 2 days apart.

49. The incident that caused the overtime occurred on

    (A) April 30th.
    (B) May 1st.
    (C) May 2nd.
    (D) September 5th.

50. What is the shield number of the officer making the request?

    (A) 407
    (B) 10896
    (C) 10986
    (D) 90594

Directions: Answer questions 51–58 based on the following data.

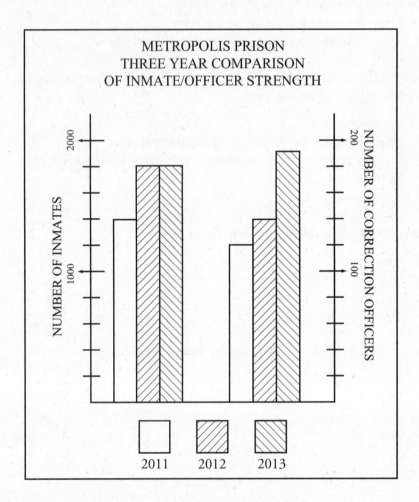

51. Which of the following is the most accurate statement concerning the number of inmates during the 3-year period shown in the data?

   (A) The number of inmates increased each year of the 3-year period.
   (B) The number of inmates decreased each year of the 3-year period.
   (C) The number of inmates increased during the first year of the 3-year period and remained about the same for the next 2 years.
   (D) The number of inmates was the greatest during the second year of the 3-year period.

52. In 2011 what was the ratio of inmates to correction officers?

   (A) about 11.6 to 1
   (B) about 1 to 11.6
   (C) about 1 to 1
   (D) cannot be determined

53. In 2013 there were

    (A) about the same number of correction officers as there were in 2011.
    (B) about 50 more correction officers than there were in 2012.
    (C) about the same number of correction officers as there were inmates in 2013.
    (D) about 35 more correction officers than there were in 2011.

54. Assume that in 2014 the inmate population increased by 100 inmates while the number of correction officers remained at the 2013 level. At the end of 2014, the ratio of inmates to officers would be

    (A) about 10 to 1.
    (B) about 15 to 1.
    (C) about 20 to 1.
    (D) not able to be determined.

55. The percentage increase in the inmate population from 2011 to 2013 was

    (A) about 10%.
    (B) about 18%.
    (C) about 29%.
    (D) not able to be determined.

56. How many correction officers would have to be added to the complement of officers during 2014 to reach a strength of 200 officers at the end of that year?

    (A) 80 officers
    (B) 60 officers
    (C) 10 officers
    (D) It cannot be determined.

57. On any given day in 2013, how many correction officers would actually be working?

    (A) 120
    (B) 140
    (C) 190
    (D) It cannot be determined.

58. Exactly how many inmates entered Metropolis Prison during 2012?

    (A) 200
    (B) 400
    (C) 600
    (D) It cannot be determined.

SECTION 6—APPLYING CORRECTION PROCEDURES

Directions: Answer questions 59–63 solely on the basis of the following information.

A *Metal Detector Search* is either a search that requires an inmate or visitor to walk through a metal detector or a search wherein a portable metal detector is passed over an inmate's or visitor's person to determine whether there are metal objects in wearing apparel or attached to the body.

A *Pat Frisk* is a search of an inmate's or visitor's person and wearing apparel while the inmate or visitor is clothed. An inmate, but not a visitor, shall be required to remove coat, hat, and shoes. The search shall include searching these items of the inmate's clothing.

A *Strip Frisk* involves a thorough visual inspection of the inmate's armpits and oral and anal cavities as well as the spreading of the legs and the forward bending of the body.

A *Body Cavity Search* is a search of an inmate's genitals, both male and female, both internally and externally, and other body cavities. This type of search is performed in absolute privacy by medical personnel. A corrections supervisor must be in attendance during the search. For security reasons, a correction officer may also attend. The supervisor and officer, however, must be of the same gender as the inmate.

59. A Metal Detector Search is permitted to be used

    (A) only when performed by medical personnel.
    (B) either on inmates or visitors.
    (C) only on inmates.
    (D) either by medical or corrections personnel.

60. It would be most appropriate to insist that medical personnel be present for a

    (A) Metal Detector Search.
    (B) Pat Frisk.
    (C) Strip Frisk.
    (D) Body Cavity Search.

61. Which of the following statements is most correct concerning a Pat Frisk?

    (A) It may include removing shoes from a visitor.
    (B) It may include removing a hat from an inmate.
    (C) It may be done only by a corrections supervisor.
    (D) It must be done in total privacy.

62. A Strip Frisk shall include all the following actions except

    (A) a visual inspection of oral cavities.
    (B) a visual inspection of the armpits.
    (C) the spreading of the legs and the forward bending of the body.
    (D) internally searching a female inmate's genitals.

63. Which of the following statements concerning Body Cavity Searches is most appropriate?

(A) They must always be performed by males.

(B) They must always be performed by females.

(C) They should always be performed by medical personnel who must be the same gender as the person being searched.

(D) A corrections supervisor must be present when they are conducted.

Directions: Answer questions 64–66 based solely on the following information.

All non-department vehicles passing through a gate shall be logged in the Gate Record of Non-Department Vehicles by the correction officer in charge of the gate. The log shall be maintained in the following manner and in the following order:

1. the gate designation;

2. the name and badge number of the officer in charge of the gate, along with the names of any officers acting as relieving officers;

3. the date and time non-department vehicles enter and leave the facility;

4. the name and address of the registered owner of the vehicle;

5. the name and address of the operator of the vehicle, along with the names and addresses of any helpers;

6. a description of the contents of the vehicles; and

7. the license plate number and make and model of the vehicle.

In addition to making entries in the Gate Record of Non-Department Vehicles, the correction officer in charge of the gate shall conduct a total vehicle search of all such vehicles. A total vehicle search requires that the correction officer enter the vehicle and conduct a search for contraband and/or unauthorized persons. The search shall also include the undercarriage of the vehicle. The search of the undercarriage shall be conducted by the use of a mirror or a mechanic's pit if available. Any irregularities shall be immediately reported to the tour commander by the correction officer in charge of the gate.

64. Officer Baker is assigned as the correction officer in charge of the gate. A private vehicle not belonging to the department is attempting to enter the gate and make a delivery. Officer Baker enters the time the vehicle enters the facility along with required preceding entries. The next entry that should be made is

(A) the name and address of the registered owner of the vehicle.

(B) the gate designation.

(C) a description of the contents of the vehicles.

(D) the name and address of the operator of the vehicle, along with the names and addresses of any helpers.

65. A total vehicle search requires all the following except that

    (A) the correction officer enter the vehicle.

    (B) a search be conducted for contraband.

    (C) a search be conducted for unauthorized persons.

    (D) a mechanic search the undercarriage of the vehicle by using a mirror.

66. As a result of a total vehicle search, irregularities are uncovered. Upon being made aware of such irregularities, Officer Baker while assigned as the correction officer in charge of the gate should immediately

    (A) effect the arrest of the driver of the vehicle.

    (B) call the owner of the vehicle.

    (C) notify the tour commander.

    (D) impound the vehicle.

Directions: Answer questions 67 and 68 based solely on the following information.

Upon admission to the Longwood Correctional Facility, any property removed from an inmate, other than property involved with a criminal offense, shall be properly identified, receipted for, and safely stored in the Facility Storage Warehouse. It shall remain there until returned to the inmate upon the inmate's discharge or given to a friend or relative of the inmate pursuant to the wishes of the inmate. When so returned, a receipt shall be obtained. An inmate may not appeal the removal of property resulting from the admissions processing. Property removed in connection with a criminal offense shall be turned over to the county prosecutor.

However, an inmate may appeal property removed as a result of a search of packages received through the mail. Such an appeal may be made by an inmate or an inmate's legal counsel. Said appeals must be made within 48 hours of the seizure of the property.

67. According to the procedures of the Longwood Correctional Facility, all property that is removed from an inmate during admissions processing must

    (A) be returned when the inmate is discharged.

    (B) be given to any relative of the inmate if such relative claims the property.

    (C) be stored in the Facility Storage Warehouse.

    (D) be receipted for if returned by the department.

68. Regarding the procedure dealing with property removed from an inmate, which of the following is least correct?

(A) An inmate may not appeal the removal of property resulting from the admissions processing.

(B) Property removed in connection with a criminal offense shall be turned over to the county prosecutor.

(C) An inmate may appeal property removed as a result of a search of packages received through the mail.

(D) In appropriate instances appeals about the removal of property must be made within 24 hours of the seizure of the property.

Directions: Answer questions 69–71 based solely on the following information.

When a prisoner in custody requires medical/psychiatric treatment, the correction officer assigned to the cell block shall notify the tour commander. If necessary, an escorting officer other than the officer assigned to the cell block shall be assigned by the tour commander to accompany the prisoner to the hospital. The officer assigned to accompany the inmate shall notify the tour commander when the prisoner actually leaves the cell block.

In all life-threatening situations the prisoner will be removed to the nearest hospital. The officer accompanying the prisoner shall prepare a Medical Treatment of Prisoner form for each inmate who:

1. receives medical/psychiatric treatment (the form shall be forwarded to the department's surgeon general) or

2. refuses treatment after claiming injury or illness (the form shall be forwarded to the city attorney) or

3. is in apparent need of treatment but makes no such request (the form shall remain with the inmate) or

4. may require prescribed medication (the form shall be forwarded to the department pharmacist).

69. One night Ray Powers, an inmate at the Jess Kegler Correctional Facility, becomes violently ill and asks for medical attention. Officer Best is the correction officer assigned to the cell block, and the tour commander is Captain Heating. The decision is made to transport the inmate to the hospital because it is a life-threatening situation. In such an instance

(A) Officer Best should accompany Inmate Powers to a hospital without consulting with anyone.

(B) Captain Heating should select Officer Best to accompany Inmate Powers to the hospital.

(C) Inmate Powers must be taken to the nearest hospital.

(D) Officer Best should notify Captain Heating when the prisoner leaves the cell block for the hospital.

70. One morning three prisoners are transported to a nearby hospital for treatment. While at the hospital, Inmate Cards receives medical treatment, Inmate Clubs refuses treatment after claiming an injury, and Inmate Towns has severe pain, which clearly requires prescribed medication. In such a situation, a Medical Treatment of Prisoner form should be prepared for

   (A) only one of the inmates.
   (B) only two of the inmates.
   (C) all three of the inmates.
   (D) none of the prisoners.

71. In the instance of an inmate who is in apparent need of treatment but makes no such request, a Medical Treatment of Prisoner form should

   (A) be prepared and forwarded to the department's surgeon general.
   (B) be prepared and forwarded to the city attorney.
   (C) be prepared and remain with the inmate.
   (D) never be prepared until help is requested by the inmate.

Directions: Answer questions 72 and 73 based solely on the following information.

A member of the Department of Correction when traveling to a location outside the state while off duty shall not carry a firearm. In such a case the member may choose to do any of the following:

1. deposit a personal firearm in the arsenal locker of the member's command or

2. deposit a personal firearm in the arsenal locker of the command that is closest to the member's private residence or

3. safeguard a personal firearm at the member's place of residence. Note that when a personal firearm is safeguarded at a member's place of residence, the firearm shall be secured in such a manner that the chance of theft is minimized as is the opportunity for others to tamper with the firearm.

Due to federal regulations, Department of Correction regulations prohibit the storing of a firearm in a bank safe deposit box.

72. According to department regulations, which of the following is least correct?

   (A) A member of the department may never carry any firearm outside the state.
   (B) A member going on vacation and traveling outside the state may choose to leave a personal firearm in the arsenal locker of the member's command.
   (C) A member going on vacation and traveling outside the state may choose to safeguard a personal firearm at the member's place of residence.
   (D) Under certain circumstances a member could deposit a personal firearm in the arsenal locker of the command that is closest to the member's private residence.

73. Correction Officer Bob Knight is planning to take some time off and take a trip out of state. His wife Pat Knight, who is also a correction officer with the same department, suggests that they leave their personal firearms in their bank safe deposit box. In this instance, Pat's advice is

   (A) good mainly because it will be very safe there.
   (B) bad mainly because officers should always be armed.
   (C) good mainly because if any theft occurs the bank will have to replace the revolvers.
   (D) bad mainly because department regulations as well as certain federal regulation prohibit such an action.

Directions: Use the information in the following reference table to answer questions 74–78. In the table each number has been associated with a letter. For each question use the relationship in the table and select the choice that correctly spells the word identified in the question.

Y	O	U	N	G	S	T	E	R	Z
1	2	3	4	5	6	7	8	9	0

74. Using the reference table, which of the following most accurately spells *GROGGY?*

   (A) 595221
   (B) 592551
   (C) 590551
   (D) 952991

75. Using the reference table, which of the following most accurately spells *STRONG?*

   (A) 679045
   (B) 679425
   (C) 679245
   (D) 679254

76. Using the reference table, which of the following most accurately spells *TESTER?*

    (A) 768789
    (B) 786987
    (C) 768769
    (D) 786789

77. Using the reference table, which of the following most accurately spells *SNORES?*

    (A) 642986
    (B) 640986
    (C) 604986
    (D) 642896

78. Using the reference table, which of the following most accurately spells *TONGUE?*

    (A) 724358
    (B) 704538
    (C) 724538
    (D) 704358

SECTION 7—JUDGMENT AND REASONING

79. Correction officers might have to evacuate inmates from a dangerous area. Under which of the following circumstances would it be most appropriate for an evacuation to take place in accordance with this rule?

   (A) An argument is occurring in the prison yard.
   (B) A hunger strike is on-going in the prison mess hall.
   (C) An asbestos fire is burning under a cell block.
   (D) A deranged inmate is being subdued in the library.

80. Correction officers, who are the first on the scene when inmates require medical assistance in life-threatening situations, must administer first aid until medical assistance arrives. In which one of the following cases should a correction officer administer first aid pending the arrival of medical assistance?

   (A) An inmate is bleeding profusely from the stomach area.
   (B) An inmate is experiencing cramps in his legs.
   (C) An inmate is complaining of a pain in his back.
   (D) An inmate has a headache.

81. A correction officer is assigned at the door of an evening showing of a movie. Attendance is optional for the inmates. The officer counted 16 inmates as they entered the theater. Right before the lights are to be lowered for the showing of the movie, the officer enters the theater, makes a quick double-check of his count and counts only 15 inmates. The officer's first action should be to

   (A) issue an alarm for one escaped prisoner.
   (B) count the inmates again before concluding that one has escaped.
   (C) notify his supervisor and await further guidance.
   (D) let the showing of the movie proceed as there is no way an inmate could have escaped.

82. To remain safe in a dangerous environment and to most effectively accomplish the goals of the prison administration, correction officers must function together as a team. The most important characteristic of teamwork is

   (A) individual accomplishment.
   (B) cooperation.
   (C) aggressiveness.
   (D) rigidity.

83. When engaged in preventive patrol in a cell block, a correction officer should try to create an impression of omnipresence. This means that inmates should be made to believe that

(A) they are always being watched by ever-present officers.
(B) it is wrong to break rules and regulations.
(C) an officer will be coming by on a regularly scheduled basis.
(D) they should behave even when they are not being watched.

84. Correction officers are sometimes required to request emergency transportation for seriously injured inmates. In which of the following situations would it be most appropriate for a correction officer to request emergency transportation?

(A) An older inmate falls down in the hallway and suffers an abrasion of the knee.
(B) A young inmate falls down a flight of stairs and is knocked unconscious.
(C) A new inmate complains of feeling faint.
(D) An inmate who is a chronic complainer says that he is experiencing difficulty eating.

85. Using inmates to help do work in the prison kitchen is a great way to economize, but it has its drawbacks. The most serious problem is caused by the fact that many essential kitchen utensils can be used as weapons. Of the following, the best and most practical way to solve this problem is to

(A) use only model inmates as kitchen help and then hope that they will not steal utensils.
(B) insist that the kitchen supervisor run the kitchen without utensils that could be used as weapons.
(C) maintain constant and careful supervision of inmates who work in the kitchen.
(D) run the kitchen without inmate help.

86. An inmate approaches a correction officer and states that he has some important information but that he will reveal the information only to the warden. When asked to reveal the information to the correction officer, the inmate refuses. Under these circumstances, of the following choices, the most correct course of action for the officer to take is to

(A) insist that the inmate reveal the information.
(B) immediately take the inmate to see the warden.
(C) inform a supervisor about the situation.
(D) take no further action.

87. An inmate approaches a correction officer and informs the officer that he has not heard from his wife in over a month. The inmate requests that the officer visit his wife on the officer's day off to find out what is going on. Under these circumstances, the best thing for the officer to do is to

(A) comply with the inmate's request as this is a good way to become popular with the inmate population.

(B) tell the inmate to ask another inmate who is about to be released to find out what is wrong.

(C) tactfully explain to the inmate that there is nothing that can be done to help him with his problem.

(D) refer the inmate to the person on the prison staff who has the responsibility to handle such situations.

88. A complaint is an allegation of an improper or unlawful act that relates to the business of a correctional facility. Which of the following is not an example of a complaint?

(A) An inmate states that an officer used excessive force on him.

(B) An inmate claims that his court-appointed lawyer did not properly represent him.

(C) An inmate contends that the officer in his cell block discriminates against him.

(D) An inmate reports that another inmate stole property from him.

SECTION 8—LEGAL DEFINITIONS

Directions: Answer questions 89–98 *solely* on the basis of the following legal definitions.

A person commits *arson* when he intentionally damages either a building or a motor vehicle by means of a fire or an explosion.

A person commits *petit larceny* when he unlawfully takes, obtains, or withholds the property of another person.

A person commits *grand larceny* when he commits petit larceny and the value of the property is more than $1,000.00 at the time of the theft.

A person commits *simple assault,* which is a misdemeanor, when he intentionally causes a physical injury to any other person.

A person commits the felony known as *felonious assault* when he intentionally causes a serious physical injury to any other person.

89. Joe is an inmate at the Foster Correctional Institution. While being transported in a Foster Correctional Institution van to attend his mother's funeral, Joe is nervously smoking a cigarette. Intending to flick the ashes from his cigarette into the van's ashtray, Joe misses the ashtray, and the burning ashes fall to the floor. Joe thereby causes damage to the interior door panels of the van. Joe has

    (A) committed arson since some damage to the vehicle has occurred.
    (B) not committed arson since only a building can be the subject of an arson.
    (C) committed arson since arson can be committed either by fire or explosion and burning ashes should be considered a type of fire.
    (D) not committed arson since he did not intentionally cause damage.

90. Which of the following statements is most appropriate according to the previously stated definitions?

    (A) Only a motor vehicle can be the subject of an arson.
    (B) Only a building can be the subject of an arson.
    (C) Either a motor vehicle or a building can be the subject of an arson.
    (D) If an arson is to occur, both a motor vehicle and a building must suffer damage.

91. Evaluate the following statements:

    1. Arson can be committed only by causing damage by an explosion.
    2. Arson can be committed by causing a fire but not by causing an explosion.

    Which of the following is most accurate concerning these two statements?

    (A) Only statement 1 is correct.
    (B) Only statement 2 is correct.
    (C) Both statements 1 and 2 are correct.
    (D) Neither statement 1 nor 2 is correct.

92. Pat reaches into Tom's pocket and secretly removes credit cards without Tom realizing what is happening. Pat then quickly walks away without being noticed by Tom. However, when Pat examines the credit cards, he throws them away because both credit cards would be difficult to use because they contain an ID photo of Tom. In such an instance, Pat would be guilty of

   (A) no crime since he never used the credit cards.
   (B) petit larceny.
   (C) grand larceny.
   (D) both grand larceny and petit larceny.

93. Terry is an inmate who is assigned to paint the state-provided residence of Warden Gibbs. While at the warden's residence, Terry sees several music albums recorded by legendary artists. The albums are very old, and, although they cost about $5 each when they were new, Terry recently saw them on sale in a collector's magazine for $200 each. As Terry is about to leave, she places six of the albums under her coat and leaves with them hidden under her coat. The next day, Terry sells the albums for $150 each to an unscrupulous prison official. If apprehended, Terry should be charged with

   (A) petit larceny because the albums only cost $5 apiece when they were new.
   (B) grand larceny because the total value of the albums at the time of the theft was more than $1000.
   (C) petit larceny since Terry sold the albums for under $1000.
   (D) grand larceny because the albums were collectibles.

94. Evaluate the following statements:

   1. Every petit larceny is also a grand larceny.
   2. Every grand larceny is also a petit larceny.

   Which of the following is most accurate concerning these two statements?

   (A) Only statement 1 is correct.
   (B) Only statement 2 is correct.
   (C) Both statements 1 and 2 are correct.
   (D) Neither statement 1 nor 2 is correct.

95. As part of an escape plan, Ray steals some gasoline from the motor transport unit of the correctional facility where he is an inmate. Using the stolen gasoline, Ray sets fire to a prison van worth $25,000 in order to cause a distraction so that his escape plan can be put into effect. If apprehended, in addition to any charges in connection with his escape plan, Ray should be charged with

   (A) only arson.
   (B) only petit larceny.
   (C) grand larceny because of the value of the van.
   (D) arson and petit larceny.

96. While exercising in the prison yard, Lou while assisting Tab in lifting free weights accidentally lets a 35-pound dumbbell slip from his hand striking Tab in his forehead. Tab was taken to the infirmary and received five stitches. In such an instance, Lou should be charged with

   (A) no crime.
   (B) felonious assault because Tab suffered a serious physical injury.
   (C) simple assault because Tab suffered only a minor injury.
   (D) felonious assault if it can be shown that Lou has a history of assaults.

97. Mary is angry at Cindy, another inmate. Mary takes a pair of scissors and, while trying to intentionally stab and seriously injure Cindy, Mary misses and stabs Ellen, causing a serious physical injury to Ellen. In such an instance, Mary is guilty of

   (A) simple assault because she did not hit her intended target.
   (B) no offense because she did not hit her intended target.
   (C) felonious assault because she intentionally caused a serious physical injury.
   (D) simple assault because it was an accident even though the act was done intentionally.

98. Evaluate the following statements:

   1. Simple assault is a misdemeanor, but felonious assault is a felony.
   2. Petit larceny is a misdemeanor, but grand larceny is a felony.

   Which of the following is most accurate concerning these two statements?

   (A) Only statement 1 is correct.
   (B) Only statement 2 is correct.
   (C) Both statements 1 and 2 are correct.
   (D) Neither statement 1 nor 2 is correct.

Gambling in correctional facilities not only violates the rules of the facility but also violates the law. For example,

Possession of Gambling Records in the second degree is a misdemeanor. A person commits Possession of Gambling Records in the second degree when such person possesses records of a kind commonly used in the operation or promotion of a bookmaking enterprise, or possesses records of a kind commonly used in the operation or promotion of a policy enterprise (the numbers game).

However, any person who possesses less than ten bets shall be presumed to possess personal bets and shall not be prosecuted under this law.

Possession of Gambling Records in the first degree is a felony. A person commits Possession of Gambling Records in the first degree when such person possesses records of a kind commonly used in the operation or promotion of a bookmaking enterprise and constituting more than five bets totaling more than $5000, or possesses records of a kind commonly used in the operation or promotion of a policy enterprise (the numbers game) constituting more than 500 plays.

A person convicted of Possession of Gambling Records in the second degree will be sentenced as a felon if the defendant has been previously convicted of the same crime within the past 5 years.

99. If Bob is arrested, charged, and convicted of Possession of Gambling Records in the first degree, it is most likely that Bob

   (A) possessed more than $5000 in policy bets.
   (B) had more than five bets totaling $500.
   (C) possessed 550 policy bets.
   (D) had eleven of his own policy bets.

100. Which of the following defendants convicted of Possession of Gambling Records in the second degree would be most appropriately sentenced as a felon?

   (A) Bugs, who was convicted of a robbery 2 years ago.
   (B) Lou, who was arrested for rape 6 years ago.
   (C) Tom, who was arrested for Possession of Gambling Records, the misdemeanor, 4 years ago.
   (D) Pat, who was convicted for Possession of Gambling Records, the misdemeanor, 4 years ago.

> **Directions:** For questions 101–105, read the five numbered sentences presented for each question and select the answer choice that contains the best way to organize these sentences into a clear and accurate paragraph.

Question 101.

1. Correction officers, while in uniform, are not allowed to smoke while performing any duties that require them to be in contact with the public or with inmates.
2. No Smoking areas must be clearly and prominently signed.
3. In addition, correction officers are prohibited from smoking in those areas that are designated as No Smoking areas.
4. Violations of this rule must result in a monetary loss.
5. The term *public* does not include other correction agency personnel.

(A) 5-4-3-2-1
(B) 3-4-5-1-2
(C) 4-1-3-2-5
(D) 1-5-3-2-4

Question 102.

1. One such requirement is for males to be cleanly shaven.
2. Officers with documented medical reasons are exempted from this requirement.
3. Correction officers are required to be well-groomed while on duty.
4. Violators of the grooming requirements must be disciplined.
5. There is, however, an exception to the clean shaven requirement.

(A) 3-1-2-5-4
(B) 3-1-5-2-4
(C) 2-1-5-4-3
(D) 4-1-3-2-5

Question 103.

1. As such, they sometimes find themselves in difficult situations that call for them to use discretion while making their decisions.
2. These guidelines and procedures are usually in written form and are made available to all correction officers.
3. These procedures, which act as guidelines, are, of course, in keeping with the overall policies of the agency.
4. Correction officers, like other law enforcement officers, often work alone and not under the direct supervision of their supervisors
5. To help and guide them in these situations, they are given procedures to follow.

(A) 1-4-5-2-3
(B) 3-4-1-2-5
(C) 4-1-5-3-2
(D) 4-3-1-2-5

Question 104.

Correction Officer Robles is giving a report to the news media regarding someone who has jumped from the roof of the detention facility where he is assigned. His report will include the following five sentences:

1. I responded to the roof, where I found the person at the edge of the roof.
2. A visitor at the facility had just reported to Sergeant Black that a man was on the roof.
3. At 5:30 P.M., the person jumped from the building.
4. My supervisor, Sergeant Black, called me at 4:50 P.M. and told me to respond to the roof of the facility.
5. I tried to talk to the person and convince him not to jump.

What is the most logical order for the above sentences to appear in the report?

(A) 1-2-4-3-5
(B) 3-4-1-2-5
(C) 2-4-1-3-5
(D) 4-2-1-5-3

Question 105.

Correction Officer Aponte is a recruitment officer. She is writing a warning notice to candidates concerning the danger of presenting false information in their employment application. This notice will include the following five sentences:

1. Such presentation of false information is a grievous and irreversible error.
2. You must understand that the factual information about yourself that you supply will be checked.
3. Sometimes candidates, in their desire to obtain employment as a court officer, will present false information about their background to investigators.
4. In many cases, this rejection is made even if the misrepresentation is no cause for automatic disqualification.
5. If a subsequent determination is made that you misrepresented your background in an attempt to deceive, you will be rejected.

What is the most logical order for the above sentences to appear in the report?

(A) 3-1-2-5-4
(B) 5-3-4-2-1
(C) 3-5-1-2-4
(D) 4-3-5-1-2

> **Directions:** Answer questions 106–108 based solely on the procedure associated with each question.

106. When a correction officer discovers a visitor to a detention facility who illegally possesses a firearm, he or she should do the following in the order shown:

1. Confiscate the firearm.
2. Properly charge the person.
3. Complete a lab examination form.
4. Bring the firearm to the lab.
5. After the lab examination, bring the firearm to the property clerk.

Correction Officer Lopez determines that Joe Brown, who is a visitor to the detention facility where Lopez works, possesses an illegal firearm. After confiscating the firearm, what should Lopez do next?

(A) Bring the firearm to the lab.
(B) Bring the firearm to the property clerk.
(C) Properly charge Brown.
(D) Complete a lab examination form.

107. When a correction officer discovers damage to agency property, other than a vehicle, he or she shall prepare a report that must contain, when appropriate, the following information in the order presented:

1. Date and time of discovery;
2. Location where damage occurred;
3. Description of damaged agency property along with extent of damage;
4. Action taken by discovering officer;
5. Name of witnesses, if any;
6. Brief description of other damaged agency property, if any;
7. Identification of other persons involved, if any;
8. Name of supervisor notified.

While working the midnight shift in Cell Block 9, Correction Officer Columbo discovers one damaged agency television set in the totally vacant cell block recreation room. As required, Officer Columbo prepares a report of the incident and lists in this order: the date and time of discovery, the location of the damaged TV set, a description of the TV set and the extent of the damage, as well as the action he took. What is the next entry Columbo should make in his report?

(A) List the name of each witness.
(B) Include a brief description of other damaged agency property.
(C) List the identity of other persons involved.
(D) Include the name of the supervisor notified.

108. When removing a prisoner to a hospital as a result of a mental health call, a correction officer shall do the following in the order shown:

1. Remove property that is dangerous to life or will aid in escape.
2. Have the prisoner removed to a hospital in an ambulance.
3. Seek the advice of a physician if an ambulance is not available.
4. Use restraining handcuffs if the prisoner is violent or upon direction of a physician.
5. Ride in the body of the ambulance along with the prisoner.
6. Ensure that a female prisoner is accompanied by a female officer.
7. Contact a member of the prisoner's family.

Correction Officer Tom Ryan is removing a violent male prisoner who is the subject of a mental health call to a hospital in an ambulance. Prior to that, Ryan removed property from the prisoner that could aid escape or be a danger to life. What should be the correction officer's next step?

(A) Use restraining handcuffs.
(B) Ask for direction from a physician.
(C) Ride in the body of the ambulance with the prisoner.
(D) Contact a member of the prisoner's family.

Directions: Answer questions 109–110 based solely on the procedure described.

When supervising a lawyer-client visit in a detention facility, a correction officer shall take the following actions in the order shown:

1. Check the lawyer's identification.
2. Record the lawyer's Bar License number in the visitor's log.
3. Remove and safeguard the lawyer's Bar License card.
4. Inspect the relevant case documents in felony cases.
5. Have a same-gender, full-body search of the lawyer performed.
6. Have all property that could facilitate an escape attempt removed.
7. Prohibit the use of electronic devices.
8. Prohibit clothing that exposes skin for female lawyers visiting male inmates.
9. Allow a face-to-face lawyer-client visit only if advance scheduling of the visit occurred.
10. Strictly enforce the time limits of any resulting visit.
11. After any face-to-face visit, have an after-the-visit frisk of the lawyer made.
12. Return the lawyer's Bar License card.
13. Have the lawyer escorted out of the facility.

109. Correction Officer Sanford is supervising a lawyer–client visit in the detention facility where he is assigned. The lawyer is Donald Josephs, and the client is Inmate Arnold Player, a 17-year-old male accused of misdemeanor rape. Sanford has just properly recorded the lawyer's Bar License number in the visitor's log. He then removed and safeguarded the lawyer's Bar License card. What is the next step the officer should take?

(A) Inspect Player's relevant case documents.
(B) Have a same-gender, full-body search of Player performed.
(C) Prohibit the use of electronic devices.
(D) Have a same-gender, full-body search of Josephs performed.

110. Correction Officer Marty McCabe is supervising a non–advanced scheduled lawyer–client visit in the detention facility where he is assigned. The lawyer is Raymond Babitch, a 60-year-old male, and the client is Inmate Daniel Merkle, a 62-year-old inmate being held on the suspicion of robbery. McCabe has properly followed procedures and has just informed Babitch that he will not be able to bring any electronic devices to the meeting. What should be the officer's next step?

(A) Prevent Babitch from wearing any clothing that exposes skin.
(B) Allow a face-to-face visit between Babitch and Merkle.
(C) Strictly enforce the time limits of any resulting visit.
(D) Have a frisk of Babitch performed.

> **Directions:** Answer questions 111–115 based solely on the following information and map. The flow of traffic is indicated by the arrows. If only one arrow is shown, traffic flows only in the direction indicated by the arrow. If two arrows are shown, traffic flows in both directions. You must follow the flow of traffic when moving from one location to another.

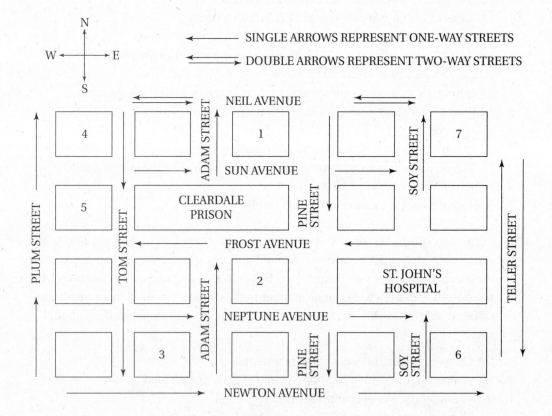

111. Correction Officer Jung is operating a prisoner van at the intersection of Tom Street and Newton Avenue. She receives a call from the dispatcher to respond to St. John's Hospital. Which of the following is the most direct route for her to take in her van, making sure to obey all traffic regulations?

    (A) Travel west on Newton Avenue for 1 block, then north on Plum Street, and then east on Neptune Avenue to St. John's Hospital.

    (B) Travel north on Tom Street, then east on Neptune Avenue, then north on Teller Street, and then west on Frost Avenue to St. John's Hospital.

    (C) Travel east on Newton Avenue for 2 blocks, then north on Pine Street for 1 block, and then east on Neptune Avenue to St. John's Hospital.

    (D) Travel east on Newton Avenue for 4 blocks, then north on Teller Street, and then west on Frost Avenue to St. John's Hospital.

112. John Jay is the warden of Cleardale Prison. On day after a tour of duty and while driving home in an official correction department vehicle, the warden pulls over at the intersection of Soy Street and Sun Avenue to take a call from the current shift supervisor at the prison. There has been a fight between two inmates, and one of the inmates is likely to die from the injuries he has sustained. The injured inmate was previously an elected official of the city who was now serving a prison sentence as a result of a bribery conviction. The press and the mayor's office have made several inquiries about the incident, so the warden decides to return to the prison to oversee an investigation of the incident. Which of the following is the most direct route for him to take in his official car, making sure to obey all traffic regulations?

    (A) Head south on Soy Street for 1 block, then east on Frost Avenue for 2 blocks, then north on Tom Street for 1 block, and then east on Sun Avenue.

    (B) Travel north on Soy Street, then west on Neil Avenue, then south on Tom Street, and then east on Sun Avenue.

    (C) Head west on Sun Avenue, then south on Pine Street, and then west on Frost Avenue.

    (D) Travel east on Sun Avenue, then south on Teller Street, then west on Neptune Avenue, and then north on Adam Street.

113. A traffic accident involving a correction van resulting in only property damage has occurred at the intersection of Frost Avenue and Plum Street. Correction Officer Daly, who is returning to the prison is in his correction van, is at the intersection of Soy Street and Newton Avenue. Officer Daly is directed to respond to the scene of the accident and assist in completing the transportation of prisoners to their destination. Which of the following is the most direct route for Daly to take in his van, making sure to obey all traffic regulations?

    (A) Travel north on Soy Street and then west on Frost Avenue to Plum Street, where the accident has occurred.

    (B) Travel west on Newton Avenue, then north on Adam Street, and then west on Frost Avenue to Plum Street.

    (C) Travel east on Newton Avenue, then north on Teller Street, then west on Neil Avenue, then south on Tom Street, and then west on Frost Avenue to Plum Street.

    (D) Travel north on Soy Street, then west on Neptune Avenue, then north on Pine Street to Frost Avenue, and then west on Frost Avenue to Plum Street.

114. You exit Cleardale Prison on Sun Avenue at Pine Street. You have been directed to drive an inmate to St. John's Hospital. It is a life and death health emergency. Therefore in this instance, you will be disregarding the designations of the streets as either one-way or two-way. Which of the following is the quickest route to the hospital?

(A) Make a right on Pine Street. Then make another right on Frost Avenue, and travel one-half block to St. John's Hospital.
(B) Head west on Sun Avenue and then south on Tom Street for 2 blocks. Now make a left, and go 1 block to the hospital.
(C) Head north on Pine Street, west on Neil Avenue, south on Plum Street, and finally east on Frost Avenue to the hospital.
(D) Head east on Sun Avenue for 1 block, make a right turn, and go 1 block to the hospital.

115. You start at point number 7 on the street map. You drive north on Soy Street, make a left onto Neil Avenue, and travel 3 blocks. Then you make a left, travel 1 block, then make another left turn, and then make your first right turn. In 1 block, you will be closest to which of the following numbered blocks on the street map?

(A) 2
(B) 3
(C) 5
(D) 6

END OF TEST

ANSWER KEY
Diagnostic Test

1.	A	30.	B	59.	B	88.	B
2.	B	31.	C	60.	D	89.	D
3.	B	32.	A	61.	B	90.	C
4.	A	33.	B	62.	D	91.	D
5.	B	34.	A	63.	D	92.	B
6.	B	35.	B	64.	A	93.	B
7.	A	36.	B	65.	D	94.	B
8.	A	37.	C	66.	C	95.	D
9.	C	38.	D	67.	D	96.	A
10.	C	39.	C	68.	D	97.	C
11.	D	40.	D	69.	C	98.	A
12.	A	41.	C	70.	C	99.	C
13.	C	42.	D	71.	C	100.	D
14.	B	43.	D	72.	A	101.	D
15.	A	44.	C	73.	D	102.	B
16.	C	45.	B	74.	B	103.	C
17.	B	46.	B	75.	C	104.	D
18.	D	47.	D	76.	D	105.	A
19.	C	48.	B	77.	A	106.	C
20.	D	49.	A	78.	C	107.	D
21.	D	50.	C	79.	C	108.	A
22.	D	51.	C	80.	A	109.	D
23.	A	52.	A	81.	B	110.	C
24.	D	53.	B	82.	B	111.	D
25.	D	54.	A	83.	A	112.	B
26.	D	55.	C	84.	B	113.	C
27.	C	56.	C	85.	C	114.	D
28.	B	57.	D	86.	C	115.	A
29.	A	58.	D	87.	D		

DIAGNOSTIC CHART

Instructions: After you score your test, complete the following chart by inserting in the column entitled "Your Number Correct" the number of correct questions you answered in each of the eight sections of the test. Then compare your score in each section with the ratings in the column entitled "Scale." Finally, to correct your weaknesses, follow the instructions found at the end of the chart.

Section	Question Numbers	Area	Your Number Correct	Scale
1	1–8	Memory (8 questions)		8 Right—Excellent 6–7 Right—Good 5 Right—Fair Under 5 Right—Poor
2	9–32	Reading Comprehension (24 questions)		24 Right—Excellent 20–23 Right—Good 16–19 Right—Fair Under 16 Right—Poor
3	33–40	Verbal and Math (8 questions)		8 Right—Excellent 6–7 Right—Good 5 Right—Fair Under 5 Right—Poor
4	41–50	Correction Forms (10 questions)		10 Right—Excellent 8–9 Right—Good 7 Right—Fair Under 7 Right—Poor
5	51–58	Graphs (8 questions)		8 Right—Excellent 6–7 Right—Good 5 Right—Fair Under 5 Right—Poor
6	59–78	Applying Correction Procedures (20 questions)		20 Right—Excellent 18–19 Right—Good 16–17 Right—Fair Under 16 Right—Poor
7	79–88	Judgment and Reasoning (10 questions)		10 Right—Excellent 8–9 Right—Good 7 Right—Fair Under 7 Right—Poor
8	89–100	Legal Definitions (12 questions)		12 Right—Excellent 10–11 Right—Good 8–9 Right—Fair Under 8 Right—Poor
9	101–115	Troublesome Question Types (15 questions)		14–15 Right-Excellent 10–13 Right-Good 8–9 Right-Fair Under 8 Right-Poor

How to correct weaknesses:

1. If you are weak in Section 1, concentrate on Chapter 3.
2. If you are weak in Section 2, concentrate on Chapter 1.
3. If you are weak in Section 3, concentrate on Chapter 2.
4. If you are weak in Section 4, concentrate on Chapter 4.
5. If you are weak in Section 5, concentrate on Chapter 5.
6. If you are weak in Section 6, concentrate on Chapter 6.
7. If you are weak in Section 7, concentrate on Chapter 7.
8. If you are weak in Section 8, concentrate on Chapter 8.
9. If you are weak in Section 9, concentrate on Chapter 9.

Note: Consider yourself weak in an area if you receive anything other than an excellent rating in it.

ANSWERS EXPLAINED

1. **(A)** Charles Adams had a $10 bill, a quarter, and a nickel. Alicia Smart did not have any money. Always count money in these types of questions.

2. **(B)** Remember that it is okay to make assumptions as long as the assumptions are based on fact. The fact here is that Alicia Smart had a subway token. There is nothing to support an assumption that Charles Adams traveled on the subway.

3. **(B)** Alicia Smart possessed mace, which, of course, is a weapon commonly carried to ward off physical attacks.

4. **(A)** According to his automobile registration, Charles Adams lives in Whitestone.

5. **(B)** If you noticed that Alicia Smart's address was in multiples of 6 (e.g., 6-18-24), you would have had an easy time with this question.

6. **(B)** Among Alicia Smart's possessions was a letter addressed to "Dear Mom" and signed "Cathy." While it is true that Cathy might not be Alicia Smart's daughter, of all the choices, the one that is *probably* correct (the wording used in the stem of the question) is choice B. The point is that when the question asks for something that is most probable, the answer does not have to be proven to a certainty; probability is all that is required.

7. **(A)** By now you should certainly understand the need to count similar items.

8. **(A)** According to the automobile registration of Charles Adams, plate number CA 221 belongs to a 1996 Buick.

9. **(C)** While standing on the southeast corner of Prison Street and 3rd Avenue, the officer heard a scream. This means, of course, that the officer was at the intersection of Prison Street and 3rd Avenue. The language used in the passage does not have to be the same as that in the choices.

10. **(C)** Note the similarity between choices A and C. To be successful, you must maintain a high level of concentration throughout the entire examination.

11. **(D)** Officers Jones and Brown arrived at the building at 1:35 P.M., but Correction Officer Smith did not join them until 1:55 P.M.

12. **(A)** The injured woman who went to the hospital, Ms. Cramdom, identified herself to the officer as the manager of the Administration Building.

13. **(C)** Although Ms. Martin arrived for work at 2:10 P.M., she was 10 minutes late. Her shift started at 2:00 P.M.

14. **(B)** Ms. Martin told the officers that Administrative Assistant Connors kept the equipment list.

15. **(A)** Mary spent the day attending school. She is a student. Although she might also work at one of the other given occupations, it is not mentioned in the passage so it cannot be the answer.

16. **(C)** The robbery took place right after the elevator doors closed.

17. **(B)** The victim described the robber as an unknown male black. He was a stranger to her.

18. **(D)** This question once again points out the necessity to answer the questions carefully. A careless reader could easily miss this rather easy question.

19. **(C)** The robber pulled a knife from under his coat.

20. **(D)** The last sentence states that at 6:15 P.M. Correction Officer Ginty filed an official report on the incident.

21. **(D)** This series of questions measures a candidate's ability to pay attention to details. The Inmate Numbers involved in the story are obviously very similar. Although the questions are not difficult, they require strict concentration. It is Inmate Cash, 420132, who has a religious problem that can be resolved by the chaplain.

22. **(D)** Don't overlook the possibility that the information needed to answer a question is not given in the passage. When that is the case, there must be a choice similar to choice D in this question.

23. **(A)** The accused inmate was identified in the fourth paragraph as Inmate Number 422213. Earlier in the passage it was stated that Inmate 422213 was Inmate Terri.

24. **(D)** This is a tricky question. Many candidates, thinking that the warden must surely be authorized to make cell changes, pick choice B, but the warden is not mentioned in the passage and can't be the answer.

25. **(D)** Careless readers often pick choice B as the answer to this question because it contains an element of accuracy. Always consider all the choices before you select an answer. Many times a tempting wrong choice will come just before the correct answer, as in this question.

26. **(D)** All the complaints were made on June 1st, but the only one that was specifically resolved was the one involving the spilling of water, which occurred at 12:45 P.M.

27. **(C)** Even though Correction Officer Ginty believed the two males might be escapees, she wasn't sure, so she did not make an arrest at 1:35 P.M.

28. **(B)** Don't let what you think is going on influence your choice of answers. It clearly states in the passage that Correction Officer Ginty decided to follow the males in the first place because they were acting suspiciously.

29. **(A)** Test writers often make it necessary to relate information from one part of the passage to another. That is what happened here. The suspect with the gun had on a black jacket. Earlier in the passage it stated that the suspect with the black jacket was a white male.

30. **(B)** According to the paragraph a fixed post is required for an extremely sensitive security problem. Hence the security problem obviously requires heightened concern. Choices A, C, and D do not necessarily bring about heightened security concerns. Choice B would bring about such concerns.

31. **(C)** Choices A, B, and D are not appropriate in that the paragraph indicates that it is a correction officer who is assigned to a fixed post.

32. **(A)** The paragraph clearly indicates that fixed posts are a result of deliberation and intuitive thinking. Such an effort would certainly have to be based on sound reasons. Hence, choice A is the most appropriate response.

33. **(B)** When finding an average, first find the sum of all the items given and then divide by the number of items.

$$
\begin{array}{r}
9 \\
6 \\
8 \\
14 \\
3 \\
17 \\
6 \\
+\ \underline{1} \\
\end{array}
$$

64 divided by 8 = 8

34. **(A)** Kites, Cross, and Hall are the three inmates with over 10 years left to serve. To find what percentage of all the inmates they represent, you must divide 3 by the number of all the inmates, which is 8. Thus 3 divided by 8 equals 0.375. To change 0.375 to a percent requires that you move the decimal point in 0.375 two places from the left to the right and add the percent sign. Thus 0.375 would now become 37.5%, or $37^1/2$%, which is the answer.

35. **(B)** To find the inmate who has served the greatest percentage of his sentence, the following steps must be taken. First, examine only the records of the inmates offered by the four choices. Then for each inmate mentioned by the choices add the number of years that inmate served in Harper to the number of years that inmate has left to serve. These sums represent the total sentence for each of the four inmates. Then take each of these four total sentences and divide each one into the number of years already served in Harper by the appropriate inmate. For example, Inmate Bellows has served 8 years in Harper. Add to that his 2 years left to serve. That equals 10 years. Then divide that 10 into 8, the number of years served in Harper. You get $^8/10$, which is 0.80 as a decimal. Changing 0.80 to a percent requires moving the decimal point two places to the right and adding a percent sign. The answer is 80%. If you follow the same steps, you would get 75% for Jay, 35% for Kites, and 75% for Sparks.

36. **(B)** Because of her other duties, Officer Reyes cannot dedicate 8 hours solely to intelligence-gathering interviews. She spends 1 hour each tour to patrol the tiers under her supervision, which is represented by V. She spends another 1 hour each tour for meals and personal necessities, which is represented by P. That means there are 2 hours, or 8 minus V and minus P, during a typical tour that Officer Reyes cannot conduct intelligence-gathering interviews. So 8 hours less V and less P gives $(8 - V - P)$. That's the number of hours Officer Reyes has available in a typical 8-hour tour to dedicate to intelligence-gathering interviews. Multiply that by the maximum number of intelligence-gathering interviews that typically can be done each hour, which is 2. Finally, multiply that by the number of tours she does during a typical month, which is 20. The correct answer is $2 \times (8 - V - P) \times 20$. Check the accuracy of your selection by substituting actual numbers. Here, $8 - 1 - 1 = 6$. Multiply that by 2, which is the number

of intelligence-gathering interviews each hour. This gives $2 \times 6 = 12$, which is the number of interviews that can be done each tour. Then multiply that by 20, which is the number of tours worked in a typical month: $12 \times 20 = 240$. So the number of interviews that Offices Reyes can conduct each month is 240. Only choice B would give you this value.

37. **(C)** Choice A is incorrect because it should state "impossible to reach you and me." Remember that, if you have difficulty evaluating this type of statement, just remove the first pronoun, in this case *you,* and then read the statement to yourself. In this case it would then read "impossible to reach I," which you can easily see is incorrect. Choice B is incorrect because it should indicate "into the holster," to show movement toward a place.

38. **(D)** Choice A should state "laid their weapons down," since it is intended to indicate a placing of something in the past. Choice B is incorrect because reclining in the past should be stated as "all the inmates lay down." Choice C should use *teach* to indicate giving knowledge. All the choices are incorrect.

39. **(C)** Choice A is unclear because it cannot be determined who was searched, the inmate or the officer. It should have stated, "After the inmate was searched." The use of "in" instead of "into" makes choice B incorrect. Choice C is correct.

40. **(D)** All statements are correctly presented.

41. **(C)** Correction Officer Frank Walker worked the overtime and made the request.

42. **(D)** Careful examination of the form shows that the officer asking for the overtime is assigned to the Beacon Facility but performed the overtime at the Carter Detention Facility because of a disturbance there.

43. **(D)** At times the information being sought by a question simply is not entered on the form.

44. **(C)** It is clearly stated on the bottom of the form that the entry was made in the log of the Carter Facility.

45. **(B)** The officer worked 12 hours on a day the officer was scheduled to work 8 hours.

46. **(B)** The option the officer selected as compensation is indicated on the form as cash.

47. **(D)** By examining the captions Date of Present Rank and Date Entered Dept., it is clear that D is the correct choice. The importance of becoming familiar with the form before answering the questions is clear when answering a question such as this.

48. **(B)** It would seem that the officer making the request would sign the form first but that is not what is indicated on the form. Remember to base your answers solely on the information provided.

49. **(A)** The disturbance occurred on April 30th.

50. **(C)** If you selected B it was probably because you were hurrying to answer the last question based on this form. Being careless allowed you to select it because it looked very similar to the shield number on the form.

51. **(C)** In 2011 there were approximately 1400 inmates, in 2012 and 2013 there were approximately 1800 inmates.

52. **(A)** In 2011 there were about 1400 inmates, and about 120 correction officers. By dividing 120 into 1400 it is determined that there were about 11.6 inmates for every correction officer. Choice B is wrong because it shows the ratio of correction officers to inmates. The question asked for the ratio of inmates to correction officers.

53. **(B)** In 2013 there were about 190 correction officers (each increment equals 20 officers). In 2012 there were about 140 officers.

54. **(A)** In 2013 there were 1800 inmates and 190 officers. That means that in 2014 there will be about 1900 inmates (an increase of 100) and 190 officers (no change). By dividing 190 officers into 1900 inmates, it is determined that in 2014 the ratio of inmates to officers will be about 10 to 1.

55. **(C)** In 2011 there were about 1400 inmates. In 2013 there were about 1800 inmates. The inmate population increased by 400. By dividing 1400 into 400, you can calculate the percentage increase, which is about 29%.

56. **(C)** If you picked either choice A or choice B, you used the wrong year. In 2013 there were about 190 officers. If 10 officers are added during 2014, there would be 200 officers on the staff in 2014.

57. **(D)** Questions 57 and 58 should make you aware of the limitations of graphs. Graphs can show only approximate numbers and are used primarily to show trends. Tables are used to show specific numbers. You must understand that, even though there are about 190 officers on the staff in 2013, it is impossible to say exactly how many of them would be working on any given day in 2013.

58. **(D)** There is no way that you can determine the answer to this question from the data shown. The word in the question that should have alerted you to this is the word *exactly.*

59. **(B)** Choice B is correct because such a search can be performed on either subject. Choice D sounds correct but is not mentioned in the procedures.

60. **(D)** A Body Cavity Search specifically requires that medical personnel perform such searches.

61. **(B)** The shoes of an inmate and not a prisoner may be searched. Choices C and D are strictly made up and are not found in the procedure.

62. **(D)** Internally searching a female inmate's genitals is part of a Body Cavity Search.

63. **(D)** This type of search is to be performed in absolute privacy by medical personnel. Nothing is mentioned about the gender of the medical personnel. But, the corrections supervisor and officer present must be of the same gender as the inmate being searched.

64. **(A)** After entering the time the vehicle enters the facility, the next required entry is as indicated in choice A.

65. **(D)** Such a search is to be done by the correction officer in charge of the gate.

66. **(C)** Remember to base your answers only on what is contained in the procedure.

67. **(D)** The use of the word *all* in the stem of the question makes choices A and C incorrect because property involved with a criminal offense shall not be returned nor stored in the Facility Storage Warehouse. Choice B is incorrect because the relative must be selected pursuant to the wishes of the inmate.

68. **(D)** Choices A, B, and C are correct statements, but choice D is incorrect and is the answer because the time frame is 48 hours.

69. **(C)** It is a life-threatening situation. Choice A is incorrect because the accompanying officer shall be assigned by the tour commander. Choice B is incorrect because an officer other than the officer assigned to the cell block shall be assigned to accompany the prisoner. Finally, choice D is incorrect because the officer assigned to accompany the inmate shall notify the tour commander when the prisoner actually leaves the cell block.

70. **(C)** All three are examples of when such a form should be prepared.

71. **(C)** As stated in the procedure, the form shall be prepared and remain with the inmate.

72. **(A)** Choice A is an incorrect statement because of the word *never*. A member of the Department of Correction is prohibited from possessing a personal firearm outside the state while off-duty. Obviously if the member was sent out of state on an assignment this procedure would not apply. Choice D describes a situation where a member could be going out of state while off-duty and wanted to leave a personal firearm in a Department of Correction arsenal that is near home and not necessarily the officer's command.

73. **(D)** As stated in the procedure, although other choices may sound logical, they are not mentioned in the procedure. Remember this type of question is not seeking to measure your judgment. The answers are in the procedures you are given.

74. **(B)** Choice D can be immediately eliminated because it indicates that the number 9 represents the first letter of the word. That is incorrect since the reference table associates 9 with the letter *R* and the word in the question begins with a *G*. If you selected choice C you made a mistake often made by candidates when answering coding questions. Often candidates confuse the letter O with the number 0.

75. **(C)** Choice A is close to choice C, but choice A is incorrect because the fourth number should represent the letter *O*. Instead the examiner tried to distract you by suggesting the number 0. Choice C is the correct answer.

76. **(D)** The letter *T* is associated with 7, *E* with 8, *S* with 6, *T* with 7, *E* with 8, and *R* with 9. Choice D, which is 786789, is correct.

77. **(A)** As indicated by the reference table.

78. **(C)** Choices B and D incorrectly suggest that *O* the second letter of the word *TONGUE* should be represented by the number 0. However the number 0 was associated by the reference table with the letter *Z*. Therefore, after quickly eliminating choices B and D, and comparing between the remaining choices A and C, you should have determined that choice C was the correct choice.

79. **(C)** Remember that fire is a threat to many people. The fire makes the area a dangerous one. Evacuation should take place.

80. **(A)** *Profuse* means a lot. Significant loss of blood always amounts to a life-threatening situation.

81. **(B)** Facts before acts. It is always best to double-check your facts before taking serious action especially when such a double-check can be quickly made.

82. **(B)** In corrections work, cooperation among officers (teamwork) is essential. Aggressiveness and rigidity are not characteristics of teamwork.

83. **(A)** The word *omnipresence* means always present. Correction officers on patrol create this feeling by passing the same location frequently but on an irregular basis. You must remember that patrol should *not* be predictable; it must be unpredictable to be effective.

84. **(B)** Unconsciousness should always be treated as a serious matter. Note that, according to the rule, the age or status of an inmate is not a factor to consider.

85. **(C)** Important matters should never be left to chance so choice A is wrong. The stem of the question indicates that the utensils involved are essential so choice B is wrong. And choice D is wrong because it is not practical to pay for kitchen help when inmates can be used.

86. **(C)** Information from inmates is an important source of intelligence in a correctional institution, but, in a semimilitary organization like a corrections agency, the chain of command must be followed.

87. **(D)** All correctional facilities have someone on staff who has the responsibility to deal with these type of requests. Remember that it is a mistake for a correction officer to get involved in the personal life of an inmate. Also remember that once an officer does a favor for one inmate, others will surely follow with similar requests for favors.

88. **(B)** The allegation in choice B does not relate to the business of the correctional facility but to the business of the courts.

89. **(D)** In order to commit arson, the damage must be caused intentionally according to the definition given. Remember that the questions must be answered *solely* on the basis of the information offered.

90. **(C)** The definition clearly states that an arson can occur if either a building or a motor vehicle is damaged. As mentioned in the part of the text explaining the strategies that should be used while answering this type of question, the importance of words such as *and/or* must be recognized.

91. **(D)** According to the definition given, neither statement is correct because arson can be committed by causing damage by means of either a fire or an explosion.

92. **(B)** Pat has unlawfully taken the property of another. Pat has not committed grand larceny since, according to the definition given, the value of the property would have to be more than $1000.

93. **(B)** The theft is grand larceny because the value of the property taken was more than $1000 (6 albums × $200 = $1200) at the time of the theft.

94. **(B)** Only statement 2 is correct because, in order for a person to commit grand larceny, the person must first commit petit larceny and then, in addition, the property must be worth more than $1000 at the time of the theft.

95. **(D)** Ray committed two separate offenses: arson, since he damaged a motor vehicle by fire, and also petit larceny, since he unlawfully took the property of another.

96. **(A)** For a proper charge of felonious assault, the act must be an intentional one. Here we are told the act that caused the injury was done accidentally.

97. **(C)** Mary intentionally caused a serious physical injury to *another* person.

98. **(A)** Only statement 1 is correct. Statement 2 sounds logical, but it is not addressed in the definitions you were given. Remember that the instructions tell you to base your answers *solely* on the following definitions.

99. **(C)** It is a felony to possess more than 500 policy plays.

100. **(D)** The information provided states that the defendant will be sentenced as a felon if the defendant was convicted, not merely arrested, for the same, not any, crime within the last 5 years.

101. **(D)** Note that the choices suggest that one of four different sentences can come first, sentences 5, 3, 4, or 1. This means that once you decide which sentence of those four comes first, you do not have to go any further. Upon reading the four suggested first sentences, it becomes clear that only sentence 1 can logically come first. Just to be sure, read the choice D sentences in order to confirm that they flow correctly. This strategy will be thoroughly addressed in Chapter 9.

102. **(B)** The choices suggest that sentence 3 (choices A and B), sentence 2 (choice C), or sentence 4 (choice D) can be the first sentence. Upon reading these sentences, it becomes clear that sentence 3 must come first. So choices C and D can be eliminated. The remaining choices, A and B, both suggest that sentence 4 comes last, so you must now examine the middle sentences. Both choices suggest that sentence 1 comes second, so the answer depends on the relationship between sentences 2 and 5, and clearly sentence 5 must precede sentence 2 as in choice B.

103. **(C)** Upon reading the suggested first sentences, it is clear that sentence 4 must come first, so choices A and B can be eliminated. Choice C suggests that sentence 2 comes last, and choice D suggests that sentence 5 comes last. All you have to do to determine the correct answer is to decide whether sentence 2 or sentence 5 comes last. Upon reading these two sentences, it is clear that sentence 2 comes last, so choice C is the answer.

104. **(D)** This is another question where deciding which sentence comes first leads you directly to the answer. In this case, sentence 4 clearly comes first. The correct answer is choice D. Some students answering this question argue that sentence 2, as in choice C, could come first. If that happens to you on your test, leave both sentences in and look at the last sentence. In this case sentence 3, as in choice D, clearly ends the action. The person jumped from the building!

105. **(A)** Upon reading the suggested first sentences, it is clear that sentence 3 comes first. This eliminates choices B and D. Since the remaining choices, A and C, both have the same suggested last sentence, you must examine the relationship of the middle sentences. Upon doing this, it becomes clear that sentence 5 must come after sentence 2. The answer is choice A.

106. **(C)** The stem of the question tells you that Officer Lopez has discovered an illegal firearm on a visitor and has confiscated that firearm. According to the procedure associated with this question, the next step for Lopez to take is properly charge Brown as stated in the answer, choice C. This question type is known as a Find The Next Step Question and is covered in detail in Chapter 9.

107. **(D)** This question exemplifies a primary rule about find the next step questions, which is the next step to take is not necessarily the next step in the procedure. Note that the stem of the question clearly states that there was only one damaged TV set and that the recreation room was totally vacant at the time of discovery. Because there is no mention of any other persons or property damage being involved, steps 5, 6, and 7 need not be performed.

108. **(A)** According to the stem of the question, Officer Ryan has already completed steps 1 and 2. Since the stem of the question describes the prisoner as being violent, the next step for the officer to take is step 4, to use restraining handcuffs. Note that since an ambulance is available, step 3 does not come into play.

109. **(D)** Remember when doing find the next step questions that the next step to take is not necessarily the next numerical step in the procedure. We mention this again because this rule comes into play in a great majority of these questions. In this question, step 4 (choice A) applies only in felony cases and Player is accused of misdemeanor rape. Choice B is incorrect since the same-gender, full-body search has to be performed on Josephs and not on Player.

110. **(C)** Choice A is incorrect since Babitch is a male lawyer. Choice B is incorrect since the visit could not be a face-to face one because it was not an advance-scheduled one. Choice D is wrong for two reasons. The first is having a frisk made is the eleventh step, while the answer, Choice C is step ten. The second is that a frisk is only required after a face-to-face visit and the visit in the question is not a face to face one since it was not scheduled in advance.

111. **(D)** Choice A is incorrect because you cannot travel west on Newton Avenue. Choice B is incorrect because Tom Street is a southbound street and thus prevents you from traveling north. Choice C is incorrect because you cannot travel north on Pine Street. Choice D is the correct route.

112. **(B)** Choice A is incorrect because Soy Street is a northbound street. Choice C is incorrect because you cannot travel west on Sun Avenue. Choice D is incorrect in that Neptune Avenue is an eastbound street upon which you cannot travel westbound. Choice B designates the correct route.

113. **(C)** Choice A is incorrect since Frost Avenue cannot be accessed by traveling north on Soy Street. St. John's Hospital presents an obstruction. Choice B is incorrect since you cannot travel west on Newton Avenue. Choice D is incorrect because you cannot travel west on Neptune Avenue and because you cannot travel north on Pine Street. Note that in some choices, there may be two actions offered that do not follow the flow of traffic, as in choice D (i.e., west on Neptune Avenue and north on Pine Street). However, for you, the candidate, only one incorrect action is enough for the choice to be eliminated as the correct route. Choice C designates the correct route.

114. **(D)** Choice A is incorrect because a left, and not a right, turn should have been made on Frost Avenue. Remember, always view the instructions in a given choice as if you were actually driving the vehicle involved. Said another way, put yourself in the driver's seat. Choice B is incorrect because following the directions still would leave you 1 block west of the hospital. Choice C is incorrect because although following the directions offered by choice C will get you to the hospital, it is not the shortest of the suggested routes.

115. **(A)** Following the directions given will lead you to numbered block 2.

Correct Your Weaknesses

Reading Comprehension Questions

1

→ **THE IMPORTANCE OF CONCENTRATION**
→ **INCREASING YOUR VOCABULARY**
→ **QUESTION STRATEGIES**
→ **UNDERSTANDING GRAPHICS**
→ **WORD SELECTION**

Reading comprehension questions are designed, as the name implies, to measure the candidate's ability to comprehend or understand written material. In effect, reading comprehension questions on a correction officer examination measure the candidate's ability to read and understand the type of written material that is used by correction officers in the performance of their everyday duties. For example, the written material could be a narrative or story about an incident, or it could be in the form of a rule or procedure that a correction officer is supposed to follow.

Reading comprehension questions appear on virtually all correction officer examinations, and they are usually the question type that accounts for the greatest number of questions. In addition, most of the other question types used also require good reading comprehension ability. Therefore, if necessary, improve your reading comprehension skills through diligent practice and make certain that you master the strategy presented in this chapter for handling reading comprehension questions.

THE IMPORTANCE OF CONCENTRATION

How often do you "read" something by looking at the words without concentrating on their meaning? This is the biggest roadblock to overcome if you want to become a good reader. Actually, letting your mind wander is not bad for light reading. However, for the kind of reading that is essential to master almost any examination, *you must learn how to concentrate on the material totally.* One way to accomplish this is to continuously ask yourself questions about what you are reading. Another way is to use your imagination and create mental impressions about what you are reading. Above all, don't let your mind wander! You must learn to concentrate exclusively on what you are reading.

A simple way to practice concentration is to read an article from the newspaper. As you read have a pencil in your hand and underline or circle key points. After reading the article, write down the key points you remember. Then return to the passage and see how well you did. You will become better with practice. Remember that the key is *concentration.*

INCREASE YOUR VOCABULARY

Concentration alone will not help if a reading passage contains a significant number of words that you don't understand. Therefore, follow these suggestions to increase your vocabulary.

1. When you read a word you don't fully understand, make a note of it along with a reminder of where you read it. Keep a special notebook for this purpose.
2. Look up the meaning of the word in the dictionary as soon as possible.
3. Return to the material where you read the word, and make sure you now understand its meaning and how it fits into the material.
4. Try to use these words in your everyday conversation.
5. Review these words periodically until you are certain you have mastered them.
6. Ask a friend or another student to test you on the meaning of these words.

STRATEGIES FOR HANDLING
READING COMPREHENSION QUESTIONS

Please note that some students do not completely understand our recommended test-taking strategies until they practice using them. It is vital, therefore, that you study each strategy and then practice using it. Throughout this book we give you practice questions with explained answers. These explanations, when appropriate, include a review of the strategy you should have used. Our experience is that, with practice, our strategies result in candidates achieving a high degree of accuracy in a minimal amount of time. But you must practice using the strategies to benefit from them. The strategies for reading comprehension questions follow.

1. **RECOGNIZE THE QUESTION TYPE.** Reading comprehension questions always have specific directions to answer the questions based *solely* on the information found in the passage. This, of course, means that you should *never* introduce personal knowledge you may have about what is being discussed in the passage.

2. **DO NOT READ THE PASSAGE FIRST.** *Never* begin by reading the passage. When you read without knowledge of what you are looking for, you tend to treat everything as important. This is why, as explained below, sensitized reading is at the heart of our strategy.

3. **LET THE STEM OF THE QUESTIONS SENSITIZE YOU.** Go right to the stem of each question (the part before the choices) and determine what the question is asking you. Circle key words in the stem and/or write key words in the test booklet to establish what information you are being asked to find to answer each question. Remember that before you begin to read the passage, it is essential that you understand what information from the passage you need to answer each question.

4. **ENGAGE IN SENSITIZED READING.** Sensitized reading occurs when you read a passage with advance knowledge of the specific information you are seeking. Sensitized reading allows you to disregard information you are not looking for no matter how important the information may seem. As you read the passage, constantly remind yourself of the information you are seeking.

5. **ANSWER QUESTIONS AS INFORMATION IS FOUND.** As you find each needed piece of information, underline it in the passage. Then go to the question involved and answer it. After you carefully record the answer to a question, remind yourself of what information you still have to find to answer the remaining questions. Continue the process until you have answered all.

Underlining the needed information as you find it in the passage serves two purposes. First, it reminds you where you left off reading the passage if you haven't yet answered all the questions. Second, it makes reviewing the questions easy should you have time after you have answered all the questions.

Finally, don't expect the questions to correspond in numerical order to the paragraphs in the passage. In order to use the right strategy, information in paragraph 4 may be needed to answer question 3, while information in paragraph 5 may be needed to answer question 2.

Note that reading comprehension questions on official exams very rarely ask more than five questions per passage. In the unlikely event that you're asked more than five questions pertaining to the same passage, modify the suggested strategy by dealing with a maximum of five questions at a time. In other words, after answering the first five questions, repeat the strategy for the next five questions.

6. **HANDLE CERTAIN QUESTIONS DIFFERENTLY.** Occasionally, a reading comprehension question will ask you to evaluate each of the four choices to determine which one is the *least* or *most* correct statement. In this rare instance, let the choices guide you. These questions must be answered one at a time. See Practice Test 2, question 66, on page 340 for an example of this type of question.

> ### QUESTION STRATEGIES
>
> Recognize the question type.
>
> Do not read the passage first.
>
> Let the stem of the questions sensitize you.
>
> Engage in sensitized reading.
>
> Answer questions as information is found.
>
> Handle certain questions differently.

UNDERSTANDING GRAPHIC WRITTEN MATERIAL

Quite often correction officer examinations contain reading comprehension questions that include the use of sketches or drawings. In other words, the written material upon which the questions are based uses a combination of words and illustrations, usually sketches, drawings, or pictures. Nonetheless, the strategy is the same. Before you look at the illustrations, you should first look at the stem of the questions to get an idea what you will be asked about. Group Three of the practice exercises in this chapter contains this type of reading comprehension question.

READING COMPREHENSION QUESTIONS INVOLVING WORD SELECTION

This type of reading comprehension question is yet another way to test if you understand what you are reading. It consists of a paragraph from which words have been left out, indicated by numbered blank spaces representing question numbers. Your task is to read the paragraph and then select from a group of words, usually four, which word most appropriately fits in the numbered blank.

Strategies for Taking Word Selection Questions

1. Scan the entire paragraph to get a sense of the overall meaning or purpose of the paragraph.
2. When initially scanning the paragraph, do not try to think of words that might fit in the blanks. It is a waste of time, since your task will be to select the word that most appropriately fits in the numbered blank from among the choices the examiner has provided.

3. When appropriate, pay particular attention to whether the paragraph is referring to only one specific person or to many people in general. Is the paragraph describing a general procedure to follow or is it referring to a specific incident? Effort here will help to decide whether a general or specific type of word should be used. For example, if you see "_____ defendant," selecting the word *this* when the paragraph is referring to any defendant in general would not be appropriate. Rather, a better selection might be _a_ defendant.

4. If a person's role is established and this person is identified by name early in the paragraph, then it would be appropriate to select that person's name when it appears later in the paragraph. But it would *not* be appropriate to suddenly select a person's name in a paragraph without the paragraph having first identified that person and what relation or role that person has to the paragraph.

5. Make sure to keep genders straight in your mind. If the paragraph is referring to a female, the use of female gender words such as *she* or *her* and not *he* or *him* would be appropriate.

PRACTICE EXERCISES

GROUP ONE

Time Allowed: 20 Minutes

> **Directions:** Answer questions 1–3 solely on the basis of the following passage.

Correction Officers Harris and Green, working an 8:00 A.M. to 4:00 P.M. shift in the Orange County Detention Facility, receive a call at 11:01 A.M. over their portable radio to investigate a theft from an automobile that was parked in the facility's visitor's parking lot on the southeast corner of Prison Row and Fourth Street. Correction Officer Harris explains to Correction Officer Green, who is new to the facility, that thefts from automobiles that are parked in the visitor's parking lot are an on-going problem that requires much of their attention. He tells Correction Officer Green that most of the thefts from this parking lot occur between 10:00 A.M. and 11:30 A.M. But, he adds that the time periods between 2:00 P.M. and 3:30 P.M. and between 7:00 P.M. and 9:00 P.M. are also times when many thefts occur. Correction Officer Harris then tells Correction Officer Green that most of the thefts from automobiles parked in the employee's parking lot occur between 10:00 P.M. and 11:30 P.M.

Turning into the visitor's parking lot, the Officers see a female waving to them. They park their patrol vehicle and approach the female. After identifying herself to the officers as Gloria Swanson, she tells them that at 9:45 A.M. she parked her car and went to visit an inmate by the name of Sam Green. At 10:45 A.M., when she returned to her car, a white 1986 Buick Riviera, she discovered that the right front vent window had been smashed and that her car radio had been stolen. She states that the radio was worth $300. She states that the thieves also stole $15 worth of tokens she had in her glove compartment. No other property was taken.

After obtaining the required information from Ms. Swanson, the officers officially report the theft, and at 11:22 A.M. they return to their normal duties.

1. Most of the thefts from automobiles parked in the employee's parking lot occur

   (A) between 10:00 A.M. and 11:30 A.M.
   (B) between 2:00 P.M. and 3:30 P.M.
   (C) between 7:00 P.M. and 9:00 P.M.
   (D) between 10:00 P.M. and 11:30 P.M.   Ⓐ Ⓑ Ⓒ Ⓓ

2. The property was stolen from Ms. Swanson's car

   (A) at 11:01 A.M.
   (B) before 9:45 A.M.
   (C) after 10:45 A.M.
   (D) sometime between 9:45 A.M. and 10:45 A.M.   Ⓐ Ⓑ Ⓒ Ⓓ

3. The total value of the property reported stolen from Ms. Swanson's car was

   (A) $300.
   (B) $15.
   (C) $315.
   (D) not given.   Ⓐ Ⓑ Ⓒ Ⓓ

Directions: Answer questions 4–7 solely on the basis of the following passage.

Regular safety inspections of cell blocks are required to ensure the safety of inmates and correctional personnel alike. Every cell in a facility, except death row cells, must be given a thorough safety inspection at least once a week. Death row cells must be inspected once each day. The inmate assigned to the cell must be present when the inspection is made. Two correction officers must be assigned to the inspecting team. Safety inspections must be made during daylight hours.

Inspecting officers are required to report any overloading of electrical sockets. Such a report must be made on form 2431. Extension cords are not allowed and should be seized immediately upon discovery. Homemade lampshades are not authorized. Any such lampshades found must be reported on form 1657 without delay to the cell block supervisor who will decide what action to take. Nothing is allowed on radiators. Anything found on a radiator must be removed immediately by the inmate. Leaking plumbing must be reported via telephone at once to the custodial staff by calling extension 4140. All such telephone reports should be followed up in writing on a form 2341. If such plumbing cannot be repaired within 2 hours of initial discovery, the inmates occupying the cell must be relocated.

If an unsatisfactory condition not mentioned previously is uncovered, the inspecting officer should instruct the inmate involved to correct the condition. If the inmate refuses to comply, the inspecting officer must notify the cell block supervisor and be guided by the supervisor's instructions.

4. Form 2341 is used for reporting

   (A) overloaded electrical sockets.
   (B) unauthorized extension cords.
   (C) homemade lampshades.
   (D) leaking plumbing.

5. Inspecting officers are required to immediately seize

   (A) anything found on radiators.
   (B) extension cords.
   (C) lampshades.
   (D) unauthorized personal property and contraband.

6. Lampshades observed during a safety inspection

   (A) must always be reported to a supervisor.
   (B) may or may not require a report to a supervisor.
   (C) must always be removed.
   (D) must always be seized.

7. Inspecting officers are specifically required to make telephone notifications concerning

   (A) refusal of inmates to take corrective action.
   (B) overloaded electrical sockets.
   (C) leaking plumbing.
   (D) homemade lampshades.   Ⓐ Ⓑ Ⓒ Ⓓ

Directions: Answer questions 8–10 solely on the basis of the following passage.

At 4:05 P.M. Correction Officer Ginty observes an inmate who is in a place in the main yard where he should not be. Correction Officer Ginty positions himself so that he can see the inmate but the inmate cannot see him. The correction officer watches the inmate for 10 minutes and then approaches him. Correction Officer Ginty moves cautiously, believing that the inmate may be armed. As the correction officer gets nearer to the inmate, he realizes that the inmate is new to the prison. The inmate greets the officer. The officer responds by saying, "Hi, you seem to have wandered off from the rest of the inmates." The inmate says, "I just wanted to be alone." The officer then says, "OK, but the area you are in is off limits to inmates. Please move back away from that gate and get nearer to the group in the yard." A little while later, at 4:30 P.M., the signal to clear the yard is given.

8. Officer Ginty originally approached the inmate at about

    (A) 4:05 P.M.
    (B) 4:15 P.M.
    (C) 4:30 P.M.
    (D) 4:45 P.M.   Ⓐ Ⓑ Ⓒ Ⓓ

9. The correction officer approached the inmate carefully because

    (A) he thought the inmate may be armed.
    (B) the inmate was trying to escape.
    (C) the inmate had a history of being violent.
    (D) all inmates must be approached cautiously.   Ⓐ Ⓑ Ⓒ Ⓓ

10. When Officer Ginty was talking to the inmate, the inmate was

    (A) with the rest of the group in the yard.
    (B) standing near a gate.
    (C) in the middle of the main yard.
    (D) in an authorized area.   Ⓐ Ⓑ Ⓒ Ⓓ

GROUP TWO

Time Allowed: 20 minutes

Directions: Answer questions 11–15 solely on the basis of the following paragraph.

It is Tuesday, March 16th. Correction Officer Ginty is working a tour of duty from 10:00 A.M. to 6:00 P.M. She is assigned as the Officer of the Day. This is the first time Officer May Ginty has worked as the Officer of the Day, so she asks her tour commander for some guidance.

Officer Ginty's tour commander, Captain Rems, informs Ginty that her major tasks as the Officer of the Day involve such things as making sure that all officers are present and assigned, making sure that all equipment is in working order, and making sure that all keys are accounted for. But, the tour commander emphasized that the most important function of the Officer of the Day is to take command when an unusual incident occurs. Captain Rems emphasized to Officer Ginty that her first responsibility when she is notified about an unusual incident is to notify the warden, Chief Gardener, and then to respond to the scene of the incident and take command. Captain Rems then told Correction Officer Ginty that the Officer of the Day is also responsible for completing an Unusual Incident Report after the incident has been declared under control.

At 1:15 P.M. Officer Ginty is notified of the occurrence of an unusual incident. It seems that two groups of inmates got involved in an argument about seating arrangements during a group counseling session. One of the groups, known as the Latin Kings, arrived late for the session and demanded to sit in seats in the front of the classroom already occupied by a group known as the Repeat Offenders. When Officer Ginty arrived at the scene of the incident at 1:22 P.M., she immediately met with Carlos Rivera, the ringleader of the Latin Kings; Danny White, the leader of the Repeat Offenders; and Dr. Jose Gonzalez, the facility's resident counsellor. After listening to the arguments of both group leaders, a compromise was reached. The leader of the Latin Kings agreed to tell his group to sit in the back of the classroom providing that they would get the preferred seats in the front of the classroom for the next training session scheduled for the following Tuesday.

At 1:45 P.M. the incident was officially declared as being under control, and the counseling session took place with no further interruption.

11. The most important function of the Officer of the Day is to

    (A) make sure that all keys are accounted for.
    (B) make sure that all equipment is in working order.
    (C) make sure that all officers are present and assigned.
    (D) take command when an unusual incident occurs.

12. Officer Ginty's first responsibility at 1:15 P.M. is to

    (A) notify the warden.
    (B) respond to the counseling session.
    (C) consult with Captain Rems.
    (D) file an Unusual Incident Report.

13. The unusual incident that occurred was settled by

    (A) adherence to prison rules.
    (B) reaching a compromise.
    (C) the direct orders of the warden.
    (D) Captain Rems. Ⓐ Ⓑ Ⓒ Ⓓ

14. The next counseling session is scheduled for

    (A) March 16th.
    (B) March 23rd.
    (C) March 30th.
    (D) April 6th. Ⓐ Ⓑ Ⓒ Ⓓ

15. At 1:45 P.M. Officer Ginty's remaining responsibility is to

    (A) complete an Unusual Incident Report.
    (B) notify the warden.
    (C) contact Captain Rems.
    (D) discipline Carlos Rivera. Ⓐ Ⓑ Ⓒ Ⓓ

On August 17th Correction Officers Frank Brown, shield number 225, and William Story, shield number 220, assigned to Vehicle number 2956, were on duty on the grounds of the Municipal Detention Facility. At approximately 10:05 A.M. the officers received a radio call to respond to a past burglary at 1248 Jailhouse Road, which is a storehouse for the facility's custodial staff. When they arrived at the storehouse at 10:10 A.M., they were met by Mr. Don Wood, a custodial assistant at the facility, who is a black male, date of birth 1/10/52. Mr. Wood informed the officers that the storehouse had been burglarized.

Mr. Wood told the officers that when he arrived for work at 10:00 A.M. he noticed that the cylinder on the lock of the door to the storehouse was removed and the door was open. Mr. Wood stated further that he did not enter the storehouse but called the dispatcher from a street phone. The officers, with guns drawn, searched the storehouse for the perpetrators with no results. While his partner notified the Crime Scene Unit from the local police department to respond to the storehouse, Officer Story instructed Mr. Wood to stay out of the building until after the Crime Scene Unit had completed its investigation. Once it was permissible for him to enter the building, he was told to prepare a listing of stolen property, if any, and to forward it to the tour commander. Officer Story then prepared an Incident Occurrence Report, and at 10:45 A.M. the officers resumed patrol.

16. At approximately what time was the call dispatched to Vehicle number 2956?

    (A) 10:05 A.M.
    (B) 10:00 A.M.
    (C) 10:10 A.M.
    (D) 10:45 A.M.   Ⓐ Ⓑ Ⓒ Ⓓ

17. Which of the following is Mr. Wood's date of birth?

    (A) 10/10/52
    (B) 1/10/52
    (C) 1/10/54
    (D) 10/10/45   Ⓐ Ⓑ Ⓒ Ⓓ

18. How was the storehouse entered?

    (A) door
    (B) window
    (C) roof
    (D) wall   Ⓐ Ⓑ Ⓒ Ⓓ

19. The Crime Scene Unit was notified by

    (A) Mr. Wood.
    (B) the dispatcher.
    (C) Officer Brown.
    (D) Officer Story.

20. The Crime Scene Unit that was notified is from

    (A) the Municipal Detention Facility.
    (B) the state police.
    (C) the local police department.
    (D) the FBI.

Directions: Answer question 21 based solely on the following information.

A correction officer should not sleep while on duty. He/she shall not engage in games of chance of any kind while on duty. Except in the line of duty, he/she shall not bring cards or dice into a correctional facility.

21. While working, a correction officer could sometimes

    (A) sleep.
    (B) play cards.
    (C) play dice.
    (D) bring a deck of cards into a prison.

Directions: Questions 22–27 are to be answered solely on the basis of the following representation of objects found in Prison Cells 1, 2, 3, and 4.

22. The cell that does not contain money is Prison Cell

   (A) 1.
   (B) 2.
   (C) 3.
   (D) 4.   Ⓐ Ⓑ Ⓒ Ⓓ

23. The inmate who has eye problems probably occupies Prison Cell

   (A) 1.
   (B) 2.
   (C) 3.
   (D) 4.   Ⓐ Ⓑ Ⓒ Ⓓ

24. A religious inmate probably occupies Prison Cell

   (A) 1.
   (B) 2.
   (C) 3.
   (D) 4.   Ⓐ Ⓑ Ⓒ Ⓓ

25. The total amount of money in all cells is

   (A) $30.
   (B) $30.05.
   (C) $40.
   (D) $40.15.   Ⓐ Ⓑ Ⓒ Ⓓ

26. The cell that has more than one drinking utensil is Prison Cell

   (A) 1.
   (B) 2.
   (C) 3.
   (D) 4.   Ⓐ Ⓑ Ⓒ Ⓓ

27. The cell that does not have a writing utensil is Prison Cell

   (A) 1.
   (B) 2.
   (C) 3.
   (D) 4.   Ⓐ Ⓑ Ⓒ Ⓓ

GROUP FOUR

Time Allowed: 10 minutes

Directions: The paragraph below contains questions 28–30 in the form of three numbered blanks. Immediately after the paragraph are lists of four word choices that correspond to these numbered blanks. Select the word choice that would most appropriately fit the numbered blank in each question.

The purpose of an arraignment in court includes formally charging a defendant with an offense and deciding the terms of bail. Bail usually is a sum of money that ___(Q 28)___ defendant deposits with the court and can lose if that defendant does not appear the next time he or she is scheduled to appear in court. Bail is therefore intended to ensure that a ___(Q 29)___ will appear at the next scheduled court date. If the defendant does not appear at the next scheduled court date, ___(Q 30)___ bail will be forfeited.

28. (A) our
    (B) that
    (C) his
    (D) a   Ⓐ Ⓑ Ⓒ Ⓓ

29. (A) lawyer
    (B) defendant
    (C) judge
    (D) correction official   Ⓐ Ⓑ Ⓒ Ⓓ

30. (A) her
    (B) his
    (C) the
    (D) their   Ⓐ Ⓑ Ⓒ Ⓓ

ANSWER KEY

1. **D**	7. **C**	13. **B**	19. **C**	25. **D**
2. **D**	8. **B**	14. **B**	20. **C**	26. **B**
3. **C**	9. **A**	15. **A**	21. **D**	27. **D**
4. **D**	10. **B**	16. **A**	22. **B**	28. **D**
5. **B**	11. **D**	17. **B**	23. **B**	29. **B**
6. **B**	12. **A**	18. **A**	24. **C**	30. **C**

ANSWERS EXPLAINED

Group One

If you followed our recommended strategy, you should have recognized from the instructions—especially the use of the word *solely*—that you were taking reading comprehension questions. Then, for questions 1–3 you should have first read the stem of the three questions and understood that you needed the following information to answer the questions:

1. the time when most thefts occur from cars parked in the *employee's* parking lot and
2. the time when the theft from Ms. Swanson's car took place and
3. the total value of property stolen from Ms. Swanson's car.

Once you knew these three pieces of information, you should have then read the passage. As you found the information needed to answer each of the three questions, you should have circled that information in the test booklet. Once you had located the information needed to answer all three questions, you should have stopped reading and answered the questions.

1. **(D)** If you selected choice A, you picked the time when most thefts occur in the visitor's parking lot. This is a common distractor used to confuse test takers. Make sure that you understand what information the question is asking for. In this case it was stated in the last sentence in the first paragraph that most thefts in the employee's parking lot occur between 10:00 P.M. and 11:30 P.M. Also note the similarity between choices A and D. You must be careful when choosing answers.

2. **(D)** Note that all the times listed in the choices appeared somewhere in the paragraph. But, since Ms. Swanson left her car at 9:45 A.M. and returned at 10:45 A.M., you must understand that the theft occurred sometime between those two times as indicated in choice D.

3. **(C)** The key word in the question was the word *total*. Because the radio was worth $300, the tokens were worth $15, and no other property was taken, the total value of property stolen was $315.

4. **(D)** Notice the similarity between form 2341, which is used to report leaking plumbing, and form 2431, which is used to report overloaded electrical sockets. When numbers are involved in the answer, be careful to select the correct ones.

5. **(B)** It states very clearly in the passage that extension cords are not allowed and should be seized immediately upon discovery. Note that while there is probably a rule somewhere that requires the seizing of unauthorized personal property, this particular passage remains silent about that. Remember that, when you are answering reading comprehension questions, the answers must be contained in the passage.

6. **(B)** Only homemade lampshades are not authorized and must be reported to a supervisor. Be careful when limiting adjectives such as *homemade* are used in the passage.

7. **(C)** Although a number of conditions in the passage would require some form of notification, only leaking plumbing specifically requires a telephone notification. Remember that the answers are there; don't read into the passage.

8. **(B)** The correction officer originally observed the inmate at 4:05 P.M. and approached him 10 minutes later at 4:15 P.M. Note that the name *Ginty* has appeared in a number of previous passages. Do not let this lead you to believe that these passages are in any way connected. This is something you must understand. The answers are based solely on the information in the passage given, not on information appearing elsewhere.

9. **(A)** The passage clearly states that the officer moved cautiously believing that the inmate may be armed. Concerning choice D, although it might be true that all inmates must be approached cautiously, the passage did not say that. When you are answering reading comprehension questions, you must answer solely on the information in the passage.

10. **(B)** In the next to last sentence in the passage, the officer asked the inmate to "Please move back away from that gate and get nearer to the group in the yard."

Group Two

Remember that you should have looked at the questions before you read the passage to determine what information you needed to answer them. Then, as you found that information, you should have circled it in the passage.

11. **(D)** While the tasks listed in choices A, B, and C are all major tasks of the Officer of the Day, to take command when an unusual incident occurs is clearly identified in the passage as being the most important function of the Officer of the Day.

12. **(A)** Captain Rems emphasized to Officer Ginty that her first responsibility when notified about an unusual incident is to notify the warden. Therefore, at 1:15 P.M., when notified about an unusual incident, her first action must be to notify the warden.

13. **(B)** The passage clearly states that a compromise was reached. It said nothing about prison rules, the warden, or Captain Rems being part of that compromise.

14. **(B)** To answer this question, it is necessary to relate information from two parts of the passage. The incident occurred on Tuesday, March 16th. This was given at the beginning of the passage. The compromise stated that the Latin Kings would get the preferred seating at the next scheduled session, which was scheduled for the following Tuesday. That means the next session is to be held on March 23rd.

15. **(A)** At 1:45 P.M. the incident was declared as being under control. When this happens, the Officer of the Day must complete an Unusual Incident Report.

16. **(A)** A call is dispatched when the officers originally receive it.

17. **(B)** This is an easy question, but work carefully when dates are involved.

18. **(A)** The cylinder on the lock of the door was removed and the door was open.

19. **(C)** While Officer Story instructed Mr. Wood, his partner, Officer Brown, notified the Crime Scene Unit.

20. **(C)** Don't assume anything. The answer is in the passage where it states that the Crime Scene Unit is from the local police department.

Please note that question 21 is what we call a rule interpretation question. This question type is sometimes included with reading comprehension questions and sometimes with procedure questions.

21. **(D)** An officer can bring a deck of cards into a prison if it is in the line of duty. In other words, it's okay if he is told to do so as part of his job.

Group Three

Please note that questions 21–26 in this group were designed to measure your ability to comprehend written material presented in graphic form.

22. **(B)** Prison Cells 1, 3, and 4 all have money depicted.

23. **(B)** Eyeglasses and eye drops are depicted in Prison Cell 2.

24. **(C)** People who read the Bible are usually religious, and there is a Bible in Prison Cell 3.

25. **(D)** Prison Cell 1 has $10, 3 has $10 and 10 cents, and 4 has $20 and 5 cents for a total of $40.15.

26. **(B)** Prison Cell 2 has a glass and a cup.

27. **(D)** Prison Cell 1 has a pen and a pencil, 2 has a pencil, and 3 has a pen. Prison Cell 4 does not have a pen or a pencil.

Group Four

Please remember that the questions in this group were designed to test your ability to select the appropriate word. You should have remembered to scan the entire paragraph to get a sense of its overall meaning or purpose. When looking at the word choices, you should have considered such things as gender and whether the word needed to be singular or plural.

28. **(D)** Choice D is the most appropriate response since the paragraph is referring to any defendant in general. Because there is no specific reference in the paragraph to any specific person or gender, choices A, B, and C are incorrect.

29. **(B)** The paragraph clearly indicates that it is the *defendant* who will lose the amount of the bail if the defendant does not appear the next time he or she is scheduled to appear in court. Choice B, therefore, is the correct response.

30. **(C)** There is no reference to one specific gender in the paragraph. Thus, Choices A and B are incorrect. Choice D is incorrect because the paragraph is referring to a single defendant. Therefore, the selection of "their," which would be describing more than one defendant, would not be appropriate.

Verbal and Mathematical Skill Questions

2

→ **WORD USAGE**
→ **ADDITION**
→ **SUBTRACTION**
→ **MULTIPLICATION**
→ **DIVISION**
→ **AVERAGES**
→ **RATIOS**
→ **PERCENTAGES**

VERBAL SKILLS

When we refer to verbal skills, we are actually referring to the skills required to write reports. Since correction officers are required to write reports, report-writing skills are often tested in entry-level correction officer examinations. Ideally an examination would require a candidate to write a report and then have the report reviewed and scored by a qualified examiner. Obviously, with large numbers of candidates taking a correction officer examination, it would be a tremendous task to score each report written by each individual candidate. Also, because many examiners would be needed, the scoring might become more subjective.

For these reasons, writing reports is tested in another manner. A candidate is required to examine written reports or written statements and indicate by answering multiple-choice questions if the reports have been written accurately and clearly. The thinking is that if a candidate can recognize clear and accurate writing, the candidate has the skill to write reports clearly and accurately.

What follows is a review of word usage often tested by examiners when testing verbal skills.

1. **Accept/Except**

    Accept means to take what is offered.

    I accept the nomination.

    Except means to exclude.

    All the prisoners except Don escaped.

2. **Adapt/Adopt**

    Adapt means to fit or adjust as needed.

    The new inmate adapted to prison life.

    Adopt means to take as one's own.

    Because of his prior conviction for child abuse, John could not legally adopt a child.

3. Affect/Effect

Affect as an action word or a verb means to influence something.

    The new rules will affect all the inmates.

Effect as an action word or a verb means to produce a result.

    The new rules will effect the needed changes.

4. Agree with/Agree to

A person *agrees with* a person.

    Officer Mays agrees with Officer Doors.

A person *agrees to* a plan.

    The Officers agree to a cut in salary.

An item or thing may *agree with* a person.

    Milk agrees with me.

5. All ready/Already

All ready means totally prepared.

    The officers are all ready to storm the gate.

Already means occurring before a specific time period.

    It is already too late for the warden to postpone the execution.

6. All together/Altogether

All together means in a group.

    The released inmate and his family will be all together for the holidays.

Altogether means totally or wholly.

    It is altogether too risky to exchange hostages.

7. Among/Between

Between is used when referring to two persons or two things.

    He was shot between his eyes.

Among is used when referring to more than two people or more than two things.

    She stood out among the twenty inmates.

8. Beside/Besides

Beside means next to or at the side of.

    The dog stood beside the officer.

Besides means in addition to.

    No one visited the inmate besides his mother.

9. Continual/Continuous

Continual means something that is repeated, often in a pattern.

    The cuckoo bird figure of the clock appeared once each hour on a continual basis.

Continuous means without interruption.

    The ticking of the clock was continuous.

10. Emigrate/Immigrate

Emigrate means to leave a country.

He was arrested as he tried to emigrate from the country without a visa.

Immigrate means to enter a country.

As soon as he immigrated into the country, he was arrested as an escaped convict.

11. Good/Well

Good is an adjective and as such usually modifies or describes names of persons, places, or things.

Because the inmate had a good record, she was given time off for good behavior.

Well is an adverb and as such usually modifies or describes action words or verbs or adjectives or other adverbs.

Because he reads well, he also writes well.

12. I/Me

I should be used when the intent is to describe the doer of an action.

I wanted to be a correction officer as soon as I heard about the job.

Me should be used when the intent is to describe the receiver of an action.

After chasing me through the exercise yard, the inmate threw a ball at me.

13. Imply/Infer

Imply means to suggest or hint.

The host tried to imply to his guests that he was tired.

Infer means to conclude by reasoning.

If you yawn and look at the clock, a guest will infer that you are tired.

14. In/Into

In means a location, place, or situation.

The inmate sat in his cell.

Into means movement toward a place.

The sun sank into the horizon.

15. Its/It's

Its means possession.

The prison has maintained its stark appearance.

It's means it is.

It's too dangerous to try a prison break.

16. Later/Latter

Later means that something is more late in time.

Officers May and Cane were both late, but Officer May arrived later.

Latter means the second of two things that were mentioned.

San Quentin and Attica are both tough institutions to serve time in, but I prefer the latter.

17. Lay/Lie

Lay means to put or place something.

   Lay your weapons on the floor.

Lie means to recline.

   I like to lie in the sun.

Note: The problem with *Lay* and *Lie* arises when different time frames are involved with the use of these two words.

EXAMPLE

Concerning the word *Lie,* meaning to recline:
In the present tense
 To lie or *lie*—I lie down when I'm sleepy.
In the past tense
 Lay—I lay down last night.
Using the past participle with words like *have* or *has*
 Lain—When tired, I have lain down on the bed.

Concerning the word *Lay,* meaning to put or place something:
In the present tense
 To lay or *lay*—Lay down your guns right now.
In the past tense
 Laid—The inmates laid down their weapons.
Using the past participle with words like *have* or *has*
 Laid—The inmate has agreed and has laid down his gun.

---

18. Learn/Teach

Learn means to get knowledge.

   I learn something every time I speak to my Dad.

Teach means to give knowledge.

   My Dad teaches me something every time he speaks to me.

19. Moral/Morale

Moral means good or virtuous conduct.

   Giving the money back was a very moral act.

Morale means spirit or the mood of someone or of an organization.

   The morale among the several hundred officers was high.

20. Practical/Practicable

Practical means useful, workable, sensible, not theoretical.

   Keeping a spare set of keys to the van is a practical idea.

Practicable means that something is possible or feasible. It is capable of being put into practice.

   The plan to escape was practicable.

21. Their/They're/There

Their shows possession relating to the word *they*.

    They ate in their dining room.

They're means they are.

    They're very happy.

There means a location.

    The correction officers never searched there.

22. To/Too/Two

To means in a certain direction.

    Inmate Cane went to the laundry.

Too means also or more than.

    Don wanted to go too, but it was too hot.

Two is a number.

    There are two inmates in each cell.

23. Which/Who

Which is used to refer to objects.

    This is the rope which was used by the inmate.

Who is used to refer to people.

    The inmate who escaped last week was captured.

24. Whose/Who's

Whose shows possession relating to the word *who*.

    The correction officer could not identify whose shoes were thrown off the tier.

Who's means who is.

    Who's using all the soap powder?

25. Your/You're

Your shows possession relating to the word *you*.

    You had better drop your weapon.

You're means you are.

    You're surrounded.

In addition to the areas of word usage explained here, the practice exercises that follow in this chapter along with the practice tests will address even more such areas of word usage commonly tested by examiners.

MATH SKILLS

In their daily duties, correction officers use basic math skills such as adding, subtracting, multiplying, and dividing. Also on occasion, correction officers are called upon to use these skills in determining averages, ratios, and percentage increases and decreases. Recognizing the use of such mathematical skills by correction officers, examiners who prepare entry-level correction officer examinations often include questions that test such mathematical skills. A candidate preparing for a correction officer entry-level examination should develop and practice such skills so that these types of questions can be answered quickly and accurately. Let's review these basic skills.

Addition

Finding
the sum

Addition is finding the sum of numbers and it requires two specific actions.

1. Properly line up or align the numbers to be added.

EXAMPLE

Add 432.5, 98, 2693.02, and 5. Remember that, when aligning numbers, 98 is the same as 98.00. So make sure that decimal points are correctly lined up. When properly aligned the numbers look like this:

$$\begin{array}{r} 432.5 \\ 98.00 \\ 2693.02 \\ +\ \ \ 5.00 \\ \hline \end{array}$$

Adding the numbers from the top down we get: 3228.52

---

2. After you have found the sum of 3228.52, check the answer by adding again, but this time from the bottom to the top.

Subtraction

Finding
the difference

Subtraction is finding the difference between two numbers. It requires two specific actions.

1. Properly align the numbers involved to make sure that the decimals are properly aligned.

EXAMPLE

Subtract 972.3 from 1009.38. (Remember that 972.3 is the same as 972.30.) When properly aligned the numbers look like this:

$$\begin{array}{r} 1009.38 \\ -\ 972.30 \\ \hline 37.08 \end{array}$$

---

2. Check your subtraction by adding. To do this add your answer (37.08) to the bottom number in your subtraction (972.30), and the sum should be 1009.38.

Multiplication

Adding the
same number
one or more
times

Multiplication is adding a number to itself several times. For example, $3 \times 6 = 18$ is the same as adding $3 + 3 + 3 + 3 + 3 + 3 = 18$, or $6 + 6 + 6 = 18$. Two specific actions are required by multiplication.

1. Align the products as you arrive at them.

2. If there are decimals in the numbers you are multiplying, add up the number of places to the decimal point from left to right and then count off an equal number in the answer from right to left and insert a decimal point there.

Multiply 47.1 × 182.33.

$$
\begin{array}{r}
182.33 \\
\times\ 47.1 \\
\hline
18233 \\
127631 \\
72932 \\
\hline
8587.743
\end{array}
$$

Note how each of the products were aligned, three places were counted off, and a decimal was inserted in the final product or answer. To check a multiplication answer merely divide the final product by one of the numbers used in the multiplication and you should get the other number originally used in the multiplication. For example, in the problem $8 \times 3 = 24$, you can check the multiplication by dividing 24 by 3 and getting 8.

Division

Division is separating a number into a certain number of equal parts. The statement 20 divided by 4 is the same as asking how many equal parts consisting of 4 are there in 20? The answer would be 5.

Separating a number into equal parts

Two specific actions are required by division:

1. Make sure that you are dividing by the right number. When asked to divide 72 by 36 that means you must divide 36 into 72.

   Also:

2. If you are dividing by a number that has a decimal in it, you must first move the decimal point as many places to the right as possible. You must also move the decimal point in the number you are dividing into the same number of places to the right. For example, to divide 392.25 by 26.15, move the decimal point in 26.15 to get 2615. The number 392.25 now becomes 39225. When you divide, the answer is 15.

To check a division problem, simply multiply the number you divided by with the answer. If you divided correctly, you will get the number you divided into. For example, 27 divided by 3 is 9. To check it, multiply 3×9, and you get 27.

Finding Averages

The arithmetic mean, or central point

To find an average number of a group of numbers,

1. find the sum of all the items in the group and

2. divide by the number of items in the group.

The weights in pounds of all the inmates in the van are 150, 190, 241, 224, and 180. What is the average weight of the inmates? The sum of 150, 190, 241, 224, and 180 is 985. Then divide by 5, the number of inmates, to determine the average weight, which in this case is 197 pounds.

Ratio

A ratio is a relationship between two numbers of the same kind. When expressing a ratio, take care to compare the same kind of items. For example, when painting a cell block, 8 quarts of primer and 4 gallons of paint were used. What is the ratio of primer to paint used to paint the cell block? To find the ratio or relationship between the same kind of items, the number of quarts must be converted to gallons so that we can compare gallons to gallons. After converting the 8 quarts to 2 gallons (there are 4 quarts to 1 gallon), we now have 2 gallons of primer used for every 4 gallons of paint. Expressed as a ratio we would have the fraction 2/4. Note that a ratio maintains its value if you multiply or divide both numbers in a ratio by the same number. In our ratio of 2/4, if we divide both numbers in the ratio 2/4 by 2, we get a ratio of 1/2, which is the same value as 2/4.

Examiners often ask a kind of question involving ratios known as a proportion question.

EXAMPLE

If 2 guards must be assigned for every 30 inmates, how many guards must be assigned for 150 inmates?

Immediately set up your ratios so that 2 guards are needed for 30 inmates as an unknown number of guards (represented by g) are needed for 150 inmates or

$$\frac{2}{30} = \frac{g}{150}$$

The solution calls for cross multiplying and dividing. First cross multiply $2 \times 150 = 300$ and then cross multiply $30 \times g = 30g$. We now have the equation $30g = 300$. We can divide by 30 as long as we do it to both sides of our equation.

$$\frac{30g}{30} = \frac{300}{30}$$

$$g = 10$$

Consequently, 10 guards must be assigned for 150 inmates.

Arithmetic Reasoning

In an arithmetic reasoning question, a situation verbally describes a fact pattern and then identifies a problem that must be solved. Four possible answer choices are given. You must then select the correct operations or solution that solves the problem. Note that the solutions or operations in the answer choices are not verbally expressed. In other words, they do not use words. Instead, the answer choices consist of either numbers or lettered symbols that must be followed to solve the identified problem. To solve an arithmetic reasoning problem, you must choose an arithmetic method, not a verbal or numerical solution.

EXAMPLE

Correction Officer Perez is required to deliver an inmate from the inner-city Metropolitan Prison to Clifton Prison, a rural facility upstate. If the officer drives at a constant rate of speed or miles per hour represented by the letter R and if the number of hours the officer travels to reach Clifton Prison is represented by the letter T, what is the distance between the two prisons expressed as the letter D?

If you know how fast (the rate of speed) Officer Perez is driving, which is R, and if you also know the number of hours he travels, which is T, multiplying the rate of speed by the time yields the distance Officer Perez travels, which is D. This can be expressed using a simple equation, which you will find in one of the answer choices:

$$T \times R = D$$

More and more, you will probably see arithmetic reasoning questions instead of traditional questions that ask for a numerical answer. The reason is simple. The use of calculators has significantly reduced reliance on rote adding, subtracting, dividing and multiplying numbers but has not lessened the need to be able to use reasoning to analyze and use data skillfully.

Percentage

Percentage increase or percentage decrease asks a candidate to examine a situation that has occurred and correctly indicate what has been the percentage increase or decrease.

A part of a whole, expressed in hundreds

EXAMPLE

Last year the number of correction officers who attended firearms training was 125. This year 150 officers attended training. What was the percentage increase in the number of officers attending training?

First, find the distance or space between the numbers being compared. In this case it is 150 – 125 = 25. Next, divide the number you just calculated, in this case 25, by the older number (the number that previously existed), in this case 125. So we now have 25/125 or 1/5, which is 20%. The numbers increased from 125 to 150 so there has been percentage increase. Remember that, in setting up this fraction, the denominator will always be the older number (the number that previously existed).

PRACTICE EXERCISES

In answering the following practice questions, try to answer them in the time allotted. After answering all the questions in a group, turn to the answers and check your work. Also make sure to review the answer explanations to help you understand why you are correct or incorrect in your choice of answers.

GROUP ONE

Time Allowed: 20 minutes

> **Directions:** In each of questions 1–10 you will be given four choices. Three of the choices—A, B, and C—contain a written statement. You are to evaluate the statement in each choice and select the statement that is most accurately and clearly written. If all or none of the three written statements is accurately and clearly written, you are to select choice D.

1. According to the directions, evaluate the following statements.

   (A) A change in cells always effects the inmates.
   (B) The correction officer was able to adapt to the transfer.
   (C) Let's keep it among us two.
   (D) All or none is accurate.   Ⓐ Ⓑ Ⓒ Ⓓ

2. According to the directions, evaluate the following statements.

   (A) It's all ready too late to register for the class.
   (B) The actions of the correction officer were all together inappropriate.
   (C) Who's book is that?
   (D) All or none is accurate.   Ⓐ Ⓑ Ⓒ Ⓓ

3. According to the directions, evaluate the following statements.

   (A) The inmate did not run the machine very good.
   (B) The captain pointed at him and I.
   (C) After questioning the inmate, I was able to infer he was innocent.
   (D) All or none is accurate.   Ⓐ Ⓑ Ⓒ Ⓓ

4. According to the directions, evaluate the following statements.

   (A) The correction officer emigrated to the United States from Ireland.
   (B) The inmate wanted to immigrate from the United States back to his homeland after serving his sentence.
   (C) The correction officer implied to the warden that he did not want a transfer to the laundry.
   (D) All or none is accurate.   Ⓐ Ⓑ Ⓒ Ⓓ

5. According to the directions, evaluate the following statements.

   (A) Its a different world in prison.
   (B) The warden is actually a very moral man.
   (C) Beans and rice are delicious, but I prefer the later.
   (D) All or none is accurate.   Ⓐ Ⓑ Ⓒ Ⓓ

6. According to the directions, evaluate the following statements.

    (A) That is to hard.

    (B) Whose using the soap?

    (C) There are two officers in the van.

    (D) All or none is accurate.   Ⓐ Ⓑ Ⓒ Ⓓ

7. According to the directions, evaluate the following statements.

    (A) They're getting away.

    (B) There is room in Cell Block D.

    (C) They went to get their car.

    (D) All or none is accurate.   Ⓐ Ⓑ Ⓒ Ⓓ

8. According to the directions, evaluate the following statements.

    (A) It's a long trip to the facility.

    (B) I agree with the cut in salary.

    (C) All the inmates accept Don wanted to exclude Frank from the team because they thought he was an informant.

    (D) All or none is accurate.   Ⓐ Ⓑ Ⓒ Ⓓ

9. According to the directions, evaluate the following statements.

    (A) The search dog lost it's way.

    (B) Your a good sport.

    (C) Morale is high among the troops.

    (D) All or none is accurate.   Ⓐ Ⓑ Ⓒ Ⓓ

10. According to the directions, evaluate the following statements.

    (A) Keeping a list of expenses is very practicable.

    (B) We are lucky that the escape was stopped because the inmates' plan was very practical.

    (C) I like to lie on my sofa.

    (D) All or none is accurate.   Ⓐ Ⓑ Ⓒ Ⓓ

GROUP TWO

Time Allowed: 20 minutes

Directions: Answer questions 11 and 12 based on the following information.

During the month of March, Inmate Ray Bats is admitted into the Bland Prison and has the following deposits made by members of his family into his prison expense account, which had an original balance of $239.89; $14.32, $65.66, $19.29, $36.36, and $102.97. In April, Bats had no deposits made into his expense account, but on the last day of April he makes his first purchases consisting of two record albums for $9.98 each, four candy bars for a total of $6.45, and three magazines totaling $7.00.

11. How much did Inmate Bats have in his prison account after making his purchases in April?

(A) $205.19
(B) $455.06
(C) $445.08
(D) $238.60

Ⓐ Ⓑ Ⓒ Ⓓ

12. The average cost of the items purchased by Inmate Bats is most nearly

(A) $3.71.
(B) $5.79.
(C) $8.35.
(D) $9.98.

Ⓐ Ⓑ Ⓒ Ⓓ

13. If the cost to house and feed an inmate in a certain facility is $16,456 for 1 year, what would be the cost for 3 years to house and feed an inmate assuming that the cost per year remained stable?

(A) $49,638
(B) $49,838
(C) $49,318
(D) $49,368

Ⓐ Ⓑ Ⓒ Ⓓ

14. If it takes 24 chickens to feed 120 inmates, how many chickens will it take to feed 600 inmates?

(A) 3000
(B) 300
(C) 120
(D) 76

Ⓐ Ⓑ Ⓒ Ⓓ

15. A certain institution currently has 2498 inmates. That is 526 more than they had last year. What is the annual percentage increase in inmate population within the institution?

(A) 21%
(B) 23%
(C) 27%
(D) 30%

Ⓐ Ⓑ Ⓒ Ⓓ

16. If 96 of the 120 correction officers who attended a training class were males, what was the ratio of females to males attending the class?

(A) 4 to 1
(B) 4 to 5
(C) 5 to 4
(D) 1 to 4

Ⓐ Ⓑ Ⓒ Ⓓ

17. Since a certain institution recently opened, the ages of the wardens who have been assigned were 57, 45, 48, 52, and 39 years old. What has been the average age of the warden?

(A) under 47 years old
(B) between 48 and 49 years old
(C) between 49 and 50 years old
(D) over 50 years old

Ⓐ Ⓑ Ⓒ Ⓓ

18. Correction Officer Ryan Ford has arrested Leo Marino, who was apprehended in connection with a failed escape plot outside the walls of Cameo Prison on Highway 33. Marino was to have provided transportation for his girlfriend Inmate Lydia Brown, who was seized inside the prison while attempting escape. Inmate Brown implicated Marino. A search of Marino and his vehicle revealed some stolen property, which was temporarily vouchered pending the arrival of the state police. The stolen property consisted of rare stamps and rare coins. If the number of these rare stamps is represented by S, if each stamp has a value of Y dollars, if the number of rare coins being vouchered is represented by C, and if each coin has a value of Z dollars, which of the following is the most accurate manner to express the total value in dollars of the vouchered stolen property represented by V?

(A) $(S \times Y) + (C \times Z) = V$
(B) $C + S + Z + Y = V$
(C) $(S \times Z) + (C \times Y) = V$
(D) $(C + S) \times (Z + Y) = V$

Ⓐ Ⓑ Ⓒ Ⓓ

Directions: Answer questions 19 and 20 based on the following information.

The inmates of a certain institution personally receive 5.25 cents for every article they prepare in the wood workshop.

19. If Inmate Hands prepares 97 such articles, how much money will the inmate earn?

(A) less than $5
(B) between $5 and $5.10
(C) between $5.15 and $5.25
(D) over $5.25

Ⓐ Ⓑ Ⓒ Ⓓ

20. If a certain inmate in the woodwork shop earns $5.0637, $6.798, $4.897, $3.459, and $3.33, in 5 consecutive days, on the average what did the inmate earn each day?

(A) $4.76
(B) $4.73
(C) $4.71
(D) $4.65

Ⓐ Ⓑ Ⓒ Ⓓ

ANSWER KEY

1. **B**	5. **B**	9. **C**	13. **D**	17. **B**
2. **D**	6. **C**	10. **C**	14. **C**	18. **A**
3. **C**	7. **D**	11. **C**	15. **C**	19. **B**
4. **C**	8. **A**	12. **A**	16. **D**	20. **C**

ANSWERS EXPLAINED

Group One

1. **(B)** *Affects* means to influence and should have been used in choice A. Choice C is wrong because *between* should be used when two people are involved.

2. **(D)** Choice A is wrong because *already* should have been used to indicate before a specific time. Choice B is wrong because *altogether* meaning totally should have been used, and choice C is wrong because *Whose* should have been used to show possession. The answer is D.

3. **(C)** Choice A is incorrect because it should indicate *very well,* not *very good.* Choice B is incorrect because it should have stated "at him and me." When not sure if *I* or *me* should be used with another pronoun or noun, remove the first pronoun or noun, in this case *him,* and you will quickly see how awkward it would be to say, "The captain pointed at I." Therefore, *me* should have been used.

4. **(C)** The word *emigrate* means to leave the country you are in presently, whereas the word *immigrate* means to enter a country. That is just the opposite of what was stated in choices A and B. *Imply* means to hint, so choice C is correct.

5. **(B)** Choice A is incorrect; *It's* should have been used. Choice C is incorrect because *later* deals with time and *latter* means the second of two things that were mentioned.

6. **(C)** Choice A incorrectly uses the word *to*; the word *too* should have been used to indicate more than. Choice B uses the word *whose* incorrectly; it should be *who's.*

7. **(D)** All are correct.

8. **(A)** Choice B is incorrect because it should state, "I agree to the cut in salary." Choice C is incorrect because it should state, "All the inmates except Don wanted to exclude Frank from the team because they thought he was an informant."

9. **(C)** Choice A should state "its way." Choice B should state "You're a good sport." Choice C is correct.

10. **(C)** Choice A should state "very practical" to indicate that it was sensible, and choice B should state "very practicable," to indicate that the plan was capable of being put into practice.

Group Two

11. **(C)** First, find how much Bats had in his prison account. Then find out how much he spent and subtract his total purchases from the balance in his account. When you do that you find that Bats had $478.49 in his account and spent $33.41 which left him with a balance of $445.08.

$239.89
14.32
65.66
19.29   2 albums @ 9.98 = $19.96
36.36   4 candy bars total of 6.45
+102.97   3 magazines total of 7.00
$478.49   Minus $33.41 = $445.08

Choice A might have been selected if a candidate did not add in the original balance of $239.89. Choice C might have been selected if a candidate did not realize that *each* album cost $9.98.

12. **(A)** First find the sum of the Inmate's purchases: $9.98 + 9.98 + 6.45 + 7.00 = $33.41. Divide the sum by the number of items, which is 9 (2 albums + 4 candy bars + 3 magazines = 9 items), and it equals $3.7122, which when rounded off to two places to represent cents is $3.71. When rounding off, if the number to the right of the number you intend to wind up with is 5 or more, then add 1 to the remaining number. For example, with a number such as 9.479, the 7 gets rounded off to an 8 because the number to the right of the 7, in this case a 9, is more than 5. If that number were less than 5 as in the example 9.472, then no number is added. The number 2 would simply be eliminated, and 9.472 would be rounded off to 9.47.

13. **(D)** Simply multiply $3 \times \$16,456 = \$49,368$.

14. **(C)** First set up the ratios that create the proportions: 24 chickens is to 120 inmates as x chickens is to 600 inmates or

$$\frac{24}{120} = \frac{x}{600}$$

Cross multiplying we get

$$120x = 24 \times 600$$

$$120x = 14400$$

$$x = \frac{14400}{120} = 120$$

15. **(C)** Usually this type of question gives the candidate two numbers and after finding the distance or space between the numbers, the candidate places that number over the old number (the number that previously existed), and then divides. However, here in this question first the old number, last year's inmate population has to be determined. You do that by subtracting 526 from 2498, which gives us 1972. Then you simply place 526 over 1972, or 526 divided by 1972. That yields 0.2667, rounded off to 0.27, which represents a 27% annual percentage increase in inmate population this year over last year. Choice A represents the result of erroneously placing 526 over 2498, which yields approximately 21%.

16. **(D)** If 96 males attended out of 120 officers, then 24 of the attendees were female. The ratio of females to males would be 24 to 96, and 24/96 reduces to 1/4 or 1 to 4. Remember that the question asked for females to males. If it had asked for males to females then the ratio would have been as choice A, 4 to 1.

17. **(B)** Adding the ages gives the sum of 241, which when divided by 5 equals 48.2, or choice B.

18. **(A)** To find the value of the vouchered property, represented by V, first multiply the number of rare stamps by the dollar value of each stamp, or $S \times Y$. Then multiply the number of rare coins by the dollar value of each coin, or $C \times Z$. Finally, add those two products together. This yields choice A, or $(S \times Y) + (C \times Z) = V$.

19. **(B)** Multiplying 97×5.25 cents = 509.25 cents. But our answer choices are in dollars. So to convert cents to dollars we must divide the cents by 100 (there are 100 cents in each dollar). 509.25/100 = $5.0925 and rounding that off yields $5.09.

20. **(C)** The sum of the monies earned is $23.5477, which when divided by 5 is $4.70954, or $4.71 when rounded off. Regarding rounding off, unless otherwise directed by the question, it should be the last calculation done.

Memory Questions 3

→ **IMPORTANCE**

→ **PICTORIAL QUESTIONS**

→ **NARRATIVE QUESTIONS**

→ **USING ASSOCIATIONS**

→ **FOCUSING ON KEY FACTS**

→ **STRATEGIES FOR RECALLING PICTORIAL DETAILS**

→ **STRATEGIES FOR RECALLING NARRATIVE MATERIAL**

In Chapter 1 we provided strategies for reading comprehension questions, which, as you now know, are questions that measure whether you understand written or pictorial information, which may be referred to when actually answering such questions.

In this chapter we go one step farther. Now you will learn to answer questions that measure whether you can understand and remember written or pictorial information, which is given to you for a period of time to study and then taken away from you while you answer questions about it. This is why we call these questions memory questions. In order to answer this type of question correctly, you must be able to commit information to memory and then retain that information long enough to answer the questions.

THE IMPORTANCE OF MEMORY QUESTIONS

In our opinion, memory questions are especially important. We feel this way for two reasons. The first is that memory questions are typically the question type that causes the greatest difficulty for test takers. In fact, statistics that we have gathered over the years indicate that the average untrained test taker misses about 50% of these questions. This means that test takers who do well on memory questions have a distinct advantage over most of the other candidates taking the test.

The second factor contributing to the importance of memory-type questions is that such questions almost always appear at the beginning of the test. When test takers experience difficulty answering these questions, it almost always has a negative impact on their performance for the rest of the examination. Conversely, those test takers who have no trouble answering memory questions tend to develop a high level of confidence, which carries over to the remainder of the test.

The bottom line is this: If you master the technique for answering memory questions and do well with them on the official test, you will be taking a giant step toward reaching your goal of becoming a correction officer.

TWO WIDELY USED TYPES OF MEMORY QUESTIONS

There are two widely used memory-question formats in general use on correction officer examinations. We call the first type pictorial memory questions, and the second type we refer to as narrative memory questions.

Pictorial Memory Questions

In pictorial memory questions you are given a drawing, sketch, or some other form of illustrated material and are permitted to study it for a specified time period, usually between 5 and 10 minutes. In the great majority of cases, the illustration you are given to study has some relationship to the job of a correction officer. You are then asked a series of questions based on information that is contained in the illustration you were given to study. In most cases, the test instructions make it clear that you are not permitted to make notes while studying the pictorial material, and you cannot refer back to it when answering the questions. In fact, the pictorial material is usually collected before the questions are started.

Narrative Memory Questions

In narrative memory questions, which are really quite similar to the pictorial memory questions, you are given written material and permitted to study it for a specified time period, usually about 10 minutes. As is the case with pictorial memory questions, the written material you are given to study should have some relationship to the job of a correction officer. You are then asked a series of questions based on information that is contained in the narrative material you were given to study. In most cases, the question instructions make it clear that you are not permitted to make notes while studying the material and that you cannot refer to it when answering the questions. In fact, as is the case with pictorial material, the narrative material is usually collected before the questions are started.

Please note that in some cases the written material you must commit to memory is distributed well in advance of the day of the test. Then, on the day of the test, a series of questions about this material is asked. As is the case with all memory questions, candidates are not allowed to refer to the material when answering the questions. As you might expect, when the narrative material that is used as the basis for memory questions is distributed in advance of test day, it is always more lengthy and somewhat more complicated than such narrative material that is distributed on the day of the test.

USING "ASSOCIATIONS"—THE KEY TO SUCCESS

Unless you are one of those very rare individuals who has a photographic memory, it is a big mistake for you to rely strictly on brute memory to remember the material, whether it is written in narrative form or presented in pictorial form. Instead, we strongly recommend that you use a memory technique that we refer to as association. Interestingly, if you learn and master the association technique, it will not only help you to be quite successful when answering memory questions on any examination, but it will also help you in the future to remember important matters in your everyday life.

PROVING OUR POINT

In the many classroom sessions we have conducted to assist students who are preparing to take memory questions, we have learned that it is important to convince those students of the value of using associations as a memory aide. That is what we intend to do with you right now by asking you to work through two practice exercises. It is important that you take these two exercises before reading the rest of this chapter.

PRACTICE EXERCISES

PRACTICE EXERCISE ONE

A list of 20 common words follows. Right now, take 5 minutes to study and commit these words to memory. At the end of 5 minutes, stop studying these words, let 10 minutes pass, and then write down as many of these words as you can to see how many you can remember. Do not take notes during your 5-minute studying period, and do not refer back to the list when you are attempting to write them all down. When you cannot remember any more of the 20 words, record the number of words you were able to remember, and resume reading this chapter starting with the next paragraph.

1.	peach	11.	automobile
2.	ring	12.	camp
3.	razor	13.	missile
4.	champion	14.	lamp
5.	lettuce	15.	children
6.	universe	16.	balance
7.	final	17.	listen
8.	teacher	18.	jump
9.	justice	19.	speak
10.	prisoner	20.	tank

PRACTICE EXERCISE TWO

In all probability you were able to remember about 10–12 of the words from Practice Exercise One after having studied them for 5 minutes. We now want you to take a similar exercise with one big difference. This time we will give you the following associations to use to help you remember the 20 words that appear in this exercise.

1. When you are studying the 20 words, be aware that there is one word in the list that begins with the letter *a*, one word that begins with the letter *b*, and so forth. For example, the *a* word is *apple*, the *b* word is *boat*, and so forth. As you study each word in the list, make sure that you take note of the first letter of each word and associate it with the alphabet. Then, later on when you are trying to remember the words, you will easily remember the first letter of each word you cannot readily recall. You will find that this will help you remember the missing words.

2. An *elephant* (word 7—the *e* word) is *gigantic* (word 17—the *g* word), usually travels in a *herd* (word 6—the *h* word), and has an occasional fight with a *lion* (word 12—the *l* word), who is the *king* (word 10—the *k* word) of the jungle and has a *queen* (word 9—the *q* word).

3. *Twenty* (word 2—the *t* word) rhymes with *plenty* (word 14—the *p* word), and is a number that is used in *mathematics* (word 8—the *m* word).

4. *Apple* (word 1—the *a* word) *jelly* (word 19—the *j* word) is *sweet* (word 15—the *s* word) and can be spread on *bread* (word 4—the *b* word).

Now take the same amount of time, 5 minutes, that you used in Practice Exercise One and study the following list of 20 words, remembering to use the suggested associations. Then, as you did for Practice Exercise One, let 10 minutes pass and see how many of the words from Practice Exercise Two you can remember. Remember that you should not make notes when studying the words and should not refer back to the list when you are trying to remember its contents. Instead, use the suggested associations to help you remember.

1.	apple	11.	dark
2.	twenty	12.	lion
3.	sun	13.	office
4.	bread	14.	plenty
5.	candle	15.	sweet
6.	herd	16.	nonsense
7.	elephant	17.	gigantic
8.	mathematics	18.	idle
9.	queen	19.	jelly
10.	king	20.	finish

Learn to Develop and Make Your Own Associations

TIP

Relate what you are trying to remember with something you already know.

In all probability, you were much more successful in Practice Exercise Two and you are now convinced of the benefit of using associations as a memory aid. You probably also understand that when we say "making associations" we mean associating (or connecting) the information you want to remember with some other information so that it is easier to recall the information you wanted to commit to memory. Association is a necessary process because trying to remember things by brute memory alone is very difficult.

The type of associations made by different people varies tremendously from individual to individual, depending upon background, interests, and imagination. This is where practice will help you the most. The technique involves associating or relating what you are trying to remember with something you already know or with something else you are trying to remember. As a further example of how this works, listed below are some facts that you might want to remember about a story or a picture and some suggested associations to help you remember them.

Facts	Possible Associations
• The prisoner is 25 years old.	• You or someone you know is 25 years old.
• Altogether 10 officers reported sick.	• They could have played a full court basketball game. (10 players needed)
• One officer was 24 and the other was 42.	• The reverse of one age equals the other age.
• The prisoner, Mike Murphy, was convicted of murder.	• Mike Murphy was convicted of Murder. This is an alphabetical which is a very useful form of association. Note the three "m" words.
• The supervisor's name is Sergeant Wright.	• The supervisor is always right (Wright)

These examples should help you understand how to use associations to aid memory. Bear in mind, however, that your degree of success with this technique depends upon practice. Incidentally, you do not need correctional material to practice. Your daily newspaper will do just fine. Study a news story for about 5–10 minutes while developing associations to remember the details of the story; then put the paper down and see how many details you can remember.

FOCUSING ON THE KEY FACTS

Every corrections officer is taught during his or her entry-level training how to capture the key facts in a story in order to write an accurate report. More often than not, the code word *NEOTWY* has been a part of this training. This code word is derived by taking the last letter from each of the six key facts that must be contained in any thorough narrative report of an occurrence.

If you answer these questions when you are investigating an occurrence (e.g., when did it happen?, where did it happen?, who was involved?, what happened?, how did it happen?, and why did it happen?), you have captured all the key information. Therefore, when you are answering memory questions, either pictorial or narrative, concentrate on remembering the information that answers these questions. To help you, we list and explain the most common kinds of information to be found in each of the six categories.

THE KEY FACTS

wheN
wherE
whO
whaT
hoW
whY

1. **WHEN.** Times and dates are favorite targets of test writers. If, for example, when looking at a pictorial representation of an inmate's cell, there is either a clock showing the time, a calendar showing the day or date, or both a clock and a calendar, you can be sure that you will be asked a when question. When the memory questions are based on a narrative, the most common dates and times used involve the time of occurrence of an incident, the time it was reported, the time escapes were made, and the time arrests were made.

2. **WHERE.** A critical element in any correctional incident is where the incident took place. If more than one incident took place, make sure that you can relate each incident to its location. A favorite pictorial memory-type where question involves the placement of items in relation to one another. For example, the question might be "where is the knife?," and the answer might be "on the inmate's bed." Incidentally, if a narrative or a pictorial representation mentions or shows any kind of weapon, you can be certain that you will be asked a question about that weapon.

3. **WHO.** There are a number of whos in every prison story, including who is the inmate, who is the escaped prisoner, who is the officer, and who is the visitor. Remember also that physical description of the various whos in the story or illustration are fair game for questions. Things such as beards, glasses, scars, and clothing are often the subject of questions. Or, if there is a vehicle of some sort involved, then it is a sure bet that you will see a question or two about the vehicle, especially its license plate number.

4. **WHAT.** The most common what question is "what is happening?" For example, "has someone been injured?, or, what kind of emergency is taking place?"

5. **HOW.** How many? is a question that is almost always asked. For example, how many weapons or how many inmates are in the picture? How things happened is also a favorite question area.

6. **WHY.** Motive is the primary why question. Why inmates do things is always of concern to the correctional staff of a prison. Always look for indications of motive when reading a story or looking at a picture. Another why question in pictorial formats involves things that are unusual. When something unusual is shown, you will be asked about it and/or the reason why the unusual condition exists.

STRATEGIES FOR RECALLING PICTORIAL DETAILS

The illustration you are given to study is never very complicated. Therefore, all you need to have to become proficient at answering these questions based on the picture is a strategy, concentration, and practice. The concentration must be developed through practice. You can practice every time you look at a picture or read a story. The strategy follows.

PICTORIAL QUESTION STRATEGIES

Standardize your study method.

Focus on key facts.

Look at all readable matter.

Look for oddities.

Use associations.

Count objects.

Concentrate.

1. **DEVELOP A STANDARDIZED METHOD OF STUDYING THE MATERIAL.** If you want to remember all the details in a pictorial representation, you must look at the picture in an organized fashion. You cannot stare at it with the mistaken belief that your mind is recording all the details. You must look at the picture methodically. You must start looking in one certain place, proceed through the picture carefully, work yourself back to the starting place, begin again, and repeat the process. You continue in this manner until your entire amount of allotted time has been used.

2. **FOCUS ON THE KEY FACTS.** As you observe the details shown in the illustration, you should focus on the NEOTWY key facts.

3. **OBSERVE ALL READABLE MATTER.** If there is information in the picture that can be read, then you probably will be asked about it. Therefore, look for these most common "readables":

   - clocks
   - signs
   - calendars
   - license plates

4. **SEARCH FOR ODDITIES.** Test writers do not only write memory questions about things that appear usual in the picture; they also write questions about things that are unusual. The following are some of the unusual things to look for:

   - weapons
   - contraband
   - things that are out of place in the scene

5. **USE ASSOCIATIONS TO REMEMBER.** Earlier we spoke a great deal about the use of associations to help you remember things. Now, as you observe key facts, you can apply the association technique to them.

6. **COUNT OBJECTS.** If there are fewer than a dozen separate items in the picture, count them. Examiners often frame questions based on the number of objects. Similarly, if there are more than one of the same type of objects, count them. Finally, if money is pictured, count the money.

7. **PAY STRICT ATTENTION TO NUMBERS IN THE PICTORIAL MATERIAL.** If there are numbers in the pictorial material, there will probably be at least one question about these numbers. Typical examples are dates, times, license plate numbers, addresses, dollar amounts, and numbers of people involved.

8. **DO NOT BREAK YOUR CONCENTRATION.** Do not stop concentrating until you have answered all the memory questions. And do not try to observe everything the first time through the picture. Go over it in a methodical way again and again.

9. **DON'T STOP CONCENTRATING WHEN YOUR TIME TO OBSERVE THE MATERIAL HAS ELAPSED.** The time between the closing of the memory booklet and the answering of the questions is the most critical time of all. It is imperative that you maintain your concentration during this time. This is the time when untrained candidates let their mind wander. As a result, they forget some of what they observed.

STRATEGIES FOR RECALLING NARRATIVE MATERIAL

Narrative memory questions are not as difficult as you may think because the written story is never a complicated one to understand. Perhaps more than any other test area, this area can be improved upon significantly by practice. So, if you work hard and adhere to the following guidelines, you will be able to do very well on this part of your examination.

1. **DON'T JUST READ THE STORY; BECOME PART OF IT!** When you are reading the story, you must clear your head of everything else except what you are reading. You must concentrate. The kind of intense concentration that is needed is best achieved by "putting yourself in the story." Create a mental picture of what is happening.

2. **RELATE THE UNKNOWN TO THE KNOWN.** You will find that it is easier to put yourself into the story if you create mental images involving persons, places, and things that you know and are familiar with. For example, if the story involves people, try to associate each person in the story with someone you know.

3. **DON'T TRY TO MEMORIZE THE ENTIRE NARRATIVE.** Some students attempt to memorize the entire story verbatim. For most of us, this is an impossible task. The trick is to identify the key facts in the story and to remember them. Don't be concerned if the story seems incomplete; it will not necessarily have a conclusion. All the test writer is interested in is giving you enough information to test your memory.

4. **USE ASSOCIATIONS TO REMEMBER.** As with the pictorial format, do not try to use brute memory. Instead, use the association techniques we discussed previously.

5. **PAY STRICT ATTENTION TO NUMBERS IN THE NARRATIVE.** If there are numbers in the narrative, there will probably be at least one question about these numbers. Typical examples are ages, license plate numbers, addresses, dollar amounts, and times.

6. **DO NOT BREAK YOUR CONCENTRATION.** Do not stop concentrating until all the memory questions are answered. And, do not try to remember everything the first time you read the story. Go over it in a methodical way again and again.

7. **DON'T STOP CONCENTRATING WHEN YOUR TIME TO OBSERVE THE MATERIAL HAS ELAPSED.** As already mentioned, the time between the closing of the memory booklet and the answering of the questions is the most critical time of all. It is imperative that you maintain your concentration during this time. This is the time when untrained candidates let their minds wander with the result that they forget some of what they have read.

GROUP ONE

Time Allowed: 25 minutes

Directions: The following story is about an occurrence involving correction officers. You are allowed 10 minutes to read it and commit to memory as much about it as you can. You are *not* allowed to make any written notes during the time you are reading. At the end of 10 minutes, you are to stop reading the material and answer 10 questions about the story without referring back to it.

MEMORY STORY—10-MINUTE TIME LIMIT

Assume that you are a correction officer working at the Municipal Detention Facility. You name is Mike Molloy. Your shield number is 6543. It is 8:00 A.M. on Sunday, April 1st, and you have been on duty for 30 minutes. You are assigned to the inmate dining room, and breakfast is being served.

Your attention is drawn by loud voices to two inmates waiting in line for their morning meal. One of the inmates, Charles Champion (Inmate Number 246810), is shaking his fist in the face of another inmate, William White (Inmate Number 765321). As you approach the two inmates, you see Champion initiate the use of force by using his right fist to hit White in the face. In an instant Inmate White, apparently unhurt by Champion's blow, struck out with his left fist and hit Champion in the stomach causing Champion to double over in apparent pain. White followed his blow to the stomach with a stinging right-handed punch to the left side of Champion's head, which knocked Champion unconscious. The altercation lasted no more than 1 minute.

As soon as you observed the first blow struck, you called for backup assistance. But, by the time help arrived, the fight was over. Your first action was to request Officer Harry Huarte to call for immediate medical assistance for Inmate Champion and then you requested Officer Sam Jones (shield number 5858) to remove Inmate White from the dining area and Officer Bob Baker (shield number 8012) to attempt to locate other witnesses to the fight. Having done this, you administered first aid to the still unconscious inmate.

Twenty minutes after the incident began, Inmate Champion was on his way to the prison hospital, and Inmate White was back in his cell. The rest of the breakfast period took place with no further incidents. Later that morning, you found out that the injured inmate had sustained a broken jaw in the fight and that Inmate White was removed from his cell and placed in isolation. At about noontime, Officer Baker reported to you that he could not determine the cause of the fight.

DO NOT PROCEED UNTIL 10 MINUTES HAVE PASSED.

1. The altercation between Inmates Champion and White took place

   (A) on Monday, April 1st at about 8:00 A.M.
   (B) on Sunday, April 2nd at about 8:20 A.M.
   (C) on Monday, April 2nd at about 8:20 A.M.
   (D) on Sunday, April 1st at about 8:00 A.M.   Ⓐ Ⓑ Ⓒ Ⓓ

2. On the day of the fight between the two inmates, Officer Molloy started his tour of duty at

   (A) 7:30 A.M.
   (B) 8:00 A.M.
   (C) 9:00 A.M.
   (D) a time not stated.   Ⓐ Ⓑ Ⓒ Ⓓ

3. Your shield number is

   (A) 6543.
   (B) 5858.
   (C) 8012.
   (D) not given.   Ⓐ Ⓑ Ⓒ Ⓓ

4. The first blow in the fight was struck by

   (A) Inmate Number 246810.
   (B) Inmate Number 765321.
   (C) Inmate Number 264801.
   (D) Inmate Number 756231.   Ⓐ Ⓑ Ⓒ Ⓓ

5. Inmate White's first blow in the fight was

   (A) a left-handed blow to the head.
   (B) a right-handed blow to the head.
   (C) a left-handed blow to the stomach.
   (D) a right-handed blow to the stomach.   Ⓐ Ⓑ Ⓒ Ⓓ

6. The officer whom you requested to call for medical assistance was Officer

   (A) Molloy.
   (B) Huarte.
   (C) Jones.
   (D) Baker.

   Ⓐ Ⓑ Ⓒ Ⓓ

7. Officer Sam Jones' shield number is

   (A) 6543.
   (B) 5858.
   (C) 8012.
   (D) not given.

   Ⓐ Ⓑ Ⓒ Ⓓ

8. Who administered first aid to the injured inmate?

   (A) Officer Molloy
   (B) Officer Huarte
   (C) Officer Jones
   (D) Officer Baker

   Ⓐ Ⓑ Ⓒ Ⓓ

9. Inmate White was back in his cell at

   (A) 8:00 A.M.
   (B) 8:20 A.M.
   (C) 9:00 A.M.
   (D) noon.

   Ⓐ Ⓑ Ⓒ Ⓓ

10. The cause of the fight

   (A) was determined to be loud talking.
   (B) was determined to be revenge.
   (C) was determined to be jealousy.
   (D) was undetermined.

   Ⓐ Ⓑ Ⓒ Ⓓ

Directions: Study the following scene of an inmate's cell for 5 minutes. Try to remember as many details in the scene as you can. Do not write or make any marks while studying the scene. After 5 minutes stop looking at the scene and answer the 10 questions that appear immediately after the scene. Do *not* refer back to the scene when answering the questions.

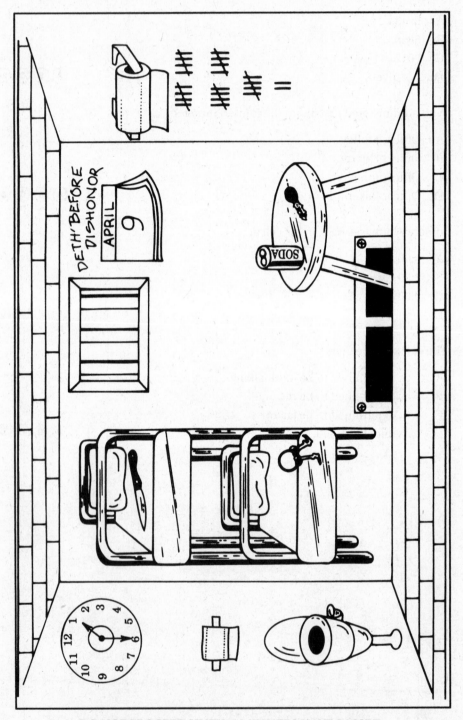

DO NOT PROCEED UNTIL 5 MINUTES HAVE PASSED.

11. Which of the following is the most accurate statement concerning the time of day depicted in the scene?

    (A) It is definitely 1:30 P.M.
    (B) It is either 6:00 A.M. or 6:00 P.M.
    (C) It is definitely 1:30 A.M.
    (D) It is either 1:30 A.M. or 1:30 P.M.

    Ⓐ Ⓑ Ⓒ Ⓓ

12. The knife in the scene is located

    (A) on the table.
    (B) on the upper bed.
    (C) on the lower bed.
    (D) on the floor.

    Ⓐ Ⓑ Ⓒ Ⓓ

13. The exact wording of the slogan written on the wall is

    (A) Death Before Dishonor.
    (B) Deth Before Dishonor.
    (C) Deth Befour Dishonor.
    (D) Death Before Dishoner.

    Ⓐ Ⓑ Ⓒ Ⓓ

14. The date shown in the scene is

    (A) April 9th.
    (B) May 10th.
    (C) June 9th.
    (D) July 10th.

    Ⓐ Ⓑ Ⓒ Ⓓ

15. How many keys are shown in the scene?

    (A) one
    (B) two
    (C) three
    (D) four

    Ⓐ Ⓑ Ⓒ Ⓓ

16. How many scratches are represented on the wall underneath the roll of paper towels?

    (A) 17
    (B) 22
    (C) 27
    (D) 32

    Ⓐ Ⓑ Ⓒ Ⓓ

17. A single key is located

    (A) on the upper bed.
    (B) on the lower bed.
    (C) on the table.
    (D) on the floor.   Ⓐ Ⓑ Ⓒ Ⓓ

18. The name of the inmate who occupies the lower bed in the cell is

    (A) James Ryan.
    (B) Charles Smith.
    (C) Don Wood.
    (D) not given.   Ⓐ Ⓑ Ⓒ Ⓓ

19. A key ring with two keys on it is located

    (A) on the upper bed.
    (B) on the lower bed.
    (C) on the table.
    (D) on the floor.   Ⓐ Ⓑ Ⓒ Ⓓ

20. The can of soda in the scene is

    (A) next to a key ring.
    (B) open.
    (C) empty.
    (D) on the table.   Ⓐ Ⓑ Ⓒ Ⓓ

GROUP THREE

Time Allowed: 20 minutes

Directions: For 5 minutes study the following illustration, which depicts items taken from two inmates immediately after they were arrested. Try to remember as many details as possible. Do not make written notes of any kind during this 5-minute period. After the 5 minutes are up, you have an additional 15 minutes to answer the 10 questions that follow immediately. When answering the questions, do *not* refer back to the illustration.

DO NOT PROCEED UNTIL 5 MINUTES HAVE PASSED.

Directions: Answer questions 21–30 solely on the basis of the preceding illustration. Do not refer back to the scene when answering these questions. You have 15 minutes to complete all 10 questions.

21. Ann Smith's address is

    (A) 246 Main Street.
    (B) 264 Main Street.
    (C) 462 Main Avenue.
    (D) 246 Main Avenue.   Ⓐ Ⓑ Ⓒ Ⓓ

22. Ann Smith's driver's license number is

    (A) 731.
    (B) 642.
    (C) 462.
    (D) 371.   Ⓐ Ⓑ Ⓒ Ⓓ

23. Both Ann Smith and John Brown have

    (A) perfume.
    (B) cigarettes.
    (C) a knife.
    (D) something to write with.   Ⓐ Ⓑ Ⓒ Ⓓ

24. Together, Ann Smith and John Brown possessed

    (A) two keys.
    (B) three keys.
    (C) four keys.
    (D) five keys.   Ⓐ Ⓑ Ⓒ Ⓓ

25. Both Ann Smith and John Brown had

    (A) car registrations.
    (B) a pen.
    (C) eyeglasses.
    (D) a $5 bill.   Ⓐ Ⓑ Ⓒ Ⓓ

26. Which of the inmates probably was experiencing headaches?

    (A) Ann Smith
    (B) John Brown
    (C) neither of them
    (D) both of them   Ⓐ Ⓑ Ⓒ Ⓓ

27. Which of the inmates clearly possessed a weapon?

    (A) Ann Smith
    (B) John Brown
    (C) neither of them
    (D) both of them   Ⓐ Ⓑ Ⓒ Ⓓ

28. What was John Brown's driver's license number?

    (A) 642
    (B) 731
    (C) 137
    (D) 317   Ⓐ Ⓑ Ⓒ Ⓓ

29. What is John Brown's address?

    (A) 31 7th Avenue
    (B) 317 Main Street
    (C) 3 17th Avenue
    (D) 31 Main Street   Ⓐ Ⓑ Ⓒ Ⓓ

30. What do Ann Smith and John Brown have in common?

    (A) They are the same age.
    (B) They were convicted of the same crime.
    (C) They live in the same town.
    (D) They drive the same make cars.   Ⓐ Ⓑ Ⓒ Ⓓ

ANSWER KEY

1. **D**	7. **B**	13. **B**	19. **B**	25. **C**
2. **A**	8. **A**	14. **A**	20. **D**	26. **B**
3. **A**	9. **B**	15. **C**	21. **A**	27. **B**
4. **A**	10. **D**	16. **C**	22. **B**	28. **B**
5. **C**	11. **D**	17. **C**	23. **D**	29. **A**
6. **B**	12. **B**	18. **D**	24. **D**	30. **C**

ANSWERS EXPLAINED

Group One

Please note that in giving the answers we will suggest associations that could have been made to recall the information needed to answer the questions. But our associations are only suggestions to help give you an idea of how associations can be made. You must remember that the development of associations is a personal matter. What works best for you is what you should follow.

1.   **(D)** The fight took place on the first of April which was a Sunday, the first day of the week. The time was 8:00 A.M. (the inmates ate at eight).

2.   **(A)** The story began at 8:00 A.M. and it was stated that Officer Molloy had already been on duty for 30 minutes, which means that Officer Molloy started his tour of duty that day at 7:30 A.M. Test writers often use this kind of question. They give you a certain time as a frame of reference (in this case 8:00 A.M.) and then say that things happened before or after this frame of reference (in this case 30 minutes before). Also note that the story made it clear that the test taker was supposed to be Mike Molloy. This could be remembered with an alphabetical association such as Me equals Mike Molloy.

3.   **(A)** The answer to this question depended for one thing on you remembering that you were told in the story to assume that you are Mike Molloy, as discussed in the answer explanation to question 2. One way of remembering your shield number is to recognize that it is 3456 in reverse—6543.

4.   **(A)** It was Inmate Champion who struck the first blow. To remember this you might have thought that a true champion would not hit first but he did. But, to correctly answer the question you must associate Champion's name with his inmate number, which was 246810 (or 2-4-6-8-10).

5.   **(C)** Inmate White left Inmate Champion doubled over when he hit him with a left fist to the stomach.

6.   **(B)** There are a couple of suggested associations to remember the fact that it was Officer Huarte who was requested to call for medical assistance. The first is to say to yourself that Officer Huarte got help for the hurt officer—notice the similarity between the words Huarte and hurt. The second way is an alphabetical association—Officer Huarte called the hospital.

7.   **(B)** The first two numbers in Sam Jones' shield number are the same as the last two.

8. **(A)** In the story it said that "you administered first aid to the still unconscious inmate." This means, of course, that Officer Molloy administered first aid because earlier it was established that you are Officer Molloy.

9. **(B)** The incident started at 8:00 A.M. Twenty minutes after it started Inmate White was already back in his cell.

10. **(D)** Officer Baker, who was requested to attempt to locate witnesses, reported to you that he was unable to determine the cause of the fight.

Group Two

11. **(D)** The clock in the scene indicates that it is 1:30 but there is no way of knowing if it is A.M. or P.M. This question highlights the importance of reading all the choices. A careless candidate who knew it was 1:30 could easily pick choice A without stopping to think about whether it was A.M. or P.M. But, a careful test taker would read all the choices and, after reading choice D would probably realize that it should indeed be either 1:30 A.M. or 1:30 P.M. Also, remember that, if the time is indicated in a memory scene, it is almost certain that you will be asked about it.

12. **(B)** A weapon in the scene is a guarantee that a question will be asked about it. A possible association is that a knife can cut you <u>up</u> and the knife was on the <u>upper</u> bed.

13. **(B)** This question emphasizes the importance of concentrating and paying attention to details. The word <u>death</u> is misspelled in the sketch. The <u>a</u> in death is <u>absent</u>.

14. **(A)** As with the time of the day, the date is a favorite question area. If you see a calendar, make sure that you remember what it says.

15. **(C)** Remember to count items in the scene, especially similar items and money.

16. **(C)** We are often asked how detailed the questions might be when answering memory questions. The answer is simple. When there are not many details depicted in a scene, as is the case in this scene, you must remember even the smallest of details. When there are a lot of details in the scene, then you should not be overly concerned with every single one of them and concentrate only on key facts. In this case, you surely should have had time to count the scratches on the wall.

17. **(C)** The <u>single</u> key is located on the table next to the can of <u>soda</u>.

18. **(D)** A favorite trick of test writers is to ask a question that does not have an answer. Of course, when they do this, one of the choices must indicate that there is no answer. Therefore, when you see a choice like choice D, always give it serious consideration.

19. **(B)** The <u>two</u> keys are located on the lower bed next to the <u>toilet</u>.

20. **(D)** The soda is where you would expect it to be, on the table. Don't be tricked by choices B and C. There is no basis for making either assumption.

Group Three

21. **(A)** 2-4-6 is certainly easy enough to remember. Hopefully you recalled it was Main Street and not Main Avenue.

22. **(B)** If you noticed that Ann Smith's driver's license number is the reverse of her house address, 642 and 246, you would have developed an association that would have helped you answer questions 1 and 2. Remember that associating one item to be remembered with another item to be remembered always pays big dividends.

23. **(D)** Ann Smith had a pen and John Brown had a pencil.

24. **(D)** Ann Smith had three keys and John Brown had two keys. Remember to count similar items.

25. **(C)** When you see this format, always notice items that both inmates possess.

26. **(B)** Assumptions can be made in these questions if they are based on facts. In this case, John Brown had aspirin. This fact can support the assumption that John Brown was probably experiencing headaches.

27. **(B)** John Brown had a knife.

28. **(B)** Choice A is Ann Smith's driver's license number. Notice the similarity among choices B, C, and D. Be careful.

29. **(A)** If you noticed the association between John Brown's driver's license number and his address, you would have earned two sure points. Always try to relate one thing in the illustration with another.

30. **(C)** Both inmates live in Bayside. There is no support in the illustration for any of the other choices.

Handling Correction Forms

4

→ **FORMS USED AS EVIDENCE**

→ **FORMS USED TO MAKE DECISIONS**

→ **FORMS USED TO PROTECT THE PUBLIC'S RIGHTS**

→ **INSERTING INFORMATION ONTO FORMS**

→ **UNDERSTANDING INFORMATION ON FORMS**

→ **INFORMATION THAT ANSWERS THE QUESTIONS WHEN? WHERE? WHO? WHAT? HOW? AND WHY?**

→ **STRATEGIES FOR ANSWERING FORMS QUESTIONS**

Correctional agencies use a variety of forms. Such forms are often

- offered as evidence in both criminal and administrative proceedings,
- used to make decisions about how to run the agency more efficiently, and
- used to protect the rights of the public, as well as inmates.

At times a correction officer is required to complete official forms, and at other times the officer will be required to comprehend and use information that has been previously recorded on official forms.

For these reasons, questions about both preparing forms and comprehending forms appear on examinations for the position of correction officer. Let's discuss each of these two question types.

In type A questions—Inserting Information onto Forms—the candidate is asked to fill in some or all the blanks of a correction form. The way this is typically done is that the candidate is given

Type A questions

- a blank correction form and
- a story about some incident or occurrence.

The candidate is then required to answer questions about the information that should be inserted in the various boxes on the correction form. It is the candidate's job to find the correct information from the story. Because the boxes of most forms are either numbered or lettered, it is not difficult to determine which box the examiner is asking about. A sample of such questions might be:

1. What information should be entered in Box A of the form?

2. What information should be entered in Boxes 25 and 26 of the form?

If the boxes on the form are not lettered or numbered, the questions might look like this:

1. What name should be inserted in the box that is labeled "witness?"

2. What address should be inserted in the box that is labeled "place of occurrence?"

The question also might ask the candidate to identify where on the form certain information from the narrative or story should be inserted. Two samples of such questions are:

1. In which of the following captions should the name Roy Smith be entered?

2. The most appropriate caption on the form to insert the address 310 West 222 Street is _____.

In either case, the information to be used in completing the form is found in the story that accompanies the question.

In type B questions—Comprehending Information from Forms—the candidate is given a completed form and is asked to answer questions by correctly comprehending and using information that has already been entered on the form.

After receiving a completed form, the candidate might typically be asked questions such as:

Type B
questions

1. At what time did the incident occur?

2. At what time was the incident reported to the correction officer?

Note that in this type of forms question, the candidate is not given a narrative or story. All the candidate receives is a completed form and questions based on that form.

Thus in a sense, in a type A forms question, the candidate is asked to transfer the story which has been provided onto the blank form, but in a type B forms question, the candidate is asked to create the story from the information already appearing on the completed form.

KINDS OF INFORMATION ON CORRECTION FORMS

Although it is true that just about anything can appear on a correction form, certain kinds of information are almost certain to appear. In the following examples you will see a sampling of the kinds of information that appear on correction forms. You should become familiar with them so that later on, when you practice answering forms questions, you will be more at ease when dealing with the information that appears on correction forms. To assist you in becoming more at ease with the information that appears on correction forms, we have broken down the information into categories that answer the questions of When?, Where?, Who?, What?, How?, and Why?

Information Dealing with When

This type of information usually deals with dates and times. Examples of this type of information include:

- when the incident happened—at 0800 hours,
- when the incident was reported to the correction officer—at 0830 hours,
- when the warden was notified—at 0900 hours,
- when the inmate was taken to the hospital—at 0845 hours.

The need to have accurate information about when the various parts of an incident took place is obvious. For example, knowing when petty thefts from the commissary occur can assist in taking action to prevent such thefts.

Information Dealing with Where

This type of information typically deals with locations and addresses. Examples of this type of information include:

- where an inmate was assaulted—in the exercise yard,
- where the visitor slipped and fell—in the waiting room,
- where the vehicle accident occurred that involved a correction bus that was transporting prisoners—at the intersection of Main Street and Wall Avenue.
- where the relatives of the escaped inmate reside—203 East 160 Street, apartment 2R.

The list of possible locations and addresses that might appear on a correction form could continue endlessly. A correction officer candidate must, therefore, be very careful and exacting when dealing with addresses and locations that appear on correction forms.

Information Dealing with Who

Information on correction forms that deals with who is expressed by the names of persons or their descriptions. Consider the following examples:

- who made the complaint—Inmate Jay Holly, prisoner number 115115,
- who was injured—Inmate Ray Bender, prisoner number 225225,
- who allegedly caused the injury—Inmate Tom Mixer, prisoner number 335553.
- who witnessed the incident—Bill Harps, 23 Marlin Place, telephone number 449-555-5445.
- who assisted in the escape—a white male, about 6 feet tall and a black male about 5 feet 6 inches tall.

Information dealing with who is a favorite topic for examiners when asking questions about correction forms. Later in this chapter, you will have plenty of opportunity to practice dealing with information on forms that require you to pay particular attention to the identities and description of persons involved in different incidents and occurrences.

Information Dealing with What

Unless someone reading a correction form is able to easily and clearly determine what occurred, the rest of the information on the form has little value. For example, was the incident an escape attempt, a fight between inmates, or an injury to a correction officer? In recording information to establish what occurred, correction officers must deal in facts.

EXAMPLE

Correction Officer Green responds to an incident in the laundry area and is informed by Inmate Marino that some detergent has splashed into his eyes. A nonfactual report of what happened would be: Some detergent splashed into Inmate Marino's eyes. A factual report of what happened would be: Inmate Marino reported to Correction Officer Green that detergent accidentally splashed into his (Marino's) eyes.

The first description of what occurred is nonfactual because the correction officer was not a witness to what occurred. The officer knows only what Inmate Marino claims has occurred. Therefore, for the information to be stated factually, it must be indicated that Officer Green was informed of the incident through Inmate Marino.

Information Dealing with How

Information on forms that indicates how something occurred can assist in preventing a reoccurrence of a bad situation or can assist in bringing about a repeat of a good situation.

EXAMPLE

Inmate Taylor reports that she tripped in a hole on the first step of stairwell B in Cell Block 29. An examination of the step revealed it was cracked and a hole 3 inches deep had formed. Information that indicates how an injury occurred can assist in determining if negligence played a part in the incident.

Information Dealing with Why

Information that reveals why something occurred can also go a long way in preventing similar incidents in the future.

EXAMPLE

An interview with inmates involved in the recent disturbance in the dayroom revealed that it occurred because the prison commissary store was not remaining open as previously scheduled. Knowing why incidents occur can certainly aid an agency in planning for the future so that similar incidents can be prevented.

Inmate Blake struck Inmate Bailes because Blake suspected Bailes of stealing cigarettes from him. In criminal matters, knowing why something occurred helps in establishing the motive for a criminal act.

Remember When?, Where?, Who?, What?, How?, and Why? The answers to these questions are what make up the information found on forms as well as the information to be inserted onto forms.

STRATEGIES FOR DEALING WITH FORMS QUESTIONS

Answering questions dealing with forms is not difficult. After all, the information to answer such questions is contained either in the story or on the form that the candidate has been given. However, such questions must be answered quickly and accurately. In order to answer such questions quickly and accurately, we recommend the following strategy.

For both type A questions—Inserting Information onto Forms—and type B questions—Comprehending Information from Forms:

- Read the title of the form that has been provided. The purpose of this is to give you an idea of what the form is all about. Quickly determine what the form is used for. Is it to report an accident, a theft, or an escape?
- Decide if you are facing type A or type B questions. Will you be required to insert information onto a blank form or are you being asked to comprehend information appearing on a completed form?

For type A questions—Inserting Information onto Forms:

- Scan the stem of the question, the lead-in part of the question, the part before the choices, to determine what kind of information you will be asked about.
- Concentrate on the story and determine the answer to such questions as:

  – When did the incident take place?
  – Where did the incident take place?
  – Who made the complaint?
  – Who was hurt?
  – Who caused the incident?
  – What actually occurred?
  – How did the incident occur?
  – Why did the occurrence happen?

- Read the question again and, this time, answer the question, referring back to the form and the story whenever necessary.

> **STRATEGIES FOR FORMS QUESTIONS**
>
> Read the title of the form.
>
> Decide if the question is Type A or Type B.
>
> *Type A*:
> Scan the question stem.
>
> Read the story, with questions in mind.
>
> Read the question again.
>
> *Type B*:
> Scan the question stem.
>
> Review the form, thinking about its purpose.
>
> Answer the questions while referring to the form.

For type B questions—Comprehending Information from Forms:

- Scan the stem of the question. See what kind of information you will be asked about.
- Carefully go over the completed form and reinforce its purpose in your mind. Also, concentrate on those parts of the form that you know you will be asked about from having just read the stems of the questions.
- Answer the questions referring to the completed form, which has been provided for you to use as often as you need.

Avoid these mistakes.

- **DO NOT ASSUME.** This means do not read information into the incident that is not given to you.
- **DO NOT MIX UP THE VARIOUS LOCATIONS.** If the question asks you to identify where the incident took place, referred to as the place of occurrence, do not confuse it with another address such as the victim's home address.
- **DO NOT MIX UP THE IDENTITIES OF THE PERSONS MENTIONED IN THE INCIDENT,** such as the names of different correction officers involved in the incident.
- **DO NOT CONFUSE THE DESCRIPTIONS OF DIFFERENT PERSONS MENTIONED IN THE INCIDENT,** such as the descriptions of different inmates. Pay particular attention to their prison numbers.
- **DO NOT ASSUME THAT ALL FORMS LOOK ALIKE.** That is one of the reasons we recommend looking over the form. You should not assume that the boxes on the form are consecutively numbered or follow in strict alphabetical order.
- **DO NOT MIX UP ANY DATES THAT ARE MENTIONED IN THE INCIDENT.** The same holds true for times. Particular attention should be given to determine if the times mentioned on a form are in military time (e.g., 0200 hours is really 2:00 A.M.). Also, do not confuse the time something happened, which is known as the time of occurrence, with the time something was reported, which is the time of reporting.
- **DO NOT AUTOMATICALLY ASSUME THAT THE PERSON WHO MAKES A COMPLAINT IS THE SAME PERSON WHO SHOULD BE CONSIDERED THE VICTIM IN THE INCIDENT.** Quite often the person who makes a complaint is NOT the victim. For one thing, the victim might be unable to make the complaint.
- **DO NOT THINK THAT EVERY CAPTION (NUMBERED OR LABELED BOX) ON THE FORM IS ABLE TO BE COMPLETED.** Sometimes the information needed to complete a certain caption on a form may not be given in the incident. In such instances, the entry in that particular caption might read "not known."
- **DO NOT IMMEDIATELY ASSUME THAT THE FIRST CHOICE THAT APPEARS TO BE CORRECT IS THE ANSWER TO A FORMS QUESTION.** When answering forms questions, it is best to examine all the choices and not only select the correct choice but be able to eliminate the wrong choices. Unfortunately, this is time consuming.

You should attempt to complete the following questions in the time allotted. After you have completed a group of questions, check your answers by using the answer key and reviewing the answer explanations provided. This should be done before moving on to the next group of questions and should be done for all the questions including the ones that you have answered correctly. Answering a question correctly is of course important, but you must make sure that you are getting the answers correct for the right reasons. If you are going to make mistakes, now is the time to make them, not on your official exam.

GROUP ONE

Time Allowed: 20 Minutes

Directions: Answer questions 1–10 based solely on the following narrative and Injury to Inmate Report form. Some of the captions on the form are numbered, and some are not. The boxes are not necessarily consecutively numbered.

On January 10, 20xx, at approximately 1440 hours, in the laundry area of the Rogers Correctional Facility of Gotham City, Inmate Tom Drake, Inmate Number 17068, assigned to Cell Block 207, cell number 158, sprained his right ankle. The details are as follows.

At the above mentioned time and place of occurrence, Inmate Drake was at his work detail in the laundry. As he was loading clothes into washing machine number 6, he slipped on a bar of soap and fell to the ground. The first correction officer present at the scene of Inmate Drake's injury was Correction Officer Bob Wills, badge number 749. Inmate Drake was removed to the infirmary and assigned injury number 456. At the infirmary he was treated by Dr. Hal Leung. Dr. Leung diagnosed Drake as having a sprained right ankle and recommended cold compresses, an elastic bandage, and light duty for three days.

The next day, January 11, 20xx, the incident was investigated by Correction Captain Frank Hotter, who interviewed both Correction Officer Wills and Inmate Drake. Correction Captain Hotter's investigation finds that Inmate Drake's injury was the result of an accidental fall and his investigation was not able to find any negligence on the part of any parties involved.

INJURY TO INMATE REPORT

CORRECTION DEPARTMENT   INSTITUTION   DATE
GOTHAM CITY   ROGERS   01-10-XX

Instructions: Prepare an Original and one copy.
Original to Legal division
Copy to Inmate folder

Inmate information
(completed by the first Correction Officer present)
Name_____[2]_____
Inmate – number_____[3]_____
Inmate – cell block and cell number_____[4]_____
Inmate – work detail_____[5]_____

DETAILS OF INCIDENT: (completed by the first Correction Officer present)
_____[1]_____
_____
_____
_____
_____
_____

Correction Officer ( ) I witnessed the injury
                 ( ) I did not witness the injury
Signature_____[6]_____ Badge #_____[7]___

To be completed by medical personnel:
Nature of Injury & Cause
_____[8]_____
Date/Time of Injury   Injury Number
_____[9]_____   _____[10]_____
Treatment   Date of Treatment
_____[11]_____   _____[12]_____

Disposition: (check one)
( ) Returned to Housing
( ) Returned to Light Duty
( ) Returned to Full Duty
( ) Admitted to Hospital

Treated by Dr._____[13]_____
                            (print)
Doctor's
Signature_____[14]_____

Inmate certification (To be completed by injured inmate)
I certify that the cause of the injury as stated herein is accurate and medical treatment was provided.
Inmate signature & number_____[15]_____

To be completed by investigating officer:
Details of Incident: [16]
_____
_____
_____
_____
_____
_____

Signature_____[17]_____ Badge #[18] Date___[19]

1. Which one of the following should be entered in caption 1?

   (A) Tom Drake
   (B) sprained right ankle
   (C) cold compress
   (D) details of the incident

   (A) (B) (C) (D)

2. It would be most appropriate to place the number 207 in which caption?

   (A) 2
   (B) 3
   (C) 4
   (D) 5

   (A) (B) (C) (D)

3. The signature of which of the following should appear in caption 6?

   (A) Tom Drake
   (B) Bob Wills
   (C) Hal Leung
   (D) Frank Hotter

   (A) (B) (C) (D)

4. To which of the following should the original copy of the Injury To Inmate Report form be sent?

   (A) the legal division
   (B) the hospital
   (C) the warden's office
   (D) the personnel office

   (A) (B) (C) (D)

5. It would be most correct to enter which of the following in caption 5?

   (A) the laundry
   (B) the hospital
   (C) Tom Drake
   (D) Gotham City

   (A) (B) (C) (D)

6. Which of the following should be entered in caption 10?

   (A) 158
   (B) 749
   (C) 456
   (D) 17068

   (A) (B) (C) (D)

7. The number 17068 should be inserted in captions

 (A) 2 and 7.
 (B) 3 and 15.
 (C) 4 and 9.
 (D) 10 and 18.

 Ⓐ Ⓑ Ⓒ Ⓓ

8. Caption 1 should be completed by

 (A) Inmate Drake.
 (B) Correction Officer Wills.
 (C) Dr. Leung.
 (D) Captain Hotter.

 Ⓐ Ⓑ Ⓒ Ⓓ

9. Which of the following would be the most appropriate entry for caption 9?

 (A) January 10 at approximately 1440 hours
 (B) January 11 at approximately 1440 hours
 (C) 456
 (D) not available

 Ⓐ Ⓑ Ⓒ Ⓓ

10. It would be most appropriate to enter which of the following in caption 18?

 (A) 158
 (B) 17068
 (C) 749
 (D) not available

 Ⓐ Ⓑ Ⓒ Ⓓ

GROUP TWO

Time Allowed: 15 minutes

Directions: Answer questions 11–20 solely on the basis of the information recorded on the following Medical Report for Visitors.

CLOVER CITY CORRECTIONAL INSTITUTION - WOMEN'S ANNEX
MEDICAL REPORT FOR VISITORS

DATE OF OCCURRENCE	AIDED SURNAME	FIRST
FEB. 08-20XX	BALL	BILL

SEX	COLOR	AGE	TIME OF OCCURRENCE
M	B	48	1350 HOURS

ADDRESS	APT NO.	AIDED #
29-84 BAY AVENUE	2E	989

PLACE OF OCCURRENCE
In the visiting room of Clover City Correctional Institution Women's Annex 889, 8th Avenue

check one ( )Dead   ( )Sick   (x)Injured   ( )Mentally Ill

NATURE OF ILLNESS OR INJURY	REMOVED TO
Concussion	Carlton Hospital

DOCTOR	HOSPITAL ADMISSION NUMBER
Willis	2399

POLICE PRECINCT NOTIFIED	RELATIVES NOTIFIED
92 Pct. Detective Bailes	The aided's brother Francis was present and notified

Details

   At the time and place of occurrence, during an altercation, aided, Bill Ball, a visitor, fell to the floor in the waiting room of Clover City Correctional Institution's Women's Annex after being struck in the head by Gene Parsons, also a visitor. While both disputants were visiting the same inmate, Tess Dubbs, inmate number 52051, an argument erupted over the affections of inmate Dubbs. Correction Officer Jones was on the scene and immediately arrested Parsons for assault.

The aided's brother Francis Ball was present and notified. The aided lives with his brother and their phone number is 555-9000.

NAME AND ADDRESS OF WITNESSES
   Barry Rems, 518 West 58 Street, tel no. 555-0000

REPORTED BY CORRECTION OFFICER + SHIELD NO. COMMAND
Jack Quayle   1889   Women's Annex.

11. What is the last name of the person who received medical assistance?

(A) Carlton
(B) Ball
(C) Clover
(D) Dubbs

Ⓐ Ⓑ Ⓒ Ⓓ

12. Who lives at 29-84 Bay Avenue?

(A) Tess Dubbs
(B) only Bill Ball
(C) Jack Quayle
(D) Francis Ball

Ⓐ Ⓑ Ⓒ Ⓓ

13. What is located at 889 8th Avenue?

(A) the 92nd Precinct
(B) the aided's home address
(C) the Carlton Hospital
(D) the women's annex

Ⓐ Ⓑ Ⓒ Ⓓ

14. The aided was

(A) dead.
(B) sick.
(C) injured.
(D) mentally ill.

Ⓐ Ⓑ Ⓒ Ⓓ

15. Barry Rems is the name of the

(A) inmate.
(B) detective.
(C) doctor.
(D) witness.

Ⓐ Ⓑ Ⓒ Ⓓ

16. The time of 1350 hours most accurately represents

(A) when the inmate arrived at the visiting room.
(B) when the altercation took place.
(C) when the police arrived.
(D) when the aided arrived at the visiting room.

Ⓐ Ⓑ Ⓒ Ⓓ

17. The number 52051 is

   (A) the aided number.
   (B) the hospital admission number.
   (C) the shield number of the correction officer who
       made the arrest.
   (D) an inmate's number.   Ⓐ Ⓑ Ⓒ Ⓓ

18. It would be most correct to state that

   (A) Jack Quayle made the arrest.
   (B) the aided has a sister named Frances.
   (C) the aided has no phone number.
   (D) the charge for the arrest which was made was assault.   Ⓐ Ⓑ Ⓒ Ⓓ

19. Detective Bailes' shield number is

   (A) 1889.
   (B) 1350.
   (C) 2399.
   (D) cannot be determined from the information provided.   Ⓐ Ⓑ Ⓒ Ⓓ

20. If someone were to dial the telephone number 555-0000,
    the person most likely to answer would be

   (A) Barry Rems.
   (B) Bill Ball.
   (C) Gene Parsons.
   (D) Dr. Willis.   Ⓐ Ⓑ Ⓒ Ⓓ

ANSWER KEY

1. **D**	5. **A**	9. **A**	13. **D**	17. **D**
2. **C**	6. **C**	10. **D**	14. **C**	18. **D**
3. **B**	7. **B**	11. **B**	15. **D**	19. **D**
4. **A**	8. **B**	12. **D**	16. **B**	20. **A**

ANSWERS EXPLAINED

Group One

If you followed our strategy you would have determined that this is a type A forms question. That means that you were given a narrative and a blank form and asked to transfer the story to the blank form. In addition, you should have determined that the purpose of the form was to capture information about injuries to inmates.

1. **(D)** Examination of the form shows that caption number 1 called for "DETAILS OF INCIDENT." If you were not careful you might have selected choice A, Tom Drake, the name of the inmate. Even though that caption appears first on the form, it is caption 2. Remember that we cautioned you about the captions. They are not necessarily numbered in sequential order.

2. **(C)** The number 207 represents the inmates cell block number. It, along with 158, the cell number, should appear in caption 4. To arrive at your answer, you should have examined only the captions that the question offered as choices. You did not need to examine all the captions to find the one where 207 should be inserted.

3. **(B)** Bob Wills was the first correction officer present.

4. **(A)** The answer appears at the top of the form in the instructions.

5. **(A)** Caption 5 asks for the inmate's work detail, which is the laundry.

6. **(C)** Caption 10 calls for the injury number, which is 456 as indicated in choice C.

7. **(B)** The number 17068 represents the inmate's number, which is called for in captions 3 and 15.

8. **(B)** The details of the incident should be inserted in Caption 1. The instructions on the form require that Officer Wills complete caption 1.

9. **(A)** Caption 9 requires that the date of the injury, January 10, be inserted. January 11 was when the incident was investigated.

10. **(D)** Correction Captain Hotter investigated the incident, but the captain's badge number was not given in the narrative. Therefore, the information is not available.

Group Two

When doing type B forms questions, which require you to extract information from an already completed form, your review of the completed form must be more thorough than your review of a blank form that is to be completed based on an accompanying narrative. This is so because all the information needed to answer the questions is contained on the form.

11. **(B)** Bill Ball suffered a concussion and received medical attention.

12. **(D)** We hope that you did not mistakenly pick B for this question. It is true that Bill Ball lives at the address given. Francis Ball, his brother, also lives at that address. It is the word *only* that makes choice B incorrect. A candidate should always be very careful when considering choices that have absolute words such as only.

13. **(D)** It is the address of the women's annex as given in the caption marked Place of Occurrence.

14. **(C)** The *x* in the parentheses next to the label "Injured" indicates that the aided was injured.

15. **(D)** Barry Rems was the witness.

16. **(B)** Choices A, C, and D might be correct, but there is nothing on the completed form to substantiate that. Remember that your instructions told you to base your answers solely on the information recorded on the form. The Details section states that the incident took place at the time of occurrence, which was previously stated on the form as 1350 hours.

17. **(D)** Once again, the information under the Details caption gives the answer. In this type of forms question, where the candidate is given a completed form, the Details caption serves as a kind of narrative to explain what occurred.

18. **(D)** Jack Quayle is the correction officer who reported the incident. The aided, who was Bill Ball, had a brother named Francis, not a sister named Frances. Notice the similarity in the spelling of the names. In this type of question, the need to read carefully is apparent. Finally the aided, Bill Ball, had a telephone number that the Details section indicates is the same telephone number as his brother. Therefore, choices A, B, and C are all incorrect. The correct statement is choice D.

19. **(D)** Do not assume. If the information is not given, it is not available. Also worth mentioning is the word *shield,* which you should have gathered by now is sometimes referred to as a badge.

20. **(A)** The phone number is that of Barry Rems.

Data Interpretation Questions

5

- → **UNDERSTANDING THE DATA**
- → **LINE GRAPHS**
- → **CIRCLE GRAPHS**
- → **BAR GRAPHS**
- → **TABLES**
- → **QUESTION STRATEGIES**

Correction officers work with data from graphs and tables. For this reason, questions about how to interpret graphs and tables appear on many correction officer examinations. Such questions are called data interpretation questions. When we mention this to students who are preparing to take such tests, many of them become uneasy. They erroneously believe that they must be a combination of engineer and mathematician to handle this type of question. Once we show them how simple such questions can really be, they actually gain confidence in their ability to deal with them. This is what we intend to do in this chapter. We will strip away the mask of difficulty that seems to surround these questions and help you develop the level of skill needed to answer them quickly and accurately.

THE CARDINAL RULE

Before discussing the major types of data interpretation questions, we discuss the cardinal rule for dealing with all such questions. The rule follows:

> **The answers are somewhere in the data. Your task is to make sure that you know what the data represent and exactly what data you are looking for.**

In a way, data interpretation questions are like reading comprehension questions. This is what we mean by the first half of the cardinal rule, "the answers are somewhere in the data." Just as the answers to reading comprehension questions are found solely in the written information given as part of the question, so are the answers to data interpretation questions found in the information that supports these questions. Let's explore this a little further with a simple example.

Suppose that you encountered the following question on a correction officer examination:

Q. The percentage of inmates who are illiterate is
15%. What percentage of inmates are illiterate?

(A) 10%
(B) 15%
(C) 20%
(D) 25%

Would such a question make you feel ill at ease? Would you find such a question to be difficult? Obviously you wouldn't. Yet, this is an example of how a data interpretation question really works. Naturally, it is not as simple as we have presented it, but that is how it works.

In actuality you will get a set of data, either in graph or table form, that contains a lot of information, most of which you do not need to answer the questions. Somewhere in that data is the fact that 15% of inmates are illiterate. Your job in this type of question, therefore, is to sift through a lot of information to find the information you are looking for.

GRAPHS AND TABLES

The data in data interpretation questions are presented either in graph or table form. Because correction officers work much more frequently with tables than with graphs, the majority of the questions you will see on your official examination will probably involve tables. For this reason, the majority of data interpretation questions in our practice examinations involve tables.

THREE TYPES OF GRAPHS

When writing data interpretation questions involving graphs, test writers generally use one of three different types of graphs:

- line graphs,
- circle graphs, and
- bar graphs.

Line Graphs

A line graph similar to those typically found on correction officer examinations is pictured here.

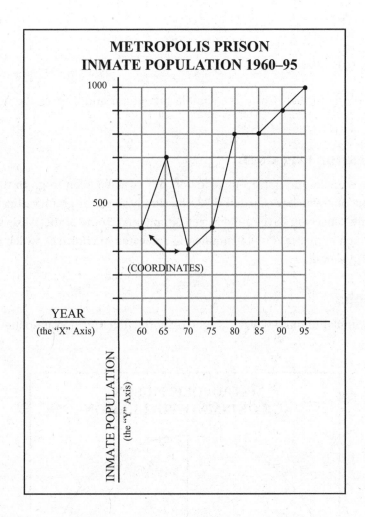

As a general rule, all graphs have a title. The title is very important because it usually tells you what the graph is about. The sample line graph is entitled Metropolis Prison, Inmate Population 1960–95. Upon reading this, you know that the data involved in the questions have something to do with the inmate population of Metropolis Prison during the years 1960 to 1995.

Line graphs have what is known as an *X*-axis and a *Y*-axis. In the sample line graph, the *X*-axis shows the years 1960 to 1995. The *X*-axis extends horizontally, from left to right. The *Y*-axis shows the inmate population and extends vertically from top to bottom. Although only two numbers are shown on the *Y*-axis, 500 and 1000, you must count the marked increments on the *Y*-axis to determine that each mark equals 100 inmates. The line graph itself is made up of a number of coordinates which are connected to each other with a line. The coordinates are usually shown as a dot or period. Each coordinate represents two values, the *X*-axis value and the *Y*-axis value. For example, the coordinate for 1960 (the *X*-axis value) corresponds to the number 400 on the *Y*-axis (the *Y*-axis value), and there is an *X*-axis coordinate for 1965 that corresponds to 700 on the *Y*-axis. Now, to see if you can read this graph, answer the following sample question.

SAMPLE QUESTION

Q1. What was the approximate inmate population of Metropolis Prison in 1980?

    (A) 500
    (B) 600
    (C) 700
    (D) 800

Do not read any further. Go to the sample line graph and answer the question; then resume reading.

SAMPLE QUESTION EXPLAINED

To answer the sample question, your first step should have been to go to the *X*-axis and find 1980. Then, once you have located 1980, you simply go up the graph vertically to find the 1980 coordinate. Once you have found it, you simply make note of the *Y*-axis value for that coordinate, which in this case is 800 inmates, as indicated in choice D, which is the answer to our sample question.

Circle Graphs

A circle graph similar to those typically found on correction officer examinations is pictured here.

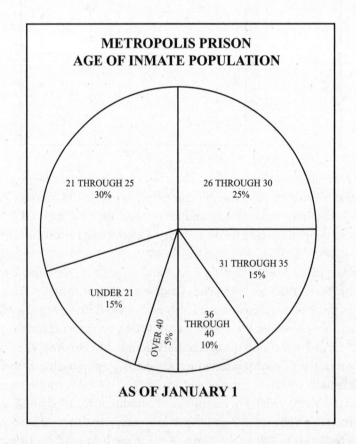

Circle graphs, which are also called pie charts, are, as their name implies, circular graphs that represent data as part of the whole. As with all graphs, the first thing you should do is read the title of the graph. In this case, the title indicates that the graph presents an analysis by age of the prison population of Metropolis Prison as of January 1.

When working with circle graphs, you must understand that the circle itself represents 100% of whatever is being depicted. We like to tell our students to think of the circle as the whole pie. For example, the circle in the sample circle graph represents the entire inmate population of Metropolis Prison. Then each segment of the circle, or each piece of the pie, represents a certain portion of the entire prison population. For example, the age group from 21 to 25 years of age represents 30% of the entire inmate population of Metropolis Prison. Now, to see if you can read this graph, answer the following sample question.

SAMPLE QUESTION

Q2.   Together the age groups 31–35 and 36–40 years of age represent

(A)   15% of the inmate population of Metropolis Prison.
(B)   10% of the inmate population of Metropolis Prison.
(C)   25% of the inmate population of Metropolis Prison.
(D)   35% of the inmate population of Metropolis Prison.

Do not read any further. Go to the sample circle graph and answer the question; then resume reading.

SAMPLE QUESTION EXPLAINED

All that you had to do to answer the sample question was locate the piece of the pie that represents the age group 31–35 and the one that represents the age group 36–40 and to add together the percentages for these two groups. Since the age group 31–35 represents 15% of the inmate population, and the age group 36–40 represents 10% of the inmate population, together they represent 25% of the entire prison population, as indicated in choice C.

Bar Graphs

A bar graph similar to those typically found on correction officer examinations is pictured here.

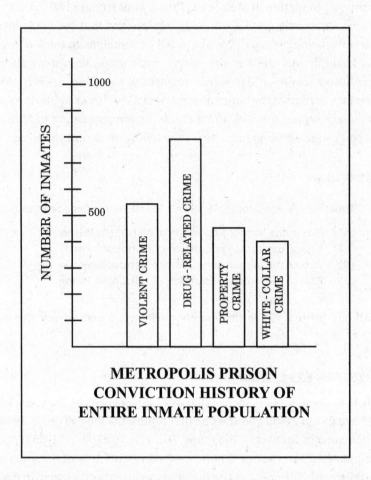

METROPOLIS PRISON CONVICTION HISTORY OF ENTIRE INMATE POPULATION

Bar graphs are, as their name implies, graphs that use bars to present data. The title of the sample bar graph reveals that it represents the conviction history of the entire inmate population of Metropolis Prison. A quick review of the individual bars shows that all convictions are divided into four categories; violent crime, drug-related crime, property crime, and white-collar crime. For example, the number of inmates who are serving time for the commission of some sort of violent crime is about 550. Now, to see if you can read this graph, answer the following sample question.

SAMPLE QUESTION

Q3. The number of inmates in Metropolis Prison who were convicted of property crimes is about

(A) 400.
(B) 450.
(C) 500.
(D) 600.

Do not read any further. Go to the sample bar graph and answer the question; then resume reading.

SAMPLE QUESTION EXPLAINED

All that you had to do to answer our sample question was to locate the bar that represented property crimes and then measure over from the top of that bar to the *y*-axis, which represents the number of inmates who were convicted of a property crime. The answer is about 450, as indicated in choice B.

TABLES

There are many different ways of presenting data in table form, but the tables that are most often used on correction officer examinations have the following characteristics in common:

- they have titles that describe the information contained in the table,
- they have vertical labels, and
- they have horizontal labels.

All three of these characteristics are shown in the following table.

NUMBER OF DISCIPLINARY CHARGES MADE FOR VARIOUS INFRACTIONS WITH DISPOSITIONS METROPOLIS PRISON			
Charge	**Total Made**	**Guilty**	**Not Guilty**
Fighting	123	112	11
Lateness	873	760	113
Contraband Possession	45	45	0
Smoking	89	87	2
Dirty Cell	1245	1201	44

As you can see, the sample table has a title that explains its contents; vertical labels, which are the various charges; and horizontal labels, which are the dispositions of the various charges. Reading the table is simple. For each charge, the vertical label, you have three pieces of information, the horizontal labels: (1) the "total made," (2) the number of "guilty" findings, and (3) the number of "not guilty" findings. For example, there were 123 charges made for fighting, of which 112 were disposed of via a finding of guilty and 11 were disposed of with a finding of not guilty. Now, to see if you can read this table, answer the following sample question.

SAMPLE QUESTION

Q4. Which of the following charges resulted in the greatest number of guilty findings?

    (A)   Fighting
    (B)   Lateness
    (C)   Smoking
    (D)   Dirty cell

Do not read any further. Go to the sample table and answer the question; then resume reading.

SAMPLE QUESTION EXPLAINED

All that you had to do to find the answer to our sample question was look under the horizontal label "guilty" and then proceed down and look for the largest number, which is 1201—the number of guilty findings for dirty cell. Having found that number you simply had to see if "dirty cell" was one of the choices. If, however, there were many more vertical labels, then it would be a better strategy to look only at the charges suggested in the choices.

STRATEGY FOR ANSWERING DATA INTERPRETATION QUESTIONS

When you are answering data interpretation questions, the first thing you must do is to study the title of the graph or table involved and to make sure that you understand the kind of information that is presented in that graph or table. The next step is to go to the question and to make sure that you know what the question is asking. After you are familiar with the graph or table and after you know what a particular question is asking, you then go to the graph or table and search for the information you need to evaluate each choice in the question. You must remain extremely careful. Attention to detail is absolutely required to maintain a high record of success when dealing with data interpretation questions. Now, compare this strategy with our cardinal rule as it was presented earlier:

> **QUESTION STRATEGIES**
>
> Read the title.
>
> Know what information is being shown.
>
> Read and understand the question.
>
> Pay attention to details.

The answers are somewhere in the data. Your task is to make sure that you know what the data represent and exactly what data you are looking for.

We hope that this cardinal rule makes much more sense to you now, after our discussion.

Math May Be Required

One final word about data interpretation questions is in order before we give you some practice exercises. It is highly likely that arriving at some of the answers to data interpretation questions will require some basic mathematics. But the math is very similar to what we reviewed in Chapter 2.

GROUP ONE

Time Allowed: 20 Minutes

Directions: Answer questions 1–10 based on the following data.

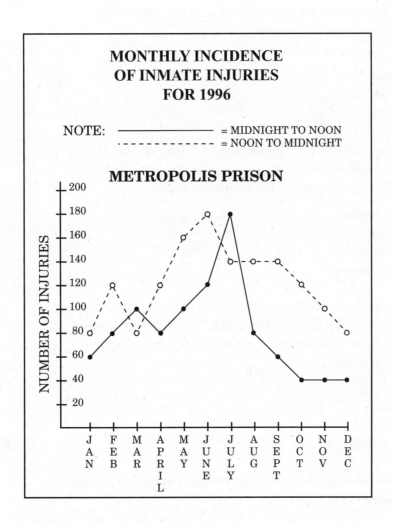

1. In what three months was the number of injuries that occurred between midnight and noon approximately the same?

   (A) July, August, and September
   (B) October, November, and December
   (C) January, February, and March
   (D) April, May, and June

   Ⓐ Ⓑ Ⓒ Ⓓ

2. In what month was the number of injuries that occurred from midnight to noon approximately the same as the number of injuries that occurred from noon to midnight?

(A) April
(B) December
(C) May
(D) There was no month in 1996 when this occurred.

Ⓐ Ⓑ Ⓒ Ⓓ

3. Approximately how many injuries occurred in Metropolis Prison in December of 1996?

(A) 40
(B) 60
(C) 80
(D) 120

Ⓐ Ⓑ Ⓒ Ⓓ

4. During which of the following months did the number of injuries that occurred between midnight and noon decrease the most as compared to the previous month?

(A) February
(B) July
(C) August
(D) November

Ⓐ Ⓑ Ⓒ Ⓓ

5. For how many months was the number of injuries that occurred during the noon to midnight period greater than the number of injuries that occurred during the midnight to noon period?

(A) eight
(B) nine
(C) ten
(D) eleven

Ⓐ Ⓑ Ⓒ Ⓓ

6. The greatest number of injuries in Metropolis Prison occurred in the month of

(A) May.
(B) June.
(C) July.
(D) August.

Ⓐ Ⓑ Ⓒ Ⓓ

7. During which of the following months was the percentage increase in the number of injuries that occurred between noon and midnight the greatest when compared to the previous month?

(A) February
(B) June
(C) August
(D) November

Ⓐ Ⓑ Ⓒ Ⓓ

8. Which of the following two month period accounted for the most injuries at Metropolis Prison?

(A) from January 1st to March 1st
(B) from May 1st to July 1st
(C) from July 1st to September 1st
(D) from October 1st to December 1st

Ⓐ Ⓑ Ⓒ Ⓓ

9. Exactly how many injuries occurred at Metropolis Prison on May 28th, 1996?

(A) 100
(B) 180
(C) 280
(D) cannot be determined

Ⓐ Ⓑ Ⓒ Ⓓ

10. Which of the following is the most accurate statement concerning inmate injuries at Metropolis Prison during 1996?

(A) They remained about the same for the entire year, although they did not remain constant.
(B) They increased during the entire year.
(C) They decreased during the entire year.
(D) They reached their peak about the middle of the year and then decreased.

Ⓐ Ⓑ Ⓒ Ⓓ

GROUP TWO

Time Allowed: 20 minutes

> **Directions:** Answer questions 11–20 based on the information presented in the following table.

CLASSIFICATION OF PRISONS IN THE STATE SYSTEM

Low Security	System Code #	Inmate Population
Downstate	1–1	435
Ellenville	1–2	545
Metropolis	1–3	576
Queensville	1–4	790
Carter	1–5	750
Lambert	1–6	1076

Medium Security	System Code #	Inmate Population
Municipal	2–10	1,090
Greensville	2–11	1,290
Kennedy	2–12	1350
Middle State	2–13	1110
Clarksville	2–14	980

High Security	System Code #	Inmate Population
Upstate	3–20	510
Myersville	3–21	374
Ottercreek	3–22	210
Farmstead	3–23	419

Explanations

1. Inmate Population listed is as of January 1st. As of that date, there were 11,505 inmates confined in the entire system.

2. Low Security Prisons are used for confining inmates who have been in the system for at least 5 years and who have compiled excellent disciplinary records. Only inmates in Low Security Prisons are eligible for Work Release Programs.

3. Medium Security Prisons are used for confining all inmates during the first 5 years of their sentence. After the fifth year in the system, all prisoners are transferred to a Low Security Prison or a High Security Prison, depending on their disciplinary records.

4. High Security Prisons are used for confining inmates who have been classified as inmates with definite disciplinary problems after the first 5 years of their confinement.

5. In accordance with a judicial ruling, the inmate population of High Security Prisons should not exceed 500 inmates.

11. Sam DeFini was just sentenced to a term of imprisonment of 6–10 years for armed robbery. His prison term is to begin immediately. Of the following, which prison would you expect him to be confined in?

    (A) number 1–1
    (B) number 2–10
    (C) number 3–20
    (D) cannot be determined ⒶⒷⒸⒹ

12. Assume that the state is opening a new Medium Security Prison. The System Code Number for this new prison would most likely be

    (A) 1–7.
    (B) 2–15.
    (C) 3–24.
    (D) It cannot be determined. ⒶⒷⒸⒹ

13. The prison in the state system that was in apparent violation of a judicial ruling on January 1st

    (A) is Upstate.
    (B) is Municipal.
    (C) is Ellenville.
    (D) cannot be determined. ⒶⒷⒸⒹ

14. How many Low Security Prisons had an inmate population of less than 700 inmates on March 1st?

    (A) three
    (B) six
    (C) seven
    (D) cannot be determined ⒶⒷⒸⒹ

15. Inmates confined in which of the following prisons are not eligible to participate in a Work Release Program?

    (A) Ellenville
    (B) Carter
    (C) Kennedy
    (D) cannot be determined ⒶⒷⒸⒹ

16. Joe Smith is an inmate who has been confined in Middle State Prison for approximately 4 years. He approaches a correction officer in Middle State and asks if he can be transferred to Lambert Prison. The correction officer would be most correct if he informed Smith that such a transfer

    (A) could possibly be made at the present time.
    (B) can never be made.
    (C) could possibly be made in about 1 year.
    (D) can definitely be made in about 1 year.   Ⓐ Ⓑ Ⓒ Ⓓ

17. As of January 1st, the Medium Security Prison that had the lowest inmate population

    (A) was Ottercreek.
    (B) was Downstate.
    (C) was Clarksville.
    (D) cannot be determined.   Ⓐ Ⓑ Ⓒ Ⓓ

18. An inmate's prison of confinement after the first 5 years of incarceration depends primarily upon

    (A) availability of space.
    (B) the age of the inmate.
    (C) the length of the inmate's sentence.
    (D) the inmate's disciplinary record.   Ⓐ Ⓑ Ⓒ Ⓓ

19. What percentage of inmates in the entire State Prison System was assigned to High Security Prisons on January 1st?

    (A) approximately 13%
    (B) approximately 26%
    (C) approximately 39%
    (D) cannot be determined   Ⓐ Ⓑ Ⓒ Ⓓ

20. After the completion of 5 years of confinement, as a general rule it can be stated that the majority of inmates in the state system

    (A) have compiled acceptable disciplinary records.
    (B) have been classified as having definite disciplinary problems.
    (C) have attempted to escape at least once.
    (D) have not had any disciplinary problems at all.   Ⓐ Ⓑ Ⓒ Ⓓ

GROUP THREE

Time Allowed: 20 minutes

Directions: Answer questions 21–30 based on the information presented in the following tables.

ROSTER OF ALL INMATES ASSIGNED TO CELL BLOCK 14 IN METROPOLIS PRISON

Name	Cell	*Inmate number	Group	Supervisor
Anthony Terri	1	113456	A	10
Louis Cassano	2	138752	A	10
Jack Hunt	3	189457	C	12
James Agresani	4	150093	B	10
William Collela	5	165727	B	10
Richie Fox	6	240093	C	12
John Heenan	7	298642	D	12
Brian Gifford	8	378653	A	10
James Holloran	9	117845	B	10
Rob Monchall	10	236902	C	12
Jim Farnocchi	11	117864	D	12
Marty McCabe	12	117863	D	12

* Inmates with inmate numbers beginning with the numeral 1 were convicted of property crimes, those with inmate numbers beginning with the numeral 2 were convicted of drug-related crimes, and those with inmate numbers beginning with the numeral 3 were convicted of violent crimes.

Cell Block 14 Commander—Lieutenant Don Rems

Supervisor # 10—Sergeant John Ginty
Supervisor # 12—Sergeant Sam Marino

DUTIES OF GROUPS ASSIGNED TO CELL BLOCK 14

Group	Duties
A	Breakfast Duty in Dining Hall 8:00–10:00 A.M.
B	Lunch Duty in Dining Hall Noon–1:30 P.M.
C	Dinner Duty in Dining Hall 5:00–7:00 P.M.
D	Library Duty 8:00 A.M.–Noon
A	Library Duty Noon–5:00 P.M.
B	Motor Pool Duty 8:00 A.M.–Noon
C	Movie Room Duty 7:30–10:00 P.M.
D	Game Room Duty 7:00–10:00 P.M.

21. The supervisor of Inmate 240093 is

    (A) Sergeant John Ginty.
    (B) Sergeant Sam Marino.
    (C) both Sergeant Ginty and Sergeant Marino.
    (D) neither Sergeant Ginty nor Sergeant Marino.   (A) (B) (C) (D)

22. An inmate is needed for a special assignment. The inmate who is selected for this assignment must be one who has not been convicted of a violent crime. Which of the following inmates would *not* qualify for this assignment?

    (A) Brian Gifford
    (B) Jack Hunt
    (C) Richie Fox
    (D) It cannot be determined.   (A) (B) (C) (D)

23. At 2:00 P.M. Inmate Cassano could most probably be located

    (A) in the library.
    (B) in the dining hall.
    (C) at the motor pool.
    (D) It cannot be determined.   (A) (B) (C) (D)

24. A new inmate is being assigned to Cell Block 14. According to the warden's instructions, the inmate must be placed under the supervision of Sergeant John Ginty. The new inmate should be assigned to

    (A) Group A.
    (B) Group C.
    (C) Group D.
    (D) It cannot be determined.   (A) (B) (C) (D)

25. Assume that you are a correction officer who has a need to discuss something with Inmate Monchall. You want to meet with him at a time when he has some time to spend with you in a private location. You should plan to meet him

    (A) at 6:30 P.M.
    (B) at 8:00 P.M.
    (C) at 11:00 A.M.
    (D) at any of the above times.   (A) (B) (C) (D)

26. Inmates in Cell Block 14

    (A) live one in a cell.
    (B) live two in a cell.
    (C) live three in a cell.
    (D) all live in the same cell. Ⓐ Ⓑ Ⓒ Ⓓ

27. Inmate McCabe

    (A) is a trained librarian.
    (B) is supervised by Sergeant Ginty.
    (C) was convicted of a property crime.
    (D) belongs to Group C. Ⓐ Ⓑ Ⓒ Ⓓ

28. Metropolis Prison

    (A) uses inmates to fix cars.
    (B) uses inmates to serve meals.
    (C) uses inmates to show movies.
    (D) may or may not use inmates to fix cars, serve meals,
        and show movies. Ⓐ Ⓑ Ⓒ Ⓓ

29. The commander of Cell Block 14

    (A) is Sergeant Ginty.
    (B) is Sergeant Marino.
    (C) is Lieutenant Rems.
    (D) cannot be determined. Ⓐ Ⓑ Ⓒ Ⓓ

30. Which of the following is the most accurate statement
    concerning the next inmate assigned to Cell Block 14?

    (A) He should be assigned to Group A.
    (B) He should be assigned to Group B.
    (C) He should be assigned to Group C.
    (D) It is unclear what group he should be assigned to. Ⓐ Ⓑ Ⓒ Ⓓ

ANSWER KEY

1. **B**	7. **A**	13. **A**	19. **A**	25. **C**
2. **D**	8. **B**	14. **D**	20. **A**	26. **A**
3. **D**	9. **D**	15. **C**	21. **B**	27. **C**
4. **C**	10. **D**	16. **C**	22. **A**	28. **D**
5. **C**	11. **B**	17. **C**	23. **A**	29. **C**
6. **C**	12. **B**	18. **D**	24. **A**	30. **D**

ANSWERS EXPLAINED

Group One

If you followed our strategy you would have taken some time before answering the questions to study the title of the graph and its contents. You should have recognized it as a line graph. Hopefully, the fact that it had two sets of lines did not confuse you. The note tells you that the solid line represents the time period from midnight to noon, and the dotted line represents the time period from noon to midnight. Then you should have observed that the X-axis represents the month of the year and that the Y-axis represents the number of injuries divided into increments of 20, from 0 to 200.

1. **(B)** If you picked choice A you failed to interpret the note carefully enough. The dotted line represents the time period from noon to midnight. The question involved the time period from midnight to noon.

2. **(D)** Graphs can also be used to indicate that something has not occurred. As in choice D, which tells us that, based on the graph, there is no month for which the number of injuries was the same for both time periods.

3. **(D)** In December of 1996 there were about 40 injuries during the midnight to noon period, and there were about 80 injuries during the noon to midnight period. This means that altogether there were 40 plus 80 injuries, which, of course, is 120.

4. **(C)** There was no need to do any math to answer this question. Concerning injuries that occurred between midnight and noon, during February, choice A, injuries increased. During July, choice B, they also increased. During November they remained the same as the previous month. Only during August did they decrease.

5. **(C)** Only in March and July were the number of injuries that occurred during the noon to midnight period less than those that occurred during the midnight to noon period.

6. **(C)** In May there were about 260 injuries. In June there were about 300. In July, the answer, there were about 320. In August there were 220.

7. **(A)** In November there was a decrease in injuries during the noon to midnight period, and in August they remained about the same. This means that choices C and D can be eliminated. In February the number of these injuries went from about 80 in January to about 120. Referring to the percentage formula in Chapter 5, this means that there was a 50% increase (120 − 80 = 40; 40 ÷ 80, the old number, = 50%). In June the injuries went from about 100 to about 120, which is an increase of about 20% (120 minus 100 divided by 100, or 20/100). The answer is choice A.

8. **(B)** Injuries reached their maximum incidence between May 1st and July 1st.

9. **(D)** If you missed this question you probably do not understand that one cannot determine exact statistics from line graphs such as the one we used for this series of questions. These line graphs are used to show trends and not to supply specific daily statistics. To completely understand this, ask yourself this question. How would I determine exactly from the graph the point at which May 28th is represented? The answer, of course, is that you can't. Exact numbers, as you will soon find out, are presented in questions involving tables.

10. **(D)** The injuries that occurred during both time periods involved started low, reached their highest levels (in other words, they reached their peak) at about the middle of the year, and then decreased.

Group Two

If you followed our strategy you would have spent some time understanding the material presented in the table prior to answering the questions. Remember that one thorough review of the table is more efficient time wise than a thorough review prior to answering each question.

11. **(B)** Two steps are required to correctly answer this question. The first is to determine from the table that Medium Security Prisons are used for confining all inmates during the first 5 years of their sentence. The second is to recognize by its system Code Number that the prison listed in choice B, Number 2–10—Municipal Prison, is a Medium Security Prison.

12. **(B)** This question emphasizes the fact that assumptions have to be made when answering some data interpretation questions. However, the rule about making assumptions for these questions is the same as with all questions that require the making of assumptions, "assumptions made *must* be based on factual information." In this case, the factual information is that all Medium Security Prisons use the numeral prefix 2 and that the next available Medium Security system Code Number is 2–15. Remember, however, that assumptions are not appropriate if the instructions tell you to answer the questions based *solely* on certain information.

13. **(A)** According to Explanation 5, there is a judicial ruling that states that the inmate population of High Security Prisons should not exceed 500. Upstate, which is a High Security Prison, had 510 inmates on January 1st.

14. **(D)** This question emphasizes the necessity to understand the limitations of the table you are basing your answers on. The exact inmate population listed is as of January 1st, 1996. There is no factual information available to support an assumption that no change in inmate population occurred between January 1st and March 1st. The answer has to be choice D.

15. **(C)** Kennedy is a Medium Security Prison. Only inmates assigned to Low Security Prisons are eligible for Work Release Programs, see Explanation 2.

16. **(C)** All inmates stay in Medium Security Prisons for 5 years. After 5 years inmates, depending on their disciplinary records, are transferred to either a Low or High Security Prison. The answer is choice C.

17. **(C)** This is a kind of data interpretation question that rewards careful test takers. Careless test takers select choice A because that is the prison with the lowest inmate population on January 1st. However, the question asked you to select the Medium Security Prison with the lowest inmate population as of January 1st. The answer is choice C. Note that the question specified "as of January 1st." If it didn't do so then the answer to the question could not be determined. When tables have effective dates, those dates will in all likelihood form the basis for a number of questions.

18. **(D)** After the first 5 years of confinement, inmates are transferred to a Low or High Security Prison depending on their disciplinary record during the first 5 years of confinement in a Medium Security Prison.

19. **(A)** Determining the correct answer to this question requires the ability to add numbers and compute percentages. As of January 1st, there were 1513 inmates confined in High Security Prisons. It was necessary for you to compute that number. Also as of January 1st, there were 11,505 inmates in the entire system. If you took the time to compute that number you wasted time because it was given to you in the table, see Explanation 1. As explained in Chapter 5, to determine the percentage you need to answer this question, you must divide 1513 inmates by 11,505 inmates. When you do, you arrive at our answer, which is approximately 13%.

20. **(A)** This is an assumption question. The correct answer, choice A, is supported by the fact that the overall population of Low Security Prisons is more than two times greater than the overall population of High Security Prisons. When this fact is viewed in light of the additional fact that, after 5 years inmates with acceptable disciplinary records are sent to Low Security Prisons and those who are classified as definite disciplinary problems are sent to High Security Prisons, it is safe to conclude that choice A is accurate.

Group Three

21. **(B)** Inmate 240093 is Richie Fox, and his supervisor is supervisor number 12, Sergeant Sam Marino.

22. **(A)** Brian Gifford's inmate number begins with the numeral 3. According to the information given, inmates with inmate numbers beginning with the number 3 were convicted of violent crimes.

23. **(A)** Inmate Cassano is in Group A. The duties of Group A require them to be in the library from Noon to 5:00 P.M.

24. **(A)** According to the roster supplied, Sergeant Ginty supervises Groups A and B. Sergeant Marino supervises Groups C and D.

25. **(C)** Inmate Monchall is in Group C. That group has dinner duty at 6:30 P.M. and movie room duty at 8:00 P.M. There is, however, no reason in the information given why you could not meet with Monchall at 11:00 A.M., as indicated in choice C.

26. **(A)** This is an interesting kind of question because it forces you to pick one of four definitive answers. Notice that the choice "cannot be determined" is not used. You must arrive at an answer, and you must have a factual basis for that answer. Because

each inmate on the roster has an individual cell number of his own, choice A is the only answer that has the needed factual support.

27. **(C)** McCabe's inmate number starts with the numeral 1. This means that he was convicted of a property crime.

28. **(D)** The factual information is that inmates perform motor pool duty, perform duty in the dining hall, and perform movie room duty. The exact nature of these duties are not specified. The answer is choice D.

29. **(C)** Sometimes the answers to data interpretation can be determined directly from a specific piece of information in the material. Don't read into the situation when this occurs. Pick the obvious answer and continue on.

30. **(D)** There are presently 12 inmates in Cell Block 14. Each group (A, B, C, D) has three inmates assigned. Therefore, there is no factual information available upon which to make an assumption as to which group the next inmate should be assigned to.

Understanding and Applying Correctional Directives, Procedures, and Regulations

6

→ **UNDERSTANDING PROCEDURES**
→ **APPLYING PROCEDURES**
→ **CODING QUESTIONS**

Correction officers often find themselves alone in work situations that call for them to use discretion in making their decisions. However, to assist them in making such decisions, they are given procedures to follow so that the discretion they are called upon to use can follow certain guidelines and agency policies. These guidelines and policies are most often written and given to the correction officers. Therefore, part of a correction officer's job is to read and understand these guidelines and policies. But that is only half of the requirement concerning such guidelines and policies. In addition, a correction officer is expected to apply them to job-related incidents correctly.

For example, a need for better detection of contraband within inmate cells might arise. A correction officer would probably then receive new guidelines for searching the cells of inmates for contraband. The officer would be expected to read and understand the new guidelines. However the officer would also be expected to be able to apply these guidelines to situations involving the detection of contraband. The problem is that each incident is not exactly alike. Each incident involves a particular situation that is happening at a specific time. This calls for the correction officer to be able to apply the overall and sometimes general policy and guidelines to a specific situation. Therefore, the questions you find in this chapter will test your ability to read, understand, and apply correction procedures.

THREE QUESTION TYPES

Three types of questions are used to test a candidate's ability to read, understand, and apply procedures. They are understanding procedures, applying procedures to situations, and answering coding questions.

Understanding Procedures

Here a candidate is given a procedure similar to what a correction officer might actually receive. The candidate is required to read and understand the procedure. Then a question or questions are asked about the procedure. This type of question tests a candidate's ability to understand the procedures. Often the question requires the candidate to identify accurate or inaccurate statements about the procedure. The candidate may refer back to the procedure if necessary.

STRATEGIES

Scan the procedure.

Scan the stem.

Read the procedure.

Use a mental picture.

Select your answer.

EXAMPLE OF AN UNDERSTANDING PROCEDURES QUESTION

Correction officers are prohibited from carrying firearms in cell block areas except in emergencies and then only when authorized by either the warden or deputy warden or ranking officer of the tour. In those emergency instances when authorized to carry firearms in cell block areas, under no circumstances will correction officers fire warning shots.

Q1.   Based solely on the information in this procedure, which of the following statements is most appropriate?

(A)   Only the warden may carry a firearm into the cell block area.
(B)   A correction officer may carry a firearm into the cell block area only, with the permission of the ranking officer of the tour.
(C)   A firearm may be carried into a cell block area even though no emergency exists.
(D)   A correction officer may never fire warning shots in an emergency situation in a cell block.

A STRATEGY FOR ANSWERING UNDERSTANDING PROCEDURES QUESTIONS

1.   **SCAN THE PROCEDURE.** The first step you should take is to read the material quickly to get an idea of what the procedure is about. A quick scan of the procedure in this example tells you that usually correction officers are not allowed to bring firearms into a cell block. However, it also tells you when and by whose authority a correction officer might be allowed to bring a firearm into a cell block. Finally, the procedure indicates that warning shots are never permitted.

2.   **SCAN THE STEM AND THE CHOICES.** You should read the stem of the question and the choices quickly. By doing this for the example given, you should have been able to determine that the question concerned itself with the use of firearms by correction officers in a cell block. The question asks you to select the most appropriate statement concerning the procedure.

3.   **CLOSELY READ THE PROCEDURE.** By closely reading the procedure, it should have become clear that one of several officials could authorize a correction officer to bring a firearm into a cell block. Also the procedure very clearly states that under no circumstances should warning shots be fired.

4.   **USE A MENTAL PICTURE.** Imagine yourself in the situation that the procedure and the question are describing. In the example given, think of a cell block where you are a correction officer without a firearm. Then imagine an emergency situation where you are given permission to carry a firearm into a cell block. Who, according to the procedure, is allowed to give you permission? All the while you are remembering that you are not allowed to fire warning shots. Put yourself into the situation that is being described so that you develop a mental image of what is going on.

5.   **SELECT YOUR ANSWER.** Selecting your answer should involve a process of elimination. For example, in this question, choice A is inappropriate because the carrying of a firearm into a cell block is not limited to only the warden. A correction officer could also do it. Put an X through choice A. Put another X through choice B, which is inappropriate. The

ranking officer of the tour is not the only person, as B suggests, who can give permission to carry a firearm into a cell block. Choice C is inappropriate and should receive an X through it because for a firearm to be carried into a cell block, an emergency must exist, and permission must be obtained. Choice D is the most appropriate choice because warning shots may never be used. Choice D is, therefore, the answer.

Applying Procedures to Situations

In this type of question, the candidate is given a typical correction procedure. In addition the candidate is given a fact pattern or narrative describing an incident or situation that a correction officer could be expected to encounter. The candidate is then asked to identify the most appropriate (or inappropriate) course of action for a correction officer to take in the situation described based on the procedure provided. The candidate is permitted to refer back to the procedure if necessary to answer the question. In some instances the candidate is required to identify what action the officer should take next based on the procedure provided and the facts of the narrative or situation described. This type of question is designed to test how well a candidate can apply procedures to situations.

EXAMPLE OF AN APPLYING PROCEDURES QUESTION

A correction officer is required to prepare form Correction 262 when, as an operator of a correction department vehicle, said correction officer is involved in a motor vehicle accident. A motor vehicle accident is one that occurs on a public highway or on a public street between building lines. Regarding accidents that occur on private property or on property to which the public does not have access, form Correction 998 shall be prepared by the operator because such incidents shall not be considered motor vehicle accidents.

Correction Officer Will Timer is driving a correction department van that is transporting several prisoners to court. Also assigned to the van as a security guard is Correction Officer Don Tombs. While backing up to an entrance to the court in a secure and private parking lot not accessible to the public, Officer Timer accidentally hits a stanchion causing some damage to the van.

> **STRATEGIES**
>
> Scan the procedure.
> Scan the narrative.
> Scan the question.
> Reread the procedure.
> Reread the narrative.
> Select your answer.

Q2. Based solely on the preceding information, it would be most appropriate for

(A) Officer Timer to prepare form Correction 262.
(B) Officer Tombs to prepare form Correction 262.
(C) Officer Tombs to prepare form Correction 998.
(D) Officer Timer to prepare form Correction 998.

A STRATEGY FOR ANSWERING APPLYING PROCEDURES QUESTIONS

1. **SCAN THE PROCEDURE.** Get a quick idea of what the procedure is about. What is the intent of the procedure? What is it describing? To whom does it apply? When should it be used?

   The intent of the procedure given in this example is to identify who is responsible for preparing a certain form and when that form should be prepared. The important parts of the procedure should be highlighted or underlined, such as the names of the forms involved, the circumstances under which they should be prepared and the persons charged with the responsibility of preparing them.

2. **SCAN THE NARRATIVE.** Quickly looking over the narrative in this example reveals that a correction van is damaged in a parking lot not accessible to the public. The incident occurs while the van driver and a security officer are transporting prisoners to court.

3. **SCAN THE QUESTION.** By looking at the stem of the question and the choices, it should be clear that the question asks which form should be prepared by which correction officer. This should sensitize you as to what to focus on when performing the next step of the strategy.

4. **CLOSELY REREAD THE PROCEDURE.** This part of the strategy should not be time-consuming because you have already underlined and highlighted the procedure when you previously scanned it. Armed with the knowledge of what part of the procedure will be asked about by the question which you have just scanned, it is an easy task to focus on the relevant part(s) of the procedure.

5. **CLOSELY REREAD THE NARRATIVE.** While now reading the narrative closely, it is recommended that you put yourself into the narrative. In this example pretend that you are the driver of the van and that the damage to the van took place while you were driving. Should this be considered a motor vehicle accident? If it should, what must you do? If it's not, what should you do?

6. **SELECT YOUR ANSWER.** Don't neglect to consider all choices. For example, in this example, choice A is inappropriate because form Correction 262 is required when the incident is an actual motor vehicle accident. This incident did not occur on a public highway or on a public street between building lines. It occurred on property to which the public does not have access. Choice B is inappropriate because regardless of where such incidents take place it is the job of the operator of the correction vehicle to prepare the necessary form. Choice C is inappropriate for the same reason. The answer is choice D. Choice D, which calls for Officer Timer to prepare form Correction 998, is correct because the incident was not a motor vehicle accident, and the operator of the correction vehicle is required to prepare form Correction 998 in such instances.

Answering Coding Questions

The other two types of questions in this chapter both dealt with following directions. This means that you were given a procedure to follow and then either asked questions about the procedure itself or were asked to apply the procedure to a situation or narrative. Therefore, in both types of questions, you were asked to do what correction officers are often asked to do, namely follow directions outlined in the form of a procedure.

There is another variation of the question type that seeks to measure how well a correction candidate can follow directions. Those questions are what we refer to as coding questions. Although it is certainly true that there is no requirement to perform the actual kinds of tasks required to answer coding questions on the job, the ability to answer coding questions is the kind of ability that correction officers need when following directions on the actual job.

There are an infinite number of types and variations of coding questions. To review each type of coding question would be impossible. However coding questions do have some basic similarities. They usually have

- a reference table,
- the specific instructions, and
- the actual questions which require you to use the table and follow the directions.

EXAMPLE OF A CODING QUESTION

Reference table: Use the information in the following reference table to answer the question. In the table each number has been associated with a letter.

R	O	Y	G	B	I	V	X	W	Z
1	2	3	4	5	6	7	8	9	0

Directions: For each question use the relationship in the table and select the choice that correctly spells the word identified in the question.

Q3.　*Question:* Using the reference table, which of the following most accurately spells *VIGOR?*

    (A)　76241

    (B)　76412

    (C)　76421

    (D)　47621

A STRATEGY FOR ANSWERING CODING QUESTIONS

STRATEGIES

Scan the reference table.

Scan the directions.

Scan the question.

Read the directions.

Look again at the reference table.

Answer the questions.

1.　**SCAN THE REFERENCE TABLE.** Get a quick idea of what is being coded. For example, are letters being associated with numbers, or, as in our example, are numbers associated with letters?

2.　**SCAN THE DIRECTIONS.** What is expected of you? Try to get a sense of what the examiner wants you to do. This is so important and is actually the key to answering coding questions. For example, does the question ask you to determine if numbers suggested in an answer choice accurately, according to the reference table provided, represent certain words? Or, are you being asked to identify, based on a reference table, whether sets of numbers accurately represent properly alphabetized letters?

    In our example, you should have found that you are to select the choice that correctly spells the word that has been identified in the stem of the question. In other words, you need to spell a word by using individual numbers that represent different letters according to the reference table. To spell the word, you had to use the reference table, which acts like a coding device. Hence, we see where the name *coding question* comes from.

3.　**SCAN THE QUESTION.** Take a quick look at the actual question. Familiarize yourself with what you will be asked to do. In our example you were asked to select the choice that most accurately spelled the word *VIGOR.*

    You should be able to complete all the steps so far fairly quickly. We suggest that you do these steps so that you can begin to point your thinking in the right direction.

4.　**READ THE DIRECTIONS CLOSELY.** Note that you do not return to the reference table yet. The directions are the key. You must understand them completely. You must know what it is that you are seeking to accomplish. In short, you must know how to use the reference table that has been provided. If you do not fully understand the directions, you will find yourself going back to the directions again and again. This will use up much of your time.

5. **TAKE ANOTHER LOOK AT THE REFERENCE TABLE.** The purpose of looking at the reference table again is to see if you understand how to use it based on the directions. Although there is no need to memorize the reference table, you should be prepared to have it ready to answer the questions. In a sense, reference tables are like the department procedures that you had to follow when answering the other type of questions in this chapter.

6. **ANSWER THE QUESTIONS.** Let the choices guide you to the answer. From scanning the stem of the above question and the choices earlier, you should have been able to ascertain that the word to be represented by the numbers was *VIGOR*. Note that choice D is the only choice that does not begin with the number 7. It begins with the number 4, which according to the reference table represents the letter *G*. You can eliminate choice D quickly. Choice B is the only remaining choice that does not end with the number 1. It ends in 2, which represents the letter *O*. Choice B can be eliminated. The difference between the remaining choices A and C lies in the third and fourth number of each choice. Examination of choice A reveals that its third number is a 2, which represents the letter *O*, and that is not the third letter of the word *VIGOR*. Once you verify the remaining choice with the reference table, you should determine that choice C is the answer.

It should be apparent that in doing coding questions it is sometimes necessary to eliminate the inappropriate choices by comparing one choice with another. Once you have decided upon an answer, you should check it using the reference table.

GROUP ONE

Time Allowed: 20 minutes

> **Directions:** Answer questions 1–10 based solely on the following 11 step procedure.

Correction Officer Uniform Regulations Procedures

1. An annual, in-depth uniform inspection and equipment inspection shall commence the first business day of May each year. The inspections shall be performed during the duty time but shall not be conducted on the 0800–1600 hours tour.

2. Officers who are on sick leave or other authorized excusal when annual uniform inspection takes place shall have their uniforms inspected within two (2) weeks after they return to duty.

3. All members of the department shall have their hair cut to a length that allows the uniform cap to be worn.

4. Mustaches and sideburns shall be maintained in a manner that reflects a professional appearance. A member of the department performing duty in uniform shall obtain permission from the commanding officer of the institution or division to which assigned before wearing a beard.

5. The only facial jewelry that is allowed while working are earrings worn on an earlobe. Such earrings shall not extend below the earlobe for safety reasons.

6. Members shall carry their shield and identification cards at all times without exception.

7. Shields shall be worn on the outermost garment when performing duty in uniform or in civilian clothes at the scene of an emergency.

8. The department regulation turtleneck sweater with official logo may be worn during winter months or during inclement weather.

9. Nameplates shall be worn on the outermost uniform garment directly over the shield. However, nameplates shall not be worn on uniform raincoats.

10. Serviceable flashlights shall be carried by all members assigned to uniform duty between the hours of 4 P.M. to 8 A.M. A serviceable flashlight shall not exceed 12 inches in length and 16 ounces in weight.

11.　Members of the department shall report the loss of their shields and/or identification cards occurring within the city limits to the ranking officer on duty at their command. In the event that such loss occurs outside the city limits, the member concerned shall notify the office of the chief of operations. In both instances it is the duty of the member suffering the loss to notify the police authorities concerned.

1.　According to the uniform regulations, which of the following statements concerning the length of a member's hair would be most accurate?

(A)　Members assigned to uniform positions have different regulations than members assigned to civilian clothes positions.
(B)　There are different regulations for male and female officers.
(C)　The shaving of one's head is prohibited.
(D)　The length of the hair must allow the uniform cap to be worn.　Ⓐ Ⓑ Ⓒ Ⓓ

2.　Ralph is a correction officer who likes to wear an earring when he socializes off duty. According to the uniform regulations, Ralph's wearing of an earring while off duty would be

(A)　inappropriate regardless of the style of the earring.
(B)　appropriate only if the earring did not extend below the earlobe.
(C)　inappropriate only if he wore a nose ring.
(D)　appropriate because the facial jewelry rule applies only to on duty officers.　Ⓐ Ⓑ Ⓒ Ⓓ

3.　It would be most appropriate to expect that annual uniform inspections shall be performed

(A)　always on the first of May.
(B)　on off-duty time.
(C)　on a 1600 × 2400 (4 P.M.–12 midnight) tour of duty.
(D)　at any time and any place selected by the warden.　Ⓐ Ⓑ Ⓒ Ⓓ

4.　If Correction Officer Timer is scheduled to undergo annual uniform inspection at a time when she will be on vacation, she will have her uniforms inspected

(A)　within 2 weeks after she returns to duty.
(B)　within 2 days after she returns to duty.
(C)　as soon as possible after she returns to duty.
(D)　before she goes on vacation.　Ⓐ Ⓑ Ⓒ Ⓓ

5. Evaluate the following statements concerning uniform regulations.

  1. If Officer Jones, who is in uniform, wishes, he may wear sideburns if they are worn in a manner that reflects a professional appearance.
  2. Officer Grey, who is assigned to a civilian clothes position, may wear a beard without seeking prior permission.

  Which of the following is most accurate concerning these two statements?

  (A) Only statement 1 is correct.
  (B) Only statement 2 is correct.
  (C) Both statements 1 and 2 are correct.
  (D) Neither statement 1 nor 2 is correct.

6. It would be least appropriate to wear the uniform turtleneck sweater with the official logo

  (A) during inclement weather in June.
  (B) anytime in February.
  (C) anytime in October.
  (D) on a sunny mild day in January.

7. According to the uniform regulations, it would be most appropriate to state that

  (A) if Correction Officer Homes loses his shield, he must always report the loss to the chief of operations.
  (B) whenever a shield is lost, it is the duty of the commanding officer of the member suffering the loss to report the loss to the police.
  (C) whenever an identification card is lost within the city limits, the member suffering the loss shall report the loss to the chief of operations.
  (D) if Correction Officer Barns loses her identification card, she must always notify the police authorities concerned.

8. Evaluate the following statements concerning uniform regulations.

1. Members must carry their identification cards at all time without exception.
2. Members must carry their shields at all times except when off duty.

Which of the following is most accurate concerning these two statements?

(A) Only statement 1 is correct.
(B) Only statement 2 is correct.
(C) Both statements 1 and 2 are correct.
(D) Neither statement 1 nor 2 is correct.

9. Which of the following statements would be most appropriate according to the uniform regulations concerning serviceable flashlights?

(A) At 4:30 P.M. all members of the department should be carrying a serviceable flashlight.
(B) Uniform members of the department must carry serviceable flashlights on all tours.
(C) Serviceable flashlights shall not exceed 12 inches in length.
(D) Serviceable flashlights shall not exceed 6 ounces in weight.

10. Evaluate the following statements concerning uniform regulations.

1. Shields shall be worn on the outermost garment when performing duty in uniform or in civilian clothes at the scene of an emergency.
2. Nameplates shall always be worn on the outermost uniform garment directly over the shield.

Which of the following is most accurate concerning these two statements?

(A) Only statement 1 is correct.
(B) Only statement 2 is correct.
(C) Both statements 1 and 2 are correct.
(D) Neither statement 1 nor 2 is correct.

Directions: The following are practice questions. Answer each question in this group solely on the basis of the information provided.

Answer questions 11–13 based solely on the following passage.

If an escape attempt by an inmate should occur while said inmate is being transported in a department vehicle on a public thoroughfare, the members concerned shall do the following in the order given:

1. The vehicle operator shall attempt to park the vehicle in a safe location.

2. The vehicle operator shall immediately notify the radio dispatcher of the following in this order:

   a. the location of the attempted escape
   b. the number of inmates involved
   c. if the escape attempt has been successful
   d. if any injuries have occurred
   e. if immediate assistance is required

3. The correction officer acting as an accompanying guard shall take necessary action to ensure that further escape attempts are not made.

4. If any inmates have been injured, the accompanying guard officer shall assist in seeking medical assistance for the inmates.

5. If outside parties assisted in the escape attempt, the accompanying guard officer shall attempt to ascertain the identities of such persons.

6. If such persons have fled the scene, the vehicle operator shall, after conferring with the accompanying guard officer, notify the dispatcher of the description of such persons and the direction and method of flight.

7. The dispatcher shall notify the police department's major case squad, which shall respond to the scene and assist in investigating the escape attempt.

11. While transporting several prisoners to court in a department bus, Correction Officer Brown, who is operating the bus, was notified by Correction Officer Cards, who is assigned as the accompanying guard officer, that an inmate attempted to kick out the rear door of the bus to escape. The bus was stopped for a signal light at the busy intersection of Main Street and Pine Avenue when Inmate Don Hatter, number 17789, attempted but failed to escape by trying to kick out the rear door. Officer Cards notified Officer Brown of the situation. Which of the following actions should occur next?

    (A) The major case squad should be notified immediately.
    (B) The dispatcher should be notified by Officer Brown.
    (C) Officer Brown should seek medical attention for any injured inmates.
    (D) Officer Brown should attempt to park the vehicle in a safe location.

12. Immediately after the radio dispatcher was notified of the location of the attempted escape, which of the following should the radio dispatcher be notified of next?

    (A) If any injuries have occurred.
    (B) The number of inmates involved.
    (C) If the escape attempt has been successful.
    (D) If immediate assistance is required.

13. Officer Cards noticed that a green sedan was attempting to assist the inmate who attempted to escape. The vehicle had been stopped behind the bus at the signal light and two men exited the vehicle and attempted to open the rear door of the bus while the inmate was trying to kick out the door. When it became apparent that the escape attempt was not going to be successful, the men fled in the green sedan. Officer Cards then notified the dispatcher of the description of such persons and the method of flight. In such an instance, the notification by Officer Cards was

    (A) appropriate because apprehension of the two men is paramount.
    (B) inappropriate because the notification should have been made by Officer Brown.
    (C) appropriate because the men might strike again.
    (D) inappropriate because the notification should have been made to the major case squad instead.

When a correction officer assigned to a tier is notified by an inmate that such inmate or another inmate is in need of medical attention, the correction officer shall do the following in the order given:

1. Notify the ranking officer present.

2. Make arrangements for medical treatment as follows:

    a. Call and make an appointment with the infirmary for all illnesses and injuries occurring during normal business hours from Monday to Friday.
    b. Call and make an appointment with the reserve department doctor on call for all illnesses and injuries occurring during other than normal business hours and on weekends.

3. Prepare a Medical Treatment form for all such requests and forward to the warden's office through channels.

14. Correction Officer Marina, while assigned to perform tier duty, is notified by Inmate Blanks that he has severe stomach pains and is in need of medical attention. Officer Marina notifies the ranking officer present at about 2 P.M. on a Sunday afternoon. The next step Officer Marina should take is to

    (A) notify the warden's office.
    (B) prepare a Medical Treatment form.
    (C) call and make an appointment with the infirmary.
    (D) call and make an appointment with the reserve department doctor on call.

Inmates shall be permitted to receive incoming mail under the following procedures:

1. Incoming inmate mail shall be delivered to the intended inmate within a 48-hour period. Upon delivery all incoming mail shall be opened and inspected in the presence of the intended inmate.

2. Printed material, photos, and money orders or bank or personal checks are permitted to be received by inmates through the mail.

3. Legal and special delivery mail must be signed for by an inmate. The housing area officer shall have the inmate receipt for such items in the Mail Logbook before allowing the inmate to take possession of it. In such instances, the housing area officer shall also sign the Mail Logbook.

4. If an inmate's mail is found to contain a prohibited article or contraband, then

    a. regarding prohibited articles, the inmate has the option of having the articles destroyed or donated to charity or returned to the sender at the expense of the inmate. The decision regarding the disposition of the prohibited article(s) is to be made by the inmate.

    b. regarding contraband or an item suspected of being narcotics or other controlled substances, the items shall be seized by the housing area officer and sealed in an envelope in the presence of the inmate. The inmate and housing area officer shall sign the flap of the sealed envelope. The envelope shall be delivered to the tour commander by the housing area officer.

5. In instances when an inmate is transferred, any mail arriving at the inmate's previous institution shall be forwarded to the inmate's new address within 24 hours.

15. Jasper is an inmate. Mail addressed to him was received at the institution on May 1st. According to department regulations it is required that the mail be delivered to Jasper within

    (A) 8 hours.
    (B) 16 hours.
    (C) 24 hours.
    (D) 48 hours.

16. Rogers is currently serving a sentence as an inmate. A legal document arrives for Rogers and is received by Correction Officer Tucker, who is assigned as the housing area officer. Officer Tucker gives the document to Rogers after advising him that it is a legal document. In this instance, the actions of Officer Tucker were

    (A) appropriate because the document may have information relating to the sentence Rogers is currently serving.
    (B) inappropriate because he should have first given it to the tour commander.
    (C) appropriate because it is specifically one of the items an inmate is permitted to receive through the mail.
    (D) inappropriate because he should have first required Rogers to receipt for it in the Mail Logbook.

    Ⓐ Ⓑ Ⓒ Ⓓ

17. Joan receives mail as an inmate. During the inspection of the mail by the housing area officer, Correction Officer Parks, a glassine envelope containing what appears to be narcotics is discovered by Officer Parks. Parks takes the glassine envelope and in the presence of the Inmate Joan places it into an envelope and seals it. In such an instance, which of the following further actions would be most appropriate?

    (A) The flap of the sealed envelope should be signed by Joan and Officer Parks.
    (B) The flap of the sealed envelope should be signed by Joan and the tour commander.
    (C) The flap of the sealed envelope should be signed only by Joan.
    (D) The flap of the sealed envelope should be signed only by Officer Parks.

    Ⓐ Ⓑ Ⓒ Ⓓ

18. Inmate Pat West is transferred to another correctional institution. Any mail arriving at her previous institution is required to be forwarded to her new address within

    (A) 8 hours.
    (B) 16 hours.
    (C) 24 hours.
    (D) 48 hours.

    Ⓐ Ⓑ Ⓒ Ⓓ

1. Prior to placing an inmate in a cell, the correction officer assigned to the housing area post shall conduct an inspection of said cell, in order to determine the condition of the fixtures, furniture, and equipment.

2. Said correction officer conducting the inspection shall prepare Form 669 to indicate the condition of the fixtures, furniture, and equipment in the cell.

3. After completion of Form 669 the officer shall have the inmate verify that entries on the form are accurate by countersigning the form. If the inmate refuses to sign, the officer shall indicate such under the caption "Details" of Form 669.

4. The officer shall give the inmate a copy of Form 669, file one copy in the inmate's folder, and forward one copy to the housing area captain.

5. When a member of the department witnesses an inmate damaging fixtures, furniture, or equipment in a cell, or has evidence of such actions, said member shall bring disciplinary action against the inmate by preparing Form 449. The member of the department shall then notify the housing area captain, if available. In all instances the tour commander will be notified by the member bringing disciplinary action against the inmate. Physical restraints may be used if required to prevent further destruction of property.

19. Prior to placing an inmate in his cell, Correction Officer Wells who is assigned to a housing area post inspects the cell to determine the condition of the furnishings of the cell. Officer Wells finds that everything is in order and records such on Form 669. Wells then sends all copies of the form to the housing area captain. In this instance, Officer Wells acted

   (A) properly because the housing area captain is required to review and countersign the forms.
   (B) improperly because it is not necessary to forward any copies of the form to the captain.
   (C) properly because the housing area captain will review and file the form in the inmate's folder.
   (D) improperly because the correction officer should have first attempted to have the inmate verify the entries.

20. Correction Officer Baker observes an inmate damaging some light fixtures. All the following would be appropriate actions for Baker to take except

   (A) notify the warden who shall bring disciplinary charges against the inmate.
   (B) notify the housing area captain, if available.
   (C) notify the tour commander in all instances.
   (D) use physical restraints if necessary.

   Ⓐ Ⓑ Ⓒ Ⓓ

GROUP THREE

Time Allowed: 20 Minutes

Directions: Use the information in the following reference table to answer questions 21–30. Each number in the table is to be associated with the letter appearing above it.

B	I	N	G	O
3	25	24	10	19
16	1	4	9	7
17	2	14	23	18
11	12	6	21	5
8	20	22	13	15

Directions: In some of the following sets of numbers, the numbers may or may not accurately reflect the letters with which they are associated according to the reference table. Compare the letters in column 1 with the numbers in column 2 and then select the choice that accurately indicates which sets of letters and numbers have been accurately associated. For each question there are four possible answers. Select the lettered choice A, B, or C that reflects the letters that have been accurately associated with the numbers. However, choice D should be selected if all or none of the sets has been accurately associated according to the reference table.

21. *Column 1*   *Column 2*

   (A) GNO   15-4-10
   (B) IOG   1-19-23
   (C) IGN   8-10-22
   (D) All or none of the sets

   Ⓐ Ⓑ Ⓒ Ⓓ

22. *Column 1*   *Column 2*

    (A) BNG   2-14-9
    (B) BGO   6-10-5
    (C) BGN   17-6-4
    (D) All or none of the sets   Ⓐ Ⓑ Ⓒ Ⓓ

23. *Column 1*   *Column 2*

    (A) NGO   14-9-7
    (B) INO   11-4-15
    (C) IGO   11-23-19
    (D) All or none of the sets   Ⓐ Ⓑ Ⓒ Ⓓ

24. *Column 1*   *Column 2*

    (A) OBN   19-3-5
    (B) BOB   3-18-1
    (C) NNN   6-24-14
    (D) All or none of the sets   Ⓐ Ⓑ Ⓒ Ⓓ

25. *Column 1*   *Column 2*

    (A) INB   12-4-16
    (B) BIN   17-2-22
    (C) NIG   6-1-9
    (D) All or none of the sets   Ⓐ Ⓑ Ⓒ Ⓓ

Directions for Questions 26–30: Select the choice containing the numbers, which when associated with their letters according to the reference table, represents the letters in best alphabetical order.

26. (A) 3, 18, 4
    (B) 3, 1, 9
    (C) 1, 4, 7
    (D) 10, 3, 19   Ⓐ Ⓑ Ⓒ Ⓓ

27. (A) 2, 7, 6
    (B) 21, 24, 1
    (C) 11, 12, 5
    (D) 21, 5, 6   Ⓐ Ⓑ Ⓒ Ⓓ

28. (A) 17, 14, 2
    (B) 17, 14, 23
    (C) 17, 18, 14
    (D) 17, 23, 2   Ⓐ Ⓑ Ⓒ Ⓓ

29. (A) 10, 25, 19
    (B) 23, 19, 14
    (C) 21, 2, 16
    (D) 17, 20, 23   Ⓐ Ⓑ Ⓒ Ⓓ

30. (A) 19, 25, 24
    (B) 18, 17, 13
    (C) 5, 9, 4
    (D) 11, 6, 7   Ⓐ Ⓑ Ⓒ Ⓓ

ANSWER KEY

1. **D**	7. **D**	13. **B**	19. **D**	25. **D**
2. **D**	8. **A**	14. **D**	20. **A**	26. **C**
3. **C**	9. **C**	15. **D**	21. **B**	27. **C**
4. **A**	10. **A**	16. **D**	22. **D**	28. **D**
5. **C**	11. **D**	17. **A**	23. **A**	29. **A**
6. **C**	12. **B**	18. **C**	24. **C**	30. **D**

ANSWERS EXPLAINED

Group One

1. **(D)** This is an example of basing an answer *solely* on the information provided. While choices A, B, and C might all seem probable, they are not mentioned in the uniform regulations upon which you must base your answers.

2. **(D)** According to the regulation dealing with facial jewelry such as earrings, the restrictions apply only when an officer is working.

3. **(C)** Choice A might have been selected if you did not read carefully. It is the first business day in May and that is not always the same as the first of May.

4. **(A)** This is as stated in the regulation number 2.

5. **(C)** If you followed our strategy and had scanned the question and the choices you would have had no problem recognizing which parts of the regulations were going to be asked about. It is those parts that you should have been underlining when you went back and reread the procedures.

6. **(C)** The uniform turtleneck sweater may be worn in the winter months and during inclement weather. Since October is in the fall, wearing it anytime in October would not always be appropriate.

7. **(D)** It is the individual member's duty to notify the police authorities.

8. **(A)** Both the shield and ID card must be carried at all times without exception.

9. **(C)** Choice A is inappropriate because it would include members of the department who are in civilian clothes. Choice B is inappropriate because uniformed members are not required to carry serviceable flashlights on all tours, only from 4 P.M. to 8 A.M. Choice D is inappropriate because serviceable flashlights may not exceed 16 ounces.

10. **(A)** Nameplates shall not be worn on a raincoat, which could be the outermost garment that an officer might wear.

Group Two

11. **(D)** This is the first action that the vehicle operator should take.

12. **(B)** If you had scanned the stem of the question and the choices when you reread the procedure, it would have been clear how important the order of these steps were.

13. **(B)** Choice A and C seem to be appropriate but are not mentioned in the procedure. Choice D is inappropriate because the notification to the major case squad should be made by the dispatcher. Choice B is the answer.

14. **(D)** The key to answering this question correctly is recognizing that the incident occurs on a weekend. Thus after step 1 was completed and the ranking officer was notified, the next step was to call and make an appointment with the reserve department doctor on call.

15. **(D)** This is as indicated in the regulations.

16. **(D)** Although a legal document is one of the items that can be received by an inmate, a receipt for it must first be made in the Mail Logbook.

17. **(A)** Both the inmate and the housing area officer are required to sign the flap of the sealed envelope.

18. **(C)** This is as indicated in regulation 5.

19. **(D)** Before a copy of the form is forwarded, the correction officer is to try to have the inmate review and countersign the form, thus verifying the entries. The officer then gives one copy to the inmate, files a copy, and sends one to the housing area captain.

20. **(A)** It is the job of the member who witnesses the inmate damaging the property to bring disciplinary charges.

Group Three

21. **(B)** Choice A should be eliminated because the letter *G* is incorrectly associated with the number 15. Eliminate choice C because the letter *I* is incorrectly associated with the number 8. A close comparison of letters with the number suggested by choice B indicates that B is the answer.

   A helpful hint in actually comparing the letters and their corresponding numbers is to use the index finger of your left hand to point to the letter in the choice you are examining. Then with your eye find the numbers in the reference table that are associated with the letter you are pointing at. If the number in the choice you are examining is not associated with that letter in the reference table, eliminate that choice. Also circle the letter along with the number in the choice which has been identified via the reference table as not being correctly associated with the letter in the answer choice you are examining. As soon as you have identified one incorrectly associated letter and number move on to the next choice. The reason for circling the incorrectly associated letters and numbers is so that when you check your work, you will be quickly reminded why you have eliminated a choice.

22. **(D)** None of the sets is accurately associated. In choices A and B, the letter B is incorrectly associated. In choice C, the letter *G* is incorrectly associated. Thus choice D is the answer.

23. **(A)** Choices B and C can both be quickly eliminated because the letter *I* in both choices was incorrectly associated with the number 11, which is inaccurate according to the reference table.

24. **(C)** Choice A is incorrect because the letter *N* is inaccurately associated with the number 5 and Choice B is incorrect because the letter B is incorrectly associated with the number 1. Choice C is accurately associated.

25. **(D)** They are all appropriately associated.

26. **(C)** The numbers in the choices represent the following (A) BON (B) BIG (C) INO (D) GBO. Choice C represents the best alphabetical order because the letter *I* comes before the letter *N* and the letter *N* comes before the letter *O*. In doing this type of coding question, we recommend that you first replace the numbers in each choice with the associated letters from the reference table. Then determine which of the individual choices is in best alphabetical order. Unfortunately each choice must be examined. That is why this type of coding question can be time-consuming.

27. **(C)** The numbers in the choices represent the following (A) ION (B) GNI (C) BIO (D) GON. Choice C represents the best alphabetical order.

28. **(D)** The numbers in the choices represent the following (A) BNI (B) BNG (C) BON (D) BGI. Choice D represents the best alphabetical order.

29. **(A)** The numbers in the choices represent the following (A) GIO (B) GON (C) GIB (D) BIG. Choice A represents the best alphabetical order.

30. **(D)** The numbers in the choices represent the following (A) OIN (B) OBG (C) OGN (D) BNO. Choice D represents the best alphabetical order.

Judgment/Reasoning Questions

7

→ GUIDELINES FOR ANSWERING CERTAIN JUDGMENT QUESTIONS
→ DIRECT RULE INTERPRETATION
→ RULE APPLICATION
→ STRATEGIES

GUIDELINES FOR ANSWERING CERTAIN JUDGMENT QUESTIONS

We have identified guidelines that examiners often rely on when writing questions that require candidates to exercise judgment. Although these guidelines will not provide the answer to all judgment-type questions, they will lead to the answer to many of them. Here are these guidelines:

1. The protection of life is the highest priority of a correction officer.

2. Situations that may cause widespread death or injury are more important than situations that may cause limited death or injury. In a sense, this requires selecting an answer choice that represents the "lesser of two evils."

3. The protection of property is the next priority of a correction officer.

4. Situations with the potential for widespread destruction of property are more important than situations that may cause limited destruction of property. Again, the answer choice that represents the "lesser of two evils" is correct.

5. Constitutional rights are more important than the reputation of the agency.

6. The needs of the agency are more important than the needs of individual officers. For example, if an officer needs a day off to attend a wedding on a day when the agency needs all officers working, the officer's request for a day off will not be approved.

7. The use of deadly force can be justified only to prevent someone from unlawfully using deadly force, and then it should be used only as a last resort.

8. The use of force by correction officers is appropriate only to defend against the illegal use of force, and then it should be used only as a last resort.

9. Unless someone's safety is at risk, discipline should be a private matter.

10. Whenever an inmate is taken out of a correctional facility, consider the possibility of escape to be high.

11. To be effective, punishment must be certain.

12. The firearm is not an offensive weapon; it is for defensive purposes.

13. Fair and consistent treatment of inmates is the hallmark of a professional correction officer.

14. The rule "facts before acts" applies in every situation that does not involve an emergency of some type.

15. Situations, like an oil spill, which are potentially life threating, must receive immediate attention.

Judgment/reasoning questions require test takers to exercise their judgment or reasoning skills to correctly answer them. There are two basic ways these questions are asked.

DIRECT RULE INTERPRETATION QUESTIONS

In the first way of asking judgment/reasoning questions, the test taker is given a rule and then asked questions about that rule. This is what we call direct rule interpretation. This question type is very similar to some reading comprehension questions involving rules. The difference is that the rule interpretation questions sometimes requires test takers to arrive at the answers by using information or knowledge not contained in the rule.

Example of a Direct Rule Interpretation Question

Q1a.   A correction officer must not be either over friendly nor overly strict with inmates. This means that a correction officer's attitude toward inmates should be

   (A)   hostile.
   (B)   neutral.
   (C)   patronizing.
   (D)   scornful.

Please note that the rule is stated in the part of the question that comes before the choices, the part that we call the stem of the question. It informs the test taker that a correction officer can't be overly friendly toward inmates nor can a correction officer be overly strict. In other words, the correction officer's attitude should be neutral toward inmates, as indicated in choice B, which is the answer.

Also note that in some jurisdictions the test writers ask this type of question in the absence of the rule. In others words, the preceding question could also be asked in the following way.

Q1b.   A correction officer's attitude toward inmates should be

   (A)   hostile.
   (B)   neutral.
   (C)   patronizing.
   (D)   scornful.

Although we do not think that this type of question (where the rule is not given) is entirely appropriate for use on an entrance test, the matter is not fully resolved. It is still in use in some jurisdictions. Therefore, we include this type of question in our practice exercises at the end of this chapter and also on our full-length practice tests.

RULE APPLICATION QUESTIONS

In this second way of asking judgment/reasoning questions, the test taker is given a rule and then asked which of four actions is in accordance with the rule, or, which of four actions is not in accordance with the rule. In other words, to answer the question correctly, the test taker is required to apply the rule.

Example of a Rule Application Question

Answer the following question based solely on the following rule.

> **Q2.** Correction officers are required to report all hazardous conditions. Which one of the following should a correction officer report?
>
> (A) Inmates are playing touch football in the main yard.
> (B) Cars are double-parked in the visitor's parking lot.
> (C) People are waiting to visit with inmates.
> (D) A large amount of oil is spilled near the prison's main boiler.

Most of the time there are two choices that simply do not apply, such as choices A and C in this example. Then there is usually one choice that could arguably apply, such as choice B. But the correct answer always clearly applies, as in choice D. For this reason it is essential that you read all choices before choosing an answer.

STRATEGIES FOR TAKING JUDGMENT/REASONING QUESTIONS

1. If a rule is given, as is the case most of the time, you must spend a little time making sure that you understand the rule before you look at the question.
2. Before reading the choices, you must know whether you are looking for an example of the rule or an example of an exception to the rule. In other words, some times there are three good statements that support the rule and one bad one and you must find the bad one. This kind of question might have a stem that reads something like this:

> Q. All the following actions are in accordance with the given
>   rule except . . .

In this case, the choices would contain three good actions and one bad one. Your job is to select the bad one. Other times there are three bad statements and one good one. This kind of question might have a stem that reads something like this:

> Q. Which one of the following actions is in accordance with the
>   given rule?

In this case, the choices would contain three bad actions and one good one. This time your job is to select the good one.

> **STRATEGIES**
>
> Understand the rule.
>
> Know what you are being asked.
>
> Label each choice as "bad" or "good."

3. Evaluate each choice as being "good" or "bad." Do this by writing *good* or *bad* in the test booklet next to each choice. If you are not sure, put a question mark next to that choice. After you have evaluated each choice, if you have three goods and one bad or three bads and one good, the answer is obvious. If, however, you have three goods and a question mark, the question mark is probably the bad choice and is the choice to select as the answer.

PRACTICE EXERCISES

GROUP ONE

Time Allowed: 20 minutes

1. Correction Officer Smith is told to notify his supervisor immediately when he observes a dangerous condition. For which one of the following should Officer Smith notify his supervisor immediately?

   (A) A motorist is stalled in the parking lot causing a traffic jam.
   (B) A parking sign on the prison facility has been painted over.
   (C) A car alarm has gone off in the employee's parking lot.
   (D) Smoke is coming out of the first floor window of the administration building.   Ⓐ Ⓑ Ⓒ Ⓓ

2. When searching visitors to a prison facility, correction officers must seize legally carried items that could very easily be used as a dangerous weapon. Which one of the following objects could very easily be used as a dangerous weapon?

   (A) a newspaper
   (B) a nail file
   (C) lipstick
   (D) tissues   Ⓐ Ⓑ Ⓒ Ⓓ

3. Correction officers should make a point of finding out about the background of new inmates. The most important reason why this is so is that

   (A) it enables officers to communicate better with new inmates.
   (B) it gives the officers an indication of which new inmates might be dangerous.
   (C) it allows officers to better rehabilitate new inmates.
   (D) it lets the officers know which inmates should get favorable treatment.   Ⓐ Ⓑ Ⓒ Ⓓ

4. All doors and gates leading to the prison arsenal shall be locked at all times and no unauthorized person shall be admitted. Which one of the following persons would be least likely to be admitted to the prison arsenal?

   (A) a correction officer
   (B) a model inmate
   (C) a member of the prison custodial staff
   (D) a warden

   Ⓐ Ⓑ Ⓒ Ⓓ

5. Only when there is a medical emergency should inmates be allowed to see the prison doctor at other than regular sick call hours. Which of the following cases is most correctly classified as a medical emergency?

   (A) An inmate's hearing aid is not working and he is having difficulty hearing.
   (B) An inmate fell down and sprained his ankle and is having some difficulty walking.
   (C) Am inmate cut himself shaving and the bleeding took 5 minutes to stop.
   (D) An inmate has severe pains in his chest and is experiencing difficulty breathing.

   Ⓐ Ⓑ Ⓒ Ⓓ

6. A correction officer observes an inmate commit a minor infraction of prison rules while he is in the presence of a group of other inmates. The best course of action for the officer to take is to

   (A) ignore the infraction since it is minor.
   (B) immediately discipline the inmate in front of the other inmates.
   (C) take action only if the inmate is a chronic offender.
   (D) take the inmate to a private area and explain to him that you will not tolerate infractions of the rules.

   Ⓐ Ⓑ Ⓒ Ⓓ

7. Handcuffs are to be used as a temporary measure when it is necessary to prevent an inmate from harming himself or others. In which one of the following situations should handcuffs be used?

   (A) It is late at night and an inmate is being loud and boisterous.
   (B) During the last 3 weeks a certain inmate has been involved in three fights.
   (C) An inmate seems to be out of control and is constantly hitting his fists against the wall.
   (D) An inmate refuses to perform his assigned duties.

   Ⓐ Ⓑ Ⓒ Ⓓ

8. More than one correction officer should be assigned to guard an inmate when the possibility of escape is significant. Which of the following situations would be least likely to require the assignment of more than one officer?

(A) An inmate is being sent to court.
(B) An inmate is being allowed to attend the funeral of a family member.
(C) An inmate is being taken to the hospital on the grounds of the prison.
(D) An inmate is being transferred to another prison.

9. Maintaining a safe and secure prison requires that inmates' cells be periodically inspected and searched. To ensure maximum effectiveness, such inspections and searches should be carried out

(A) on the same day each week but at different times.
(B) at the same time of day but not always on the same day of the week.
(C) on the same day each week and always at the same time.
(D) on a frequent but irregular basis using different days of the week and different times of the day.

10. When escorting a group of prisoners, it is a prison rule that a correction officer walk behind the group. The most important reason for such a rule is to

(A) totally prevent any escape attempts.
(B) promote the safety of the officer.
(C) eliminate the need for the assignment of a second officer.
(D) prevent inmates from fighting among themselves.

GROUP TWO

Time Allowed: 20 minutes

11. It would be appropriate for an armed correction officer to shoot at an inmate

(A) only if the inmate is trying to escape.
(B) who has just punched another correction officer.
(C) who is committing a serious violation of rules.
(D) who is using or about to use deadly physical force against the officer.

12. Punishment is effective only if it is

   (A) severe.
   (B) certain.
   (C) delayed.
   (D) uniform.   Ⓐ Ⓑ Ⓒ Ⓓ

13. A correction officer should be open-minded. This means that an officer should

   (A) consider both sides of a story.
   (B) impose her will on others.
   (C) never exercise discretion.
   (D) never believe an inmate.   Ⓐ Ⓑ Ⓒ Ⓓ

14. A correction officer is required to report all dangerous conditions to a supervisor immediately. Which of the following would require such an immediate report?

   (A) An officer notices a strong smell of gas in a cell block.
   (B) A broken bottle is found in the kitchen.
   (C) An inmate is found sleeping in the toilet area.
   (D) A shower head is discovered leaking in the shower area.   Ⓐ Ⓑ Ⓒ Ⓓ

15. To be effective, a correction officer must be

   (A) an extremely physically strong person.
   (B) a thinking person.
   (C) a very emotional person.
   (D) an inflexible person.   Ⓐ Ⓑ Ⓒ Ⓓ

16. Correction officers should not view their firearms as offensive weapons. This means that firearms would best be used

   (A) to prevent escapes.
   (B) to maintain order.
   (C) to promote discipline.
   (D) to defend against a threat to life.   Ⓐ Ⓑ Ⓒ Ⓓ

17. Tool control in a correctional work shop absolutely requires an accurate inventory of the tools presently in use. This means that

   (A) a listing and current status of all tools on hand must be available.
   (B) only nondangerous tools should be distributed to inmates.
   (C) inmates must be strip searched at the conclusion of each work period.
   (D) each tool must have a definite place where it is stored.   Ⓐ Ⓑ Ⓒ Ⓓ

18. A correction officer is preparing a wanted poster for an escaped inmate. Of the following information, which would most likely lead to that inmate's capture?

(A) At the time of his escape, the inmate was wearing prison clothing.
(B) The escaped inmate is about 5 feet, 10 inches tall.
(C) The escaped inmate has long black hair.
(D) The escaped inmate has a 5-inch scar underneath his left eye. Ⓐ Ⓑ Ⓒ Ⓓ

19. A correction officer must not, under any circumstances, accept a gift or a favor from any inmate. The main justification for such a rule is that acceptance by a correction officer of a gift or a favor could possibly

(A) damage the reputation of the inmate giving the gift or favor.
(B) put pressure on other inmates to give gifts or do favors.
(C) lead inmates to believe that gifts and favors will be returned by the officer.
(D) lower the morale of those officers who do not receive gifts or favors. Ⓐ Ⓑ Ⓒ Ⓓ

20. Key control is an essential element of safe and effective correctional operations. This most likely means that

(A) there should not be more than one key for any lock.
(B) inmates should not be permitted to have any keys.
(C) there should be specific regulations concerning the possession of keys.
(D) only certain correction officers should have keys in their possession. Ⓐ Ⓑ Ⓒ Ⓓ

GROUP THREE

Time Allowed: 20 minutes

21. A correction officer should treat all inmates

(A) in a fair and consistent manner.
(B) in a manner comfortable to the officer.
(C) in the same manner.
(D) in the same manner that the inmates treat them. Ⓐ Ⓑ Ⓒ Ⓓ

22. Report writing is an essential part of the job of a correction officer. The most important characteristic of a good report is

    (A) brevity.
    (B) accuracy.
    (C) subjectivity.
    (D) good grammar.

    Ⓐ Ⓑ Ⓒ Ⓓ

23. Occasionally, correction officers may require backup assistance from other officers. In which of the following situations would it be most appropriate for an officer to request backup assistance?

    (A) An argument about a parking space is taking place in the visitor's parking lot.
    (B) A fight between two groups of inmates is taking place in the recreation room.
    (C) An inmate is making a grievance about treatment he received in the prison hospital.
    (D) An inmate is quite upset about a recent decision of the parole board.

    Ⓐ Ⓑ Ⓒ Ⓓ

24. The most important reason why a correction officer must remain especially alert when supervising a large group of inmates during a recreational period is

    (A) to ensure that all inmates get an equal opportunity to engage in recreational activities.
    (B) that a correction officer must always be especially alert that the sports equipment is not damaged.
    (C) that recreation time is the best time for inmates to attempt to escape.
    (D) that the presence of a large group of inmates in one place always requires extra caution.

    Ⓐ Ⓑ Ⓒ Ⓓ

25. During a routine search of a prisoner, a correction officer discovers an object that he is not sure the prisoner is authorized to possess. Even though the object does not present a threat to anyone's safety, the officer believes it might be against prison rules for the inmate to have it. Under these circumstances, the best course of action for the officer to follow would be to

    (A) let the inmate retain possession of the object.
    (B) confiscate the object immediately.
    (C) determine if it is or is not a violation to possess the object before taking action.
    (D) discipline the inmate on the spot.

    Ⓐ Ⓑ Ⓒ Ⓓ

26. A correction officer is sometimes authorized to exercise discretion when enforcing rules and regulations. This means that

   (A) an officer can sometimes choose the best way to deal with an apparent violation.
   (B) an officer must always handle rule violations in the same manner.
   (C) an officer should always consult with a supervisor when engaged in rule enforcement.
   (D) an officer is always free to handle rule violations any way she sees fit.

   Ⓐ Ⓑ Ⓒ Ⓓ

27. Control of eating utensils is an important task of the correctional staff. The importance of this task is caused mainly by the fact that

   (A) humane treatment mandates that inmates be given every opportunity to enjoy their meals.
   (B) constant loss of eating utensils creates a significant financial loss.
   (C) eating utensils are sometimes used by inmates as weapons.
   (D) a shortage of eating utensils always generates a significant number of legitimate grievances.

   Ⓐ Ⓑ Ⓒ Ⓓ

28. Correction officers are required to maintain a neat and clean appearance. The primary justification for this rule is that

   (A) a neat and clean appearance tends to win the respect and cooperation of the inmates.
   (B) officers can be disciplined for presenting an unkempt appearance.
   (C) the directions of sloppy officers are never followed.
   (D) correction officers are paid to be neat and clean.

   Ⓐ Ⓑ Ⓒ Ⓓ

29. When an inmate consistently refuses a routine order of a correction officer, the officer should

   (A) insist on compliance.
   (B) use force to gain compliance.
   (C) confine the prisoner and inform a supervisor.
   (D) immediately punish the inmate.

   Ⓐ Ⓑ Ⓒ Ⓓ

30. An inmate comes to a correction officer and accuses another inmate of stealing property. Under these circumstances the first step the officer should take is to

(A) search the cell of the accused inmate immediately.

(B) inform the accused inmate of the allegation and ask if it is true.

(C) ask the inmate making the allegation for the specific facts in the matter.

(D) notify a supervisor immediately.

ANSWER KEY

1. **D**	7. **C**	13. **A**	19. **C**	25. **C**
2. **B**	8. **C**	14. **A**	20. **C**	26. **A**
3. **B**	9. **D**	15. **B**	21. **A**	27. **C**
4. **B**	10. **B**	16. **D**	22. **B**	28. **A**
5. **D**	11. **D**	17. **A**	23. **B**	29. **C**
6. **D**	12. **B**	18. **D**	24. **D**	30. **C**

ANSWERS EXPLAINED

Group One

1. **(D)** The possibility of fire is always to be considered as an extremely dangerous situation. Fire in a building can injure or kill many people. Also, remember the old adage, "Where there is smoke, there is fire."

2. **(B)** A nail file is a relatively sharp metal instrument that could be used as a weapon.

3. **(B)** Basic character change in adults is rare. Inmates with a past history of violent behavior are more likely to be violent in prison than inmates with no past history of violence. Note that choice A presents a benefit of finding out the background of an inmate, but safety is always the paramount reason why correction officers do the things that they do.

4. **(B)** Arsenals are weapons storehouses. Under no circumstances should inmates be allowed access to weapons.

5. **(D)** The situation described in choice D is clearly life-threatening.

6. **(D)** A correction officer should not tolerate infractions of the rules, but, unless someone's safety is at risk, discipline should be a private matter. Also remember that to discipline an inmate for a minor infraction in front of other inmates could lead to a dangerous situation for a correction officer.

7. **(C)** Regarding choice D, handcuffs should never be used to discipline inmates.

8. **(C)** Choices A, B, and D all involve leaving the confines of the prison. Whenever an inmate is taken out of a correctional facility, consider the possibility of escape to be high.

9. **(D)** If the timing of inspections is predictable, then inmates can plan for them. Inspections must come when they are not expected. They must be scheduled on an irregular but frequent basis.

10. **(B)** When an officer is positioned in the rear of a group, he has all the inmates in view and cannot be the victim of a surprise attack. Once again the importance of safety dictates an answer. Note that choice A is too strong. Remember our previous advice about being wary of choices with strong absolute words such as *totally* and *never*.

Group Two

11. **(D)** Shooting a firearm is employing deadly force. The use of deadly force can be justified only to prevent someone from unlawfully using deadly force on another. Regarding choice C, punching someone is not the same as using deadly force.

12. **(B)** It is a mistake to believe that punishment must be severe to be effective. The truth is that it must be certain. In other words, the feeling among inmates should be that if an inmate violates the rules, it is a certainty that punishment will follow.

13. **(A)** A person with an open mind is flexible and not rigid. Such a person considers all the facts, including both sides of a story.

14. **(A)** Remember that the protection of life is more important than anything else and that the protection of many lives takes precedence over the protection of one life.

15. **(B)** While a correction officer must be sound in mind and body, the word *extremely* makes choice A incorrect. The ability to think on one's feet is, however, an essential attribute of a correction officer.

16. **(D)** The firearm is not an offensive weapon. It is for defensive purposes. And, remember, even when used to protect lives, firearms should be used only as a last resort.

17. **(A)** Inventory means listing. To control tools effectively, a correction officer must have a listing of all of the tools presently in use, and their current status, e.g., the whereabouts of the tools. Regarding choice D, even though it represents an effective tool control procedure, it does not explain the statement that good tool control requires an accurate inventory. To be an answer, a statement must be accurate, but it must also respond to the question.

18. **(D)** Clothing can be changed, many people are 5 feet, 10 inches tall, and hair can be cut, but a facial scar is quite difficult to conceal.

19. **(C)** In the mind of the inmate giving the gift or doing the favor, acceptance of a gift or favor by an officer easily obligates an officer to return it. Remember that it is absolutely wrong for a correction officer to play favorites. Fair and equitable treatment is the order of the day.

20. **(C)** To be effective, controls must be specific. They should also be well publicized so that unintentional violations can be avoided.

Group Three

21. **(A)** Fair and consistent treatment of inmates is the hallmark of a professional correction officer. Remember that fair treatment is synonymous with equitable treatment. Regarding choice C, it is wrong because consistent treatment alone is inappropriate if it involves unfair treatment.

22. **(B)** A report loses its value if it is not accurate. Concerning choice C, subjectivity is another word for *bias* and should be viewed as having negative connotations. On the other hand, objectivity connotes fairness and should be viewed as having positive connotations.

23. **(B)** Choice B describes an on-going situation of physical violence between two groups of inmates. It is clearly a situation that would require backup assistance.

24. **(D)** The key to answering this question was the fact that there was a very large group of inmates involved. In this instance, what they were doing was not the issue. Large groups always present more potential problems than small groups from the same prison population.

25. **(C)** The rule "facts before acts" applies in every situation that does not involve an emergency of some type. In an emergency situation, any decision is better than no decision. In all other situations, it is best to find out the facts in the matter before taking action.

26. **(A)** To have the authority to exercise discretion is the same as being able to choose for yourself. Note, however, the use of the word *sometimes* in the rule. It is that word that makes choice A correct and choice D incorrect, since choice D contains the word *always.*

27. **(C)** Maintaining a safe environment is always a paramount consideration, and keeping weapons and potential weapons out of the hands of inmates always has the highest of priorities.

28. **(A)** Study after study has confirmed the fact that a professional appearance increases the possibility of gaining respect and cooperation. Choice C is incorrect because of the use of the word *never.*

29. **(C)** The use of force by correction officers is appropriate only to defend against the use of force, and then it should be used only as a last resort; therefore, choice B is wrong. It is not a proper function of officers to unilaterally punish an inmate so choice D is wrong. To insist on compliance after repeated refusals often aggravates the situation, so choice A is wrong.

30. **(C)** This is yet another way for a test writer to see if you know that, in nonemergency situations, it is important to gather facts before taking action.

Understanding Legal Definitions

8

→ **LEGAL TERMINOLOGY**

→ **LITTLE WORDS WITH BIG MEANINGS**

→ **TWO TYPES OF LEGAL DEFINITION QUESTIONS**

→ **PRACTICE EXERCISES**

This chapter will help you deal with questions designed to determine if you can understand and apply legal definitions. These legal definitions are the kinds that correction officers are called upon to be familiar with while performing their duties. You should note that at times the definitions are exactly as they actually appear in the law concerned, and at times they are not. Sometimes on civil service examinations the definitions have been slightly changed by exam writers to make it easier for them to ask questions about the law. This is important to understand because most legal definitions questions ask the candidate to answer such questions solely on the basis of the information appearing before them in the examination question. Therefore, as a candidate taking an entry-level correction officer examination, you should not rely on anything that you might already know about the law but rather should answer legal definitions questions solely on the basis of the information given.

LEGAL TERMINOLOGY

The following legal terminology list contains terms that are often used in a correctional setting and sometimes used on correction officer exams. They are included here because some correction officer exam writers include these terms in the test questions they write. In addition, some job orientation booklets indicate that legal terminology might be asked on official examinations. This is unusual since entry-level examinations are not supposed to contain questions involving knowledge to be acquired after appointment. Nonetheless, to be safe, you should familiarize yourself with this legal lexicon as part of your test preparation:

- **Acquittal**—The setting free from the charge of an offense by verdict, sentence, or other legal process.
- **Adjourn**—To suspend until a later stated time.
- **Appearance Ticket**—A written notice issued by a public servant requiring a person to appear before a court to answer a charge made against him or her.
- **Arraignment**—The time when a defendant against whom an accusatory instrument has been filed appears before the court for the purpose of having such court acquire and exercise control over said defendant.
- **Bail**—The temporary release of a prisoner in exchange for security given for the prisoner's appearance at a later hearing.
- **Bailiff**—An officer of the court usually serving the needs of the judge.

- **Conviction**—The entry of a plea of guilty or a verdict of guilty to a criminal charge.
- **Defaulted**—Failed to appear at the required time in a legal proceeding.
- **Defendant**—The person charged in a criminal action.
- **Dismiss**—To put out of judicial consideration.
- **Judge**—Any judicial officer who is a member of or constitutes a court.
- **Judge's Charge**—The instructions given to a jury by the court before the jury retires to consider the evidence and render a verdict.
- **Judgment**—A conviction and the sentence imposed.
- **Lien**—A charge upon real or personal property to satisfy some debt or duty; ordinarily arises by operation of law.
- **Magistrate**—An official entrusted with administration of the law who often performs judicial functions.
- **Oath**—An affirmation and every other mode authorized by law of attesting to the truth of what is stated.
- **Parole**—A conditional release of a prisoner serving an unexpired sentence.
- **Peace Officer**—A public servant who has police powers while performing official duties.
- **Plaintiff**—A person who brings a legal action.
- **Plea**—A defendant's answer to a criminal charge, such as "guilty" or "not guilty."
- **Police Officer**—A public servant who has police powers at all times.
- **Probation**—A sentence not involving confinement that imposes certain conditions on the convicted criminal.
- **Prosecutor**—A public servant who represents the people in a criminal action.
- **Respondent**—One who answers in various legal proceedings.
- **Sentence**—The imposition of a punishment upon a conviction.
- **Sergeant at Arms**—An officer of a court of law who preserves order and executes commands.
- **Summons**—The process of a court requiring a defendant to appear before that court for the purpose of arraignment.
- **Surcharge**—An additional tax, cost, or monetary punishment.
- **Trial**—The time from the selection of a jury, which includes all further proceedings, through the rendition of a verdict.
- **Verdict**—The announcement by a jury or the court of its decision concerning the defendant's guilt or innocence.
- **Warrant of Arrest**—A court process directing a police officer to arrest a defendant and to bring him or her before the court for the purpose of arraignment.

Note that when a Legal Definition question gives you a legal definition to interpret, do not let your knowledge of the above definitions affect your answer.

LITTLE WORDS WITH BIG MEANINGS

Two words will help you to understand and successfully master legal definition questions. One is *and*; the other is *or*.

Most laws have more than one required circumstance. This means that often, before someone is considered to have violated such laws, several circumstances must exist. In order to tell people that more than one circumstance is required before a violation of a particular law has occurred, law makers use the word *and*.

The crime of robbery is committed when an armed person enters a store with the intent to remove some property illegally *and* such armed person illegally removes the property from the store.

In this example, more than one circumstance must exist before the crime of robbery can be committed. Here, according to the legal definition supplied, an armed person must enter a store with the intent to illegally remove some property and must illegally remove the property from the store.

The point is that more than one circumstance must exist, or, as law students say, must be satisfied before the crime of robbery can take place. How then can a candidate know that more than one circumstance must exist before the crime of robbery can be committed? The answer is by being sensitive to the use of the word and. In our example of a robbery definition, an armed person must first enter a store with the intent to remove some property illegally *and* then the armed person must illegally remove the property from the store. In this sample definition of robbery, both circumstances must exist; otherwise, no robbery has occurred.

Let's now take the same definition of robbery, change it ever so slightly, and examine what takes place.

The crime of robbery is committed when an armed person enters a store with the intent to remove some property illegally *or* when an armed person illegally removes the property from the store.

Here only one circumstance must occur for a robbery to take place. If the armed person enters a store with the intent to remove some property illegally, then that is enough for a robbery to have been committed. But if an armed person illegally removes property from the store, then that is also enough for a robbery to have been committed. The point here is that either circumstance can be satisfied for the crime of robbery to take place. How then can a candidate know that either circumstance and not both must be satisfied for the crime of robbery to be committed? The answer is by being sensitive to the use of the word or.

Use caution and stay particularly alert when you see the words *and/or* used in legal definitions. You must make sure that you understand how each word can change a legal definition.

TWO TYPES OF LEGAL DEFINITION QUESTIONS

Direct Questioning About a Legal Definition

In this type of legal definition question, you are asked to review one or several legal definitions. Then you are required to select accurate or inaccurate statements about the legal definitions or to indicate which of several situations is the best example of the legal definition. Once again it is important to note that the instructions usually tell you to answer questions based *solely* on the information contained in the legal definitions that are provided. Also note that you are permitted to go back and review the legal definitions while answering the questions.

STRATEGY FOR ANSWERING DIRECT QUESTIONING ABOUT A LEGAL DEFINITION

STRATEGIES

Scan the definitions.

Read the stem.

Carefully read the definitions.

Reread the question.

Answer the question.

1. **QUICKLY SCAN THE LEGAL DEFINITION OR DEFINITIONS WITH YOUR PENCIL.** This means that you should quickly read the legal definition(s). This will help you understand what crimes or situations are being described by the legal definitions. Are you being given the definition of an escape? Of an assault? Or is this the definition of what is considered contraband? While you are scanning, you should identify and underline important parts of the definition(s) and key words such as *and/or.* In addition note numerical amounts that have to do with ages, dollar amounts, weights, and times because they are favorite topics for test writers to ask about. Two examples of how to underline while scanning follow:

   Q1. A person is guilty of <u>assault in the second degree</u> when with <u>intent</u> to cause <u>serious physical injury</u> to <u>another</u> person, <u>he causes such</u> injury <u>to such person</u> <u>or</u> a <u>third person.</u>

   A person is guilty of grand larceny when <u>he steals</u> the <u>property of another</u> <u>and</u> the <u>property</u> costs <u>more than $1000.00.</u>

2. **QUICKLY READ THE STEM**, the part of a multiple-choice question that comes before the choices. This will tell you what part or parts of the legal definitions you will be asked about. Also it is helpful to take a quick look at the choices for the same reason. It is the question and its choices that hold the clues to what the test writer is testing you on. There is not enough time for the test writer to ask you about all parts of a legal definition or definitions if you are given more than one. Therefore, it is a waste of valuable test time for you as the candidate to try to remember all parts of a legal definition. It is much better to focus only on what the test writer might ask you about. And you can do this quickly by reading the stems of the questions and their choices before actually answering legal definitions questions. You do this to get an idea of what parts of the legal definition the test writer intends to test you about.

3. **CAREFULLY AND FULLY READ THE LEGAL DEFINITION OR DEFINITIONS.** As you now carefully read the definitions involved, you should be focusing on those parts of the definitions that the test writer will ask you about. Once again, how will you know what part of the definition(s) the test writer will ask you about? You will have already discovered this by scanning the stems and the choices of the questions. Now when you recognize parts of the definitions that will be important in answering the questions, you should be circling the parts of the definitions that you now feel you will be using in answering the actual questions.

4. **REREAD AND ANSWER THE QUESTIONS.** As you again read the questions along with the choices that are being offered, you should go back to those parts of the definitions that you have circled and underlined to help you select the correct answer to each question.

EXAMPLE OF DIRECT QUESTIONING ABOUT A LEGAL DEFINITION

The crime of menacing occurs when by means of a physical object a person intentionally places another person in fear of imminent physical injury or imminent death.

Q1. Based solely on the preceding information, which of the following is a correct statement concerning the crime of menacing?

(A) Menacing is a felony.
(B) A person who commits menacing must act intentionally.
(C) The use of a physical object is not required to commit menacing.
(D) For the crime of menacing to be committed, someone must receive an injury.

If you followed our strategy for answering a Direct Questioning About a Legal Definition type of question, you should have selected choice B as the answer.

Applying a Narrative to a Legal Definition

In this type of legal definitions question, you as the candidate will be given a legal definition followed by a narrative or brief story that describes actions that someone has taken. This is then followed by the actual question, which asks you to compare the details of the narrative or brief story to the legal definition to determine what, if any, criminal acts have occurred.

STRATEGY FOR ANSWERING APPLYING A NARRATIVE TO A LEGAL DEFINITION

> **STRATEGIES**
>
> Scan the definition.
>
> Scan the narrative.
>
> Scan the question and answer choices.
>
> Reread the definition.
>
> Reread the narrative.
>
> Answer the question.

1. **YOU SHOULD BEGIN AGAIN BY SCANNING THE LEGAL DEFINITION WITH YOUR PENCIL AND QUICKLY READING THE LEGAL DEFINITION.** As you read the definition try to see someone actually doing what is being described. Use your pencil to identify and underline parts of the definition and key words.

2. **SCAN THE NARRATIVE OR BRIEF STORY TO GET AN IDEA OF WHAT KIND OF SITUATION IS BEING DESCRIBED.** You scan the narrative to find out what kind of connection the narrative has to the legal definition, which you have already scanned.

3. **SCAN THE QUESTION BY QUICKLY READING THE QUESTION AND ITS CHOICES.** This is done so that when you reread the definition and the narrative, you will focus on the important parts of them. This points you in the right direction when answering the question.

4. **REREAD THE DEFINITIONS.** This time zero in on the parts that you have already underlined and that you see as important based on your scanning of the narrative and questions.

5. **READ THE NARRATIVE ONE MORE TIME.** You should put yourself in the story and try to actually picture what is being described. You know what the definition is about. You have also discovered what the question will ask about, so now you should be concentrating on that part of the narrative that deals with what you know the question will ask.

6. **ACTUALLY ANSWER THE QUESTION.** Go back and use the parts of the definition and narrative that you have underlined to answer the question. Remember to examine each choice. When you eliminate a choice or select one as the answer, you should be able to support it based on what was given in the legal definition.

Most candidates have trouble with legal definitions questions because they spend too much time scanning. Scanning does not mean studying the material. When you scan, the only thing you should be trying to do is to get a general idea of what the definition, question, and, when applicable, the narrative are about.

EXAMPLE OF APPLYING A NARRATIVE TO A LEGAL DEFINITION

Murder in the First Degree—An inmate of a correctional institution is guilty of murder in the first degree when an inmate who is eighteen (18) or older intentionally causes the death of someone who the inmate knows is a correction officer.

Q2. Joe Young is an inmate of a correctional institution. While serving his sentence in the institution, Young intentionally kills an on duty correction officer who is not in full uniform but is known to Young as a correction officer. Young then escapes but is recaptured before his eighteenth (18th) birthday. In such a situation Young is

(A) guilty of murder in the first degree because he intentionally killed the correction officer.
(B) not guilty of murder in the first degree because the correction officer was not in uniform.
(C) guilty of murder in the first degree because he was an inmate of a correctional institution at the time of the killing.
(D) not guilty of murder in the first degree because he was not yet eighteen (18) years of age when he caused the death of the correction officer.

If you followed our strategy for answering this type of question, you should have selected choice D as the answer.

PRACTICE EXERCISES

Directions: Answer questions 1–20 in the time limits provided. Answers are to be based on the information provided and not on any other knowledge of the law you may possess. The information that is provided may be referred to when answering questions. Also note that, when used, the pronoun he refers to either gender and that, when gender is a specific element of any definition, the appropriate masculine or feminine pronoun will be used such as *he* or *she*.

GROUP ONE

Time Allowed: 20 minutes

Directions: Answer question 1 solely on the basis of the following legal definition.

Reckless endangerment occurs when a person knows what he is about to do creates a large risk of serious physical injury to another person, but the person goes ahead and does it anyway.

1. Which of the following is the best example of reckless endangerment?

 (A) Larry, an inmate, is working alone painting a walkway. While no one is around, he refuses to wear a safety harness, which could prevent him from falling to his death.

 (B) Tom, an off-duty correction officer, while firing back at a robber who is firing at him, strikes a young boy who just turned the corner where the gunfire was taking place.

 (C) Joe, an inmate in the exercise yard, is practicing hand-stands, and slips and falls on a correction officer who Joe had no way of knowing was near him.

 (D) Curly, a correctional employee making repairs, leaves his tools on the edge of a building scaffold after the foreman tells him not to do so because of the danger to passersby four stories below.

Directions: Answer question 2 solely on the basis of the following legal rule.

A correction officer may stop and search an inmate of a correctional institution when the correction officer reasonably believes that the inmate is in possession of contraband or has, is, or is about to violate the rules and regulations of the institution.

2. Correction Officer Brown observes Fred Carter, an inmate of the institution, working in the machine shop. Carter is observed continually looking around as if he is waiting for something to happen. If Correction Officer Brown wishes to legally search Carter, Brown should

 (A) wait until Carter actually commits a crime.
 (B) be absolutely sure that Carter is violating a rule or regulation of the institution.
 (C) obtain the permission of his supervisor.
 (D) reasonably believe that Carter possesses contraband.

Directions: Answer questions 3–10 solely on the basis of the following legal definitions.

Offense—An act that is prohibited by the penal code and for which you may be imprisoned and/or receive a fine. An offense may be either a felony, a misdemeanor, or a violation.

Felony—An offense for which a person is to be imprisoned for more than one year.

Misdemeanor—An offense for which a person may be imprisoned for more than 15 days but not more than 1 year.

Violation—An offense for which a person may be imprisoned for up to and including 15 days.

Crime—An offense that is either a felony or a misdemeanor but not a violation.

Physical Injury—A condition that causes the victim substantial pain or some type of physical impairment.

Serious Physical Injury—A physical injury that brings someone close to death or damages an organ or that will last for a long period of time.

Deadly Weapon—A gun that is loaded and operable and that can cause a serious physical injury; or a gravity knife, dagger, switchblade knife, billy, blackjack, or metal knuckles.

Dangerous Instrument—Anything (including a vehicle) that is capable of causing death or other serious physical injury because of the way it is being used.

3. The least severe punishment is given for a

   (A) felony.
   (B) misdemeanor.
   (C) violation.
   (D) crime. Ⓐ Ⓑ Ⓒ Ⓓ

4. Which of the following is the best example of a deadly weapon?

   (A) a blackjack
   (B) a kitchen knife
   (C) a tractor trailer
   (D) any gun Ⓐ Ⓑ Ⓒ Ⓓ

5. A crime is

   (A) either a violation or a misdemeanor.
   (B) always a misdemeanor.
   (C) always a felony.
   (D) either a felony or a misdemeanor. Ⓐ Ⓑ Ⓒ Ⓓ

6. Based on the preceding legal definitions, felonies, misdemeanors, and violations are

   (A) all crimes.
   (B) each punishable by at least 30 days imprisonment.
   (C) all offenses.
   (D) each punishable by at least 6 months in jail. Ⓐ Ⓑ Ⓒ Ⓓ

7. Concerning the legal definitions of injuries, which of the following statements is inaccurate?

   (A) If a victim suffers an impairment of a physical condition, then a physical injury has occurred.
   (B) If a victim suffers substantial pain, then a physical injury has occurred.
   (C) Every physical injury is also a serious physical injury.
   (D) Every serious physical injury is also a physical injury.   Ⓐ Ⓑ Ⓒ Ⓓ

8. Which of the following statements is most accurate regarding the legal definitions dealing with deadly weapons and dangerous instruments?

   (A) Under certain circumstances a soda bottle could be a deadly weapon.
   (B) Under certain circumstances a vehicle could be a deadly weapon.
   (C) Under certain circumstances a soda bottle could be a dangerous instrument.
   (D) Under certain circumstances anything, except a vehicle, could be a dangerous instrument.   Ⓐ Ⓑ Ⓒ Ⓓ

9. A correction officer discovers several weapons on the person of someone who is attempting to visit an inmate. Which of the weapons found on the visitor is least likely to be considered a deadly weapon?

   (A) metal knuckles
   (B) a blackjack
   (C) a razor that has been hidden in an cigarette pack
   (D) a gravity knife   Ⓐ Ⓑ Ⓒ Ⓓ

10. Several inmates of a correctional institution, aided by outside accomplices, attempt escape from the institution. However, quick action on the part of the correction officers prevents them from being successful. During the escape attempt, Correction Officer May Shore is struck by one of the inmates and suffers a great deal of pain to her back for several hours. A search of one of the inmates involved, Ted Harps, revealed a spoon filed into the shape of a dual-edged knife and a set of metal knuckles. Each inmate involved in the escape attempt is to be charged with a felony in addition to any previous charges for which they have been found guilty. Concerning this situation, which of the following statements is least accurate?

   (A) Correction Officer Shore suffered a physical injury.
   (B) Inmate Ted Harps was in possession of a dangerous instrument.
   (C) Inmate Ted Harps was in possession of a deadly weapon.
   (D) Each inmate involved in the escape attempt will receive an additional imprisonment penalty of at least 5 years.   Ⓐ Ⓑ Ⓒ Ⓓ

GROUP TWO

Time Allowed: 20 minutes

Directions: Answer questions 11–15 solely on the basis of the following legal definitions.

A **detention facility** means any place used for the confinement of a person whom a court has charged or convicted of a criminal offense.

Legal custody means restraint by a public servant as a result of an authorized arrest or a court order.

Contraband means any article that a person in a detention facility is prohibited from having according to a law or rule of the detention facility.

Dangerous contraband means contraband that is capable of endangering the safety of any person in a detention facility or endangering the security of a detention facility.

Escape in the third degree. A person is guilty of escape in the third degree when he escapes from custody. This crime is a misdemeanor.

Escape in the second degree. A person is guilty of escape in the second degree when he escapes from a detention facility or, having been originally arrested for a felony, he escapes from custody. This crime is a felony.

Escape in the first degree. A person is guilty of escape in the first degree when, having been originally arrested for a felony, he escapes from a detention facility. This crime is a felony that carries a more severe penalty than escape in the second degree.

11. Which of the following is the best example of legal custody as it applies to the restraint of criminals?

 (A) A private citizen captures someone who has broken into a home and is now holding the person until the authorities arrive.
 (B) A police officer made an unauthorized arrest and is bringing the person arrested to the station house.
 (C) A correction officer is transporting an inmate to a hospital as a result of a court order.
 (D) A parent holds a youth who has broken a school window until school security personnel arrive on the scene.

12. Which of the following most accurately describes a detention facility?

    (A) A room in a court house where a person is held before he appears before a judge for the first time after being arrested.

    (B) Any police station house.

    (C) Any police car that has a metal screen to separate the officer from persons who have been arrested.

    (D) Any place used to confine a person whom a court has convicted of an offense.

    Ⓐ Ⓑ Ⓒ Ⓓ

13. Which of the following items possessed by inmates in a correctional facility is the best example of dangerous contraband?

    (A) June keeps perfume in her cell.

    (B) Jess keeps food in her cell in violation of the rules of the facility.

    (C) Tom has a set of dice, which he uses to gamble illegally with other inmates.

    (D) Don has a ballpoint pen cartridge, which can be used to open handcuffs.

    Ⓐ Ⓑ Ⓒ Ⓓ

14. Frank was recently charged with a criminal offense by a court and arrested. If Frank now breaks out of a department of corrections' prisoner van used to confine prisoners, then as a result of his actions

    (A) Frank could be charged only with escape in the third degree no matter for what he was originally arrested.

    (B) Frank could be charged with escape in the first degree if he had been originally arrested for a felony.

    (C) Frank could not be charged with escape in the second degree unless he had been originally taken into custody as a result of a court order.

    (D) Frank could be charged only with escape in the second degree regardless of his previous arrest record.

    Ⓐ Ⓑ Ⓒ Ⓓ

15. Which of the following statements is most accurate concerning the crime of escape?

    (A) Escape has three degrees.

    (B) Escape is always a felony.

    (C) Each degree of escape requires escape from a detention facility.

    (D) The most serious charge of escape involves an escape from custody and not a detention facility.

    Ⓐ Ⓑ Ⓒ Ⓓ

Resisting Arrest. A person is guilty of resisting arrest when he intentionally prevents or attempts to prevent a police officer or peace officer from effecting an authorized arrest of himself or another person.

16. Correction Officer Don Flick is assisting in the process of allowing visitors to visit inmates at the facility to which he is assigned. Officer Flick notices that one of the visitors, Frank Mays, is in possession of some marijuana, which Mays is attempting to smuggle into the facility. As Correction Officer Flick is attempting to legally arrest Mays, April Goods, also a visitor and a friend of Mays, attempts to prevent Flick from arresting Mays by grabbing Officer Flick's arm. However, Officer Flick is quite strong and is easily able to subdue Goods and continues to arrest Mays. In this situation

    (A) Goods has committed some offense but not resisting arrest.
    (B) Goods has committed resisting arrest.
    (C) Goods would have committed resisting arrest but only if Goods had been successful in actually preventing the arrest.
    (D) Goods would have committed resisting arrest but only if Officer Mays was attempting to arrest her personally.

17. Correction Officer June Rivers, who is a peace officer, is assigned to the Gotham Correctional Facility. One day while returning to the facility from duty in court, she observes Tom Mixer snatching a handbag from an elderly female. Rivers pursues Mixer and places him under arrest. Frank Keys, a friend of Mixer, happens to be in the area and approaches Officer Rivers and asks her, "What has Mixer done?" As Rivers turns to talk to Keys, Mixer bolts away. Officer Rivers chases Mixer for several blocks and then finally apprehends him. Under these circumstances

    (A) Mixer should be charged with resisting arrest but Keys should not.
    (B) Keys should be charged with resisting arrest but Mixer should not.
    (C) both Mixer and Keys should be charged with resisting arrest.
    (D) neither Mixer nor Keys should be charged with resisting arrest.

    Ⓐ Ⓑ Ⓒ Ⓓ

Benefit—A benefit is any gain or advantage for yourself or for another person you select. A benefit could include, for example, money, or it could be clothing or even a good job for you or someone you select.

Bribe Receiving—A public servant such as a correction officer is guilty of bribe receiving when he asks for, accepts, or agrees to accept any benefit from another person based on an understanding that the public servant's future official actions will be influenced.

Receiving Reward for Official Misconduct—A public servant such as a correction officer is guilty of receiving reward for official misconduct when the public servant asks for, accepts, or agrees to accept any benefit from another person for having violated his duty as a public servant.

Receiving Unlawful Gratuities—A public servant such as a correction officer is guilty of receiving unlawful gratuities when the public servant asks for, accepts, or agrees to accept any benefit from another person for having done his authorized duties knowing that he was not authorized to receive any special or extra compensation for doing these duties.

18. Correction Officer Neil Bailes is assigned to the Palm Way Correctional Institution. While at work one day, Officer Bailes is approached by Don Day, one of the inmates. He tells the officer that he will give Bailes $100 dollars a week if Bailes will look the other way and not interfere with an illegal gambling operation that Day is running using other inmates as his customers. Bailes agrees, but before any actual money passes hands between Bailes and Day, the warden finds out and the plan is interrupted. In this situation Officer Bailes committed

    (A) bribe receiving.
    (B) receiving reward for official misconduct.
    (C) receiving unlawful gratuities.
    (D) no crime since money never passed hands between Bailes and Day.

19. Vivian Bailes is a correction officer assigned to the Whitestone Correctional Facility. Every Sunday when Mrs. Russle comes to visit her son, Officer Bailes is very kind to Mrs. Russle and escorts her to the visiting area, which is part of Officer Bailes's normal duties. To show her appreciation, Mrs. Russle gives Officer Bailes a wristwatch worth $85. Correction Officer Bailes accepts the wristwatch. In this situation Correction Officer Bailes's actions were

(A) appropriate because all Mrs. Russle wanted to do was show her appreciation.
(B) inappropriate because she has committed receiving unlawful gratuities.
(C) appropriate because no money was involved.
(D) inappropriate because she has committed bribe receiving.

20. Jay Wiser is an organized crime member who is serving a sentence in El Perro Correctional Facility where Frank Firmer is assigned as a correction officer. One night, Officer Firmer observes Inmate Wiser beating another inmate for not showing Wiser enough respect. Officer Firmer does nothing and looks the other way. The next day Firmer visits Wiser and informs him of what he observed and tells him he thinks that what he did should be worth $500. Wiser refuses and tells Officer Firmer that he doesn't know what he is talking about. In this situation Officer Firmer

(A) has committed no offense because his request was refused by Wiser.
(B) has committed bribe receiving.
(C) has committed no offense because his official conduct had already been influenced.
(D) has committed receiving reward for official misconduct. Ⓐ Ⓑ Ⓒ Ⓓ

ANSWER KEY

1. **D**	5. **D**	9. **C**	13. **D**	17. **A**
2. **D**	6. **C**	10. **D**	14. **B**	18. **A**
3. **C**	7. **C**	11. **C**	15. **A**	19. **B**
4. **A**	8. **C**	12. **D**	16. **B**	20. **D**

ANSWERS EXPLAINED

Group One

1. **(D)** Choice A is incorrect because the danger of serious physical injury must be toward another. Choices B and C are incorrect because there was no way of knowing that a large risk of serious physical injury to another person was being created. The answer is choice D.

2. **(D)** Nothing in the given information mentions waiting until a crime is committed or obtaining the permission of a supervisor before a search can be conducted. Remember that the directions to this type of question usually require answering the question based solely on the information given. According to that information, a correction officer does not have to be absolutely sure before he can search. Here the level of certainty required is only that he reasonably believes.

3. **(C)** A person can be sentenced to no more than 15 days for a violation.

4. **(A)** A blackjack is the only one of the choices offered that is specifically listed as a deadly weapon. Any gun is not a deadly weapon because it must be loaded and be operable; that is, it must work.

5. **(D)** Crimes can be either a felony or a misdemeanor.

6. **(C)** Violations are not crimes, so choice A is incorrect. However, offenses do include felonies, misdemeanors, and violations.

7. **(C)** Every serious physical injury is in the first instance a physical injury, but many physical injuries never amount to serious physical injuries.

8. **(C)** Only certain specific weapons are legally considered deadly weapons; however, anything including a vehicle, or even a soda bottle, could be a dangerous instrument depending on the way it is being used.

9. **(C)** A razor is not one of the listed deadly weapons. The fact that it is hidden in a pack of cigarettes has no bearing on whether it is a deadly weapon. Remember that, when the instructions tell you to base your answer solely on the information given, that is what you must base your answer on.

10. **(D)** Do not assume that because an escape attempt sounds very serious that a penalty of an additional 5 years of imprisonment must be correct. Remember that your answer must be based solely on the information provided, and in this situation the only information given says that each inmate involved in the escape attempt is to be charged with an additional felony. The sentence for a felony could be as little as a year and a day since the definition merely stated that the sentence would be more than 1 year.

Group Two

11. **(C)** Only a public servant can legally hold someone in legal custody, and when a public servant such as a police officer holds someone in custody as a result of an arrest, the arrest must be authorized.

12. **(D)** For a place to be considered a detention facility, it must act as a place of confinement for a person whom a court has charged or convicted of an offense.

13. **(D)** Dangerous contraband is capable of endangering the safety of any person in a detention facility *or* endangering the security of a detention facility. It's easy to see how important words like *and/or* are.

14. **(B)** According to the definitions and information provided in the stem of the question, in this situation, the correction van described is a detention facility. Thus when Frank escapes from a detention facility he commits escape in the first degree if he was originally arrested for a felony.

15. **(A)** Escape can be a misdemeanor; escape in the third degree merely requires an escape from custody; escape in the first degree requires escape from a detention facility.

16. **(B)** If someone merely tries to prevent the arrest of oneself or another person, that is resisting arrest.

17. **(A)** Only Mixer, by running away, tried to prevent the correction officer from making an authorized arrest.

18. **(A)** For the crime of bribe receiving to take place, all that is required is an agreement that the official conduct of the public servant will be influenced.

19. **(B)** If the public servant accepts a benefit, such as a wristwatch, for performing authorized duties for which no extra or special compensation is allowed, then the public servant commits receiving unlawful gratuities.

20. **(D)** To commit receiving reward for official misconduct, a public servant such as Officer Firmer merely needs to ask for a benefit for having already violated his official duty as a public servant.

Troublesome Question Types

9

→ **ABOUT TROUBLESOME TYPES OF QUESTIONS**
→ **TROUBLESOME TYPES OF QUESTIONS**
→ **HOW TO DEAL WITH TROUBLESOME QUESTION TYPES**
→ **RECOMMENDED THREE STEP STRATEGY**
→ **FIND THE NEXT STEP QUESTIONS**
→ **SPATIAL ORIENTATION QUESTIONS**

ABOUT TROUBLESOME TYPES OF QUESTIONS

Since the publication of the fourth edition of this book, your authors have been monitoring major entrance examinations given throughout the country for correctional titles. We have noted that, although the types of questions outlined in the Fourth Edition have continued to be used on these examinations, there are some variations of the original types of questions that are being used and which seem to give candidates difficulty. This chapter provides a strategy for dealing with such questions.

It is extremely important to note that the Testing Agency in the jurisdiction conducting the exam you will be taking informs the general public about an upcoming corrections officer test via a document that is usually called either a "Job Announcement," a "Preparation Guide," or a "Job Orientation Booklet." When the test involved is professionally developed and administered, this document will contain significant information about the test you will be taking and it is strongly recommended that you obtain and study this document. This information is sometimes found in a link within the Job Announcement under the tab often entitled "Subject Matter." or "Test Content."

TROUBLESOME TYPES OF QUESTIONS

1. **SENTENCE ORDERING QUESTIONS.** In this type of question, the candidate is given a series of randomly numbered sentences, usually five, and then tested to determine if he or she can arrange those sentences in the most logical sequence.

2. **FIND THE NEXT STEP QUESTIONS.** Find the Next Step Questions are already found in Chapter Six of this text where we deal with applying procedures questions. They can also be found in the Diagnostic Test and the Practice Tests. However, they have recently grown in popularity to the extent that we decided to designate them as a separate question type with their own specific answering strategy.

    Find the Next Step Questions start by presenting law enforcement procedures in the strict order in which they must be performed. Candidates are then given a narrative describing procedural steps a corrections officer has already taken and asked to determine the "next step" which must be followed based on the sequence of steps specified in the actual procedure.

3. **SPATIAL ORIENTATION QUESTIONS.** To test spatial orientation, examiners use what we refer to as Traffic Map Questions. Here, you are given a street map which usually contains: an indication of the main compass points, although sometimes only one main point is given, usually the north point; a legend which tells you the location of certain buildings or other places of interest on the map; and a number of named one-way and two-way streets. In the typical traffic map question you are told you are at a certain location and then asked to select from several alternatives the best way to go by vehicle from that location to another location on the map. You are usually directed to obey traffic regulations. Sometimes, however, you are told to go from one location to another without regard to traffic regulations as you might do in an emergency situation.

HOW TO DEAL WITH TROUBLESOME QUESTION TYPES

1. **SENTENCE ORDERING QUESTIONS.** In this question type you are typically given a series of five randomly numbered facts concerning an incident about which you, as a corrections officer, might have to make a report. Your task is to arrange the numbered sentences (facts) in logical order as if you were preparing a written or oral report about the incident. Often all you have to do is arrange the details in chronological (time) sequence. Once in a while there is no clear time order. In that case, the details should be arranged in an order that represents a logical reporting of an incident.

An Example of a Sentence Ordering Question

This is what a typical sentence ordering question looks like. Remember, learn to recognize the various question types because in order to use the right strategy, you must first be able to recognize the various question types on your exam.

EXAMPLE

Q.   Correction Officer Club was home one evening when a burglar broke into his home which resulted in Officer Club physically confronting the burglar. After the confrontation was over, Officer Club called the local police. Police Officer Bardo responded to the scene and wrote a report of the incident. Officer Bardo's report of the incident will contain the following five sentences:

1. When Officer Club attempted to stop the burglar by grabbing him, he was pushed to the floor.
2. The burglar had apparently gained access to the premises by forcing open the third floor bedroom window.
3. Officer Club sustained a head injury in the scuffle and the burglar left the home via the front entrance.
4. Finding nothing in the dresser, the burglar proceeded downstairs to the first floor where he was confronted by Officer Club, who was reading in the library.
5. Once inside he searched the bedroom dresser.

The most logical order for the above sentences to appear in the report is

(A)   5, 4, 1, 2, 3
(B)   2, 5, 4, 1, 3
(C)   2, 4, 5, 3, 1
(D)   3, 2, 1, 5, 4

Note: You will see this question answered in the practice questions below.

RECOMMENDED THREE STEP STRATEGY

There are a few ways to approach the answering of sentence ordering questions, but most of them can be very time consuming. Our recommended three step strategy relies on the fact that the correct order of the sentences must be listed for you as one of the choices. Since this is so, **use the suggested choices as a guide for arriving at the right answer.**

The First Step

Concentrate initially on the suggested first sentences in the ordering arrangement of each choice from A to D. It is usually always easiest to figure out what happened first in an incident. Look at the suggested first sentences in the choices from A to D and eliminate those choices that clearly have inappropriate sentences coming first. Approximately 20 percent of the time, this is all you will have to do. In other words, you will be able to answer the question, not by ordering the entire five sentences, but merely by deciding which sentence comes first. In any case, you will almost always be able to eliminate one or two choices with this first step. Once you have eliminated an answer choice, cease considering that choice any further. Instead, consider only the remaining choices you have not eliminated.

Note that, although we call it a "three step strategy", quite often these sentence ordering questions can be answered by using only the first or second steps. This is what makes it a great time saving strategy.

The Second Step

If you get to this step, that means there is more than one choice with the same correct suggested first sentence. The sentence that come last in a report is also rather easy to determine. Therefore, go through the same process as in Step One to eliminate those remaining choices with obviously wrong last sentences. Approximately 70 percent of the time, after this step you will have arrived at the correct choice and need go no further. Additionally, even if you have not arrived at the correct choice, you have almost always eliminated at least two of the choices.

The Third Step

If you have come to this step, that means that you have two (or more) choices with the same correct suggested first and last sentences. Therefore, for each remaining choice you should now compare the second sentence with the first sentence. Select as your answer the choice that is the one that offers a second sentence that most logically follows the first. After doing this you will almost always have arrived at the answer. Once in a while, however, you will have two choices with the same first, last, and second sentences. When this occurs, to determine the answer, you simply have to compare the relationship between the third and fourth sentences in the remaining choices and select the choice that contains the most logical relationship.

Note that in very rare cases we have seen Sentence Ordering Questions with six suggested sentences. If this occurs, follow the same concept of comparing the first, last, and middle sentences to arrive at the correct answer.

HELPFUL HINT

Learn to take advantage of the words "the" and "a" or "an." They are articles that are used with nouns. However, the first time the noun is mentioned in a report, the article "a" or "an" is used. The next time the same noun is used, the article "the" is used. For example:

CORRECT ORDER
1. A car has been stolen.
2. The car belongs to John.

INCORRECT ORDER
1. The car has been stolen.
2. A car belongs to John.

This hint can help you many times over. However, once in a great while the sentences you are given may sometimes reflect a portion of the middle of a report so this rule does not always apply. Just the same, in the great majority of the time it can be relied on.

An Example of the First Sentence Providing the Answer

EXAMPLE

Q. Correction Officer Al Vittorio is part of an Escaped Prisoner Recapture Task Force when he observes an incident involving a female being held hostage by an estranged lover. Since the female was in immediate danger, Officer Vittorio took immediate action. His report will contain the following five sentences.

1. I saw a male holding a .38 caliber revolver to a woman's head, but he did not see me.
2. I then broke a door down and gained access to the house.
3. As I approached the house on foot, a gunshot rang out, and I heard a scream.
4. A decoy auto brought me as close as possible to the house where a female was being held hostage.
5. I ordered the man to drop his weapon, and he released the woman and was taken into custody.

The most logical order for the above sentences to appear in the report is

(A) 1, 3, 2, 4, 5
(B) 4, 3, 2, 1, 5
(C) 3, 2, 1, 4, 5
(D) 5, 1, 2, 3, 4

Answer: (B) According to the choices, which as mentioned above, you should use to guide you to the correct answer, the following sentences come first in this report:

Choice A—Sentence 1 comes first.
Choice B—Sentence 4 comes first.
Choice C—Sentence 3 comes first.
Choice D—Sentence 5 comes first.

This is one of those questions where all you have to do is to decide which sentence comes first and you arrive at the answer. This is because each of the four choices lists a different first sentence. Choice A says sentence 1 comes first, Choice B says sentence 4 comes first, Choice C says sentence 3 comes first, and Choice D says sentence 5 comes first. Upon reading sentences 1, 3, 4, and 5, it should be obvious to you that sentence 4 starts the actions and logically comes first. Before the action in the other sentences can occur, the officer has to be in the vicinity of the house. Therefore, sentence 4 comes first and the correct answer is Choice B. And, remember, you arrived at the correct answer simply by choosing the first sentence, and not by ordering all five into the correct sequence. In this case you save considerable time and effort.

An Example of the Last Sentence Providing the Answer

In the above example, the first sentence gave you the answer. Now let's look at an example of a question type where the last sentence provides the key to answering the question.

EXAMPLE

Q.   Correction Officer Club was home one evening when a burglar broke into his home which resulted in Officer Club physically confronting the burglar. After the confrontation was over, Officer Club called the police. Police Officer Bardo responded to the scene and wrote a report of the incident. Officer Bardo's report of the incident will contain the following five sentences:

1. When Officer Club attempted to stop the burglar by grabbing him, he was pushed to the floor.
2. A burglar had apparently gained access to the premises by forcing open the third floor bedroom window.
3. Officer Club sustained a head injury in the scuffle and the burglar left the home via the front entrance.
4. Finding nothing in the dresser, the burglar proceeded downstairs to the first floor where he was confronted by Officer Club, who was reading in the library.
5. Once inside, he searched the bedroom dresser.

The most logical order for the above sentences to appear in the report is

(A) 5, 4, 1, 2, 3
(B) 2, 5, 4, 1, 3
(C) 2, 4, 5, 3, 1
(D) 3, 2, 1, 5, 4

Answer: (B) Following our strategy, we can quickly eliminate choices A and D because sentences 5 (choice A) and 3 (choice D) could not logically come first in the report. This leaves us with choices B and C, both of which start with sentence 2, which makes sense because all of the action takes place after the burglar gained access to the premises. Note the use of the article "a" at the start of Sentence 2 to refer to the noun "burglar" for the first time in the report. As previously mentioned, this should have helped you decide that sentence 2 comes first.

The next step (Step Two) we take is to look at the last sentence for the two remaining choices, B and C. If sentence 3 logically occurs last, then choice B is the answer. If sentence 1 occurs last, then the answer is choice C. Please note how easy it is to make this decision. In sentence 3 the burglar left the premises. In sentence 1 the burglar was still in Mr. Club's home. Sentence 3 surely comes last, and the answer has to be choice B.

And, remember that you arrived at the answer without ordering all of the sentences.

An Example of a Question Where the Middle Sentences Provide the Answer

Now let's take a look at a question which requires you to look to the middle sentences to arrive at an answer. Remember, as mentioned above, if you have come to this step, that means that you have two (or more) choices with the same suggested first and last sentences. When this happens you should first check out the relationship between the suggested second sentence and the first sentence in each choice that you have not yet eliminated, and only go to sentences 3 and 4 if it is necessary.

EXAMPLE

Q. Correction Officer Garcia is completing a report about a robbery in the visitor's parking lot at the detention facility where she is assigned. Her report contains the following five sentences.

1. Mr. Aponte gave me a complete description of the robber.
2. Ray Aponte, owner of the Royal Coach Taxi Company, called the correction dispatcher to report he had just been robbed in the visitor's parking lot.
3. I then notified all vehicles on patrol to look for a black male in his early twenties wearing red pants and a blue shirt.
4. I arrived at the scene after being directed by the dispatcher to investigate a robbery.
5. Fifteen minutes later, a man fitting the description was arrested by a correction officer at the main gate.

The most logical order for the above sentences to appear in the memo book is

(A) 2, 1, 4, 3, 5
(B) 2, 4, 3, 1, 5
(C) 2, 4, 1, 3, 5
(D) 2, 4, 1, 5, 3

Answer: (C) All four choices suggest sentence 2 as coming first, so in accordance with Step Two of our Three Step Strategy, you must now look at the last suggested sentence in all four choices. A comparison of these suggested last enables you to eliminate choice D since sentence 3, which describes the robber, cannot occur after sentence 5, which indicates the arrest of the robber. You now have to move on to Step Three of our strategy. A comparison of the relationship between the first and second sentences in choices A, B, and C allows you to eliminate choice A since Officer Garcia has to be on the scene (sentence 4) before Mr. Aponte can give her a description (sentence 1). Since choices B and C both have the same first, second, and last sentences, we must look at the relationship between the third and fourth sentences. If sentence 1 comes before sentence 3, then choice C must be the answer. And since the officer has to have the description (sentence 1) before she can broadcast it (sentence 3), the answer is choice C.

Time Allowed: 10 minutes

> **Directions:** For questions 1–5 read the five sentences presented for each question and select the answer choice that contains the most correct way to organize the sentences into a clear and accurate paragraph.

Question 1.

1. When a defendant in a criminal action has been found guilty, the courts have a number of sentencing options.
2. One of these options is probation which is defined as a sentence not involved confinement that imposes certain conditions on the convicted criminal.
3. It is the most common since over half of convicted felons are given a sentence of probation.
4. Finally, when a person is sentenced to probation, the courts retain the authority to resentence the offender.
5. In fact, the most commonly used sentencing option is probation.

(A) 1-2-5-3-4
(B) 2-5-4-3-1
(C) 3-1-4-5-2
(D) 5-4-2-3-1

Question 2.

1. The counsel may be of the juvenile's own choosing or appointed by the court.
2. Therefore, a correction officer who finds it necessary to arrest a juvenile must give notice of the juvenile's right to counsel.
3. Finally, such notice must be given both verbally and in writing.
4. This notice must be clearly understood by both the juvenile and at least one of the juvenile's parents or legal guardians.
5. The courts have ruled that a juvenile who has been accused of a crime has a right to counsel.

(A) 5-4-2-3-1
(B) 4-3-2-5-1
(C) 5-1-2-4-3
(D) 4-5-1-2-3   Ⓐ Ⓑ Ⓒ Ⓓ

Question 3.

    1. He is shopping in Astoria.

    2. While shopping, he observes two males he believes may be bail jumpers.

    3. Consequently, Officer Ryan arrests the two bail jumpers.

    4. Correction Officer Ryan is off duty.

    5. Officer Ryan knows he is authorized to make off duty arrests of bail jumpers.

    (A)   4-1-2-5-3

    (B)   4-2-5-1-3

    (C)   4-5-1-2-3

    (D)   4-3-2-1-3

Question 4.

    1. When this occurs, the presiding magistrate has the ultimate responsibility for maintaining the dignity of the court.

    2. This is so because the danger of overcrowding in a court building is much greater than outside.

    3. Also, the people in courthouses are most often orderly and calm.

    4. As a general rule, court buildings are not permissible locations for public demonstrations.

    5. However, once in a while, cohesive groups enter the courthouse with the specific purpose of creating disruption.

    (A)   4-3-5-1-2

    (B)   4-2-1-5-3

    (C)   4-2-3-5-1

    (D)   4-1-2-5-3

Question 5.

    1. This special legal authority applies only in places of detention.

    2. Also note, correction officers who are also peace officers are legally entitled to make mistakes when they arrest someone if the arrest is in their performance of duty.

    3. Most correction officers are peace officers.

    4. Those correction officers who are peace officers have special legal authority to make arrests.

    5. Nonetheless, when correction officers do make arrests in the performance of their duty, they may be upon to testify about the arrest at a criminal trial.

    (A)   3-4-1-2-5

    (B)   5-1-2-3-4

    (C)   3-1-4-2-5

    (D)   5-3-4-1-2

ANSWER KEY

1. **A**
2. **C**
3. **A**
4. **C**
5. **A**

ANSWERS EXPLAINED

1. **(A)** You should smile to yourself when you see a question like this one since all of the choices suggest a different first sentence. Upon examination, it is clear that sentence 1 should come first. Therefore, the answer is **Choice A**.

2. **(C)** Choice A and C suggests sentence 5 comes first while Choices B and D suggest sentence 4 comes first. Clearly, sentence 5 comes first so Choices B and D can be eliminated. Choice A suggests sentence 1 comes last while Choice C suggests sentence 3 comes last. The word "finally" in sentence 3 identifies it as the last sentence. The answer is **Choice C**.

3. **(A)** In this question all choices suggest the same first and last sentences. You must, therefore, check the relationship between the first and second sentences. When you do this you should realize that sentence 1 flows best after sentence 4. The answer is **Choice A**.

4. **(C)** All four choice suggest the same first sentence. So, we now look at the last sentences and determine that Choices B and D can easily be eliminated, but it is not that clear that Either Choices A or C can be eliminated. When this occurs, look at the relationship between the first and second sentence. When you do this it becomes clear that the answer is **Choice C**.

5. **(A)** Choices A and C suggest sentence 3 comes first while Choices B and D suggest sentence 5 comes first. Clearly sentence 3 comes first so Choices B and D can be eliminated. Both Choices A and C suggest sentence 5 comes last so we have to look at the relationship between the suggested first and second sentences in Choices A and C. Upon doing this it becomes clear that **Choice A** is the answer.

FIND THE NEXT STEP QUESTIONS

These questions start by presenting a law enforcement multistep procedure as a lead-in to the question. Then, in the stem of the question, you are presented with the narrative of an officer following that procedure up to a certain point. Your job is to determine from the narrative the step in the procedure the officer has just completed and then select from among the choices the next step the officer should take in accordance with the provided procedure.

An Example of a Find the Next Step Question

The following example is a typical Next Step Question. The answer to this question appears in the practice exercises. Learn to recognize the various question types. In order to use the right strategy, you must be able to recognize the various question types on your exam.

Answer the question question below solely on the basis of the following procedure.

When a correction officer is assigned to screening visitors to a detention facility, he or she should, in the following order:

1. Properly identify the visitor.
2. Determine the identity of the inmate to be visited.
3. Check to see if the inmate is allowed visitors.
4. Determine if the inmate wants to see the visitor except if the inmate is under 18 years old.
5. Perform a full-body search of the visitor, and confiscate any contraband found.
6. Send for the inmate.
7. Allow the visitor to have 15 minutes alone with the inmate.
8. After 15 minutes, search the inmate and the visitor.
9. Return the inmate to detention.
10. Allow the visitor to depart.

Q. Officer Tigro is assigned to screening visitors to the Westside Detention Facility where adult inmates are housed in the Peterson Building and where inmates under 18 are housed in the Washington House. At about 1400 hours, a properly identified visitor arrives to visit George Fowler, who is identified to be an inmate in the Washington House. After checking that Inmate Fowler is allowed visitors, what is the next step the officer should take?

(A) Determine if Fowler wants to see the visitor.
(B) Perform a full-body search of the visitor.
(C) Refuse to allow the visitor to visit Fowler.
(D) Send for Fowler.

Note: You will see this question answered in the practice exercises.

KEY POINTS ABOUT FIND THE NEXT STEP QUESTIONS

1. Bear in mind that unlike applying procedures questions found in Chapter Six, Find the Next Step Questions do not involve evaluating an officer's actions. Rather, as the name implies, they simply ask you to determine what to do next.

2. Find the Next Step Questions, like most questions involving applying policy and procedures, at times require the test taker to exercise judgment.

3. Out of sequence steps are often offered as a choice. Therefore, you must pay attention to the exact order in which steps are to be taken.

4. Pay close attention to contingency words in the given procedure that create the possibility that a certain step might not be necessary, such as *except, unless, if,* and *or.* Because of words like these, the next step is often not the next numerical step. It is in this area that the exercising judgment is often required. For example, a certain step in a procedure might be to "handcuff the prisoner if the circumstances warrant." This step, of course, requires you to examine the circumstances in the stem of the question and make a judgment as to whether those circumstances require handcuffing. The practice exercises will clarify this for you if needed.

5. You must not make assumptions when answering a Find the Next Step Question. For example, if a certain step in a procedure is to "record damage to other property, if applicable" and the question does not mention the presence of other property, do not assume there was such damaged property. Skip that step.

6. Be aware that one step in a procedure might require an officer to take more than one action. For example, the next step to be followed might be to "put out the accident flares and the cones." So if the last step taken in the stem of the question was putting out the flags, the next step would be to put out the cones.

STRATEGY FOR FIND THE NEXT STEP QUESTIONS

1. Recognize the question type as a Find the Next Step Question. This is the first step in all answering strategies. You must learn to recognize very quickly the various question types you will encounter on your exam so you can employ the right strategy.

2. Quickly review the sequential steps in the given procedure to determine the situation encountered in the procedure.

3. Compare the steps that the officer in the stem of the question has already taken with the steps required by the given procedure. Accept the fact that the steps the officer has already taken conform to the procedure.

4. Determine the last step taken by the officer in the stem of the question.

5. Use the procedure and the information in the question to determine the next step the officer should take. Remember that the next step the officer should take is not necessarily the next step in the procedure. As previously mentioned, some steps are required only under certain circumstances.

PRACTICE EXERCISE

Time Allowed: 10 minutes

> **Directions:** Answer questions 1 and 2 solely on the basis of the following procedure.

When a correction officer is assigned to screening visitors to a detention facility, he or she should, in the following order:

1. Properly identify the visitor.
2. Determine the identity of the inmate to be visited.
3. Check to see if the inmate is allowed visitors.
4. Determine if the inmate wants to see the visitor except if the inmate is under 18 years old.
5. Perform a full-body search of the visitor, and confiscate any contraband found.
6. Send for the inmate.
7. Allow the visitor to have 15 minutes alone with the inmate.
8. After 15 minutes, search the inmate and the visitor.
9. Return the inmate to detention.
10. Allow the visitor to depart.
11. Make an accurate record of the entire visit.

1. Officer Tigro is assigned to screening visitors to the Westside Detention Facility where adult inmates are housed in the Peterson Building and where inmates under 18 are housed in the Washington House. At about 1400 hours, a properly identified visitor arrives to visit George Fowler, who is identified to be an inmate in the Washington House. After checking that Inmate Fowler is allowed visitors, what is the next step the officer should take?

    (A) Determine if Fowler wants to see the visitor.
    (B) Perform a full-body search of the visitor.
    (C) Refuse to allow the visitor to visit Fowler.
    (D) Send for Fowler.

2. Officer Tigro has allowed the visitor to have 15 minutes alone with George Fowler and has just completed a search of Fowler. What is the next step for the officer to take?

    (A) Return Inmate Fowler to detention.
    (B) Allow the visitor to depart.
    (C) Search the visitor.
    (D) Make an accurate record of the entire visit.

When an on-duty correction officer discovers a visitor who illegally possesses a firearm, he or she should, in the following order:

1. Confiscate the firearm.
2. Properly charge the person.
3. Complete a request to have the firearm examined in the state lab.
4. Bring the firearm to the state forensic lab.
5. After lab examination, bring the firearm to the property clerk.
6. Document all of the above in a report to the commanding officer.

3. While on duty, Correction Officer Garcia discovers an illegally possessed firearm on a visitor to the Smithtown Detention Center. After he confiscates the firearm, what is the next step for Officer Garcia to take?

   (A) Disarm the firearm.
   (B) Properly charge the visitor.
   (C) Notify his supervisor.
   (D) Complete a request to have the firearm examined in the forensic lab.

There is a specific procedure that must be followed to report damage to correction department property other than agency automobiles. The correction officer who discovers the damaged property must make an entry in his or her memo book and report the information to his or her immediate supervisor. The officer then must prepare an original and three copies of a report on official letterhead, which must include the following information in the sequential order indicated below:

1. Date and time of occurrence
2. Place of occurrence
3. Description of department property involved
4. Description of damage to other property, if applicable
5. Owner of other property, if applicable
6. Action taken by discovering officer
7. Identity of witnesses, if applicable
8. Brief description of injury involved, if any
9. Name of supervisor notified, including date and time of notification

4. Correction Officer Ann Zaruba discovers a damaged department portable radio and makes a memo book entry concerning this property. She then immediately reports the information to her immediate supervisor. After properly following procedure, Officer Zaruba then prepares an original and three copies of a report on official letterhead about the incident. After properly following procedure, she describes the department property involved in her report. What is the next required entry she must make in this case?

(A) Describe the damage to other property.
(B) List the name of the owner of the other damaged property.
(C) Indicate what action she took upon discovering the damaged property.
(D) List the identity of witnesses.

5. Which of the following steps in the above procedure must always be included in the official report an officer has to make upon discovering damaged department property?

(A) steps 1, 2, 3, 6, and 9
(B) steps 1, 2, 3, 4, 6, and 8
(C) steps 1, 3, 6, 8, and 9
(D) steps 1, 2, 3, 5, 6, and 9

ANSWER KEY

1. **B**
2. **C**
3. **B**
4. **C**
5. **A**

ANSWERS EXPLAINED

1. **(B)** The stem of the question tells you that inmates under 18 are housed in the Washington House. Since the visitor wants to visit George Fowler, who is an inmate in the Washington House, you must recognize that Fowler is under age 18. Step 3 of the procedure, therefore, does not apply in this case. So the next step in this specific situation, which is to check to see if the inmate is allowed visitors, is not step 4 (choice A) but, instead, is step 5 (choice B). Fowler's age makes it unnecessary to perform step 4. This is why when answering this question type, you must pay attention to contingency words such as "except."

2. **(C)** Once again, a contingency word has dictated the correct answer, as will be the case in almost all find the next step questions. In this case, the contingency word is "and," which appears in step 8. That step requires a search of both the inmate and the visitor. Since only Fowler was already searched, the next step for the officer to take is to search the visitor, choice C. This is why you must be aware that one step in a procedure might require an officer to take more than one action.

3. **(B)** There are no contingency words involved in this question. The next step after a correction officer discovers an illegally possessed firearm on a visitor is to do as stated in choice B, which is the answer. However, note the fact that the question writer tried to distract you by including choices A and C, which describe steps that seem logically correct. Remember that you must read and follow the directions carefully and specifically. Here, you are told in the directions to answer solely on the basis of the given procedure.

4. **(C)** Do not make assumptions when you answer Find the Next Step Questions. The question makes no mention of other property. Therefore, skip over choices A and B. The next entry in the directions is choice C, the action she took upon discovering the damaged property.

5. **(A)** Steps 4, 5, 7, and 8 all contain the contingency word "if." They may or may not be included in the report depending on the circumstances. Steps 1, 2, 3, 6, and 9 must always be included in the report.

SPATIAL ORIENTATION QUESTIONS

Correction officer exams have recently asked questions that test a candidate's ability to determine one's location in relation to the surrounding area when the person is at rest. The candidate must also make such a determination both when a person is moving and after that person has moved. This is sometimes referred to as spatial orientation ability. The question type used to test this ability is also described as traffic map questions.

Traffic map questions require a candidate to find the best route to follow when driving from one location on a map to another location. A correction officer needs this skill when transporting an inmate. For example, a correction officer may be directed to leave a certain correctional facility indicated on a map, drive to a hospital or another location, and then transport an inmate back to the original correctional facility or to a different location indicated on the same map.

KEY POINTS ABOUT SPATIAL ORIENTATION QUESTIONS

1. This question type tests your ability to understand and follow directions as well as recognize your position in relation to changing surroundings.
2. For this question type, a street map is provided, which usually contains:
   a. The main compass points: north, south, east, and west. At times, only one compass point will be indicated. In that case, you must fill in the other three compass points.
   b. A legend that tells you the location of places of interest on the map.
   c. A number of named, one-way and two-way streets along with dead-end streets, cul-de-sacs, and governmental and private-sector buildings.
3. The question will place you in a motor vehicle at one location on the map. You will be directed to respond to another location on the map. You must then select from several listed choices, usually four, the most direct route while obeying traffic regulations. In this question type, that translates to following the traffic flow by not going the wrong way on one-way streets.
4. In rare instances, such as in an emergency situation, the directions will permit you to disobey traffic regulations. You must then simply get to the location indicated by following the shortest route among the given choices.

Strategy For Spatial Orientation Questions

1. Read the directions carefully. Make certain you know exactly what the ground rules are.
2. Look for any legends and codes that accompany the map, and be certain you understand them.
3. Find the compass points on the map. Fill in all four of the compass points if you're given only one of the points. You must know the relationship between north, east, south and west. It is a relationship that never changes while answering the questions that follow. Sometimes, however, you will simply be directed to make left and right turns and to travel a certain number of blocks on named streets without any reference to north, south, east, and west.
4. Using your fingers as a guide, initially take a quick trip through the map while taking notice of one-way streets, two-way streets, dead ends, detours, excavations, any road repairs that may be temporarily closing streets, and both public and private installations and buildings.
5. Remember that most questions will require you to obey all traffic regulations. Note, though, that some questions might state that there is an emergency. It will then tell you to disregard traffic regulations and simply find the shortest route between one point and another.
6. There are no shortcuts to answering this question type; you must consider all choices to eliminate the incorrect choices. However, once you determine that a part of a choice is incorrect, stop considering that choice and move on. While there may be more than one part of a choice that contains an improper direction, you only need one improper direction to eliminate a choice. If you are taking a pencil-and-paper exam, you should

use your pencil to trace lightly on the map the route suggested by each choice. After determining the answer to one question, completely erase all pencil marks on the map before starting on the next question.

7. When you eliminate an answer choice, make note of the part that led you to conclude that the choice is not correct. An example is an answer choice that recommends traveling the wrong way on a one-way street. These notes will expedite any review you have time to make later.

8. Often there is more than one legal route from one point to another among the choices. When this occurs, you must select the most direct route as your answer. This is one more very important reason why you must consider all choices before selecting an answer.

9. Always imagine yourself in the driver's seat of the vehicle as you travel around the map. In this way when you are told to turn right, you will, in fact, be making a right turn from the perspective of the driver referred to by the question. This is especially important when the vehicle is traveling downward on the map in front of you. Remember, a right or a left turn must be made from the perspective of the person driving the vehicle.

10. As a final note, be aware that examiners writing this question type often suggest you travel the wrong way on a one-way street in more than one of the answer choices to the same question. Don't be surprised if you see this.

PRACTICE EXERCISE

Time Allowed: 10 minutes

Directions: Answer questions 1–5 based solely on the following information and map. The flow of traffic is indicated by the arrows. If only one arrow is shown, traffic flows only in the direction indicated by the arrow. If two arrows are shown, traffic flows in both directions. You must follow the flow of traffic when moving from one location to another.

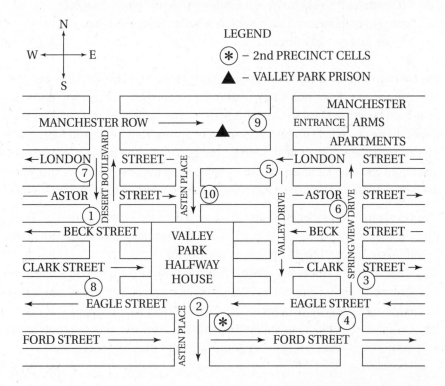

1. You're the driver of a prisoner transportation vehicle at Astor Street and Spring View Drive. The correction dispatcher directs you to meet and assist another prisoner transportation unit that has become disabled and needs assistance. That vehicle is located at the intersection of Beck Street and Desert Boulevard. While obeying traffic regulations and following the flow of traffic, which of the following is the most direct route for you to take?

    (A) Go 1 block north on Spring View Drive, then 3 blocks west on London Street, and then 2 blocks south on Desert Boulevard.
    (B) Go west for 3 blocks on Astor Street and then 1 block south on Desert Boulevard.
    (C) Go south for 1 block on Spring View Drive, and then go 3 blocks west on Beck Street.
    (D) Go south for 3 blocks on Spring View Drive, then 3 blocks west on Eagle Street, and then 2 blocks north on Desert Boulevard.   Ⓐ Ⓑ Ⓒ Ⓓ

2. You are assigned as the warden's driver and are currently at Clark Street and Desert Boulevard. The warden directs you to take him to Clark Street and Spring View Drive to rendezvous with some city officials who have gathered there for a ceremony to honor war veterans who have recently returned from duty overseas. While obeying traffic regulations and following the flow of traffic, which of the following is the most direct route for you to take?

    (A) Go northbound for 2 blocks on Desert Boulevard, then 3 blocks east on Astor Street, and then 2 blocks south on Spring View Drive.
    (B) Go 1 block south on Desert Boulevard, then east for 3 blocks on Eagle Street, and then 1 block north on Spring View Drive.
    (C) Go northbound for 2 blocks on Desert Boulevard, then 2 blocks east on Astor Street, and then 3 blocks south on Valley Drive.
    (D) Go north for 2 blocks on Desert Boulevard, then 2 blocks east on Astor Street, then south for 2 blocks on Valley Drive, and then 1 block east on Clark Street.   Ⓐ Ⓑ Ⓒ Ⓓ

3. You are in a correction vehicle at the entrance to the Manchester Arms Apartments on Manchester Row. A few hours ago, an inmate escaped from the prison and is believed to be held up in the Manchester Arms Apartments. Suddenly, you are directed to respond in your vehicle to the intersection of Spring View Drive and Eagle Street where the inmate has just been seen loitering. Without the use of lights and sirens that might alert the inmate and also while obeying traffic regulations and following the flow of traffic, which of the following is the most direct route for you to take?

    (A) Go south for 5 blocks on Valley Drive, and then for 1 block go east on Eagle Street.
    (B) Go south for 2 blocks on Valley Drive, then east for 1 block on Astor Street, and then south for 3 blocks on Spring View Drive.
    (C) Go south for 5 blocks on Valley Drive, then west for 1 block on Eagle Street, then 1 block south on Asten Place, then 1 block east on Ford Street, and then 1 block north on Spring View Drive.
    (D) Go south for 1 block on Valley Drive, then 2 blocks west on London Street, then 4 blocks south on Desert Boulevard, and then 3 blocks east on Eagle Street.   Ⓐ Ⓑ Ⓒ Ⓓ

4. You are parked on Eagle Street in your official correction vehicle in front of the
    2nd Precinct cells. You must respond immediately to the Valley Park Prison on
    Manchester Row where several inmates have overpowered the driver and assigned
    guard of another correction vehicle. In this instance if you are able to respond
    without following any traffic regulations or the flow of traffic, which of the following
    is the shortest route for you to take?

    (A) Go eastbound on Eagle Street to Spring View Drive, then travel 5 blocks south
         on Spring View Drive, and then turn left onto Manchester Row.
    (B) Go west on Eagle Street to Desert Boulevard, then north for 4 blocks to
         Manchester Row, and then turn right onto Manchester Row.
    (C) Go east for 2 blocks to Spring View Drive, then north for 4 blocks to London
         Street, then west on London Street for 3 blocks to Desert Boulevard, then north
         for 1 block to Manchester Row, and then turn east onto Manchester Row.
    (D) Go east on Eagle Street to Valley Drive, then 5 blocks north on Valley Drive, and
         then turn west onto Manchester Row.   Ⓐ Ⓑ Ⓒ Ⓓ

5. You are in a correctional vehicle located at point 7 on the map. If you travel south for
    1 block, then turn left and travel 2 blocks, then turn south and travel 2 blocks, and
    then turn east and travel 1 block, which point will you be closest to?

    (A) 2
    (B) 3
    (C) 4
    (D) 6   Ⓐ Ⓑ Ⓒ Ⓓ

ANSWER KEY

1. **A**
2. **D**
3. **C**
4. **D**
5. **B**

ANSWERS EXPLAINED

1. **(A)** Choice B is wrong because it requires traveling west on Astor Street, which is a one-way eastbound street. Choices C and D are wrong because they both require going south on Spring View Drive, a one-way northbound street. Choice A designates the correct route.

2. **(D)** Choice A is wrong because you cannot go south on Spring View Drive since it is a one-way northbound street. Note that in the previous question, two answer choices were incorrect because they also recommended going south on Spring View Drive. If you had noted that going south on Spring View Drive is prohibited, you would have answered this question that much faster. Choice B is wrong since Eagle Street is a one-way westbound street. Choice C is wrong since it does not get you to Spring View Drive. Choice D has the correct route.

3. **(C)** Choices A and D require you to go the wrong way on Eagle Street. Choice B requires you to go the wrong way on Spring View Drive. Choice C has the correct route.

4. **(D)** In this question, you are looking for the quickest route without regard for any of the flow of traffic directions. Choice A is wrong because traveling south for 5 blocks on Spring View Drive would take you off the map. Choice B is wrong because Manchester Row is 5 blocks (not 4) away from Eagle Street. Choice C would get you there, but it is not as direct and therefore not as quick as the route suggested by the correct choice, which is choice D.

5. **(B)** Simply trace the route with your pencil. You will wind up on Spring View Drive and Clark Street, which is location 3, making choice B the correct answer. Remember in this question that when you travel south or down the map from point 7 and turn left, you wind up going in an eastbound direction. You must always consider right and left turns from the perspective of the person driving the vehicle. This is especially tricky when following directions that are bringing you in a downward direction on a traffic map.

The Oral Interview

10

- → **TRUTHFULNESS**
- → **UNDERSTANDING THE PROCESS**
- → **THE PANELISTS**
- → **THE QUESTIONS**
- → **SCORING**
- → **A SAMPLE RATING FORM**
- → **ADVANCED PREPARATION**
- → **QUESTIONS AND ANSWERS**
- → **INTERVIEW DAY**

In an earlier chapter you were told that oral interviews are often a part of the process used in selecting correction officers. Therefore, candidates who are seeking employment with a state or local correction agency that uses the oral interview as a formal component of its entry-level selection process must attach great importance to the information presented in this chapter. The information in this chapter is of importance to you even if the agency you are interested in does not have a formal oral interview component. The qualities measured in a formal oral interview are always evaluated. If they are not specifically evaluated in a structured oral interview, then they are evaluated as part of the probationary period. Said another way, correction agencies know the abilities and attitudes they want their officers to have and how they want them to conduct themselves. In many cases they use a formal process to determine this. In other cases they make this determination in other, less formal ways through observation of the candidate during the probationary period. But they always make that determination before granting you full civil service tenure. Your job is to find out the kind of person they want you to be, and then, insofar as possible, to be that person.

THE IMPORTANCE OF TRUTHFULNESS

Sometimes candidates, in their desire to obtain employment as a correction officer, will present false factual information about their background to investigators. This is a grievous and irreversible error. You must understand that the factual information about yourself that you supply will be checked. If a subsequent determination is made that you misrepresented your background in an attempt to deceive, you will be rejected. In many cases, the rejection is made even if the information you misrepresented is not cause for automatic disqualification. The bottom line is this: Be truthful and accurate about your background. You will not be judged solely on any one fact but on the total of all of the facts.

UNDERSTANDING THE PROCESS

Your chances of success on an oral interview are increased if you have a good working knowledge of the oral interview process. Please understand that we cannot describe for you the exact process as it exists in each jurisdiction. There are simply too many variations of the process. But, there are certain concepts that are the same regardless of the exact process, and it is these concepts that you should understand.

Why Are Oral Interviews Needed?

The first thing you should understand is the reason oral interviews are needed. There are certain attitudes and abilities that a correction officer must have that cannot be measured by a written examination. For example, during an oral interview, an evaluator can measure your communication abilities. In addition, your attitude, which means your approach toward law enforcement work, can also be identified during an oral interview. These attitudes and abilities are not measured as effectively on a written test.

Are Oral Interviews Part of All Selection Models?

No! Some jurisdictions do not include an oral component in their selection process. In most cases when they are not used, the reason is economics. Oral interviews are costly; therefore, they are not used in some jurisdictions, especially in larger ones where hundreds—even thousands—of prospective candidates would have to be interviewed. On the other hand, some jurisdictions rely heavily on oral interviews and not on written tests.

Who Are the Panelists on the Oral Board?

To begin with, most oral interviews are usually conducted by a panel of three people, although you might see anywhere from one to five panelists. In almost all cases you can expect to have someone on the board who has a background in the corrections field and someone from the state personnel agency. Quite often an attempt is made to have community representation on the board, and in some instances the services of a psychologist are used. If you are furnished ahead of time with information about the composition of the board, you should display this knowledge during the interview, since it will probably help you score better.

Are the Questions You Are Asked Standardized?

Yes! There are mandatory questions that must be asked of each candidate. Think of the interview as being quite structured. Panelists do not ask different questions of candidates based on how the interview goes; they ask each candidate the same basic questions. These questions must, of course, be legal. For example, questions about marital status, religious affiliation, or political beliefs would be illegal. Questions must also be job related. For this reason, you should secure a copy of the job description (also known as a position description) for the correction officer title in the jurisdiction where you are applying. This description is very often included as part of the job announcement (sometimes called the test announcement) that is published when the correction officer test is scheduled. The job description is important to you with respect to the oral interview because it tells you those typical tasks of a correction officer that are emphasized in the jurisdiction where you are applying. The persons responsible for formulating the questions asked

ILLEGAL QUESTIONS

Marital status

Religious affiliation

Political beliefs

during the oral interview almost always use the job description to develop interview questions. It is, therefore, relatively safe for you to assume that some of the questions during your oral interview will be related to those tasks that are included in the job description.

How Are Oral Interviews Scored?

Each board member is an evaluator and is trained in the scoring process. From the start of the interview until its conclusion you will probably see board members making notes as you speak. They are recording positive or negative comments about you in accordance with the guidelines that were established during their training. Immediately after each interview, the panelists independently arrive at a numerical rating within an agreed upon range, such as from one to ten, with, for example, one being the lowest rating and ten being the highest. Then, after each board member has arrived at a score for the interview, a group discussion is held to guard against the possibility that one of the members missed some very important negative or positive information. Although consensus among the raters is not required, quite often the ratings have to fall within a certain range of each other.

Is the Scoring Process Subjective or Objective?

From the preceding discussion of the scoring process, it is now quite apparent to you that the scoring of oral interviews is a subjective process. Unlike a written multiple-choice examination, there is not just one correct answer to each question asked during an oral interview. Although evaluators are trained to be as objective as possible, to overlook the fact that the process is subjective is a big mistake. Therefore, you should not answer questions from your perspective of what the ideal correction officer should be. Rather, your goal should be to convince the board members that you will be the kind of correction officer they think is ideal. And you can rest assured that they are very traditional in their beliefs. They have a fixed idea of how a correction officer should behave and how a correction officer should present himself/herself. This includes appearance. This is why it is a good idea to find out in advance whatever you can about the composition of the board. This will be discussed in more detail later.

Would It Be Helpful to See a Sample Rating Form?

Yes. Reviewing a sample rating form allows a candidate to see at a glance the attitudes and abilities that are typically measured during an oral interview for the position of correction officer. A sample oral interview rating form is shown below. Remember, however, when you review this form that it is only a sample of what a rating form typically looks like. It is meant only to give you a general idea of what the form used in your jurisdiction might be.

CORRECTION OFFICER CANDIDATE
ORAL INTERVIEW RATING FORM

1. APPEARANCE AND BEARING   SCORE _____
   Has appropriate general appearance,
   poise, confidence, level of enthusiasm.

2. COMMUNICATION SKILLS   SCORE _____
   Speaks with clarity of expression,
   good tone of voice; uses body language;
   has the ability to listen.

3. JUDGMENT   SCORE _____
   Statements are logical, reasonable, and
   supported by facts.

4. UNDERSTANDING OF POSITION   SCORE _____
   Shows a good grasp of the duties
   and responsibilities of a correction officer.

5. ATTITUDE   SCORE _____
   Displays a service attitude and a desire to
   serve society.

6. SELF-ASSURANCE   SCORE _____
   Recognizes the essence of questions and
   responds with confidence.

7. INTERPERSONAL SKILLS   SCORE _____
   Indicates an understanding of the point of
   view of others; shows a level of tolerance
   for those with different values.

8. PERSONAL INTEGRITY   SCORE _____
   Answers show a high level of personal
   integrity.

9. OBJECTIVITY   SCORE _____
   Displays the ability to keep subjective
   feelings out of the decision-making
   process.

10. EMPATHY   SCORE _____
    Displays concern for those victimized by
    events beyond their control.

ADVANCE PREPARATION—THE KEY TO SUCCESS

In those departments that use a formal oral interview as part of their selection process, you will often be told by those conducting the examination that you cannot prepare for it. In some jurisdictions you will be told to simply appear at the appointed time and to be yourself. This is bad advice. The truth is that there are a number of steps you can take ahead of time that can greatly increase your chances of being selected.

1. **STUDY THE JOB ANNOUNCEMENT.** The correction officer job announcement for your jurisdiction usually contains statements concerning the knowledge, skills, and abilities required for the job. It also contains examples of the typical tasks performed by correction officers in that jurisdiction. The oral board members are very often given the job announcement as the source for the questions they develop for the interview. The job announcement, therefore, contains many clues to the type of questions you will be asked and the responses you should give. Study this announcement, anticipate questions from it, and frame tentative answers.

> **PRE-INTERVIEW STRATEGIES**
>
> Study the job announcement.
>
> Review the job applicaiton.
>
> Learn about the particular correction agency.
>
> Be a volunteer.
>
> Enroll in a criminal justice program.
>
> Talk to correction officers.
>
> Practice answering questions.
>
> Work on your personal appearance.
>
> Learn suggested responses.

2. **REVIEW YOUR JOB APPLICATION.** You may very well be asked questions during your interview about information you included on your job application. You should be quite familiar with that information so that you will be able to answer promptly and coherently when asked about it. Also consider the possibility that you could be asked to elaborate on some portion of the job application at the interview. You should, therefore, be prepared to do so.

3. **LEARN ABOUT THE CORRECTION AGENCY INVOLVED.** Make an effort to gain knowledge about the agency you want to join. Know the salary, fringe benefits, retirement policy, and promotional opportunities. Also try to gain an understanding of the current critical issues the department is trying to deal with. As explained below, this information will probably be discussed during the interview if it becomes relevant to the interview, and it should.

4. **TAKE PART IN VOLUNTEER PROGRAMS.** Many correction agencies use civilian volunteers to supplement the work of its paid members. Insofar as possible, you should participate in such a volunteer program.

5. **ENROLL IN A CRIMINAL JUSTICE PROGRAM.** If you have the opportunity, you should enroll in a criminal justice program at an accredited college or university. This would not only help you at the interview, but by doing so you would be taking the first step toward getting promoted after you are appointed.

6. **SPEAK TO SOMEONE WHO SUCCESSFULLY COMPLETED THE PROCESS.** Seek out relatives or friends who are members of the agency involved and discuss the process with them. Unless they are prohibited from doing so, and that is unlikely, they can give you a lot of insight and valuable information about the interview they had. Although the specific questions asked from test to test usually differ, the structure of the interview usually remains fixed. Find out the type of questions that are asked and then prepare yourself to answer them as discussed below.

7. **WORK ON YOUR METHOD OF ANSWERING QUESTIONS.** It is a mistake to believe that having the correct response to a question is the only thing that matters. Of course accuracy is important, but your method of answering questions is also of great importance. Your answer must reflect organized thought. Where appropriate, introduce your answer, give your answer, and then conclude your answer. In other words, employ a format that includes an introduction, a body, and a conclusion. In addition, using the above sample rating form as your guide:

a. Present a good appearance.
b. Show enthusiasm.
c. Speak loudly enough to be heard, but remember to modulate your tone of voice. Candidates who speak in a monotone lose points.
d. Use appropriate hand gestures to make a point. Don't sit with your arms crossed or with your hands folded in front of you.
e. Maintain eye contact with the board members.
f. Display empathy for crime victims and other unfortunate people, such as the homeless.
g. Have tolerance for the lifestyles of others.

8. **PREPARE TO MAKE A GOOD PERSONAL APPEARANCE.** Your personal appearance at your interview is of critical importance. Board members expect you to dress in proper business attire. Any departure from that mode of dress can hurt your chances. Remember, appearance is the first thing noticed about you when you enter the interview room, and first impressions are extremely important. If you do not own appropriate business attire, borrow it, rent it, or buy it, and then be sure to wear it.

9. **LEARN SOME SUGGESTED RESPONSES.** Below are listed some interview responses. Practice working these responses, rephrased in your own words, into the interview. Couple these responses with information gleaned from the job announcement, your job application, your knowledge of the correction agency, your volunteer efforts, your college experience, and your correction officer contacts in answering general questions you might be asked. Then, ask a friend to help you, and, with your friend acting as the interviewer, practice answering a series of general questions. To facilitate this, included below is a list of general questions often asked during the interview of correction officer candidates. We strongly urge that you videotape these practice interviews, listen to your answers, observe your body language, and then strive to improve on the content of your answers as well as your method of delivery.

Suggested Responses

Remember, learn to use only those responses that apply to your situation.

1. I have a relative (or friend) who has been a correction officer for quite a long time and over the years I have discussed his (or her) work a lot with him (or her). These discussions led me to admire the work being done by correction officers and to want to become one myself.
2. My interest led me to do volunteer work with a correction agency, and/or to enroll in a college level criminal justice program, and that experience served to increase my interest in becoming a correction officer.

3. Correction officers should be extremely honest and have ethical standards that are beyond reproach. I feel this way because of the fact that correction officers are entrusted with a great deal of authority, which gives them an even greater responsibility to the society they serve.

4. Correction officers should be mature individuals who possess and employ a great deal of common sense. I feel this way because I realize that it is impossible to have a standard procedure for every situation encountered in correctional facilities.

5. If I am fortunate enough to earn the job of correction officer, I will be guided by the rule that it is never appropriate to be anything except courteous and respectful to those whom I deal with in an official capacity.

6. All my life I have enjoyed helping people. It makes me feel good. And working as a correction officer is certainly a good way to help people.

7. Correction officers should be able to communicate well. This certainly includes listening. A correction officer who doesn't take the time to listen carefully to what others are telling him is not doing his job properly.

8. Correction officers must be extremely tolerant of the viewpoints of others. They must understand that just because a person is different from them, that doesn't mean they are not entitled to fair treatment.

9. If I were forced to choose, I would have to say that having high ethical standards is the most important characteristic a correction officer should possess.

10. In my opinion, a correction officer should use force only as an absolute last resort, when it is absolutely necessary to protect someone. And, even then, the amount of force used should be the minimum necessary to deal with the situation at hand.

11. The protection of life is clearly the most important responsibility of a correction officer, and it takes precedence over all other matters.

12. While I might occasionally drink alcoholic beverages at social functions, I would not, under any circumstances, use illegal drugs. Nor would I attend any function where such drugs were being used.

13. When a correction officer is off duty, he or she must remain mindful of the fact that he or she is still a correction officer. For this reason, a correction officer's off-duty conduct must be beyond reproach.

14. If someone offered me money to violate my oath of office, I would follow the legal mandates of my agency. If the agency's policy was to make an immediate arrest, I would not hesitate to do so.

15. If I had knowledge that another correction officer was involved in a criminal activity, such as taking a bribe, I would follow the policy of my department in that situation. If the policy was to make an immediate arrest, I would not hesitate to do so. In my opinion, it is doubly wrong for a correction officer to commit a crime, and I simply would not tolerate it.

16. There is no question that I am interested in the salary, pension, and other fringe benefits that go with the job of a correction officer, but my interest in being a correction officer involves more than just these material considerations. I want a job that will give me a feeling that I am contributing to the betterment of society, and that, more than anything else, is why I want to be a correction officer.

General Questions

The following is a list of general questions that are often used during oral interviews for the correction officer's job.

1. Tell us about your background and life experience.
2. Why do you want to be a correction officer?
3. Are you prepared to be a correction officer?
4. Why would you make a good correction officer?
5. What is it about the correction officer's job that appeals to you?
6. What kind of person should a correction officer be?
7. What would you do if you were offered a bribe?
8. What would you do if a friend of yours committed a crime and you knew about it?
9. How do you feel about alcohol and drugs?
10. How should a correction officer conduct himself while off duty?

INTERVIEW STRATEGIES

Dress appropriately.

Arrive early.

Be professional.

Know what to expect in the interview room.

Listen.

Be polite, professional, and confident.

Thank the panelists for the interview.

INTERVIEW DAY

You have done everything possible to prepare yourself for your interview. You have learned a lot and it is now the time for all of your effort to pay off. It would be a tragedy if all of that work was wasted because of a foolish mistake you made on the day of your interview. Listed below are recommendations for you to follow to prevent that from happening.

1. **DRESS APPROPRIATELY.** We discussed the importance of appearance, but it is important enough to mention once again. Don't dress to be overly stylish. Dress the way the board members think you should be dressed; that is neatly in proper business attire. Also, be sure to bring notes with you to use as last minute reminders of things you wish to include in your interview room strategy. Review them just before the interview.

2. **PLAN TO ARRIVE EARLY.** You absolutely must arrive on time for your interview. Arriving late, or even at the last minute, is a big mistake. Punctuality is the hallmark of a reliable correction officer. Make sure you know the route you are going to take and how much travel time is involved in the trip to the interview site. If you are using public transportation, make sure you know the bus or train schedules for the day you are being interviewed. Remember that in other than peak rush hour times, there are fewer buses and trains running. If you are traveling by car, make sure you are aware of the traffic patterns involved at the time of your trip, and make sure you know ahead of time where you will park upon arrival. For all of the above reasons, we recommend that you make a practice run one week before the day of your interview at the exact times you will be making the trip on interview day. All of this may seem excessive, but there have been many instances where people lost their opportunity because they did not take the necessary precautions against arriving late for their interview. If it turns out that you have to wait to have your interview, take that time to review your interview room strategy.

3. **MAINTAIN A PROFESSIONAL DEMEANOR FROM START TO FINISH.** Be courteous and dignified from the time you walk into the interview site to the time you leave. Don't make the mistake of believing that you will be judged solely during the actual interview.

Quite often the impression you make upon arrival and while you are waiting for your interview can help you or hurt you. Remember that first impressions are quite often lasting impressions.

4. **GET A START TO THE INTERVIEW.** When you are finally called into the interview room, here is what you can expect. You will see the board members, and they will probably be sitting down. Don't sit down until you are invited to do so. And, be sure to thank whoever extends that invitation to you. You may or may not be introduced to the board members. If you are introduced, listen carefully to their names. If, during the interview, you refer to board members by their names you will enhance your chances. Expect to see a recording device on the desk, as well as notepads and other papers.

5. **LISTEN.** Although this may seem to be basic, it is the most important recommendation for you to follow while you are being interviewed. Don't anticipate the question. Listen attentively and make sure you understand the question before you answer.

6. **BE GUIDED BY THE FOLLOWING SUGGESTIONS:**

    a. Sit up straight.
    b. Maintain eye contact with the board members.
    c. Use simple but complete sentences while responding.
    d. Maintain an appropriate volume of speech.
    e. Inflect your voice when appropriate.
    f. Use hand gestures appropriately to emphasize important points.
    g. Use only words you can pronounce and fully understand.
    h. Be confident but not cocky.
    i. Don't display nervous mannerisms.
    j. Don't fold your arms in front of you.
    k. Don't make jokes.
    l. Don't ever interrupt a board member.
    m. Think for a moment before responding.
    n. Don't be overly repetitious.

7. **THANK EVERYONE PRESENT AT THE END OF THE INTERVIEW.**

A FINAL WORD

This chapter has given you an overview of what to expect in a typical oral interview for the correction officer position. We have explained concepts to incorporate into a strategy for you to follow to achieve your optimal score. But you must remain flexible on the day of the interview. Apply those concepts that are appropriate to your interview as it unfolds. Don't get flustered if the interview involves a format you are not expecting. Stay calm. Your attitude should be one that reflects an empathetic approach toward those who, whether by choice or by circumstance, now require care, custody, and control as inmates of a correctional institution. Regardless of the format, if you come across as possessing the attributes discussed in this chapter, you should do well. Good luck.

Test Yourself

Practice Test 1

When you took the Diagnostic Test you took the first of six tests we have provided for you. This is your first practice test. Four more practice tests follow.

Be sure to develop and use a time management plan for each test and to take each test in one sitting. This test, Practice Test 1, contains 115 questions with a 4 hour time limit. The remainder of the Practice Tests each contain 100 questions to be answered in 3½ hours.

Remember, It is imperative that you become accustomed to concentrating for the length of time required to complete an entire test. Be sure to review the test-taking strategy outlined in the Introduction before taking this test, and use the strategy when working on the exam, and then record your answers on the following Answer Sheet.

ANSWER SHEET
Practice Test 1

Follow the instructions given in the test. Mark only your answers in the circles below.

WARNING: Be sure that the circle you fill is in the same row as the question you are answering. Use a No. 2 pencil (soft pencil).

BE SURE YOUR PENCIL MARKS ARE HEAVY AND BLACK. ERASE COMPLETELY ANY ANSWER YOU WISH TO CHANGE.

DO NOT make stray pencil dots, dashes, or marks.

1. Ⓐ Ⓑ Ⓒ Ⓓ	30. Ⓐ Ⓑ Ⓒ Ⓓ	59. Ⓐ Ⓑ Ⓒ Ⓓ	88. Ⓐ Ⓑ Ⓒ Ⓓ
2. Ⓐ Ⓑ Ⓒ Ⓓ	31. Ⓐ Ⓑ Ⓒ Ⓓ	60. Ⓐ Ⓑ Ⓒ Ⓓ	39. Ⓐ Ⓑ Ⓒ Ⓓ
3. Ⓐ Ⓑ Ⓒ Ⓓ	32. Ⓐ Ⓑ Ⓒ Ⓓ	61. Ⓐ Ⓑ Ⓒ Ⓓ	90. Ⓐ Ⓑ Ⓒ Ⓓ
4. Ⓐ Ⓑ Ⓒ Ⓓ	33. Ⓐ Ⓑ Ⓒ Ⓓ	62. Ⓐ Ⓑ Ⓒ Ⓓ	91. Ⓐ Ⓑ Ⓒ Ⓓ
5. Ⓐ Ⓑ Ⓒ Ⓓ	34. Ⓐ Ⓑ Ⓒ Ⓓ	63. Ⓐ Ⓑ Ⓒ Ⓓ	92. Ⓐ Ⓑ Ⓒ Ⓓ
6. Ⓐ Ⓑ Ⓒ Ⓓ	35. Ⓐ Ⓑ Ⓒ Ⓓ	64. Ⓐ Ⓑ Ⓒ Ⓓ	93. Ⓐ Ⓑ Ⓒ Ⓓ
7. Ⓐ Ⓑ Ⓒ Ⓓ	36. Ⓐ Ⓑ Ⓒ Ⓓ	65. Ⓐ Ⓑ Ⓒ Ⓓ	94. Ⓐ Ⓑ Ⓒ Ⓓ
8. Ⓐ Ⓑ Ⓒ Ⓓ	37. Ⓐ Ⓑ Ⓒ Ⓓ	66. Ⓐ Ⓑ Ⓒ Ⓓ	95. Ⓐ Ⓑ Ⓒ Ⓓ
9. Ⓐ Ⓑ Ⓒ Ⓓ	38. Ⓐ Ⓑ Ⓒ Ⓓ	67. Ⓐ Ⓑ Ⓒ Ⓓ	96. Ⓐ Ⓑ Ⓒ Ⓓ
10. Ⓐ Ⓑ Ⓒ Ⓓ	39. Ⓐ Ⓑ Ⓒ Ⓓ	68. Ⓐ Ⓑ Ⓒ Ⓓ	97. Ⓐ Ⓑ Ⓒ Ⓓ
11. Ⓐ Ⓑ Ⓒ Ⓓ	40. Ⓐ Ⓑ Ⓒ Ⓓ	69. Ⓐ Ⓑ Ⓒ Ⓓ	98. Ⓐ Ⓑ Ⓒ Ⓓ
12. Ⓐ Ⓑ Ⓒ Ⓓ	41. Ⓐ Ⓑ Ⓒ Ⓓ	70. Ⓐ Ⓑ Ⓒ Ⓓ	99. Ⓐ Ⓑ Ⓒ Ⓓ
13. Ⓐ Ⓑ Ⓒ Ⓓ	42. Ⓐ Ⓑ Ⓒ Ⓓ	71. Ⓐ Ⓑ Ⓒ Ⓓ	100. Ⓐ Ⓑ Ⓒ Ⓓ
14. Ⓐ Ⓑ Ⓒ Ⓓ	43. Ⓐ Ⓑ Ⓒ Ⓓ	72. Ⓐ Ⓑ Ⓒ Ⓓ	101. Ⓐ Ⓑ Ⓒ Ⓓ
15. Ⓐ Ⓑ Ⓒ Ⓓ	44. Ⓐ Ⓑ Ⓒ Ⓓ	73. Ⓐ Ⓑ Ⓒ Ⓓ	102. Ⓐ Ⓑ Ⓒ Ⓓ
16. Ⓐ Ⓑ Ⓒ Ⓓ	45. Ⓐ Ⓑ Ⓒ Ⓓ	74. Ⓐ Ⓑ Ⓒ Ⓓ	103. Ⓐ Ⓑ Ⓒ Ⓓ
17. Ⓐ Ⓑ Ⓒ Ⓓ	46. Ⓐ Ⓑ Ⓒ Ⓓ	75. Ⓐ Ⓑ Ⓒ Ⓓ	104. Ⓐ Ⓑ Ⓒ Ⓓ
18. Ⓐ Ⓑ Ⓒ Ⓓ	47. Ⓐ Ⓑ Ⓒ Ⓓ	76. Ⓐ Ⓑ Ⓒ Ⓓ	105. Ⓐ Ⓑ Ⓒ Ⓓ
19. Ⓐ Ⓑ Ⓒ Ⓓ	48. Ⓐ Ⓑ Ⓒ Ⓓ	77. Ⓐ Ⓑ Ⓒ Ⓓ	106. Ⓐ Ⓑ Ⓒ Ⓓ
20. Ⓐ Ⓑ Ⓒ Ⓓ	49. Ⓐ Ⓑ Ⓒ Ⓓ	78. Ⓐ Ⓑ Ⓒ Ⓓ	107. Ⓐ Ⓑ Ⓒ Ⓓ
21. Ⓐ Ⓑ Ⓒ Ⓓ	50. Ⓐ Ⓑ Ⓒ Ⓓ	79. Ⓐ Ⓑ Ⓒ Ⓓ	108. Ⓐ Ⓑ Ⓒ Ⓓ
22. Ⓐ Ⓑ Ⓒ Ⓓ	51. Ⓐ Ⓑ Ⓒ Ⓓ	80. Ⓐ Ⓑ Ⓒ Ⓓ	109. Ⓐ Ⓑ Ⓒ Ⓓ
23. Ⓐ Ⓑ Ⓒ Ⓓ	52. Ⓐ Ⓑ Ⓒ Ⓓ	81. Ⓐ Ⓑ Ⓒ Ⓓ	110. Ⓐ Ⓑ Ⓒ Ⓓ
24. Ⓐ Ⓑ Ⓒ Ⓓ	53. Ⓐ Ⓑ Ⓒ Ⓓ	82. Ⓐ Ⓑ Ⓒ Ⓓ	111. Ⓐ Ⓑ Ⓒ Ⓓ
25. Ⓐ Ⓑ Ⓒ Ⓓ	54. Ⓐ Ⓑ Ⓒ Ⓓ	83. Ⓐ Ⓑ Ⓒ Ⓓ	112. Ⓐ Ⓑ Ⓒ Ⓓ
26. Ⓐ Ⓑ Ⓒ Ⓓ	55. Ⓐ Ⓑ Ⓒ Ⓓ	84. Ⓐ Ⓑ Ⓒ Ⓓ	113. Ⓐ Ⓑ Ⓒ Ⓓ
27. Ⓐ Ⓑ Ⓒ Ⓓ	56. Ⓐ Ⓑ Ⓒ Ⓓ	85. Ⓐ Ⓑ Ⓒ Ⓓ	114. Ⓐ Ⓑ Ⓒ Ⓓ
28. Ⓐ Ⓑ Ⓒ Ⓓ	57. Ⓐ Ⓑ Ⓒ Ⓓ	86. Ⓐ Ⓑ Ⓒ Ⓓ	115. Ⓐ Ⓑ Ⓒ Ⓓ
29. Ⓐ Ⓑ Ⓒ Ⓓ	58. Ⓐ Ⓑ Ⓒ Ⓓ	87. Ⓐ Ⓑ Ⓒ Ⓓ	

THE TEST

Time: 4 hours
115 questions

MEMORY STORY—10-MINUTE TIME LIMIT

Correction Officer Green, shield 1256, has just learned that four new inmates are being assigned to the cell block under his supervision. He receives the following information about the new inmates.

Inmate Number 1, Bill Smith, Number 12789, is a white male, age 46. He is an accountant by profession. He was convicted of embezzlement and given a 5-year prison term. This will be his first time in prison. According to his probation report, he is a nonviolent person, and it is not anticipated that he will create any special problems for Officer Green. His only apparent vice is that he is a chronic gambler. In fact, it was his gambling debts that caused him to engage in embezzlement. Inmate Smith is married with three children.

Inmate Number 2, Peter Block, Number 21654, is a white male, age 26. He is a skilled auto mechanic. His criminal specialty is picking pockets. He was convicted of larceny and given a 3-year term of imprisonment. This will be his second stay in prison having previously served a 2-year term for larceny. Although his special skills as a mechanic make it easy for him to find employment, his salary as a mechanic is not enough to sustain his chronic drug use problem. According to his records, he was a model prisoner during his first prison term and developed a reputation as a peacemaker. He is single with no known relatives.

Inmate Number 3, Don Hurte, Number 87543, is a white male, age 36. He has no special skills and has never held a legitimate job. He has lived a life of crime and has served three previous prison terms. His present conviction is for armed robbery, and his sentence is for 10 years. He is a very violent person, and during his last stay in prison he created many special problems. He is married with eight children.

Inmate Number 4, Frank Wood, Number 33555, is a black male, age 26. He is a union carpenter, but he is also a con man. He specializes in swindling elderly people out of their life savings. Because of his three previous convictions and short prison terms, the sentencing judge for his latest conviction threw the book at him. He was given 10 years. He is a passive person who deplores violence. He is married with one child.

DO NOT PROCEED UNTIL 10 MINUTES HAVE PASSED.

1. Bill Smith is

   (A) an accountant.
   (B) an auto mechanic.
   (C) a bank teller.
   (D) a taxi driver.

2. Of the four inmates, the one who has violent tendencies is

   (A) Bill Smith.
   (B) Peter Block.
   (C) Don Hurte.
   (D) Frank Wood.

3. Peter Block is

   (A) an automobile mechanic.
   (B) an accountant.
   (C) unskilled.
   (D) a carpenter.

4. Of the following inmates, which one is a black male?

   (A) Bill Smith
   (B) Peter Block
   (C) Don Hurte
   (D) Frank Wood

5. Of the following inmates, which one is not married?

   (A) Bill Smith
   (B) Peter Block
   (C) Don Hurte
   (D) Frank Wood

6. Frank Wood is

   (A) an automobile mechanic.
   (B) a carpenter.
   (C) an accountant.
   (D) a lawyer.

7. The inmate who will be serving his first prison term is

    (A) Bill Smith.
    (B) Peter Block.
    (C) Don Hurte.
    (D) Frank Wood.

8. The inmate who swindles elderly people is

    (A) Bill Smith.
    (B) Peter Block.
    (C) Don Hurte.
    (D) Frank Wood.

Directions: Answer questions 9–11 solely on the basis of the following passage.

The policy of the state correction department requires correction officers who are going to arrest any inmate for a criminal act that occurs in any state correction facility to first notify the warden of the facility where the criminal act occurred of their intention to make such an arrest. If the warden is not available, the notification must be made to the tour commander on duty at the time. When, in the opinion of the warden or the tour commander, the arrest is not appropriate, no arrest shall be made. In such cases, the correction officer involved shall be notified, in writing, of the reason why the arrest is not appropriate. This written notification must be made within 24 hours of the officer's initial notification of his/her intent to make the arrest. Correction officers can appeal a decision that prohibits them from making an arrest to the department's grievance section. Such appeals must be made in writing.

9. A correction officer of the state correction department who is going to arrest an inmate for a criminal act must first notify the warden or an on-duty tour commander

    (A) in all cases.
    (B) only if the criminal act occurred in a state correction facility.
    (C) only if the arrest is for a felony.
    (D) only if the arresting officer is off duty.

10. When a warden or a tour commander decides an arrest of an inmate is not appropriate

    (A) the officer can still make the arrest.
    (B) the officer must receive a written notice.
    (C) the decision cannot be appealed.
    (D) the officer must be disciplined.

11. An officer can appeal a decision that stops him from making an arrest, but the appeal must be made

    (A) to the courts.
    (B) to the department's grievance section.
    (C) to the warden.
    (D) to the officer's tour commander.

Directions: Answer questions 12–14 solely on the basis of the following information.

Correction officers constantly receive requests from inmates. Some of these requests will be legitimate and others will not be. When a request is legitimate, the worst thing an officer can do is to ignore it. However, before an officer responds to a legitimate request, he should always consider all the available facts. One fact that must always be considered is the rules or regulations of the institution. An officer must never grant an inmate a request that amounts to a violation of such rules and regulations. A request that must never be ignored is one that involves a possible health problem. When an officer has to refuse an inmate's request, it is essential that the officer explain the reason for the refusal to the inmate. Explaining the reason for refusals is the best way to minimize future grievances.

12. An officer should respond to a legitimate request

    (A) immediately.
    (B) only after all the available facts have been considered.
    (C) only if the request involves an inmate's health.
    (D) only after checking with a supervisor.

13. A request to go to the infirmary, which is made by an inmate who is complaining of a health problem,

    (A) should always be granted.
    (B) should always be referred to a doctor.
    (C) should never be ignored.
    (D) should be reduced to writing.

14. The best way to minimize future grievances is for an officer to

    (A) grant all legitimate requests.
    (B) explain why requests are refused.
    (C) respond to all requests.
    (D) gather all available facts.

Most crimes fall into one of two categories, felonies or misdemeanors. Felonies are more serious than misdemeanors. They are considered serious enough to deserve severe punishment or even death. At one time the distinction between felonies and misdemeanors was based on the fact that all felonies were capital offenses punishable by death. The present day distinction between a felony and misdemeanor in the United States is usually based on the length of the sentence imposed. Felony convictions require a sentence of more than one year in prison. Misdemeanors, however account for a great majority of arrests made. There are almost three million misdemeanor arrests made each year. A misdemeanor conviction involves a sentence of 1 year or less. Convictions for either felonies or misdemeanors can result in the assessment of a fine.

15. Misdemeanors are

(A) less serious than felonies.
(B) punishable by more than 1 year in prison.
(C) sometimes punishable by death.
(D) capital offenses.

16. In the United States the difference between felonies and misdemeanors is usually based

(A) on the length of the sentence imposed.
(B) on the location where confinement takes place.
(C) on the intent of the criminal.
(D) on the amount of fine that can be imposed.

17. Which of the following is the most accurate statement concerning fines?

(A) They may be imposed only for misdemeanor convictions.
(B) They may be imposed only for felony convictions.
(C) They may be imposed for both felony and misdemeanor convictions.
(D) They may not be imposed for felony convictions.

Directions: Answer questions 18–20 based solely on the information contained in the following passage.

The criminal justice system is comprised of four separate components—police, prosecutor, courts, and corrections. Each of these four components has its own specific tasks. A major problem for the overall system is that each of the four components acts independently of one another. This is so despite the fact that what happens in one component definitely impacts on what happens in the other three. For example, an increase in arrest activity by the police always results in an increased workload for the rest of the system. And, if corrections does not do its job properly, the police become overloaded with repeat offenders. The problem is made worse by the fact that the four components of the system compete with one another for funding. By far, the component that receives the most funding is the police, and the most underfunded component is corrections. This is a difficult fact to understand because it is corrections that has the most complex problems. Clearly, however, the most powerful component is the courts. The police, the prosecutor, and corrections are all responsible to and supervised by the courts.

18. The component of the criminal justice system that receives the most money to operate is the

   (A) police.
   (B) prosecutors.
   (C) courts.
   (D) corrections.

19. The courts

   (A) have the most complex problems.
   (B) receive less money than the other three components.
   (C) exercise authority over the other three components.
   (D) have fewer problems than the other three components.

20. A major problem of the criminal justice system is that

   (A) there are insufficient funds available.
   (B) there are many complex problems to solve.
   (C) the amount of crime is increasing drastically.
   (D) there is a lack of coordinated action.

Correction officers are many times required to punish inmates. It is important, therefore, that they understand the guidelines for administering effective punishment. It must be understood that punishing an inmate does not guarantee improved future conduct. To be effective, punishment for an infraction of the rules must be certain. Certainty of punishment is unquestionably the greatest deterrence to future misbehavior. However, punishment must not only be certain, but it must also be swiftly administered. Delay in the punishment process is never desirable. The most difficult concept for correction officers to understand is that severity of punishment is not an important consideration. In fact, overly severe punishments create more problems than they solve. On the other hand, punishments that are excessively lenient can also cause problems. The rule that must be followed is that the amount of punishment should be that which is needed to prevent future misbehavior. Finally, it should be remembered that punishment is actually a form of training for all inmates.

21. Prevention of future misbehavior depends mostly on

    (A) the severity of punishment.
    (B) the swiftness of punishment.
    (C) the certainty of punishment.
    (D) the fairness of punishment.

22. Severity of punishment is

    (A) an effective deterrent.
    (B) an unimportant consideration.
    (C) very important.
    (D) never creates problems.

23. Lenient punishments

    (A) are always desirable.
    (B) sometimes cause problems.
    (C) create more problems than they solve.
    (D) are sometimes necessary.

When a defendant in a criminal action has been found guilty, the courts have a number of sentencing options. The most commonly used sentencing option is probation. Over half of convicted felons are given a sentence of probation. Probation is defined as a sentence not involving confinement that imposes certain conditions on the convicted criminal. When a person is sentenced to probation, the courts retain the authority to resentence the offender if these certain conditions are violated. Probation has many advantages for offenders. It allows them to work, keep their families together, and avoid the stigma of going to prison. It must be remembered, however, that people on probation are not completely free to do as they choose. They remain under the supervision of a probation officer for their entire probation period. While probation has many critics and people on probation often create serious crime problems, it is indispensable. Society could not afford the financial cost of sending all convicted persons to prison.

24. Probation is

    (A) the most frequently used sentencing option.
    (B) not an effective way to rehabilitate repeat offenders.
    (C) very expensive.
    (D) unfair to convicted felons.

25. People on probation

    (A) must spend some time in confinement.
    (B) find it difficult to keep their families together.
    (C) sometimes create serious crime problems.
    (D) are completely free to do as they choose.

26. Probation is a necessary sentencing option because it

    (A) allows offenders to work.
    (B) reduces the level of crime.
    (C) usually rehabilitates the offender.
    (D) is not as expensive as incarceration.

The following guidelines for key control must be adhered to in order to maintain effective control and custody of inmates:

1. Inmates should never have keys for any reason. A thorough investigation must be made whenever an inmate is found to be in the possession of a key of any kind.

2. Keys should never be left in any lock in the cell block area.

3. Correction officers should never carry personal keys while they are working.

4. Correction officers should keep the work keys they are carrying on their person, but they must be kept out of the sight of inmates. They should be carrying only those keys that are necessary for them to perform their required duties.

5. Correction officers assigned to the key room must know the location of all work keys.

6. A separate key log should be maintained for every cell block in the facility. The responsibility for maintaining that log must be fixed with one officer on each tour.

27. When an inmate is found to have a key,

(A) the inmate must be disciplined.
(B) it should be taken away only if the possession of the key is not authorized.
(C) an investigation must be conducted.
(D) an investigation is sometimes required.

28. A prison facility with 16 cell blocks should have

(A) one master key log.
(B) 4 key logs.
(C) 8 key logs.
(D) 16 key logs.

29. Correction officers should never

(A) carry personal keys.
(B) carry work keys on their person.
(C) leave a key in a lock in the cell block area.
(D) write in the key log.

Directions: The paragraph below contains questions 30–32 in the form of three numbered blanks. Immediately following the paragraph are lists of four word choices that correspond to these numbered blanks. Select the word choice that would MOST appropriately fit the numbered blank in each question. Base your answers solely on the information contained in the paragraph.

During his tour of duty, Correction Officer Green was called to the scene of an injured visitor because he was the only correction officer on duty in that area of the jail. The visitor, Mr. Tom Roe, had slipped on some water that was leaking from a public water fountain. Upon arrival at the scene, _____(Q 30)_____ called his supervisor, Sergeant Carter, and requested that an ambulance respond to the jail house to examine the injured Mr. Roe. An ambulance responded from Bayside Hospital with Emergency Medical Technician Bailes. _____(Q 31)_____, who was injured, was taken to the hospital for treatment of a dislocated shoulder. Doctor Smith treated Mr. Roe, who was _____(Q 32)_____ later in the day and went home.

30. (A) Smith
    (B) Carter
    (C) Green
    (D) Someone

31. (A) Green
    (B) Bailes
    (C) Roe
    (D) Smith

32. (A) hospitalized
    (B) released
    (C) transported
    (D) examined

Directions: Answer questions 33–36 based solely on the following information.

INFRACTIONS BY INMATES CONFINED IN THE BELL CORRECTIONAL FACILITY FOR WOMEN

Infraction	Last Year	This Year
Petty Thefts	52	39
Disorderly Conduct	86	100
Possession of Narcotics	38	26
Assaults (Nonsexual)	32	48
Sexual Assaults	16	12
Possession of Weapons	69	46
Unauthorized Uniforms	75	90
Refusal of Work Assignments	7	3

33. Which of the following represents the greatest percentage increase of infractions when comparing this year to last year?

    (A) Petty Thefts
    (B) Disorderly Conduct
    (C) Assaults (Nonsexual)
    (D) Unauthorized Uniforms

34. Which of the following represents the greatest percentage decrease of infractions when comparing this year to last year?

    (A) Possession of Narcotics
    (B) Sexual Assaults
    (C) Possession of Weapons
    (D) Refusal of Work Assignments

35. If all the infractions were added up and a comparison were made between this year and last year, it would be most correct to state that

    (A) there has been a percentage increase of 2.9%.
    (B) there has been a percentage decrease of 3.02%.
    (C) there has been a percentage decrease of 2.9%.
    (D) there has been a percentage increase of 3.02%.

36. Examining the infractions that occurred this year and those of last year, which of the following infractions occurred most frequently?

    (A) Petty Thefts
    (B) Assaults (Nonsexual)
    (C) Possession of Weapons
    (D) Unauthorized Uniforms

Directions: In each of questions 37–40, you will be given four choices. Each of the choices, A, B, and C, contains a written statement. You are to evaluate the statement in each choice and select the statement that is most accurately and clearly written. If all or none of the three written statements is accurately and clearly written, you are to select choice D.

---

37. According to the directions, evaluate the following statements.

    (A) The escape was not planned well.
    (B) Please except my apology for not following the plan.
    (C) Among the two of them, they could not come up with a plan.
    (D) All or none of the choices are accurate.

38. According to the directions, evaluate the following statements.

    (A) Whose afraid of the warden?
    (B) Having entered her car, the windows were quickly rolled up.
    (C) I could not hear the warden good from the last row.
    (D) All or none of the choices are accurate.

39. According to the directions, evaluate the following statements.

    (A) The captain had a wonderful award for Officer Walls and myself.
    (B) The inmate whom you know committed the infraction was punished.
    (C) This is the file which was used by the inmate.
    (D) All or none of the choices are accurate.

40. According to the directions, evaluate the following statements.

    (A) You can be stronger than him.
    (B) I am as happy in my job as her.
    (C) You're talking nonsense.
    (D) All or none of the choices are accurate.

(FRONT)
WORK ACTIVITIES RECORD
CELL BLOCK D

Week of March 12–18

INMATE	SUN	MON	TUES	WED	THUR	FRI	SAT
Walls	3	2/2	4/6	3/8	RDO	RDO	10
Hill	6	6	RDO	88	5	2	RDO
Apex	RDO	9	9	10	4/1	88	RDO
Ranter	1	3	4/1	RDO	RDO	2	88
Ford	10/9	RDO	88	6	2/3	2	RDO
Marino	1	1	10	9	RDO	RDO	4
Ginty	9/8	2	1	RDO	RDO	4	1
Bailes	9/8	1	2	RDO	RDO	2	1
Kegler	10/9	RDO	88	6	2/3	2	RDO

(REAR)

When describing work activities use Job Reference Number given below:

Job Reference Number:	Job Description:
1	Wash cell block floors
2	Wax library floor
3	Dust and wax office furniture
4	Laundry duty
5	Sweep visiting area
6	H.S. Equivalency Diploma class
7	College level class
8	Vocational trade study
9	Foundry duty
10	Machine shop duty

(Each of the above jobs shall be assigned to an inmate for a 3-hour block of time. More than one reference number per day means the inmate received more than one assignment that day.)

88	Sick for entire day
RDO	Excusal—Entire day off

Date	Cell Block Correction Officer
March 20, 20xx	C.O. – Don Tops/Shield Number 749

41. Which of the following statements would be most correct regarding Inmate Kegler's work activities?

(A) Kegler is currently studying college-level courses.
(B) The activity done most often by Kegler during the period indicated is waxing the library floor.
(C) Kegler never reports sick.
(D) No other inmate had the same work activities as Kegler.

42. Which of the following inmates was the only one to sweep the visiting area?

(A) Walls
(B) Hill
(C) Ginty
(D) Bailes

43. The number of hours spent by all inmates dusting and waxing the office furniture was

(A) 10.
(B) 12.
(C) 15.
(D) 18.

44. The number of hours spent in work activities by Inmate Walls was

(A) 24.
(B) 21.
(C) 18.
(D) 15.

45. On Tuesday, Inmate Apex performed which of the following duties?

(A) washing the cell block floors
(B) laundry
(C) machine shop duty
(D) foundry duty

46. Which of the following activities was done most frequently by the inmates during the period indicated by the form?

    (A) washing the cell block floors
    (B) attending High School Equivalency classes
    (C) laundry duty
    (D) machine shop duty

47. Which of the following activities was not performed on Thursday?

    (A) waxing the library floor
    (B) dusting and waxing office furniture
    (C) laundry duty
    (D) vocational trade study

48. Of the following inmates, the one with the most sick time was

    (A) Ginty.
    (B) Bailes.
    (C) Kegler.
    (D) Walls.

49. Of the inmates listed on the form, the number of inmates who already have a high school diploma

    (A) is 4.
    (B) is 5.
    (C) is 6.
    (D) cannot be determined from the information given.

50. Which of the following statements would be least correct regarding Inmate Marino's work activities?

    (A) Only Marino worked in the machine shop.
    (B) Marino had to wash the cell block floors.
    (C) Only Marino worked in the foundry on Wednesday.
    (D) Marino had laundry duty during the week.

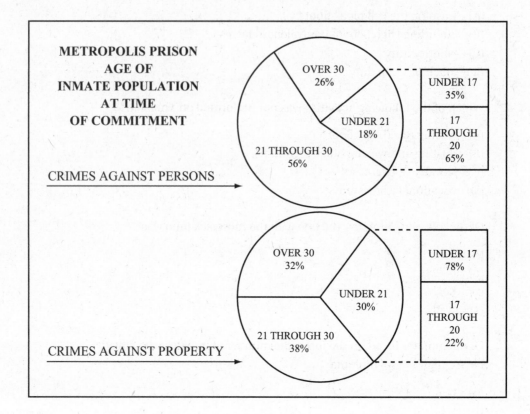

METROPOLIS PRISON
AGE OF
INMATE POPULATION
AT TIME
OF COMMITMENT

CRIMES AGAINST PERSONS

OVER 30
26%

UNDER 21
18%

21 THROUGH 30
56%

UNDER 17
35%

17
THROUGH
20
65%

CRIMES AGAINST PROPERTY

OVER 30
32%

UNDER 21
30%

21 THROUGH 30
38%

UNDER 17
78%

17
THROUGH
20
22%

51. Most of the inmates who are committed to Metropolis Prison after being convicted of the crime of robbery are

(A) under 21.
(B) 21–30.
(C) over 30.
(D) of an age that cannot be determined from the data given.

52. Of all the inmates who are committed to Metropolis Prison as a result of being convicted of crimes against persons, the majority of them

(A) are under 21.
(B) are between 21 and 30.
(C) are over 30.
(D) cannot be determined.

53. Of all the inmates under 21 who enter the prison after being convicted of a crime against a person, most of them

(A) are under 17 years old.
(B) are 17–20 years of age.
(C) are 18 years old.
(D) cannot be determined.

54. Of all the inmates under 21 who enter the prison after being convicted of a crime against property, most of them

   (A) are under 17 years old.
   (B) are 17–20 years of age.
   (C) are 16 years old.
   (D) cannot be determined.

55. Assuming that current trends concerning the age of inmates at the time of commitment continues, if 1000 new inmates entered Metropolis Prison during the next year as a result of a conviction of a crime against property, then about

   (A) 320 of them would be over 30 years of age.
   (B) 560 of them would be between 21 and 30 years old.
   (C) 180 of them would be under 21 years of age.
   (D) 63 of them would be under 17 years of age.

56. If in the next year 1000 new inmates entered Metropolis Prison as a result of being convicted of a crime against a person, approximately how many of them would be between 17 and 20 years of age?

   (A) 180
   (B) 300
   (C) 117
   (D) cannot be determined

57. What percentage of the new inmates entering Metropolis Prison after being convicted of a crime against a person are over 21 years of age?

   (A) 56%
   (B) 26%
   (C) 82%
   (D) cannot be determined

58. On June 1st, what percentage of the inmate population of Metropolis Prison was under 21 years of age?

   (A) 18%
   (B) 30%
   (C) 48%
   (D) cannot be determined

Directions: Answer questions 59 and 60 based solely on the following procedure governing items permitted to be in the possession of inmates.

1. All powdered items shall be purchased in the facility's commissary.

2. Jewelry is limited to wedding rings, watches, bracelets, religious medals, necklaces, and other jewelry of a type typically worn in public in general civilian situations. However, any type, number, or size of jewelry which is capable of simulating a weapon or facilitating escape is prohibited.

3. Regarding recreational items, an inmate may possess board games without dice, balls other than those with a hardcover, dominoes, and jigsaw puzzles.

4. Cigars, cigarettes, and smoking tobacco must be purchased at the facility's commissary.

59. Regarding the possession of personal property by an inmate, it would be most correct to state that

(A) jewelry is permitted, but the only qualification is that it be of a type typically worn in public in general civilian situations.
(B) powdered items received through the mail are permitted if still in the original undisturbed wrappers.
(C) any ball may be possessed.
(D) dominoes may be possessed.

60. Evaluate the following statements:

1. An inmate may possess jigsaw puzzles.
2. An inmate may possess any board game.

Which of the following is most accurate concerning these two statements?

(A) Only statement 1 is correct.
(B) Only statement 2 is correct.
(C) Both statements 1 and 2 are correct.
(D) Neither statement 1 nor 2 is correct.

When a correction officer conducts a search of living quarters of inmates, the officer shall record the following information in the cell block log in the following order.

1. The date and time of the search;

2. the specific area searched;

3. who supervised the search (A captain or above must be present.);

4. who specifically conducted search (A correction officer must conduct the search.);

5. if any contraband was found and where it was found; and

6. what follow-up action was taken, such as the preparation of

   - Form 109 (Recommendation for Criminal Charges),
   - Form 2235 (Report of Inmate Infraction),
   - Form 207 (Request for Lab Analysis),
   - Form 699 (Intelligence Report).

61. One Saturday morning, Correction Officer Singer is making entries in the cell block log after conducting a search of inmate living quarters. After performing all required actions and then entering the name of the correction officer who conducted the search, the next entry should be

    (A) the date and time of the search.
    (B) the specific area searched.
    (C) if any contraband was found and where it was found.
    (D) who supervised the search.

62. If based on the results of the search, Officer Singer wished to make a recommendation for criminal charges, which of the following forms should be prepared?

    (A) Form 699
    (B) Form 109
    (C) Form 2235
    (D) Form 207

63. In the search involving Officer Singer, who else was required to be present?

    (A) the tour commander
    (B) at least two members of the department at the rank of correction officer
    (C) at least two inmates as witnesses
    (D) a supervisor at the rank of captain or above

The following procedures shall be complied with by correction department personnel and enforced by the correction officers assigned to entry gates.

1. Persons not having department identification shall undergo a metal detector search.

2. Metal detectors shall be tested daily by the officer assigned to the midnight shift.

3. At the discretion of the tour commander any person in the facility may be required to undergo a metal detector search.

4. Employee vehicles parked in employee parking lots adjacent to the gates shall be securely locked and shall not contain weapons, money, or contraband.

5. All briefcases or other containers in the possession of visitors shall be opened and searched by the officer assigned to the gate. If the search proves negative, they shall be returned to the visitor.

6. Items deemed inappropriate for entry into the facility shall be removed from visitors, held in storage and returned upon the departure of the visitor.

7. If an officer assigned to duty at the gate has a reasonable suspicion that a person may be carrying contraband, the first action shall be to notify a supervisor. Upon the supervisor's approval, a hand-held metal detector search shall be conducted.

64. Metal detectors shall be tested

(A) weekly.
(B) monthly.
(C) on the midnight tour by the tour commander.
(D) daily by an officer assigned to the gate.

65. While on duty as the gate officer, Correction Officer Bell is approached by a male visitor who is carrying a briefcase. In this instance it would be most appropriate if Officer Bell

(A) turned the visitor away.
(B) told the visitor that he should leave the briefcase in his car.
(C) allowed the visitor to bring the briefcase into the facility if a search of the briefcase proves negative.
(D) in all instances held on to the briefcase until the visitor completed the visit.

66. Officer John Bell has a reasonable suspicion that a female visiting her husband may be carrying contraband. Bell immediately conducts a hand-held metal detector search. He then notifies his supervisor of the results of the search. In such an instance, Officer Bell acted

(A) properly because reasonable suspicion is all that is required to search for contraband.

(B) improperly because he should have first notified his supervisor.

(C) properly because a hand-held metal detector is more sensitive than a walk-through metal detector.

(D) improperly because he should have had a female correction officer conduct the search.

Directions: Answer questions 67 and 68 based solely on the following information.

An inmate shall be denied possession of an item of jewelry under the following circumstances:

• the item could be used as a weapon;

• the inmate's physical or mental condition raises the reasonable likelihood that the inmate could be harmed by the jewelry;

• the item is clearly expensive and would increase the possibility of theft; or

• the item does not fit the department's definition of inmate jewelry.

Inmate jewelry is defined as any nonhollow ornamental piece that includes but is not limited to wedding rings, necklaces, wrist or pocket watches, costume jewelry or religious jewelry illustrating a religious theme.

Decisions that deny inmates possession of jewelry shall be made at time of admission into the facility by the facility admissions corrections captain. Correction officers conducting admissions procedures shall immediately refer all questions concerning denial of inmate jewelry to said captain before removing any jewelry from inmates.

An inmate who has been denied jewelry may appeal the decision by submitting three written copies of Request for Reevaluation (Form 333) to the assistant warden within 3 days of the original denial.

67. While on admissions duty, Correction Officer Lee is made aware that Slick Movers, an inmate being admitted, is wearing a very expensive wristwatch. The officer immediately removes the watch from Inmate Movers who protests saying the watch was a wedding gift. Officer Lee's actions were

(A) appropriate because the watch would increase the possibility of a theft.

(B) inappropriate because Officer Lee should have referred the issue to the facility admissions corrections captain.

(C) appropriate because the glass face of the watch could be used as a weapon.

(D) inappropriate because the watch could have been in lieu of a wedding ring.

68. Unhappy with having his watch removed, Slick Movers advises Officer Lee that he would like to appeal. In such a situation, Officer Lee would be most correct to advise Movers that

(A) the decision is final and there is no appeal procedure.

(B) he should speak to the assistant warden.

(C) he has 3 days from the original denial to submit his appeal.

(D) Form 333 should be submitted to the facility admissions corrections captain.

Directions: Answer questions 69–73 based solely on the following information.

When an inmate is sick or injured and requires medical attention at a hospital, the following procedure shall be followed.

The tour commander shall assign an escort officer to bring the inmate to the hospital. The escort officer shall sign out in the command log, which is maintained at the correctional facility. The time they left and the destination should be part of the entry.

The escorting officer shall:

1. Handcuff the inmate with hands in rear before transporting to reduce the inmate's freedom of motion.

2. If possible, remain with the inmate at all times in the hospital.

3. Request a room change from the hospital administrator if security in the treatment room is inadequate. Admitting clerks have no such authority; therefore, such requests should not be directed to them.

4. Not remove handcuffs, unless requested by the attending physician.

   a. If requested to remove handcuffs, immediately inform physician of the inmate's background prior to removing the handcuffs.

    b. If the physician still wants them removed, remove the handcuffs. After removing the handcuffs, call the tour commander and request that an entry be made in the command log. Put the handcuffs back on the inmate at the completion of the examination.

    5.   Remain immediately outside the room and attempt to maintain visual contact even if requested to leave the examination room.

69. Correction Officer Days is directed by the tour commander to escort Inmate Jacks to the hospital for treatment for a gall bladder condition. Before leaving, Officer Days makes an entry in the command log. In such a situation, the actions of Officer Days were

    (A) proper mainly because it is Officer Days' duty to enter the time of departure as well as the destination.
    (B) improper mainly because entries in the command log must be made by any supervisor.
    (C) proper mainly because the treating physician will want to examine the command log.
    (D) improper mainly because only the tour commander is permitted to make entries in the command log.

70. While Officer Days is transporting Inmate Jacks to the hospital, Officer Days permits Jacks to smoke a cigarette but insists that Jacks hands remain handcuffed in front of his body. In such an instance the actions of Officer Days were

    (A) proper mainly because handcuffing the inmate in such a manner permits the prisoner to hold his own cigarette.
    (B) improper mainly because smoking could aggravate the inmate's condition.
    (C) proper mainly because the inmate is going to the hospital and undue attention should not be drawn to the inmate.
    (D) improper mainly because greater freedom of motion, which could facilitate escape, is given to the inmate.

71. While at the hospital, Officer Days is asked by the attending physician to remove the handcuffs from Inmate Jacks. In this situation, Officer Days should immediately

    (A) refuse to remove the handcuffs under any circumstances.
    (B) call the tour commander.
    (C) advise the physician of the inmate's background.
    (D) handcuff one of the inmate's wrists to a fixed object.

72. If security in the treatment room is inadequate, Officer Days should request a room change from the

    (A) hospital administrator.
    (B) tour commander.
    (C) treating physician.
    (D) admitting clerk.

73. During the examination, Officer Days is requested to leave the examination room. In such an instance it would be most correct for Officer Days

    (A) to refuse to leave.
    (B) to handcuff the prisoner to a bed.
    (C) to remain immediately outside the room and attempt to maintain visual contact.
    (D) to leave the room as requested and use the time for a quick coffee break.

Directions: Use the information in the following reference table to answer questions 74–78. In the table each number has been associated with a letter. For each question you are to select the choice that correctly spells the word identified in the question.

R	O	U	N	D	M	E	A	T	S
1	2	3	4	5	6	7	8	9	0

74. Using the reference table, which of the following most accurately spells *TREMOR?*

    (A) 917612
    (B) 917621
    (C) 917601
    (D) 197601

75. Using the reference table, which of the following most accurately spells *MOUNDS?*

    (A) 623450
    (B) 603452
    (C) 623405
    (D) 603542

76. Using the reference table, which of the following most accurately spells *MOROSE?*

    (A) 620207
    (B) 621027
    (C) 621207
    (D) 601027

77. Using the reference table, which of the following most accurately spells *STORER?*

    (A) 092171
    (B) 092711
    (C) 090171
    (D) 090711

78. Using the reference table, which of the following most accurately spells *RANDOM?*

    (A) 184502
    (B) 184506
    (C) 184562
    (D) 184526

79. Mandatory inmate line-ups shall be held upon the written request of a police supervisor, but an attorney must be present when the line-up is conducted in order to protect the interests of the inmate. Which of the following is NOT a correct interpretation of this rule?

    (A) Sometimes an inmate line-up can be held in the absence of an attorney.
    (B) Inmate line-ups must be requested in writing.
    (C) Inmate line-ups must be requested by a police supervisor.
    (D) An inmate cannot refuse to stand in a line-up.

80. During a prison disorder, it is essential that the leaders of the disorder be dealt with immediately for the purpose of negating their influence on other inmates. In accordance with this rule, when a disorder occurs, the leaders of the disorder must be

    (A) disciplined immediately and publicly.
    (B) arrested and charged with inciting a riot.
    (C) transferred on the spot to another institution.
    (D) identified as quickly as possible.

81. A correction officer is informed that a new regulation that changes a long-standing regulation concerning the movement of inmates is being implemented. Prior to enforcing the new regulation, the officer must first

    (A) make sure to issue a number of warnings.
    (B) make sure that all the inmates understand the new regulation by explaining it to them.
    (C) wait to see if the new regulation will be effective.
    (D) make sure to post the new regulations in a conspicuous place.

82. A new policy has been implemented in a certain prison. The policy is unpopular with the inmates and correction officers alike. It was explained at a training session for correction officers that the change is one that the warden strongly believes is necessary. Under these circumstances, when enforcing the new regulation, a correction officer should tell the inmates that

    (A) although he does not personally agree with the new policy it must be enforced.
    (B) he will be enforcing the policy because that is the way the warden wants it.
    (C) he will ignore all but the most serious violations of the new policy.
    (D) that he supports the new policy and will enforce it fairly and equitably.

83. A correction officer believes she knows of a better way of accomplishing a certain task than the way that task is now being officially accomplished. That officer should

    (A) experiment with her way of doing the task.
    (B) submit her recommendation for change along with her reasons through the institution's employee suggestion system.
    (C) wait until she assumes a position of greater responsibility and then implement the change.
    (D) make an unofficial attempt at convincing other officers that she has a good idea.

84. Public relations is an important matter. A correctional institution is often visited by members of the public such as friends and relatives of inmates, media representatives, and elected officials. When dealing with members of the public, a correction officer should act

    (A) in an aloof manner.
    (B) in a courteous and tactful manner.
    (C) in a somewhat friendly yet very stern manner.
    (D) in a dignified but unfriendly manner.

85. Assume that you are a correction officer in a prison that has just experienced a newsworthy incident. A reporter approaches you while you are on duty and asks you to comment on that incident. Under these circumstances, you should

(A) make only "off the record" statements.
(B) ask the reporter to contact you when you are off duty.
(C) refer the reporter to the person in the chain of command whose job it is to deal with the media.
(D) simply say, "No comment."

86. You are the correction officer in charge of the arsenal. During a routine inspection you discover a firearm that you are sure has been recently fired. You check the appropriate records and determine that there has been no official report of a firearms discharge. You should

(A) immediately inform your supervisor.
(B) take no action.
(C) make an unofficial inquiry whenever you get a chance.
(D) make an immediate notification to the office of the warden.

87. Except in emergency situations, correction officers shall not be armed when they are in direct contact with the inmate population. Such a rule is needed primarily

(A) to prevent officers from using their weapons to gain compliance with their orders.
(B) to guard against the possibility of inmates obtaining a weapon by overpowering an officer.
(C) to create an acceptable environment for the rehabilitation of inmates.
(D) to develop much needed rapport between officers and inmates.

88. Correction officers are required to unload their firearms prior to entering any area in the psychiatric ward of any hospital. Such a rule is necessitated primarily by

(A) the need not to disturb patients in the ward.
(B) the unpredictable mental state of many of the patients in such a ward.
(C) the importance of maintaining good public relations.
(D) the need to protect the rights of hospitalized persons.

The term *culpable mental state* means acting intentionally or recklessly or with criminal negligence.

Conduct means the act or omission a person does plus the person's accompanying mental state.

A person acts *intentionally* when the object of this person's actions is to cause a certain result.

A person acts *recklessly* when such person is aware of a risk and takes action that indicates a conscious disregard of that risk.

A person acts with *criminal negligence* when such person takes action which indicates that such person failed to perceive a risk caused by the action the person took.

When a *pure defense* is raised at a trial by a defendant, the state has the burden of disproving such defense beyond a reasonable doubt.

An *affirmative defense* must be raised at a trial by a defendant. When this occurs, the defendant has the burden of establishing such defense by a preponderance of the evidence. That means that it must be shown that it is more than 50% certain that what the defendant is claiming is true.

Under the law, a person less than 16 years of age is not criminally responsible for conduct, except that certain 13-, 14-, and 15-year-olds are criminally responsible for their conduct for very serious crimes such as murder and kidnapping.

89. The term *culpable mental state* is most accurately defined as

    (A) acting intentionally only.
    (B) acting recklessly only.
    (C) acting with criminal negligence only.
    (D) either acting intentionally or recklessly or with criminal negligence.

90. Evaluate the following statements.

    1. Conduct includes only the actions a person takes plus the person's accompanying mental state.
    2. Conduct includes only the actions a person fails to take plus the person's accompanying mental state.

    Which of the following is most accurate concerning the statements above?

    (A) Only statement 1 is correct.
    (B) Only statement 2 is correct.
    (C) Both statements 1 and 2 are correct.
    (D) Neither statement 1 nor 2 is correct.

91. Joe, an inmate at the Ferris Correctional Facility, wants to strike Pat in the face. Joe waits for his opportunity. One day in the exercise yard Joe strikes Pat in the face. Joe has acted

    (A) recklessly.
    (B) with criminal negligence.
    (C) intentionally.
    (D) either intentionally or recklessly depending on the nature of the injury.

92. Inmate Don has repeatedly been warned about leaning weights against a railing leading to the second tier. One afternoon he disregards what he has been warned against doing and again leaves some barbells leaning against a stair railing. The barbells begin to roll and fall over 20 feet to the tier below. There they strike Frank, another inmate, in the back, seriously injuring Frank. In such an instance, Don has acted

    (A) intentionally.
    (B) with criminal negligence.
    (C) recklessly.
    (D) properly and has no culpable mental state.

93. Frank is an independent contractor who has been hired to do some maintenance work at a correctional facility. He digs a large hole to repair some water pipes. At the end of the day, thinking that there was no risk involved, Frank leaves the hole open, unattended and unprotected. To the average person, however, it would be quite apparent that to do so would create a hazard in that someone could easily fall into the unprotected hole and receive an injury. That night a correction officer conducting an inspection falls into the hole and is injured. In such an instance, Frank has acted

(A) only intentionally.
(B) with criminal negligence.
(C) only recklessly.
(D) either intentionally or recklessly.

94. When a pure defense is raised at a trial by a defendant, then

(A) the defendant has the burden of establishing the pure defense beyond a reasonable doubt.
(B) the state has the burden of disproving the pure defense beyond a reasonable doubt.
(C) the defendant has the burden of establishing the pure defense by a preponderance of the evidence.
(D) the state has the burden of disproving the pure defense by a preponderance of the evidence.

95. At a trial, an affirmative defense must be raised by

(A) the defendant.
(B) the state.
(C) either the defendant or the state.
(D) neither the state nor the defendant.

96. Proving an issue by a preponderance of evidence means that

(A) absolute certainty exists concerning the matter attempted to be proven.
(B) it is more than 50% certain that what is attempted to be proven is certain.
(C) it is equally possible that what is attempted to be proven can be either true or false.
(D) it is highly unlikely that what is being attempted to be proven is true.

97. Mark, who is 15 years old, is visiting an inmate at a correctional facility. While visiting, Mark gets into an argument with another visitor. As a result of the argument, Mark shoves the other visitor, injuring the other visitor very, very slightly. Which of the following statements would be most correct concerning such an instance?

(A) Mark is criminally responsible the same as any other person.

(B) Mark is not criminally responsible for such an action.

(C) Mark could be criminally responsible if he has previously been arrested for similar actions.

(D) Mark could never be criminally responsible for his criminal actions no matter what he does because of his age.

98. Which of the following persons would be most likely to be considered criminally responsible for actions such person might take?

(A) Pat, who is 15 and commits a robbery.

(B) Jay, who is 14 and commits a larceny.

(C) Tom, who is 13 and commits a kidnapping.

(D) Frank, who is 12 and commits a murder.

Directions: Answer question 99 based solely on the following legal definition.

Sodomy in the first degree occurs when a person engages in deviate sexual intercourse with another person

1. by forcible compulsion or

2. who is incapable of consent by reason of being physically helpless or

3. who is less than 11 years old.

Deviate sexual intercourse means sexual conduct between persons not married to each other consisting of contact between the penis and the anus, the mouth and the penis, and the mouth and the vulva.

99. Joe, who is an inmate participating in a work release program, is accused of having deviate sexual intercourse. Joe insists he has committed no crime. Joe would not have committed sodomy in the first degree if he engaged in deviate sexual intercourse with

(A) a 10-year-old male.

(B) his girl friend who was physically unconscious.

(C) a 30-year-old male.

(D) a strange female whom he forced into submission.

Detention facility   A place used for the confinement of persons convicted of a crime.

Custody   Restraint by a public servant pursuant to an order of a court or an authorized arrest.

Escape in the third degree   Occurs when a person escapes from custody.

Escape in the second degree   Occurs when a person escapes from a detention facility or, having been arrested for a Class C, D, or E felony, escapes from custody.

Escape in the first degree   Occurs when, having been convicted of a felony, a person escapes from a detention facility or, having been arrested for a Class A or B felony, escapes from custody.

100.   Inmate Ray Satin saws through some bars at the White Horse Correctional Facility and makes good his escape. His escape is the first ever at the facility, which was constructed to house dangerous convicts. Ray had been serving a sentence for being convicted of an E felony. If arrested, which of the following would be the most appropriate charge against Ray?

(A)   escape in the first degree
(B)   escape in the second degree
(C)   escape in the third degree
(D)   the appropriate degree of escape depending on the amount of resistance Ray offers at the time of arrest

Question 101.

1. After identifying herself to the officer as Gloria Swanson, the female tells the officer that at 9:45 A.M. she parked her car and went to visit an inmate by the name of Sam Green.
2. No other property was taken.
3. While patrolling the visitor's parking lot, a correction officer observes a female waving to her.
4. Then, at 10:45 A.M. when she returned to her car, she discovered that the right front vent window had been smashed and that her car radio had been stolen.
5. The officer parks her patrol vehicle and approaches the female.

(A) 3-5-1-4-2
(B) 1-3-2-4-5
(C) 2-3-4-1-5
(D) 3-1-5-2-4

Question 102.

1. Death row cells must be inspected once each day.
2. Every cell in a facility, except death row cells, must be given a thorough safety inspection at least once a week.
3. Safety inspections must be made during daylight hours.
4. The inmate assigned to the cell must be present when the inspection is made.
5. Regular safety inspections of cell blocks are required to ensure the safety of inmates and correctional personnel alike.

(A) 5-2-1-4-3
(B) 4-5-3-1-2
(C) 3-1-2-4-5
(D) 1-5-3-2-4

Question 103.

1. Officer Bardo watches the inmate for 10 minutes and then approaches him.
2. As the correction officer gets nearer to the inmate, he realizes that the inmate is new to the prison.
3. Bardo then tells the new inmate to move to an authorized area, and the inmate complies.
4. A little while later, at 4:30 P.M., the signal to clear the yard is given.
5. At 4:05 P.M., Correction Officer Bardo observes an inmate who is in a place in the main yard where he should not be.

(A) 5-4-3-2-1
(B) 5-1-2-3-4
(C) 5-3-4-1-2
(D) 5-2-1-4-3

Question 104.

1. On August 17, Correction Officer Frank Brown was on duty on the grounds of the Municipal Detention Facility.
2. At approximately 10:05 A.M., the officer received a radio call to respond to a storehouse at 1248 Jailhouse Road.
3. When he arrived at the storehouse at 10:10 A.M., he was met by Mr. Don Wood, a custodial assistant at the facility.
4. Officer Brown then started an investigation.
5. Mr. Wood informed the officers that the storehouse had been burglarized.

(A) 1-2-3-5-4
(B) 1-3-2-5-4
(C) 1-5-2-3-4
(D) 1-3-5-2-4

Question 105.

1. If at any time, equipment is properly passed from one officer to another, the last officer to receive the equipment shall be responsible for it.
2. Finally, the last officer leaving an office is responsible for turning off all nonessential lights and electrical appliances.
3. Additionally, whenever file cabinets are made available to correction officers, all official documents and records must be placed therein overnight.
4. Correction officers are responsible for the proper care and maintenance of agency equipment and/or property issued for their use.
5. Officers placing such documents and records into file cabinets must close and lock the cabinets when finished.

(A) 4-2-1-5-3
(B) 4-5-2-3-1
(C) 4-2-3-1-5
(D) 4-1-3-5-2

Directions: Answer question 106 based solely on the following information.

When a correction officer arrives at the scene of an apparently dead human being, he or she should do the following in the order given:

1. Request, through the radio dispatcher, that an ambulance and a correction supervisor respond.

2. Obtain names of witnesses, and detain them at the scene if circumstances indicate a suspicious death.

3. If in a public place, screen the area from public view if possible.

4. Cover the body with waterproof covering if publicly exposed.

5. Ascertain the facts, and notify the duty officer as soon as possible.

6. Request that the assisted person be removed to the hospital or that a hospital doctor be dispatched if a pronouncement of death by an ambulance attendant is questioned by anyone.

106. It is 0250 hours, and Correction Officer Larkin is on duty in the private rooms section of the detention facility. While performing a routine check of Private Room 206, Officer Larkin discovers that the elderly inmate alone in the room is apparently dead from natural causes. Officer Larkin immediately requests, through the radio dispatcher, that an ambulance and a correction supervisor respond to the scene. What is the next step the officer should take?

(A) Ascertain the facts, and notify the duty officer as soon as possible.
(B) Screen the area from public view.
(C) Cover the body with a waterproof covering.
(D) Obtain names of witnesses, and detain them at the scene.

Directions: Answer question 107 based solely on the following information.

Upon arresting a person for an offense, the following procedure must be followed by the arresting officer in the order given:

1. Inform the individual being arrested of your authority.

2. Advise the prisoner of the cause of the arrest except when:

   a. Arrested in the actual commission of an offense, or

   b. pursued immediately after an escape.

3. Using discretion and sound judgment, handcuff the prisoner only when circumstances require.

4. Search the prisoner for weapons, evidence, or contraband.

5. Advise the prisoner of his or her rights before questioning.

6. Take the prisoner to the designated arrest-processing area.

7. Request backup, if necessary.

8. Safeguard property owned or operated by the prisoner before removing him or her from the scene.

9. Bring the prisoner before the arraignment judge as soon as possible after processing.

107. Correction Officer Lina Wu has just discovered an illegal weapon on the person of a pregnant female confined to a wheelchair who was attempting to visit an inmate. After Wu informed the visitor of her arrest authority, Officer Wu placed the visitor under arrest. What is the next step Correction Officer Wu should take?

(A) Advise the prisoner of the cause of the arrest.
(B) Handcuff the prisoner.
(C) Search the prisoner for weapons, evidence, or contraband.
(D) Advise the prisoner of her rights before questioning.

Directions: Answer question 108 based solely on the following information.

Upon arriving at a location where a person is threatening to jump from a building, a correction officer should do the following in the order given:

1. Notify the communications unit, and request an emergency service unit to respond.

2. Attempt to persuade or prevent the person from jumping.

3. Seek assistance from the person's relatives, friends, or clergy if they are on the scene.

4. Confine the person to the side of the building facing the street.

5. Rope off the area below, and prevent persons from entering the area.

6. Prepare a complaint report, and make appropriate memo book entries.

108. Correction Officer Tom Samuels is notified that an inmate is on the roof of the 12-story detention facility where he works and that the inmate has threatened to jump. Officer Samuels goes to the roof of the building. The inmate sees him and shouts, "You come any closer and I'll jump!" Officer Samuels radios the communications unit and requests an emergency service unit to respond. Officer Samuels then attempts to persuade the man not to jump. What is the next step Officer Samuels should take?

(A) Prepare a complaint report, and make appropriate memo book entries.
(B) Rope off the area below, and prevent persons from entering the area.
(C) Confine the person to the side of the building facing the street.
(D) Seek assistance from the person's relatives, friends, or clergy.

Directions: Answer question 109 based solely on the following information.

When a correction officer stops a vehicle on agency property and discovers that the operator is driving with a suspended or revoked driver's license, the following should be done in the order given:

1. Confiscate the driver's license.

2. Prepare a seized driver's license receipt/report.

3. Give the operator of the vehicle a receipt for the license.

4. If the driver has two or more unrelated suspensions or if his or her license has been revoked for any reason, arrest the driver and take him or her to central booking.

5. Do not mark or mutilate the license in any manner.

6. Have the violator's vehicle parked in a safe and legal parking area until the registered owner can arrange to have the vehicle removed from the scene by a licensed operator.

109. Correction Officer Mia Lopez is on patrol on the grounds of the detention center where she is assigned. She has just stopped a visitor's vehicle and, while correctly following procedures, discovered that the operator is driving with a revoked driver's license. Officer Lopez arrests the operator after correctly investigating and following the mandated procedure. What is the next thing for Lopez to do in this instance?

    (A) Refrain from marking or mutilating the arrested person's driver's license.
    (B) Take her prisoner to central booking.
    (C) Park the violator's vehicle in a legal spot.
    (D) Prepare a seized driver's license receipt/report.

Directions: Answer question 110 based solely on the following information.

Correction officers who observe a person carrying a rifle or shotgun on agency property should do the following in the order given:

1. Determine if the person has a valid permit.

2. If there is no permit:

    a. Inform the person that he or she may surrender the firearm to the officer at the scene or at correction headquarters.

    b. Serve a summons for violation or make an arrest.

    c. Prepare a receipt for the firearm, and give a copy to the owner.

    d. Send the firearm to the gun lab if it is believed to have been used in a crime, or safeguard it at headquarters.

    e. Tell the owner to apply for a permit.

110. After stopping Mr. Jones for carrying a rifle on agency property, Correction Officer Scott determines that Mr. Jones owns the rifle but does not have a valid permit. What should Officer Scott do next?

    (A) Give a copy of the receipt to Jones.
    (B) Send the rifle to the gun lab.
    (C) Tell Mr. Jones to surrender his rifle.
    (D) Tell the owner to apply for a permit.

Directions: Answer questions 111–115 based solely on the following information and map. The flow of traffic is indicated by the arrows. If only one arrow is shown, traffic flows only in the direction indicated by the arrow. If two arrows are shown, traffic flows in both directions. You must follow the flow of traffic when moving from one location to another.

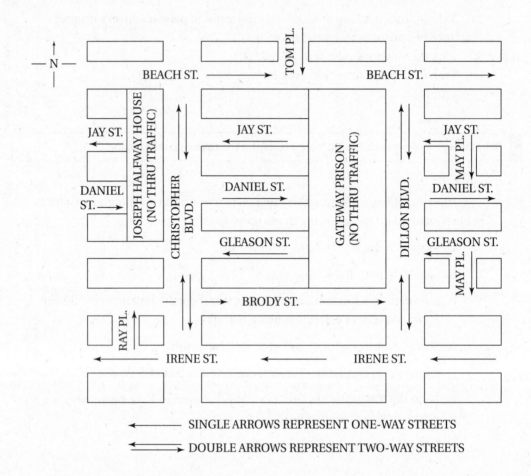

SINGLE ARROWS REPRESENT ONE-WAY STREETS

DOUBLE ARROWS REPRESENT TWO-WAY STREETS

111. You are in your official department of correction vehicle proceeding west on Gleason Street toward Gateway Park. You proceed to the next street where you are able to make a right turn and do so. You continue straight ahead for 3 blocks and then make a left turn and continue straight ahead. At that point, you would be

(A) heading east.
(B) going against traffic.
(C) traveling on a two-way street.
(D) heading north.

112. You are in a department of correction van, legally parked on Christopher Boulevard facing south in front of the Joseph Halfway Houses at Daniel Street. You receive an assignment to meet the warden at May Place and Daniel Street. Which of the following is the most direct route for you to take in your vehicle, making sure to obey all of the traffic regulations?

(A) Make a left onto Daniel Street, and head east until you reach May Place.
(B) Head south to Brody Street, make a right onto Brody Street, continue to Dillon Boulevard, and then head north on Dillon Boulevard to Daniel Street where you make a right to May Place.
(C) Continue straight to Brody Street, head east on Brody Street to Dillon Boulevard, and then head north to Daniel Street where you make a right to May Place.
(D) Head south on Christopher Boulevard to Irene Street, head east on Irene Street to Dillon Boulevard, and then head north on Dillon Boulevard to Daniel Street where you head east to May Place.

113. While you are legally parked facing the Joseph Halfway Houses at the intersection of Jay Street and Christopher Boulevard, you are directed to respond to Irene Street and Dillon Boulevard to help in removing prisoners from a disabled prisoner transport van. Which of the following is the most direct route for you to take in your vehicle, making sure to obey all of the traffic regulations?

(A) Turn south and continue on Christopher Boulevard to Brody Street, head east on Brody Street to Dillon Boulevard, and then head south on Dillon Boulevard to Irene Street.
(B) Turn north and continue on Christopher Boulevard to Beach Street, head east on Beach Street to Dillon Boulevard, and then head south on Dillon Boulevard to Irene Street.
(C) Turn south and continue on Christopher Boulevard to Irene Street, and then head east on Irene Street to Dillon Boulevard.
(D) Turn south and continue on Christopher Boulevard to Brody Street, and then make a right and continue to Dillon Boulevard where you should make another right to Irene Street.

114. While at Tom Place and Beach Street, you are directed to respond to the Joseph Halfway Houses. Which of the following is the most direct route for you to take in your vehicle, making sure to obey all of the traffic regulations?

(A) Head west on Beach Street to Christopher Boulevard, and then head south on Christopher Boulevard to the Joseph Halfway Houses.
(B) Head east on Beach Street to Dillon Boulevard, head south on Dillon Boulevard to Jay Street, and then head west on Jay Street to the Joseph Halfway Houses.
(C) Make a left onto Beach Street and head east to Dillon Boulevard, go south on Dillon Boulevard to Gleason Street, head west on Gleason Street to Christopher Boulevard, and then head north on Christopher Boulevard to the Joseph Halfway Houses.
(D) Head east on Beach Street to Dillon Boulevard, head south on Dillon Boulevard to Irene Street, then head west on Irene Street to Christopher Boulevard, and then head north on Christopher Boulevard to the Joseph Halfway Houses.

115. If you are traveling south in your vehicle at the intersection of Gleason Street and May Place, what is your only legal option upon reaching Brody Street?

(A) Head north.
(B) Make a right.
(C) Head directly south for another 2 blocks.
(D) Make a left.

END OF TEST

ANSWER KEY
Practice Test 1

1. **A**	30. **C**	59. **D**	88. **B**
2. **C**	31. **C**	60. **A**	89. **D**
3. **A**	32. **B**	61. **C**	90. **D**
4. **D**	33. **C**	62. **B**	91. **C**
5. **B**	34. **D**	63. **D**	92. **C**
6. **B**	35. **C**	64. **D**	93. **B**
7. **A**	36. **D**	65. **C**	94. **B**
8. **D**	37. **A**	66. **B**	95. **A**
9. **B**	38. **D**	67. **B**	96. **B**
10. **B**	39. **C**	68. **C**	97. **B**
11. **B**	40. **C**	69. **A**	98. **C**
12. **B**	41. **B**	70. **D**	99. **C**
13. **C**	42. **B**	71. **C**	100. **A**
14. **B**	43. **C**	72. **A**	101. **A**
15. **A**	44. **A**	73. **C**	102. **A**
16. **A**	45. **D**	74. **B**	103. **B**
17. **C**	46. **A**	75. **A**	104. **A**
18. **A**	47. **D**	76. **C**	105. **D**
19. **C**	48. **C**	77. **A**	106. **A**
20. **D**	49. **D**	78. **D**	107. **C**
21. **C**	50. **A**	79. **A**	108. **C**
22. **B**	51. **D**	80. **D**	109. **B**
23. **B**	52. **B**	81. **B**	110. **C**
24. **A**	53. **B**	82. **D**	111. **B**
25. **C**	54. **A**	83. **B**	112. **C**
26. **D**	55. **A**	84. **B**	113. **A**
27. **C**	56. **C**	85. **C**	114. **D**
28. **D**	57. **C**	86. **A**	115. **D**
29. **C**	58. **D**	87. **B**	

DIAGNOSTIC CHART

Instructions: After you score your test, complete the following chart by inserting in the column entitled "Your Number Correct" the number of correct questions you answered in each of the eight sections of the test. Then compare your score in each section with the ratings in the column entitled "Scale." Finally, to correct your weaknesses, follow the instructions found at the end of the chart.

Section	Question Numbers	Area	Your Number Correct	Scale
1	1–8	Memory (8 questions)		8 Right—Excellent 6–7 Right—Good 5 Right—Fair Under 5 Right—Poor
2	9–32	Reading Comprehension (24 questions)		24 Right—Excellent 20–23 Right—Good 16–19 Right—Fair Under 16 Right—Poor
3	33–40	Verbal and Math (8 questions)		8 Right—Excellent 6–7 Right—Good 5 Right—Fair Under 5 Right—Poor
4	41–50	Correction Forms (10 questions)		10 Right—Excellent 8–9 Right—Good 7 Right—Fair Under 7 Right—Poor
5	51–58	Graphs (8 questions)		8 Right—Excellent 6–7 Right—Good 5 Right—Fair Under 5 Right—Poor
6	59–78	Applying Correction Procedures (20 questions)		20 Right—Excellent 18–19 Right—Good 16–17 Right—Fair Under 16 Right—Poor
7	79–88	Judgment and Reasoning (10 questions)		10 Right—Excellent 8–9 Right—Good 7 Right—Fair Under 7 Right—Poor
8	89–100	Legal Definitions (12 questions)		12 Right—Excellent 10–11 Right—Good 8–9 Right—Fair Under 8 Right—Poor
9	101–115	Troublesome Question Types (15 questions)		14–15 Right-Excellent 10–13 Right-Good 8–9 Right-Fair Under 8 Right-Poor

How to correct weaknesses:

1. If you are weak in Section 1, concentrate on Chapter 3.
2. If you are weak in Section 2, concentrate on Chapter 1.
3. If you are weak in Section 3, concentrate on Chapter 2.
4. If you are weak in Section 4, concentrate on Chapter 4.
5. If you are weak in Section 5, concentrate on Chapter 5.
6. If you are weak in Section 6, concentrate on Chapter 6.
7. If you are weak in Section 7, concentrate on Chapter 7.
8. If you are weak in Section 8, concentrate on Chapter 8.
9. If you are weak in Section 9, concentrate on Chapter 9.

Note: Consider yourself weak in an area if you receive anything other than an excellent rating in it.

ANSWERS EXPLAINED

1. **(A)** The name *Bill* opens the door to a number of associations, such as accountants always send you a bill. We hope that you are using associations to help you do these memory questions. The more you practice creating and using them, the better you get at it.

2. **(C)** Don Hurte's name is perfect for an association to remind you that he is violent. Hurte likes to hurt people. None of the other three inmates are linked to violence in any way.

3. **(A)** Peter Block is an automobile mechanic. One might say that Peter Block works on engine blocks.

4. **(D)** Smith, Block, and Hurte are all white males. Remember that, when one of a group of people in a memory story is different from others, that difference is probably going to be the subject of a question.

5. **(B)** Once again the question centered around the difference among the four inmates.

6. **(B)** Hopefully you recognized the obvious association between Frank Wood's name and his occupation. Carpenters, of course, work with wood.

7. **(A)** Bill Smith was the first inmate to be discussed and is serving his first prison term. Remember that anything that works for you can serve as a good association. Just practice making associations and your memory will improve.

8. **(D)** It is Frank Wood who is the swindler.

9. **(B)** The rule applies only to arrests for criminal acts that occur in a state correction facility. When rules are the subject of reading questions, you must read them very carefully.

10. **(B)** In this situation, the officer involved shall be notified in writing of the reason why the arrest is not appropriate.

11. **(B)** The passage clearly states that the appeal must be made to the department's grievance section.

12. **(B)** Before an officer responds to a legitimate request, he should always consider all the available facts.

13. **(C)** The passage does not indicate that all requests that involve a possible health problem must be granted. It does say that such requests must never be ignored.

14. **(B)** Explaining the reason for refusals is the best way to minimize future grievances.

15. **(A)** Felonies are the more serious of the two categories of crime.

16. **(A)** The present day distinction between a felony and misdemeanor in the United States is usually based on the length of the sentence imposed.

17. **(C)** Convictions for either felonies or misdemeanors can result in the assessment of a fine.

18. **(A)** By far, the component that receives the most funding is the police.

19. **(C)** The other three components are supervised by the courts.

20. **(D)** A major problem for the overall system is that each of the four components acts independently of the other.

21. **(C)** Certainty of punishment is unquestionably the greatest deterrent to future misbehavior.

22. **(B)** Severity of punishment is not an important consideration. This, of course, means that it is unimportant.

23. **(B)** Punishments that are excessively lenient can cause problems. Therefore, lenient punishments sometimes cause problems. Regarding choice D, although common sense dictates that this is a good statement, nothing in the paragraph supports this answer. Never introduce your own knowledge when answering reading comprehension questions. As the instructions state, you should base your answers solely on the information in the passage.

24. **(A)** Probation is the most commonly used sentencing option.

25. **(C)** People on probation often create serious crime problems.

26. **(D)** Society could not afford the cost of sending all convicted persons to prison. For this reason probation is indispensable.

27. **(C)** Inmates should never have keys for any reason. A thorough investigation must be made whenever an inmate is found to have a key of any kind.

28. **(D)** A separate key log should be maintained for every cell block in the facility.

29. **(C)** You must understand why choice A is not the answer. It is a partially correct statement of the kind often used by test writers as a wrong choice. The rule states that correction officers should never carry personal keys while they are working. It is the "while they are working" part of the rule that was left out in choice A.

30. **(C)** Green is the name of the correction officer who called his supervisor and requested an ambulance.

31. **(C)** Roe is the name of the injured party.

32. **(B)** After being *released*, the injured Mr. Roe went home.

33. **(C)** To find a percentage increase first select the two quantities to be compared. In the case of Assaults (Nonsexual), they would be 32 for last year, increasing to 48 for this year. Now find the distance between these two numbers, which is 16. Divide 16 by 32, which is the older number since it represents last year. The result is 0.5, which is the same as 50%. Because the numbers went up from 32 to 48, it is a percentage increase. The same procedure may be followed for the other three choices. Only the infractions offered by the choices should be considered in determining the greatest percentage increase. Petty Thefts can be eliminated because it represents a percentage decrease; Disorderly Conduct increased slightly over 16% and Unauthorized Uniforms increased only 20%. Choice C is the answer.

34. **(D)** The formula is the same as the previous question. Find the distance between the two quantities and then divide by the old number. If the quantities increased from last year to the current year, then a percentage increase occurred. If the quantities decreased, then a percentage decrease has occurred. For Refusal of Work Assignments, the quantities were 7 and 3 or a distance of 4. Divide 4 by 7, which was the quantity from last year or the old number, and the result is a little more than 57%. Possession of Narcotics is not quite a 32% decrease with Sexual Assaults decreasing only 25% and Possession of Weapons decreasing about 33%.

35. **(C)** After adding up all the infractions of last year, which is 375, and those of this year, which is 364, find the distance between them which is 11. Remember to divide 11 by the old number, or last year's infractions, which is 375. This comes to 2.9%. Because the infractions have decreased, it is a percentage decrease of 2.9%. If you erroneously divided by the number of this year's infractions, you would have been dividing 11 by 364, which gave you 3.02%. The answer is C.

36. **(D)** Counting both this year and last year there were 165 incidents of Unauthorized Uniforms as compared with 91 Petty Thefts, 80 Assaults (Nonsexual), and 115 Possession of Weapons.

37. **(A)** Choice B is incorrect because it should state, "accept my apology." Choice C is incorrect because it should state, "Between the two of them."

38. **(D)** Choice A is incorrect; it should state, "Who's afraid," to indicate Who is afraid. It is unclear in choice B who entered the car. It would be clearer if it stated, "Having entered her car, she rolled the windows up quickly." Choice C is incorrect; it should state, "hear the warden well."

39. **(C)** Choice A is incorrect because it should state, "for Officer Walls and me." Words such as *myself, herself, himself,* and *themselves* are known as reflexive pronouns and cannot be used in place of *me, her, him,* or *them.* They should be used to reflect back to the doer of the action, such as I love myself, He cut himself, and They injured themselves. Choice B is incorrect because it should indicate, "who you know committed the infraction." With this type of statement, it is best to remove words such as "you know" when analyzing the statement. Then the statement is easier to examine. By doing this you are left with, "The inmate whom committed the infraction." That is obviously not correct. Choice C is correct because *which* should be used to refer to objects.

40. **(C)** Choice A is incorrect because it should state, "stronger than he." Such statements are understood to mean that you can be stronger than he (is). The word *is* is understood. That is why it would be correct to state stronger than he is. Choice B is incorrect for the same reason, namely that *is* is also understood. What is understood is the statement "I am as happy in my job as she (is)." Choice C is stated correctly.

41. **(B)** Kegler attended a high school equivalency diploma class on Wednesday, not a college-level course. Also Kegler was sick on Tuesday and had the exact same work activities as Ford.

42. **(B)** Inmate Hill swept the visiting area on Thursday.

43. **(C)** Walls did it two times, and Ranter, Ford, and Kegler each did it once, for a total of five occasions. Remember that, according to the information on the rear of the form, each job is to be assigned for a 3-hour block of time. Therefore, five occasions multiplied by 3 hours for each occasion equals a total of 15 hours. Also if each job is to be assigned for a 3-hour block of time, Choice A should have been ruled out immediately because it cannot be divided by 3.

44. **(A)** Walls had eight activities times 3 hours each, which equals 24 hours.

45. **(D)** Reference 9 on Tuesday represents foundry duty.

46. **(A)** In selecting the correct choice you should have examined only the choices offered by the question. Our strategy, which recommends scanning the choices of the question and then examining the form, would have been a great help in answering this question. Of the choices offered, the most frequently done activity was washing the cell block floors.

47. **(D)** Only the activities listed on Thursday should be examined in answering this question.

48. **(C)** Kegler was the only inmate among the inmates mentioned in the choices who was sick during the period covered by the form.

49. **(D)** If you tried to answer this question by first finding the number of inmates who attended high school equivalency classes and then subtracted that number from the total number of inmates because you assumed that anyone who was not attending these classes already had a high school diploma, you made an error. Nothing on the form stated that attendance at the high school equivalency classes was mandatory for all those without a high school diploma.

50. **(A)** Other inmates, for example Apex, also worked in the machine shop. Also read carefully. The question asked for the least correct statement.

51. **(D)** There is no specific data given that deals with the crime of robbery.

52. **(B)** 56% of inmates who enter the prison after being convicted of crimes against persons are 21–30 years of age. A majority is more than half. Choice B is the answer.

53. **(B)** 65% of those under 21 who enter the prison after being convicted of crimes against a person are between 17 and 20 years of age. Because most means more than half, choice B is the answer. Concerning choice C, there is no way of determining from the data any specific information about persons who are 18 years of age. The 18-year-old inmates are included in the overall category of 17–20.

54. **(A)** 78% of those persons under 17 who enter the prison after a conviction of a crime against property are under 17.

55. **(A)** Choices B, C, and D would all be correct if the category involved was crimes against persons. However, the category was crimes against property. In the over 30 age group for the category crimes against property, 32% of the new inmates are over 30. 1000 new inmates multiplied by 0.32 (32% in decimal form) equals 320, as indicated in Choice A.

56. **(C)** This is a difficult question because it involves making two calculations. You must first determine the approximate number of new inmates convicted of crimes against persons who are under 21. This is accomplished by multiplying 1000 (the total number of new inmates) by 0.18 (the decimal equivalent of 18%). By doing this you determine that the number of new inmates under 21 entering as a result of a conviction for a crime against a person is 180. Of that number, 65% of them are 17 through 20 years of age. This means that 117 of them are 17 through 20 years of age (180 multiplied by 0.65, the decimal equivalent of 65%).

57. **(C)** To determine the answer to this question, all you had to do was to pick the answer off of the graph. Over 21 includes two categories, 21–30 and over 30. Because 56% are between 21 and 30 and 26% are over 30, simply add the two percentages to arrive at the answer, which is 82%, as indicated in choice C.

58. **(D)** Once again we have included a question that cannot be answered based on the data supplied. Test writers do this often, and we want you to be prepared. The data you were given to answer this series of questions was about the age of inmates entering the prison. You simply cannot use that data to answer any questions about the overall population of the prison at any specific point in time.

59. **(D)** Jewelry that simulates a weapon or facilitates escape is prohibited. Thus Choice A is incorrect. Hardcover balls are also prohibited, and powdered items must be purchased in the commissary.

60. **(A)** Statement 2 is incorrect because board games containing dice are not permitted.

61. **(C)** Choice C is the next step.

62. **(B)** Form 109 is a Recommendation for Criminal Charges.

63. **(D)** Choices A, B, and C are not mentioned in the procedure. Choice D is found in the procedure.

64. **(D)** The metal detector is to be tested on the midnight tour but not by the tour commander as suggested in choice C. Choice D is the best selection.

65. **(C)** If the search is negative, the briefcase may be returned to the visitor.

66. **(B)** According to the procedure, the first action to be taken under these circumstances is to notify a supervisor. Regarding choice D, there is no requirement that a female conduct the search.

67. **(B)** The action that should be taken immediately in such a situation is to refer all questions concerning denial of inmate jewelry to the captain.

68. **(C)** The appeal consists of submitting three written copies of Request for Reevaluation (Form 333) to the assistant warden within 3 days of the original denial.

69. **(A)** The entry is to be made by Officer Days, the escorting officer.

70. **(D)** According to the procedure, such inmates should be rear cuffed.

71. **(C)** Choice B is incorrect because it is not done immediately. Choice A is incorrect because it violates the procedure. Choice D is not found in the procedure.

72. **(A)** Questions where the answer is very clear and straightforward should show you the benefit of that part of our strategy calling for you to first scan the questions and the answer choices before rereading the procedure. This allows you to focus on what the examiner feels is important in the procedure.

73. **(C)** This is as stated in the procedure.

74. **(B)** The letter *T* is associated with the number 9, *R* with 1, *E* with 7, *M* with 6, *O* with 2 and *R* with 1.

75. **(A)** The letter *M* is associated with the number 6, *O* with 2, *U* with 3, *N* with 4, *D* with 5, and *S* with 0.

76. **(C)** The letter *M* is associated with the number 6, *O* with 2, *R* with 1, *O* with 2, *S* with 0, and *E* with 7.

77. **(A)** The letter *S* is associated with the number 0, *T* with 9, *O* with 2, *R* with 1, *E* with 7, and *R* with 1.

78. **(D)** This is as indicated by the reference table.

79. **(A)** The rule clearly states that an attorney must be present to protect the interests of the inmate.

80. **(D)** Choices A, B, and C all involve instant judgment and punishment, which is *never* a recommended approach in our democratic society. The action described in Choice D satisfies completely the stated rule.

81. **(B)** Change must be explained. Understanding must never be assumed, nor should an officer assume that posted regulations are understood.

82. **(D)** Officers are required to support the policies of the administration. If they do not agree with them, they should communicate this along with their reason to their supervisors, but as long as the policy remains in place, the officers are obligated to support it completely.

83. **(B)** In official matters, officers must follow the chain of command to implement change. If there were no employee suggestion system, the officer would properly present her idea to her supervisor. But, until official change is made, the existing procedure must be followed. Unofficial experimentation or unofficial attempts at convincing others is never appropriate.

84. **(B)** Acting with courtesy and tact is a mark of a true professional.

85. **(C)** "Off the record" statements are always inappropriate. Only with prior permission should an officer make detailed work-related statements to the media. Saying "No comment" is often misconstrued. The correct course of action is as stated in choice C.

86. **(A)** It is a definite responsibility of all correction officers to keep their supervisors informed of all important developments. Choice C is incorrect because such a serious situation warrants official and immediate action. Choice D is wrong because the chain of command must be maintained.

87. **(B)** Inmates almost always outnumber officers. If officers were armed, it would be a relatively easy task for inmates to attack a lone officer and take his firearm.

88. **(B)** Patients in psychiatric wards are often not responsible for their actions, and some may tend to be inclined toward violence.

89. **(D)** Once again we see the importance of the word *or* in our definition.

90. **(D)** Conduct includes both acts and omissions (the things a person does as well as the things a person fails to do), along with the mental state that accompanies the act or omission.

91. **(C)** The object of Joe's action was exactly the result he caused. Choice D might seem to have merit, but it's not in the information provided. Remember to base your answer solely on the information given.

92. **(C)** Don was aware of the risk and disregarded it.

93. **(B)** Frank failed to perceive the risk caused by his leaving the hole unattended and unprotected.

94. **(B)** The state must disprove a pure defense beyond a reasonable doubt.

95. **(A)** It is the defendant's responsibility to raise an affirmative defense.

96. **(B)** This is as stated in the given definitions.

97. **(B)** Mark is not criminally responsible for the actions described because of his age. Choice D is incorrect because a 15-year-old such as Mark could be criminally responsible if he committed certain very serious crimes.

98. **(C)** A 13-, 14-, or 15-year-old who commits murder or kidnapping is criminally responsible for the action such person takes.

99. **(C)** Choice C does not indicate force, physical helplessness, or a child under 11 years old.

100. **(A)** Ray has escaped from a detention facility after being convicted of a felony—that is, escape in the first degree.

101. **(A)** The answer choices suggest that the first sentence is either sentence 3 (choices A and D), sentence 1 (choice B), or sentence 2 (choice C). Upon reading the sentences, it is clear that sentence 3 must come first. So choices B and C can be eliminated. Choice A suggests sentence 2 comes last, and choice D suggests sentence 4 comes last. Comparing these two sentences easily reveals that sentence 2 must come last. Note that in sentence 3, the article "a" is used when referring to the correction officer. This should have helped you decide that sentence 3 should come first.

102. **(A)** Since each answer choice lists a different first sentence, you can arrive at the correct answer to this question very quickly. Clearly, sentence 5 comes first. Choice A is the answer.

103. **(B)** Since all four answer choices suggest the same first sentence, check the last sentence. All four choices suggest a different last sentence. Your job at this point is to decide which sentence should logically come last. Upon reading all four suggested last sentences, it is clear that sentence 4 comes last. The answer is choice B. Note that when times are involved, as in this question, they can prove to be quite helpful since information in law enforcement reports is usually reported in chronological sequence.

104. **(A)** Hopefully you recalled that when all the answer choices suggest the same first and last sentences, as in this question, you must go to the middle sentences to find the answer. You should start with the relationship between the first and second sentences. Note that all four choices have a different second sentence. This means that when you find the correct second sentence, you find the answer. Here it is clear upon reading that sentence 2 comes after sentence 1 since sentences 3, 4, and 5 all occur after the officer received the call to respond to the storehouse.

105. **(D)** All four answer choices suggest the same first sentence, so look at the last sentence in each answer choice. You should realize that all four suggested last sentences are different. This means that selecting the correct last sentence means selecting the correct answer. This selection is made rather simple by the word "finally" in sentence 2.

106. **(A)** Steps 2, 3, and 4 are called contingency steps. They need to be performed only under certain circumstances. Under the circumstances described in the stem of the question, none of these steps applies. The death was not described as being suspicious, and it did not occur in a public place. The stem of the question reveals that the officer has already completed step 1. Since steps 2, 3, and 4 do not apply, the next step is step 5.

107. **(C)** This is an example of a question requiring the exercise of judgment. The officer has just completed step 1. Step 2 is not needed since the visitor was arrested in the actual commission of an offense. Now comes the judgment part. Step 3 says, "Using discretion and sound judgment, handcuff the prisoner only when circumstances require." Considering that the visitor is a pregnant female in a wheelchair, sound judgment dictates that the handcuffing can be waived. The next step to be taken is step 4.

108. **(C)** This question invokes the "no assumptions" rule. The question does not mention the presence of the inmate's relatives, friends, or clerg. Do not assume they are on the scene. Skip step 3.

109. **(B)** You are told that the officer arrested the operator while correctly following procedures. So you should realize that steps 1, 2, and 3 have already been completed. However, simply arresting the violator does not complete step 4. The officer still has to take the arrested person to central booking.

110. **(C)** According to step 2a, the next step is to inform Mr. Jones that he may surrender the firearm to Officer Scott at the scene or at correction headquarters.

111. **(B)** When you turned right from Gleason Street, you were heading north on Dillon Boulevard, which is a two-way street. After continuing straight ahead for 3 blocks, you were at Beach Street, which is a one-way street heading east. The suggestion for counting blocks is to count from one intersection to another. If you made a left turn at this point, you would be going west on Beach Street and, as such, going against traffic.

112. **(C)** To be legally parked facing south, the van has to be parked on Christopher Boulevard. Choice A can be eliminated because heading east on Daniel Street is blocked by Gateway Prison, which prohibits thru traffic. Choice B is incorrect because making a right on Brody Street would have you heading west on Brody Street, which not only is an eastbound street but would also have you heading away from the required destination of Daniel Street and May Place. Choice D is incorrect because heading east on westbound Irene Street would be against the flow of traffic.

113. **(A)** Although choice A is the most appropriate, in this type of question you still must examine all the choices. Following choice B will get you to the correct destination, but it is not as direct as following the directions given in choice A. Choice C is incorrect because it directs you to head east on Irene Street, which is a westbound street. Choice D is incorrect because it directs you to make a right at Brody Street after heading south on Christopher Boulevard. This would cause you to go against traffic on Brody Street as well as head off the map.

114. **(D)** Choice A is incorrect because you are required to head west on Beach Street, which is an eastbound street. Choices B and C are incorrect because they both require that you go through Gateway Prison, an area that does not permit thru traffic.

115. **(D)** Under such circumstances, the only action that would be in keeping with the traffic regulations would be to make a left and thus legally head east on Brody Street. Remember that when you are given directions that require you to make right or left turns or to head north, south, east, or west, you must imagine yourself in the driver's seat of the vehicle.

Practice Test 2

This is the second of five practice tests that you will be taking. Don't forget to

1. take the test in one sitting. You have 3½ hours to answer all 100 questions.

2. use the test-taking strategies outlined in the Introduction. Make certain to develop and use a time management plan.

3. complete the diagnostic chart that appears at the end of this test after you score this practice examination.

4. use the answer sheet we have provided to record your answers.

ANSWER SHEET
Practice Test 2

Follow the instructions given in the test. Mark only your answers in the circles below.

WARNING: Be sure that the circle you fill is in the same row as the question you are answering. Use a No. 2 pencil (soft pencil).

BE SURE YOUR PENCIL MARKS ARE HEAVY AND BLACK. ERASE COMPLETELY ANY ANSWER YOU WISH TO CHANGE.

DO NOT make stray pencil dots, dashes, or marks.

1. (A) (B) (C) (D)
2. (A) (B) (C) (D)
3. (A) (B) (C) (D)
4. (A) (B) (C) (D)
5. (A) (B) (C) (D)
6. (A) (B) (C) (D)
7. (A) (B) (C) (D)
8. (A) (B) (C) (D)
9. (A) (B) (C) (D)
10. (A) (B) (C) (D)
11. (A) (B) (C) (D)
12. (A) (B) (C) (D)
13. (A) (B) (C) (D)
14. (A) (B) (C) (D)
15. (A) (B) (C) (D)
16. (A) (B) (C) (D)
17. (A) (B) (C) (D)
18. (A) (B) (C) (D)
19. (A) (B) (C) (D)
20. (A) (B) (C) (D)
21. (A) (B) (C) (D)
22. (A) (B) (C) (D)
23. (A) (B) (C) (D)
24. (A) (B) (C) (D)
25. (A) (B) (C) (D)

26. (A) (B) (C) (D)
27. (A) (B) (C) (D)
28. (A) (B) (C) (D)
29. (A) (B) (C) (D)
30. (A) (B) (C) (D)
31. (A) (B) (C) (D)
32. (A) (B) (C) (D)
33. (A) (B) (C) (D)
34. (A) (B) (C) (D)
35. (A) (B) (C) (D)
36. (A) (B) (C) (D)
37. (A) (B) (C) (D)
38. (A) (B) (C) (D)
39. (A) (B) (C) (D)
40. (A) (B) (C) (D)
41. (A) (B) (C) (D)
42. (A) (B) (C) (D)
43. (A) (B) (C) (D)
44. (A) (B) (C) (D)
45. (A) (B) (C) (D)
46. (A) (B) (C) (D)
47. (A) (B) (C) (D)
48. (A) (B) (C) (D)
49. (A) (B) (C) (D)
50. (A) (B) (C) (D)

51. (A) (B) (C) (D)
52. (A) (B) (C) (D)
53. (A) (B) (C) (D)
54. (A) (B) (C) (D)
55. (A) (B) (C) (D)
56. (A) (B) (C) (D)
57. (A) (B) (C) (D)
58. (A) (B) (C) (D)
59. (A) (B) (C) (D)
60. (A) (B) (C) (D)
61. (A) (B) (C) (D)
62. (A) (B) (C) (D)
63. (A) (B) (C) (D)
64. (A) (B) (C) (D)
65. (A) (B) (C) (D)
66. (A) (B) (C) (D)
67. (A) (B) (C) (D)
68. (A) (B) (C) (D)
69. (A) (B) (C) (D)
70. (A) (B) (C) (D)
71. (A) (B) (C) (D)
72. (A) (B) (C) (D)
73. (A) (B) (C) (D)
74. (A) (B) (C) (D)
75. (A) (B) (C) (D)

76. (A) (B) (C) (D)
77. (A) (B) (C) (D)
78. (A) (B) (C) (D)
79. (A) (B) (C) (D)
80. (A) (B) (C) (D)
81. (A) (B) (C) (D)
82. (A) (B) (C) (D)
83. (A) (B) (C) (D)
84. (A) (B) (C) (D)
85. (A) (B) (C) (D)
86. (A) (B) (C) (D)
87. (A) (B) (C) (D)
88. (A) (B) (C) (D)
39. (A) (B) (C) (D)
90. (A) (B) (C) (D)
91. (A) (B) (C) (D)
92. (A) (B) (C) (D)
93. (A) (B) (C) (D)
94. (A) (B) (C) (D)
95. (A) (B) (C) (D)
96. (A) (B) (C) (D)
97. (A) (B) (C) (D)
98. (A) (B) (C) (D)
99. (A) (B) (C) (D)
100. (A) (B) (C) (D)

THE TEST

Time: 3½ hours
100 questions

> **Directions:** Answer questions 1–8 based on the following illustration, which depicts items taken from two inmates immediately after they were arrested. You are permitted 5 minutes to study the illustration. Try to remember as many details as possible.
>
> Do not make written notes of any kind during this 5-minute period. At the end of 5 minutes, stop studying the illustration, turn the page, and answer questions 1–8 *without* referring back to the illustration.

DO NOT PROCEED UNTIL 5 MINUTES HAVE PASSED.

1. Which of the inmates is probably a sports fan?

    (A) Ron Tonso
    (B) William Judd
    (C) neither Ron Tonso nor William Judd
    (D) both Ron Tonso and William Judd

2. Which of the following statements is most correct concerning money possessed by the inmates?

    (A) Ron Tonso had the most money.
    (B) William Judd had the most money.
    (C) They both had an equal amount of money.
    (D) Neither of them had any money.

3. Which of the inmates is probably experiencing difficulties with his private residence?

    (A) Ron Tonso
    (B) William Judd
    (C) neither Ron Tonso nor William Judd
    (D) both Ron Tonso and William Judd

4. Which of the inmates is probably planning a trip?

    (A) Ron Tonso
    (B) William Judd
    (C) neither Ron Tonso nor William Judd
    (D) both Ron Tonso and William Judd

5. Which of the inmates is probably experiencing a medical problem?

    (A) Ron Tonso
    (B) William Judd
    (C) neither Ron Tonso nor William Judd
    (D) both Ron Tonso and William Judd

6. The plate number of William Judd's car is

    (A) QND 160.
    (B) 1632.
    (C) 804 QND.
    (D) not given.

7. Both Ron Tonso and William Judd had

    (A) a $10 bill.
    (B) a weapon.
    (C) at least one key.
    (D) aspirins.

8. Which inmate possessed a weapon?

    (A) Ron Tonso
    (B) William Judd
    (C) neither Ron Tonso nor William Judd
    (D) both Ron Tonso and William Judd

Directions: Answer questions 9–14 solely on the basis of the following passage.

Correction Officer Ginty, shield 24758, assigned to the visitors arrival station at the Municipal Island Detention Facility and working a 4 P.M. to 12 P.M. tour on August 17th, is told by a visitor at 5:10 P.M. that an elderly woman who came over to the island on the bus is still outside on the bus and is in need of medical assistance.

Officer Ginty notified the dispatcher that she was responding to the bus stop on the corner of Prison Row and 10th Street.

Correction Officer Ginty arrived at the bus stop at 5:15 P.M. and found three buses parked at that location. The officer asked the driver of Bus Number 2356 if he had any knowledge of an elderly woman in need of medical assistance. The driver directed the officer to Bus Number 2365, which was parked at the southeast corner of Prison Row and 10th Street. At 5:20 P.M., the officer located Bus Number 2365 and found the sick woman inside, the sick woman's niece, and two paramedics. The paramedics had arrived 5 minutes before the officer, having been called to the scene by the driver of the bus, Jack Hunt. Paramedics Green Number 7890 and Brown Number 1630 stated to the officer that the woman identified as Pat White, age 66, date of birth, 4/12/30, was in need of medical treatment, but she was refusing medical assistance.

Correction Officer Ginty tried but failed to convince the woman to go to the hospital. Mrs. Mary Martin, age 36, niece of Mrs. White, who resides at 1492 Columbus Avenue, apartment 12F, was also present, and she was able to convince her aunt to go to the hospital.

Mrs. White was removed from the bus at 6:00 P.M. and was put in ambulance Number 1889 and taken to Municipal Hospital. The ambulance arrived at the hospital at 6:15 P.M., and Mrs. White received the medical attention she needed so urgently.

9. Officer Ginty was initially informed about the sick woman on the bus by

(A) the radio dispatcher.
(B) a bus driver.
(C) a visitor.
(D) the sick woman's niece.

10. Which of the following is the correct time that Officer Ginty arrived at Bus Number 2356?

(A) 5:15 P.M.
(B) 5:20 P.M.
(C) 6:00 P.M.
(D) 6:10 P.M.

11. At what time did the paramedics arrive on Bus Number 2365?

(A) 5:15 P.M.
(B) 5:20 P.M.
(C) 6:00 P.M.
(D) 6:10 P.M.

12. Which of the following is the correct name of the sick woman's niece?

(A) Pat White
(B) Pat Martin
(C) Mary Martin
(D) Mary White

13. Which of the following is the correct date of birth of Mrs. Pat White?

(A) 4/12/30
(B) 4/22/30
(C) 12/4/30
(D) 1/12/30

14. The paramedics were called to the scene by

(A) Officer Ginty.
(B) Jack Hunt.
(C) Mary Martin.
(D) a visitor.

Correction Officers Harris, shield 2234, and Smits, shield 3324, are assigned as a search team to conduct living quarters searches in cell block 14. The captain on duty is Captain Rems. It is 10 A.M.

Unit 1 in cell block 14 is occupied by Inmate Smith, Inmate Number 22567. Prior to the search of Unit 1 and in compliance with existing regulations, Inmate Smith is placed outside the immediate area to be searched and is given a Pat Frisk search. A Pat Frisk search is a search of an inmate's person and wearing apparel while the inmate is clothed. Its sole purpose is to detect weapons. Once the officers determine that Inmate Smith has no weapons on his person, he is permitted to observe the search of his quarters. During the living quarters search, however, Inmate Smith attempts to disrupt the search so he is removed from the area of the search and the search is then continued. During the living quarters search, which is being conducted in full accordance with written procedural guidelines, all departmental property and all the inmate's personal property are examined carefully and objectively. The search reveals no violations, and Inmate Smith is returned to his cell.

The search team then proceeds to unit 2 of cell block 14, which is occupied by Inmate Green, Inmate Number 24589. At 10:30 A.M., after the required Pat Frisk search of Inmate Green was conducted, the search of his livings quarters was started. About 5 minutes after the start of the search, Officer Harris uncovers a small amount of marijuana hidden in an open pack of cigarettes. An immediate notification is then made to Captain Rems and the officers stop the search to await the arrival of the captain. The captain arrived at the scene 10 minutes later.

15. The only purpose of a Pat Frisk search is to detect

    (A) evidence.
    (B) contraband.
    (C) weapons.
    (D) marijuana.

16. Marijuana was found

    (A) in a pack of cigarettes belonging to Inmate Smith.
    (B) during a Pat Frisk search of Inmate Green.
    (C) in unit 2 of cell block 14.
    (D) by Officer Smits.

17. The inmate who became disruptive during the search of his living quarters was Inmate

    (A) Smits.
    (B) Green.
    (C) Harris.
    (D) Smith.

18. When making living quarters searches, Pat Frisk searches of inmates are required

    (A) by regulations.
    (B) only when officers feel they are in danger.
    (C) only when there is a specific need.
    (D) whenever contraband is found.

19. What time was it when Captain Rems arrived at unit 2 of cell block 14?

    (A) 10 A.M.
    (B) 10:30 A.M.
    (C) 10:35 A.M.
    (D) 10:45 A.M.

Directions: Answer question 20 based solely on the following rule.

Correction officers may apply for an interview with the warden, in writing, either directly or through official channels.

20. Correction officers

    (A) can telephone and ask for an interview with the warden.
    (B) can forward a written request for an interview with the warden through their supervisors.
    (C) must have a good reason for requesting an interview with the warden.
    (D) must inform their supervisors when they want to have an interview with the warden.

Unless such action interferes with their prescribed duties, correction officers in uniform must stand at attention and render a hand salute before speaking to a supervisor or when spoken to by a supervisor.

21. Correction officers

 (A) must always salute their supervisors before talking to them.
 (B) must always stand at attention when speaking with their supervisors.
 (C) who are not in uniform are not required to salute their supervisors.
 (D) who are in uniform must always salute their supervisors before speaking with them.

Correction officers shall not behave with disrespect toward a supervising officer.

22. For a correction officer to behave in a disrespectful way when dealing with a supervisor

 (A) is never permissible.
 (B) is sometimes allowed.
 (C) is always tolerated.
 (D) may or may not be permissible.

Correction officers are responsible for the proper care and maintenance as well as the serviceable condition of agency equipment and/or property issued for their use. If at any time equipment is properly passed from one officer to another, the last officer to receive the equipment shall be responsible for it. Whenever file cabinets are made available to correction officers, all official documents and records must be placed therein overnight. The last officer leaving an office is responsible for turning off all nonessential lights and electrical appliances. Windows must be closed overnight in all offices that are not used at night.

23. Correction officers

 (A) can be held responsible for the maintenance of all agency equipment.
 (B) are responsible for the serviceable condition of all agency property.
 (C) must take care of agency equipment that has been issued for their use.
 (D) are not responsible for the maintenance of any agency equipment.

24. When equipment is properly passed from one officer to another

   (A) responsibility for that equipment belongs to everyone who used it.
   (B) the first officer who used it is responsible for it.
   (C) the last officer who had the equipment is responsible for it.
   (D) no officer can be held responsible for it.

25. The last officer leaving an office

   (A) must always turn off all the lights.
   (B) must always turn off all electrical devices.
   (C) does not have to always close the windows.
   (D) must always close all windows.

Directions: Answer question 26 based solely on the following rule.

   Correction officers shall not convert to their own personal use any property belonging to any inmate or to the department of corrections.

26. Correction officers

   (A) cannot ever use any property belonging to inmates.
   (B) can sometimes adapt inmate property for their own personal use.
   (C) cannot ever use any property that is owned by the department of corrections.
   (D) can sometimes use department of corrections property.

Directions: Answer question 27 based solely on the following rule.

   Correction officers shall not carry packages into or from any prison without the prior authorization of the warden or a deputy warden.

27. Correction officers

   (A) always need permission from the warden to take packages out of a prison.
   (B) must get permission ahead of time to carry a package into a prison.
   (C) can sometimes carry packages into or out of a prison without anyone's permission.
   (D) can never carry packages into or out of a prison.

Disciplinary charges may be made against any Correction Officer who fails to pay his or her just debts.

28. Correction officers

   (A) may or may not be disciplined for failing to pay their debts.
   (B) must pay all their debts.
   (C) do not have to pay all their debts.
   (D) must be punished for nonpayment of debts.

Correction officers shall not accept an award or gift for departmental services without the written consent of the warden.

29. Gifts given to correction officers

   (A) must sometimes be refused.
   (B) can only be accepted with written permission of the warden.
   (C) are all subject to the above rule.
   (D) are treated differently than awards.

A complaint is an allegation of an improper or unlawful act committed by a correction officer provided that the act relates to the business of the correctional agency that employs the officer. A complaint shall be thoroughly investigated by the supervisor to whom it is referred, and if the condition complained of actually exists, it shall be corrected and steps shall be taken to prevent its recurrence.

30. Complaints

   (A) must involve an unlawful act.
   (B) must relate to the business of a correctional agency.
   (C) must be promptly made.
   (D) must be made in person.

31. Complaints

   (A) must be investigated by a supervisor.
   (B) cannot be anonymously made.
   (C) must all result in some form of corrective action.
   (D) do not all have to be investigated.

Correction officers shall not intercede with any court for the discharge of or change of sentence for any inmate.

32. Correction officers

    (A) need permission to intercede with a court concerning the discharge of an inmate.
    (B) are prohibited from asking a court to modify the sentence of an inmate.
    (C) can sometimes petition the courts to have an inmate's sentenced reduced.
    (D) can sometimes petition the courts to have an inmate's sentenced increased.

33. The inmates in a certain institution are seeking an increase in the free weights available in their exercise room. They are seeking a 20% increase over the current weight of their free weights, which is 1850 pounds. If their request is granted, the total weight of the free weights would be

    (A) 370 pounds.
    (B) 2220 pounds.
    (C) 1480 pounds.
    (D) 2520 pounds.

34. In cell block D 10 inmates shower at one time for a 5-minute shower period. Assuming that there are 150 inmates in cell block D, how long would it take for all the inmates to take a shower?

    (A) 1 hour
    (B) 1¼ hours
    (C) 1½ hours
    (D) 2 hours

35. Three inmates must equally share a 5 feet 9 inch long wood plank in an arts and craft class. In order for each inmate to receive an equal length of wood, how long should each length of wood be?

    (A) 19 and ⅔ inches
    (B) 20 inches
    (C) 1 foot and 11 inches
    (D) 2 feet

36. Inmate Don Bell has the following monies deposited into his commissary account: $15.85, $2.95, $36, $34.86, and $29.34. However, Inmate Bell also makes purchases from the commissary that amount to $17.31, $32, $0.89, $16.31, and $12.04. How much money is still in Inmate Bell's commissary account?

(A) $39
(B) $40.45
(C) $52.65
(D) $78.55

Directions: In each of questions 37–40 you will be given four choices. Each of the choices, A, B, and C, contains a written statement. You are to evaluate the statement in each choice and select the statement that is most accurately and clearly written. If all or none of the three written statements is accurately and clearly written, you are to select choice D.

37. According to the directions, evaluate the following statements.

(A) The principle of the high school sent textbooks to the facility.
(B) The principle reason for rules is to maintain order.
(C) The principal of equal treatment for all demands an investigation.
(D) All or none of the choices are accurate.

38. According to the directions, evaluate the following statements.

(A) The inmate went in the bathroom to take a shower.
(B) He is the inmate whom I think broke the refrigerator.
(C) The warden would not see the officers about their complaints.
(D) All or none of the choices are accurate.

39. According to the directions, evaluate the following statements.

(A) The drug has no side effects.
(B) Stress affects a person's appetite.
(C) The effect of the prison break on the inmates surprised me.
(D) All or none of the choices are accurate.

40. According to the directions, evaluate the following statements.

(A) The tour commander merely adapted the new plan from the old plan.
(B) The argument was among the warden and his deputy.
(C) I told the warden when the officers were already.
(D) All or none of the choices are accurate.

USE OF FIREARM BY CORRECTION EMPLOYEE
FIREARMS DISCHARGE REVIEW REPORT

SECTION ONE—Employee Information

RANK	DATE OF BIRTH	FACILITY
Correction Officer		Highs Detention

SHIELD NO.	SURNAME	FIRST
23987	Bomber	Don

PRESENT ASSIGNMENT	DATE ASSIGNED
Kitchen	08-05-xx

SECTION TWO—Firearms Information
Make [Colt]   Model [Military]   Serial Number [XN1923]
Type: Revolver [x]   Pistol [ ]   Other [ ]
Firearms Removed From Officer   [ ] Yes   [x] No

SECTION THREE —Details Of Firearms Discharge

Date of Firearms Discharge	Location of Shooting
March 17, 20xx	Highs Detention Facility

Firearms

Case Number	Time of Firearms Discharge	Injuries
26	1150 Hours	Yes [ ] No [x]

DETAILS: At the time and place of occurrence, Correction Officer Don Bomber did discharge his service revolver. While outside the main gate and receiving food deliveries from Mark and Sons, a private vendor, Officer Bomber was approached by two males who demanded the release of one of the inmates unloading foodstuffs from the van of the private vendor. One of the males displayed what appeared to be a sawed off shotgun and aimed it at the corrections officer who drew his revolver and fired one shot at the male. Both males fled the scene in a late model white sedan. A search of the area by the police of the 2nd Precinct and correction officers did not reveal any injuries or property damage. The investigation to identify the two males is continuing under Police Complaint number 4768 and Department of Correction Criminal Case number 6478.

SECTION FOUR – FIREARM DISCHARGE REVIEW BOARD FINDINGS
Date Hearing Held: March 30, 20xx
Hearing Officer: Deputy Warden Frank Long
Finding: Officer acted properly under the Defense of Justification of Deadly Physical Force found in the State Penal Code.
Recommendation: Officer should continue in present assignment and Department Medical Officer Ray Shine to arrange Post Trauma Counseling sessions prior to 05-10-20xx.

41. What is the last name of the officer who discharged a firearm?

   (A) Long
   (B) Bomber
   (C) Shine
   (D) Mark

42. What is the firearm case number?

   (A) 26
   (B) 62
   (C) 4768
   (D) 6478

43. Concerning the firearm discharge, on what law did the hearing officer base the finding?

   (A) The State Criminal Procedure Law
   (B) The United States Title Codes
   (C) The Rules and Regulations of the Department of Correction
   (D) The State Penal Code

44. The type of weapon that was discharged was a

   (A) Colt pistol.
   (B) Smith and Wesson revolver.
   (C) Colt revolver.
   (D) Smith and Wesson pistol.

45. What was the date of the hearing?

   (A) March 17
   (B) March 30
   (C) 08-05
   (D) 05-10

46. What is the date of birth of the officer who discharged the firearm?

   (A) January 10th
   (B) January 15th
   (C) June 10th
   (D) cannot be determined from the information provided

47. The investigation concerning the identification of the two males is continuing under which of the following?

(A) Police Complaint number 4768
(B) Department of Correction Criminal Case 4768
(C) Police Complaint number 6478
(D) Police Complaint number 6478 and Department of Correction Criminal Case 4768

48. It would be most correct to state that the number 23987 represents

(A) a case number.
(B) a police officer's shield number.
(C) a serial number.
(D) a correction officer's shield number.

49. Which of the following most accurately represents the serial number of the firearm that was discharged?

(A) NX1293
(B) NX1923
(C) XN1923
(D) XN1293

50. The firearm that was discharged was

(A) removed from the officer.
(B) not removed from the officer.
(C) never found.
(D) stolen by the two males.

WEEKLY PAYROLL FOR INMATES
ASSIGNED TO CELL BLOCK 16
WEEK OF MAY 15TH

Inmate	Assignment Code	Hours Worked	Current Rating
F. Day	1	28	A
J. Brown	4	32	B
F. White	1	18	A
D. Smith	2	22	D
C. Beach	3	0	C
G. May	4	40	A
J. Fine	2	30	D
M. Branch	4	24	Unrated
S. Sweet	1	20	A
L. Waters	3	10	B

Note: Supervisors of unrated inmates must submit Form 221 each week that the inmate remains unrated. Until an inmate is rated he will be assigned a temporary rating of A.

ASSIGNMENT CODES

Code	Basic Salary	Added Bonus for Hours in Excess of 20 Each Week
1	$2.00/hour	$1.00/hour
2	$3.00/hour	$1.50/hour
3	$4.00/hour	$2.00/hour
4	$5.00/hour	$2.50/hour

RATING BONUS

Rating	Bonus
A	5% of total weekly salary
B	10% of total weekly salary
C	15% of total weekly salary
D	20% of total weekly salary

51. Inmates who have the potential to earn the most money are the ones who have an assignment code of

    (A) 1 and a rating of A.
    (B) 4 and a rating of A.
    (C) 1 and a rating of D.
    (D) 4 and a rating of D.

52. Assume that you are the correction officer who is the supervisor of inmates assigned to cell block 16. Concerning Inmate Branch, at the end of each week you have a specific responsibility to

    (A) train him.
    (B) rate him.
    (C) discipline him.
    (D) submit a Form 221 concerning him.

53. Which of the following inmates received the lowest salary, including bonuses, for the week of May 15th?

    (A) Inmate Day
    (B) Inmate Brown
    (C) Inmate White
    (D) Inmate Beach

54. An inmate who has an assignment code of 3 is eligible for a bonus for hours worked in excess of 20 hours. This bonus represents

    (A) an increase of 10% over the basic salary.
    (B) an increase of 20% over the basic salary.
    (C) an increase of 50% over the basic salary.
    (D) an increase of 100% over the basic salary.

55. How much money did Inmate Waters earn during the week of May 15th?

    (A) $30
    (B) $40
    (C) $44
    (D) cannot be determined

56. How much was Inmate May's rating bonus for the week of May 15th?

    (A) $12.50
    (B) $25
    (C) $50
    (D) cannot be determined

57. How much did Inmate Branch earn during the week of May 15th?

    (A) $6.50

    (B) $130

    (C) $136.50

    (D) cannot be determined

58. How much did Inmate Sweet earn during the week of March 15th?

    (A) $84

    (B) $42

    (C) $21

    (D) cannot be determined

Directions: Answer questions 59–63 based solely on the following information.

When a death occurs for which a member of the department is entitled to personal leave with pay, the member shall prepare a Request for Leave Report. If the member is unable to make personal application, the command clerk shall prepare the Request for Leave Report and submit it to the member's commanding officer. The member making the request shall be excused with pay for four consecutive scheduled tours of duty.

A member shall be entitled to such leave for the death of any of the following:

1. an immediate family member or
2. a domestic partner or
3. the covered relative of a domestic partner.

The immediate family shall include a spouse; biological, adoptive, foster, or step parent; child; brother or sister; father-in-law, mother-in-law, or any relative residing in the household.

Domestic partners shall include two (2) persons, both of whom are twenty-one (21) years of age or older and neither of whom is married, who have a close and personal relationship including shared responsibilities, who have lived together for a period of two (2) years or more on a continuous basis at time of death, and who have registered with the city department of personnel as domestic partners and have not terminated the registration in accordance with procedures established by the city department of personnel.

A covered relative of a domestic partner includes a parent or child of such domestic partner, or a relative of such domestic partner who resides in the household.

Any member of the department of correction who is turned down after seeking domestic partner status for someone and wishes to appeal must submit a written appeal within 30 days directly to the department's counsel general stating the reasons for the appeal.

59. When a death occurs for which a member of the correction department is entitled to a personal leave, a Request for Leave Report shall be prepared by

(A) the member's commanding officer.
(B) an immediate member of the member's family.
(C) only the member seeking the leave.
(D) the member seeking the leave or the command clerk.

60. When a death occurs for which a member of the department is entitled to personal leave, the member shall be excused

(A) with pay for any four tours of duty selected by the member.
(B) without pay for four consecutive scheduled tours of duty.
(C) with pay for four consecutive scheduled tours of duty.
(D) without pay for any four tours of duty selected by the member.

61. A member of the department of correction would be least likely to be granted a personal leave based on the death of which of the following?

(A) a grandmother who raised the employee and now lives out of town
(B) a cousin who lives in the employee's household
(C) a domestic partner of the same gender
(D) a mother-in-law

62. Raymond has never been married and is a 24-year-old male correction officer. According to department of correction's procedure, which one of the following would most qualify to become Raymond's domestic partner?

(A) Terry, a 20-year-old female, who has never been married
(B) Louise, a 36-year-old female, who is married
(C) Sherry, a 23-year-old female, who is divorced and whom Raymond has lived with for 1 year
(D) Albert, a 24-year-old male, who is currently unmarried and whom Raymond has lived with for 3 years

63. Harriet is a female correction officer. She applies for domestic partner status with Roy. Her application requesting such status is turned down. She prepares a written appeal. She would be most correct if she submitted the appeal to

(A) her commanding officer within 30 days.
(B) the department's counsel general within 10 days.
(C) her commanding officer within 10 days.
(D) the department's counsel general within 30 days.

The following general regulations shall govern the behavior of correction officers.

A member of this Department performing the duties of a correction officer shall

1. Perform all duties as directed by competent authority.

2. Remain at assigned post until properly relieved.

    a. Notify the tour commander and, if possible, make entry in the cell block log before leaving post.
    b. Make entry in the cell block log upon return to post and notify the tour commander.

3. Make accurate, concise entries in department records in chronological order, without delay, using black ink.

4. Sign department reports or forms with full first name, middle initial, and surname.

5. Make corrections on department records by drawing an ink line through incorrect matter. Enter correction immediately above and initial change.

6. Use numerals when entering dates on department forms (e.g., 1/5/95).

7. Use abbreviation "Do" for ditto.

8. Start serial numbers with one (1) at beginning of each year for official forms or reports, unless otherwise specified.

64. Correction Officer Neil Harry Bailes is assigned to the Del Ray Correctional Facility. When signing an official department form, Officer Bailes would be most correct if he signed his name in which of the following formats?

    (A) N. Bailes
    (B) N.H. Bailes
    (C) Neil H. Bailes
    (D) Neil Harry Bailes

65. Correction Officer Roller is assigned to cell block 15. The officer's assistance is required by a correction officer assigned to an adjacent cell block. Officer Roller makes an entry in the cell block log and then immediately leaves cell block 15 to assist the officer in the adjacent cell block. Upon returning to his post, Officer Roller notifies the tour commander. In this situation Officer Roller's actions were

(A) proper, mainly because an entry was made in the cell block log prior to leaving the cell block.

(B) improper, mainly because no entry is ever required in the cell block log prior to leaving the cell block.

(C) proper, mainly because the tour commander was notified upon return to the cell block.

(D) improper, mainly because the tour commander was not notified prior to leaving the cell block and no entry was made in the cell block log upon returning to the cell block.

66. In connection with department of correction regulations which of the following statements is most correct?

(A) Official reports must be completed in black ink and serial numbers always begin with the number 1 at the beginning of the year.

(B) Official reports may be completed in blue or black ink and serial numbers begin with the number 1 at the beginning of the year unless otherwise specified.

(C) Official reports must be completed in black ink and serial numbers begin with the number 1 at the beginning of the year unless otherwise specified.

(D) Official reports may be completed in blue or black ink and serial numbers begin with the number 1 at the beginning of the year.

67. If the current date is the sixth day of June, and the year is 1996, then which of the following is the most appropriate entry when entering such a date on a department form?

(A) June 6, 1996
(B) June 06, 96
(C) 06/06/1996
(D) 6/6/96

68. Correction Officer Goods is preparing an official department form. The officer makes an error and wishes to correct one of the entries she made. In such a situation, the officer would be most correct if she

(A) circled the error and entered the correction immediately below the change and initialed it.
(B) drew an ink line through the error and entered the correction immediately below the change and initialed it.
(C) circled the error and entered the correction immediately above the change and initialed it.
(D) drew an ink line through the error and entered the correction immediately above the change and initialed it.

Directions: Answer question 69 based solely on the following.

An inmate who is either new or direct admission to a department facility shall be searched and identified in front of a correction officer by the escorting officer turning the prisoner over to the department facility. Before the correction officer concerned accepts the prisoner, that correction officer shall take the following actions in this order:

1. inspect all documents mandating the commitment of the prisoner,

2. pat frisk the prisoner before accepting the prisoner,

3. record the prisoner's name on the Inmate Intake Sheet,

4. record the prisoner's state criminal identification number.

69. A police officer arrives at the End Zone Correctional Facility with a prisoner. Correction Officer Dawns has the escorting police officer search and identify the prisoner in front of both officers. Which one of the following should Officer Dawns do next?

(A) Record the prisoner's state criminal identification number.
(B) Pat frisk the prisoner before accepting the prisoner.
(C) Record the prisoner's name on the Inmate Intake Sheet.
(D) Inspect all documents mandating the commitment of the prisoner.

Directions: Answer questions 70 and 71 based solely on the following information.

A correction officer assigned to a tower observation point shall be particularly aware of suspicious vehicles in the vicinity of the institution. A correction officer should take the following steps in this order when a suspicious vehicle is observed:

1. record a description of the vehicle, paying particular attention to the type of vehicle, color, and if possible the license plate number;

2. notify the tour commander of the exact location of the vehicle;

3. make a note of the description of the occupants;

4. notify all officers assigned at all entry gates.

However, if the occupants of the vehicle exit the vehicle, then the tour commander shall be notified immediately before any other action is taken.

70. At 1730 hours, while on duty at an observation tower, Correction Officer Bends observes a suspicious car loitering in the vicinity of the institution. Officer Bends further observes two males getting out of the car each carrying a long package. Officer Bends should immediately

   (A) record a description of the vehicle.
   (B) notify all officers assigned at all entry gates.
   (C) notify the tour commander.
   (D) make a note of the description of the occupants.

71. At about 1800 hours, Officer Bends again observes a suspicious car in the vicinity of the institution. It is a different car than the one earlier observed by Officer Bends. In such a situation which of the following actions should the correction officer take first?

   (A) Take down the license plate number if possible.
   (B) Notify the tour commander.
   (C) Notify all officers assigned at all entry gates.
   (D) Make a note of the description of the occupants.

When a correction officer is authorized to make an arrest whether on or off duty, the officer shall comply with the following in the order given:

1. inform the person of the reason for the arrest unless the person who has been arrested has attempted to escape or has physically resisted;

2. immediately rear cuff the prisoner;

3. field search the prisoner for evidence, weapons, and other contraband;

4. advise the prisoner of Miranda Rights before questioning such prisoner.

72. Correction Officer Parks is off duty and sees a man breaking into Officer Parks' automobile. The officer approaches the man and lawfully places him under arrest. The male bolts from the officer and tries to escape. After a brief chase and struggle Officer Parks is able to subdue the man. Which of the following actions must Officer Parks take next?

(A) Advise the prisoner of Miranda Rights before questioning such prisoner.
(B) Field search the prisoner for evidence, weapons, and other contraband.
(C) Immediately rear cuff the prisoner.
(D) Tell the prisoner why he has been arrested.

73. Evaluate the following statements concerning arrests made by correction officers.

1. A field search of a prisoner for evidence, weapons, and other contraband should be conducted by the correction officer.

2. A prisoner arrested by a correction officer must always be given Miranda Rights.

Which of the following is most accurate concerning the statements above?

(A) Only statement 1 is correct.
(B) Only statement 2 is correct.
(C) Both statements 1 and 2 are correct.
(D) Neither statement 1 nor 2 is correct.

PRACTICE TEST 2

A	B	C	D	E	X
1	2	3	4	5	0

EXAMPLE

Which of the following choices contains the letters that add up to 10 after they are converted to numbers?

    (A) A, C, E
    (B) B, D, E
    (C) A, D, E
    (D) C, D, E

Choice C contains letters A, D, and E, which, according to the reference table, are associated with 1, 4, and 5. When added together, they equal 10.

74. Which of the following choices contains the letters that add up to 6 after they are converted to numbers?

    (A) A, B, D
    (B) A, B, C
    (C) A, B, E
    (D) B, C, D

75. Which of the following choices contains the letters that add up to 14 after they are converted to numbers?

    (A) D, D, E
    (B) D, E, E
    (C) A, B, C, D, E
    (D) D, D, E, X

76. Which of the following choices contains the letters that add up to 19 after they are converted to numbers?

    (A) E, D, E, X, E
    (B) E, E, E, A, B
    (C) A, B, C, D, E, X
    (D) D, D, E, C, D

77. Which of the following choices contains the letters that add up to 11 after they are converted to numbers?

(A) A, E, B, D
(B) B, C, D, A, X
(C) X, B, E, D
(D) B, A, X, E, D

78. Which of the following choices contains the letters that add up to 17 after they are converted to numbers?

(A) X, B, E, D, C
(B) A, E, E, B, E, X
(C) C, C, X, E, D
(D) E, X, D, C, E

79. Carelessness on the part of an on- or off-duty correction officer in the carrying or safekeeping of firearms shall be deemed neglect of duty and is subject to disciplinary action. The primary intent of such a rule is to

(A) deter carelessness in the carrying or handling of firearms.
(B) to punish careless officers.
(C) protect the general public.
(D) prevent civil suits.

80. There are times when correction officers must give testimony about an inmate at a criminal trial. Of the following steps you take to prepare for giving such testimony, by far the MOST important step for you to take is to

(A) refresh your memory about the case by reviewing your personal notes and any other available information.
(B) go over your testimony with the prosecutor assigned to the case.
(C) make sure your uniform is neat and clean so that you make a professional appearance on the witness stand.
(D) anticipate questions that you might be asked and answers you might give.

81. Assume that you are a correction officer and that you have just given an inmate instructions concerning an important new regulation. It is essential that the inmate understand the regulation. To determine if she does in fact understand, the best course of action for you to take is to

(A) ask her if she understands.
(B) ask her if she has any questions.
(C) ask her to repeat the instructions back to you in her own words.
(D) give her a copy of the regulations and tell her to study it.

82. Assume that you are a correction officer. An inmate approaches you and asks you to recommend an accountant to him to straighten out his wife's income taxes. Under these circumstances, the best course of action for you to take is to

(A) give the inmate the name of a good accountant if you know of one.
(B) tell the inmate that he should not worry about his wife's income taxes until after he is released from prison.
(C) explain to him that, while you would like to help him, you simply cannot comply with his request.
(D) tell him that you wouldn't help him with any of his personal problems.

83. Assume that you are a correction officer and you know that an inmate under your supervision has an officially documented medical problem that limits his ability to perform a full range of physical activities. You should

(A) give him no special consideration.
(B) exempt him from all physical activities.
(C) assign him only tasks that he can safely perform.
(D) perform some of his physical duties for him.

84. A correction officer should expect

(A) to be treated with respect by all inmates.
(B) to be the subject of insolent verbal attack.
(C) to be able to reason with all inmates.
(D) to have all inmates always yield to your authority.

85. Inmates have their own language. For a correction officer to speak that language constantly when dealing with inmates

(A) is highly recommended.
(B) may or may not be advisable.
(C) is necessary.
(D) is not recommended.

86. Correction officers will hear many inmate complaints. Concerning inmate complaints, the best way for an officer to deal with them is to

(A) make an official record of each one.
(B) disregard all but the most serious ones.
(C) make a thorough investigation of each one.
(D) analyze each one before deciding what to do.

87. It is prohibited by correctional policy for correction officers to socialize with inmates. The primary reason for this rule is that when an officer socializes with an inmate

 (A) he puts the inmate in danger of physical attack from other inmates.
 (B) he invariably winds up helping the inmate to escape.
 (C) he often becomes less attentive about his ever-present responsibility to guard prisoners.
 (D) he always creates the impression that he sympathizes with the plight of all inmates.

88. Assume that you are a correction officer on duty in the prison library when an inmate becomes violent. He begins to throw books off the library shelf while complaining loudly that he is never able to find the law books he needs. You should immediately

 (A) offer your assistance to find the needed books.
 (B) try to calm the inmate by reasoning with him.
 (C) tell the other inmates present to leave.
 (D) have the inmate removed from the library.

Directions: Answer questions 89–93 based solely on the following legal definitions.

A parent or other such person entrusted with the care of a child under the age of 21 years old may use physical force, but not deadly physical force, when the parent or other such person reasonably believes it necessary to maintain discipline or to promote the welfare of such child.

Deadly physical force is different from physical force in that deadly physical force is the kind of force that can produce death or other serious physical injury.

A warden or other authorized official of a jail, prison, or correctional institution may, in order to maintain order and discipline, use physical force.

A person such as a correction department bus driver responsible for the maintenance of order in a common carrier of passengers such as a bus, or a person acting at the direction of such a bus driver, may use physical force when and to the extent that this person reasonably believes it necessary to maintain order. However, deadly physical force may be used only to maintain order on a common carrier such as a bus if such person reasonably believes it necessary to prevent death or other serious physical injury.

A person acting under a reasonable belief that physical force is needed to prevent another person from committing suicide may use physical force but not deadly physical force intended to protect such a suicidal person from serious physical injury.

89. Evaluate the following statements:

1. Only a warden of a jail, prison, or correctional institution may, in order to maintain order and discipline, use physical force.
2. Physical force and deadly physical force have the same meaning.

Which of the following is most accurate concerning the statements above?

(A) Only statement 1 is correct.
(B) Only statement 2 is correct.
(C) Both statements 1 and 2 are correct.
(D) Neither statement 1 nor 2 is correct.

90. Leslie is a correction officer in a correctional institution. While performing a tour of duty one night, she observes an inmate attempting to commit suicide. In such an instance, it would be most correct for Leslie

(A) to use only physical force to prevent the inmate's suicide.
(B) to use only deadly physical force to prevent the inmate's suicide.
(C) to use physical force or deadly physical force to prevent the inmate's suicide if the inmate is facing the death penalty.
(D) to use deadly physical force and physical force if she reasonably believed that the inmate's attempt at suicide might be successful.

91. Jill wants to discipline her son Mark who is 17 years old. In such an instance, Jill

(A) may not use physical force since Mark is over 16 years old.
(B) may use deadly physical force since Mark is more than 16 years old.
(C) may use physical force because of her relationship with Mark and also because of Mark's age.
(D) may use physical force to discipline Mark but only until he is 18 years old.

92. If a bus driver wishes to maintain order on the bus, it would be most appropriate for the driver

(A) to use deadly physical force in all instances.
(B) to use only physical force in all instances.
(C) to never direct any of the passengers to use physical force in seeking to maintain order on the bus.
(D) to use deadly physical force only if he reasonably believes it necessary to prevent death or serious physical injury.

93. Evaluate the following statements:

1. In order for deadly physical force to occur, a death must result.

2. If John shoots at Mary and misses, no deadly physical force is considered to have occurred.

Which of the following is most accurate concerning the statements above?

(A) Only statement 1 is correct.

(B) Only statement 2 is correct.

(C) Both statements 1 and 2 are correct.

(D) Neither statement 1 nor 2 is correct.

Directions: Answer questions 94–98 based solely on the following information.

A person may use physical force upon another person when and to the extent he reasonably believes such to be necessary to defend himself or a third person from what he reasonably believes to be the use or imminent use of unlawful physical force by such other person.

A person may use physical force when he reasonably believes such to be necessary to prevent or terminate the stealing of property or the damage to property, except such person may use deadly physical force to prevent or terminate an arson or attempted arson.

A private person may use deadly physical force when necessary to arrest another person who has in fact committed the crime of murder, manslaughter in the first degree, robbery, forcible rape, or forcible sodomy and who is in immediate flight therefrom.

When necessary a peace officer in the course of making an arrest may use deadly physical force against a person who the peace officer reasonably believes committed kidnapping, burglary in the first degree, escape in the first degree, and arson.

94. Tom is a peace officer and is attempting to arrest Pat who is in the act of committing a certain offense. It would be most appropriate for Tom as a peace officer to use deadly physical force if the offense being committed by Pat is

(A) larceny.

(B) assault in the third degree.

(C) escape in the first degree.

(D) any burglary.

95. It would be least appropriate for Harriet, who is a peace officer, to use deadly physical force when effecting the arrest of someone who is committing

(A) kidnapping.
(B) arson.
(C) criminal mischief in the first degree.
(D) burglary in the first degree.

96. Mary is forcibly raped by Tom while Mary is home alone in her apartment. Louise, Mary's sister, is forced to watch the horrible ordeal. Tom flees the scene unapprehended and unidentified. Frightened by this experience, Louise begins to carry a sharp pair of scissors in her handbag. Several weeks after the rape, Louise spots Tom on a bus. She follows him off the bus intending to arrest him and stabs him in the stomach, thus using deadly physical force against Tom. In such an instance, the use of deadly physical force by Louise was

(A) justified because Tom had committed a forcible rape.
(B) not justified because Tom was no longer in immediate flight from the rape.
(C) justified because Louise was trying to arrest Tom.
(D) not justified because Louise had not been the victim of the forcible rape.

97. A private person may use deadly physical force to arrest a person for certain crimes if that person is in immediate flight from such crimes. Which of the following is not one of these crimes?

(A) murder
(B) manslaughter in the first degree
(C) robbery
(D) any sodomy

98. Pat is walking along the street when she suddenly sees a man trying to commit arson by setting fire to a building Pat does not own or even live in. Pat is, however, licensed to carry a firearm. She draws her gun and yells to the man to stop. He yells back that he wants to get even with the landlord and continues to try to set fire to the building. Pat fires her gun, striking and killing the man, thereby using deadly physical force against him. In such an instance, Pat was

(A) justified mainly because she was licensed to carry a firearm.
(B) not justified mainly because she did not own the building.
(C) justified mainly because she was preventing or terminating an arson.
(D) not justified mainly because the arson was only being attempted and was never actually completed.

Contraband is any article or thing that a person confined in a detention facility is prohibited from obtaining or possessing by law, rule, regulation, or order. An example of contraband is alcohol.

Dangerous contraband means contraband that is capable of being used to endanger the safety or security of a detention facility or any person in a detention facility. An example of dangerous contraband is a rope ladder.

A person who brings contraband into a detention facility or a person who, while confined in a detention facility, makes contraband is guilty of a misdemeanor. However, if a person brings dangerous contraband into a detention facility or a person who is confined in a detention facility makes dangerous contraband, then such person is guilty of a felony.

99. Correction Officer Winters notices a bulge under the shirt of Pat Walker, a visitor at the Bakers Detention Facility. Subsequent investigation revealed that Walker was bringing in a tool capable of making keys that could then be used to open cell doors. In this instance, it would be most appropriate to charge Walker with

(A) a felony.

(B) a misdemeanor.

(C) either a misdemeanor or a felony depending on Pat Walker's previous criminal record.

(D) no crime since Pat Walker is not an inmate.

A person renders criminal assistance when, knowing that another person has committed a crime and is being sought by law enforcement officials, such person hides or harbors the person being sought.

Any person who renders such criminal assistance to someone sought in connection with a felony is guilty of hindering prosecution in the second degree, which is a misdemeanor.

Hindering prosecution becomes more serious and is a felony when a person renders criminal assistance by hiding another person being sought for a Class A felony.

100. Which of the acts, if committed by an adult person, would be most appropriately considered a felony?

(A) Hiding a wanted fugitive who escaped from a detention facility while awaiting trial for a misdemeanor.

(B) Hiding oneself after escaping from a holding pen in a courtroom while on trial for the Class A felony of murder.

(C) Hiding a wanted fugitive who was being detained in a correctional institution for a Class A felony.

(D) Hiding oneself after escaping from the police for a misdemeanor.

STOP

END OF TEST

ANSWER KEY
Practice Test 2

1. **D**	26. **D**	51. **D**	76. **A**
2. **C**	27. **B**	52. **D**	77. **C**
3. **B**	28. **A**	53. **D**	78. **D**
4. **A**	29. **A**	54. **C**	79. **A**
5. **A**	30. **B**	55. **C**	80. **A**
6. **D**	31. **A**	56. **A**	81. **C**
7. **C**	32. **B**	57. **C**	82. **C**
8. **B**	33. **B**	58. **D**	83. **C**
9. **C**	34. **B**	59. **D**	84. **B**
10. **A**	35. **C**	60. **C**	85. **D**
11. **A**	36. **B**	61. **A**	86. **D**
12. **C**	37. **D**	62. **D**	87. **C**
13. **A**	38. **C**	63. **D**	88. **D**
14. **B**	39. **D**	64. **C**	89. **D**
15. **C**	40. **A**	65. **D**	90. **A**
16. **C**	41. **B**	66. **C**	91. **C**
17. **D**	42. **A**	67. **D**	92. **D**
18. **A**	43. **D**	68. **D**	93. **D**
19. **D**	44. **C**	69. **D**	94. **C**
20. **B**	45. **B**	70. **C**	95. **C**
21. **C**	46. **D**	71. **A**	96. **B**
22. **A**	47. **A**	72. **C**	97. **D**
23. **C**	48. **D**	73. **A**	98. **C**
24. **C**	49. **C**	74. **B**	99. **A**
25. **C**	50. **B**	75. **B**	100. **C**

DIAGNOSTIC CHART

Instructions: After you score your test, complete the following chart by inserting in the column entitled "Your Number Correct" the number of correct questions you answered in each of the eight sections of the test. Then compare your score in each section with the ratings in the column entitled "Scale." Finally, to correct your weaknesses, follow the instructions found at the end of the chart.

Section	Question Numbers	Area	Your Number Correct	Scale
1	1–8	Memory (8 questions)		8 Right—Excellent 6–7 Right—Good 5 Right—Fair Under 5 Right—Poor
2	9–32	Reading Comprehension (24 questions)		24 Right—Excellent 20–23 Right—Good 16–19 Right—Fair Under 16 Right—Poor
3	33–40	Verbal and Math (8 questions)		8 Right—Excellent 6–7 Right—Good 5 Right—Fair Under 5 Right—Poor
4	41–50	Correction Forms (10 questions)		10 Right—Excellent 8–9 Right—Good 7 Right—Fair Under 7 Right—Poor
5	51–58	Graphs (8 questions)		8 Right—Excellent 6–7 Right—Good 5 Right—Fair Under 5 Right—Poor
6	59–78	Applying Correction Procedures (20 questions)		20 Right—Excellent 18–19 Right—Good 16–17 Right—Fair Under 16 Right—Poor
7	79–88	Judgment and Reasoning (10 questions)		10 Right—Excellent 8–9 Right—Good 7 Right—Fair Under 7 Right—Poor
8	89–100	Legal Definitions (12 questions)		12 Right—Excellent 10–11 Right—Good 8–9 Right—Fair Under 8 Right—Poor

How to correct weaknesses:

1. If you are weak in Section 1, concentrate on Chapter 3.
2. If you are weak in Section 2, concentrate on Chapter 1.
3. If you are weak in Section 3, concentrate on Chapter 2.
4. If you are weak in Section 4, concentrate on Chapter 4.
5. If you are weak in Section 5, concentrate on Chapter 5.
6. If you are weak in Section 6, concentrate on Chapter 6.
7. If you are weak in Section 7, concentrate on Chapter 7.
8. If you are weak in Section 8, concentrate on Chapter 8.

Note: Consider yourself weak in an area if you receive anything other than an excellent rating in it.

ANSWERS EXPLAINED

1. **(D)** Ron Tonso was carrying a baseball schedule, and William Judd was carrying football tickets.

2. **(C)** Ron Tonso had a $20 bill and a quarter. William Judd had two $10 bills, two dimes, and a nickel. They both had $20.25.

3. **(B)** William Judd was in possession of an eviction notice. Ron Tonso was not in possession of any items that would lead one to believe he was having difficulties with his private residence.

4. **(A)** Ron Tonso had a plane ticket in his possession. William Judd was not in possession of any item that would lead one to believe he is planning a trip.

5. **(A)** Ron Tonso had a prescription and aspirin in his possession. William Judd was not in possession of any item that would lead one to believe he is experiencing a medical problem.

6. **(D)** William Judd did not possess any item that indicated the plate number of his car.

7. **(C)** Ron Tonso had one key. William Judd had two keys. They both had at least one key.

8. **(B)** William Judd had a knife.

9. **(C)** It was a visitor who was the first to inform the correction officer about the sick woman on the bus.

10. **(A)** Bus Number 2356 was the first bus the correction officer found, and that was at 5:15 P.M.

11. **(A)** Correction Officer Ginty arrived at Bus Number 2365 at 5:20 P.M., and the paramedics had arrived 5 minutes earlier.

12. **(C)** The sick woman's niece was Mary Martin.

13. **(A)** Answering this question is nothing more than an exercise in paying attention to detail.

14. **(B)** It was the driver of the bus, Jack Hunt, who called the paramedics to the scene.

15. **(C)** The sole, or only, purpose of a Pat Frisk search is to detect weapons.

16. **(C)** The marijuana was found in a pack of cigarettes in Inmate Green's cell, which is unit 2 of cell block 14. Notice how the test writer tried to trick you in choice A.

17. **(D)** Once again you can see the importance of being careful when doing reading comprehension questions. Lazy candidates select choice A, which is the name of one of the officers. It was Inmate Smith who became disruptive.

18. **(A)** It states in sentence two of paragraph two that the Pat Frisk search was made in compliance with existing regulations.

19. **(D)** The search of unit 2 began at 10:30 A.M. The marijuana was found 5 minutes later, and an immediate notification was made to the captain. The captain arrived on the scene 10 minutes later; that would be at 10:45 A.M.

20. **(B)** According to the rule, requests must be in writing, and they can be made directly to the warden, or they may be sent through official channels (up the chain of command). There is nothing in the rule that mentions the reason for the request. Even though choice C is a logical answer, it is not supported in the rule.

21. **(C)** The entire rule is aimed only at correction officers who are in uniform. And, even those in uniform are not covered by the rule if saluting and standing at attention interferes with their duties, such as during an emergency.

22. **(A)** This is what we call an absolute rule. It has no exceptions. Note the similarity between choices B and D. When you see such similarity between two choices, you must recognize that neither one can be the answer.

23. **(C)** The key to this question are the words "issued for their use." These were the limiting words that established the answer.

24. **(C)** If at any time, equipment is properly passed from one officer to another, the last officer to receive the equipment shall be responsible for it. The last officer leaving an office is responsible for turning off all nonessential lights and electrical appliances.

25. **(C)** Only those lights and electrical appliances which are nonessential must be turned off. Windows have to be closed only in offices that are not in use overnight.

26. **(D)** The rule prohibits correction officers from converting (or adapting) inmate or department of corrections property for their own use.

27. **(B)** Choice A is wrong because permission can also be obtained from a deputy warden. Choice B is correct because prior permission is always required.

28. **(A)** The key word in the rule is *may*. This is a flexible rule. It would be more inflexible if the words *must* or *shall* were used in place of *may*. Also, the rule has to do with just debts and not all debts.

29. **(A)** If the gift is one that is given for departmental services, and the warden does not give his approval, then that gift must be refused. The rule applies only to gifts given for departmental services. But the rule is the same for gifts as it is for awards, and that is why choice D is wrong.

30. **(B)** Complaints can involve either improper or unlawful acts. But they must relate to the business of some correctional agency. Choices C and D are not mentioned in the rule.

31. **(A)** A complaint shall be thoroughly investigated by the supervisor to whom it is referred. If the condition complained of actually exists, it shall be corrected, and steps shall be taken to prevent its recurrence.

32. **(B)** This is an absolute rule. It has no exceptions. Correction officers cannot intercede with a court for the discharge of or change (modification) of sentence for any inmate.

33. **(B)** A 20% increase of 1850 pounds would be 1850 × 0.2 = 370. Add 370 to 1850 and you arrive at 2220 pounds.

34. **(B)** Let's review the facts. There are 150 inmates, and 10 inmates shower at one time. Therefore, all 150 inmates showering 10 at a time would require 15 showering sessions (150/10 = 15). Each showering session lasts 5 minutes for a total of 75 minutes (15 × 5 = 75 minutes). Expressed in hours this is 1 hour and 15 minutes or 1¼ hours.

35. **(C)** The wood plank is 5 feet 9 inches long. That equals 69 inches (5 × 12 = 60 + 9 = 69). Dividing 69 by 3 we get 23 inches for each inmate, and 23 inches is the same as 1 foot and 11 inches as expressed by choice C.

36. **(B)**

Deposits	Purchases
$15.85	$17.31
2.95	32.00
36.00	0.89
34.86	16.31
+ 29.34	+ 12.04
$119.00	Less $78.55 = $40.45

37. **(D)** Choices A, B, and C are incorrect. When seeking to indicate the leader of an institution or the main purpose of something as in choices A and B, respectively, the use of the word *principal* would be correct. However, when seeking to indicate a basic truth, as in choice C, the use of the word *principle* would be correct.

38. **(C)** Choice A is incorrect because it should state, "went into the bathroom." Choice B is incorrect because it should state, "who I think broke the refrigerator." Words like "I think," "I know," "he feels," and so on do not affect the pronouns to be used, such as *who,* as seen in this example. The statement is more easily analyzed by mentally eliminating the words "I think" and changing it to read . . . He is the inmate whom broke the refrigerator. This makes it easier to determine that the use of the pronoun whom is incorrect. Choice C is correct.

39. **(D)** All choices are correctly stated. Remember that when *effect* is used as a noun (the name of a person, place, or thing), it represents a result. When *affect* is used as a verb (an action word), it means to influence.

40. **(A)** Choice B is incorrect because of the use of the word *among;* it should be "an argument between them." Choice C is incorrect because *already* means occurring before a specific time. Here, where the intent was to indicate that the officers were totally prepared, *all ready* should have been used.

41. **(B)** The surname of the correction employee who discharged his revolver is Bomber.

42. **(A)** The firearm case number is 26.

43. **(D)** The hearing officer found that the correction officer acted properly under the Defense of Justification of Deadly Physical Force found in the State Penal Code.

44. **(C)** The correct information appears under the caption Firearms Information.

45. **(B)** The firearm discharge took place on March 17, but the hearing took place on March 30.

46. **(D)** The information required by Section One concerning the date of birth of the employee is not provided by the form.

47. **(A)** The investigation to identify the two males is continuing under both Police Complaint number 4768 and Department of Correction Criminal Case number 6478. In choices B, C, and D the numbers are incorrectly presented.

48. **(D)** It is Correction Officer Don Bomber's shield number.

49. **(C)** The choices attempted to rearrange the serial number of the firearm. The correct serial number is XN1923.

50. **(B)** This is as indicated by the information found in Section Two.

51. **(D)** Inmates with an assignment code of 4 make $5.00 and a bonus of $2.50 an hour for hours worked in excess of 20 hours each week, and those who also have a rating of D receive an additional 20 per cent of the total weekly salary.

52. **(D)** Inmate Branch is unrated. Supervisors of unrated inmates are required to submit Form 221 each week an inmate remains unrated. There is nothing factual anywhere in the data to support choices A, B, or C.

53. **(D)** This is a very easy question, but many students will learn an important lesson from it. If you didn't realize from the beginning that Inmate Beach did not work any hours at all, you probably wasted time figuring out the salary earned by the inmates in choices A, B, and C. On a timed test like the one you will be taking, any time saved is a big plus. When you review the tables prior to answering the questions and notice something unusual, as in this case an inmate who did not work at all, you should make a mental note of it.

54. **(C)** An inmate with assignment code 3 earns a basic salary of $4/hour, with a bonus for excess hours of $2/hour, which is a 50% increase over the basic salary.

55. **(C)** Inmate Waters worked 10 hours at an hourly rate of $4 per hour (assignment code 3) for a total of $40. However, Inmate Waters has a B rating, which entitles him to an additional 10% of his total weekly salary, which amounts to an extra $4. Inmate Waters earned $40 plus $4, or $44, as indicated in choice C.

56. **(A)** Inmate May, who has an assignment code of 4, worked 40 hours at a basic hourly rate of $5/hour. That amounted to $200. His excess hour bonus added another $2.50/hour for 20 hours, or an additional $50. Because he has an A rating, his rating bonus amounts to 5% of $250 (his basic salary plus his excess hour bonus). Therefore, his rating bonus is $12.50.

57. **(C)** Branch worked 24 hours at $5/hour (assignment code 4). That is $120. He worked 4 hours in excess of 20, so he receives an additional $2.50/hour for each of these 4 hours, for an additional $10. He is unrated so he is given a temporary rating of A, which entitles him to an additional 5%. He has a grand total for the week of $136.50 ($120 plus $10 plus $6.50). If you picked choice C, you probably did not see the note under the rating bonus information.

58. **(D)** If you selected choice B, you probably didn't notice that the question asked about the week of March 15th, while the data is for the week of May 15th. Be careful!

59. **(D)** If the member is unable to prepare the Request for Leave Report, then the command clerk shall prepare it.

60. **(C)** Examiners often attempt to distract a candidate by changing one or more words of a procedure to test a candidate's ability to follow directions closely.

61. **(A)** The grandmother would have to live in the employee's household as does the cousin in choice B. There is no requirement that domestic partners be of the opposite gender, and a mother-in-law is considered an immediate family member according to the procedure.

62. **(D)** Terry in choice A is too young to be a domestic partner, Louise in choice B is still married, and Sherry in choice C has lived with Raymond for only 1 year. Albert in choice D meets all the criteria.

63. **(D)** The department's counsel general should get such an appeal within 30 days.

64. **(C)** The rule requires that department reports or forms be signed with full first name, middle initial, and surname.

65. **(D)** The tour commander must be notified before leaving and upon returning. Entries in the cell block log must be made, if possible, before leaving, but they must be made upon return.

66. **(C)** The use of the word *always* makes choices A and D incorrect. Because the ink must be black, choice B, as well as choice D, is incorrect. Choice D is therefore obviously incorrect for both stated reasons. Choice C is in keeping with the regulations.

67. **(D)** When entering such a date on a department form, only the last two digits of the year are required to be entered. Thus choice C is incorrect. Choice D is the answer.

68. **(D)** An ink line is drawn through the incorrect material, the correct entry is entered above the correction, and the change is initialed.

69. **(D)** The first action to be taken after the search by the escorting officer is a document inspection.

70. **(C)** The tour commander must be notified immediately when occupants exit a suspicious vehicle.

71. **(A)** Among other steps aimed toward identifying the car such as the type of vehicle and color, the license plate should be recorded if possible.

72. **(C)** There is no requirement to advise a prisoner who has resisted or attempted to escape the reason for his arrest. The next step is to handcuff the prisoner with his hands behind him.

73. **(A)** An officer is required to give a prisoner Miranda Rights only if the officer intends to question the prisoner.

74. **(B)** The letters *A*, *B*, and *C* are associated respectfully with the numbers 1, 2, and 3, which when added together equal 6, the number sought by the question.

75. **(B)** Choice D, consisting of *D, D, E,* and *X,* if analyzed represents 4, 4, 5, and 0, which when added together equals 13, and is therefore incorrect. Choice B is the correct choice because D = 4, E = 5, and E = 5, which when added together equals 14.

76. **(A)** Choice A contains three *E*s, which equals 5 + 5 + 5 = 15, plus one *D,* which has a value of 4. The letter *X* is valued at 0. Thus choice A adds up to 19.

77. **(C)** *X* = 0; *B* = 2; *E* = 5; *D* = 4. Combining all the values adds up to 11. Choice C is correct.

78. **(D)** According to the reference table, the letter *X* should be associated with the number 0, which adds nothing to the sum. Therefore, it can be completely ignored in this exercise.

79. **(A)** Officers are less apt to be careless with their firearms if they are certain that carelessness will not be accepted as an excuse for accidental discharge or loss of their firearms.

80. **(A)** It is absolutely essential to be as familiar as possible with the facts in the case when you take the stand. You must also be familiar with the background and prison record of the inmate. So, while the actions described in choices B, C, and D are all beneficial, the most important step is as described in choice A.

81. **(C)** The single best way to ensure understanding is to have the instructed person repeat the instructions back to you in her own words. Regarding choice D, while giving a copy of the regulation to the inmate is a good idea, it is *not* the best way to ensure understanding. You must make sure that you understand the question before you select an answer.

82. **(C)** This is a favorite question of test writers. Often the question involves recommending a lawyer, but it doesn't matter. Recommending professional assistance is never appropriate. Choice D is wrong because of the use of the word *any.*

83. **(C)** You should understand the nature of his medical problem and be guided accordingly. But, in all other matters, that inmate should be treated in the same way all other inmates are treated.

84. **(B)** The most important thing to keep in mind is that a correction officer must keep an even temper even in the face of insolent and rude verbal attack.

85. **(D)** A correction officer should make it a point to speak clearly and properly when dealing with inmates.

86. **(D)** As the question states, as a correction officer you will hear many inmate complaints. Some require further action; some don't. It would be impossible to investigate each one thoroughly. Therefore, the first step is to analyze each one and decide which ones merit further investigation.

87. **(C)** Officers who develop friendships with inmates often become lax about the performance of their duties.

88. **(D)** It is a long-standing prison rule to isolate out-of-control inmates to prevent the possibility of the inappropriate behavior spreading to the other inmates. Disruptive prisoners must be removed from a group setting as quickly and nonviolently as possible.

89. **(D)** In addition to a warden, other authorized officials may use physical force. Also, physical force is not as severe as deadly physical force.

90. **(A)** Only physical force may be used. Certainly deadly physical force, which includes inflicting death, should obviously not be used to prevent a suicide.

91. **(C)** Parents can use physical force but not deadly physical force to discipline their children as long as the children are under 21 years old.

92. **(D)** Such a driver could direct others to assist in maintaining order. Physical force can be used to achieve such order but deadly physical force may be used only to prevent death or serious physical injury.

93. **(D)** Deadly physical force occurs when the force used is readily capable of producing death or other serious physical injury. Thus even though no injury actually results, the mere fact that the force used was capable of causing either death or serious physical injury is enough to consider the force used as deadly physical force.

94. **(C)** Only choice C is specifically mentioned in the information concerning peace officers that has been provided.

95. **(C)** Choice C was not mentioned in the information provided concerning peace officers; choices A, B, and D were mentioned.

96. **(B)** In order for a private person to use deadly physical force to arrest a person for a forcible rape, the person must be in immediate flight from the forcible rape.

97. **(D)** It must be a forcible sodomy, which means that it was committed by force.

98. **(C)** The arson does not have to be completed; merely being attempted is enough. Choices A and B are not found in the material on which the answers were to be based.

99. **(A)** Such a tool would be considered dangerous contraband because it would threaten the security of the detention facility, and such an action would be considered a felony.

100. **(C)** Choices B and D can be quickly eliminated because hindering prosecution concerns hiding or harboring another person. Choice A can be eliminated because hindering prosecution must involve hiding another person being sought in connection with at least a felony. Choice C is the best choice.

Practice Test 3

This is the third of five practice tests that you will be taking. Don't forget to

1. take the test in one sitting. You have 3½ hours to answer all 100 questions.

2. use the test-taking strategies outlined in the Introduction. Make certain to develop and use a time management plan.

3. complete the diagnostic chart that appears at the end of this test after you score this practice examination.

4. use the answer sheet we have provided to record your answers.

ANSWER SHEET
Practice Test 3

Follow the instructions given in the test. Mark only your answers in the circles below.

WARNING: Be sure that the circle you fill is in the same row as the question you are answering. Use a No. 2 pencil (soft pencil).

BE SURE YOUR PENCIL MARKS ARE HEAVY AND BLACK. ERASE COMPLETELY ANY ANSWER YOU WISH TO CHANGE.

DO NOT make stray pencil dots, dashes, or marks.

1. Ⓐ Ⓑ Ⓒ Ⓓ
2. Ⓐ Ⓑ Ⓒ Ⓓ
3. Ⓐ Ⓑ Ⓒ Ⓓ
4. Ⓐ Ⓑ Ⓒ Ⓓ
5. Ⓐ Ⓑ Ⓒ Ⓓ
6. Ⓐ Ⓑ Ⓒ Ⓓ
7. Ⓐ Ⓑ Ⓒ Ⓓ
8. Ⓐ Ⓑ Ⓒ Ⓓ
9. Ⓐ Ⓑ Ⓒ Ⓓ
10. Ⓐ Ⓑ Ⓒ Ⓓ
11. Ⓐ Ⓑ Ⓒ Ⓓ
12. Ⓐ Ⓑ Ⓒ Ⓓ
13. Ⓐ Ⓑ Ⓒ Ⓓ
14. Ⓐ Ⓑ Ⓒ Ⓓ
15. Ⓐ Ⓑ Ⓒ Ⓓ
16. Ⓐ Ⓑ Ⓒ Ⓓ
17. Ⓐ Ⓑ Ⓒ Ⓓ
18. Ⓐ Ⓑ Ⓒ Ⓓ
19. Ⓐ Ⓑ Ⓒ Ⓓ
20. Ⓐ Ⓑ Ⓒ Ⓓ
21. Ⓐ Ⓑ Ⓒ Ⓓ
22. Ⓐ Ⓑ Ⓒ Ⓓ
23. Ⓐ Ⓑ Ⓒ Ⓓ
24. Ⓐ Ⓑ Ⓒ Ⓓ
25. Ⓐ Ⓑ Ⓒ Ⓓ

26. Ⓐ Ⓑ Ⓒ Ⓓ
27. Ⓐ Ⓑ Ⓒ Ⓓ
28. Ⓐ Ⓑ Ⓒ Ⓓ
29. Ⓐ Ⓑ Ⓒ Ⓓ
30. Ⓐ Ⓑ Ⓒ Ⓓ
31. Ⓐ Ⓑ Ⓒ Ⓓ
32. Ⓐ Ⓑ Ⓒ Ⓓ
33. Ⓐ Ⓑ Ⓒ Ⓓ
34. Ⓐ Ⓑ Ⓒ Ⓓ
35. Ⓐ Ⓑ Ⓒ Ⓓ
36. Ⓐ Ⓑ Ⓒ Ⓓ
37. Ⓐ Ⓑ Ⓒ Ⓓ
38. Ⓐ Ⓑ Ⓒ Ⓓ
39. Ⓐ Ⓑ Ⓒ Ⓓ
40. Ⓐ Ⓑ Ⓒ Ⓓ
41. Ⓐ Ⓑ Ⓒ Ⓓ
42. Ⓐ Ⓑ Ⓒ Ⓓ
43. Ⓐ Ⓑ Ⓒ Ⓓ
44. Ⓐ Ⓑ Ⓒ Ⓓ
45. Ⓐ Ⓑ Ⓒ Ⓓ
46. Ⓐ Ⓑ Ⓒ Ⓓ
47. Ⓐ Ⓑ Ⓒ Ⓓ
48. Ⓐ Ⓑ Ⓒ Ⓓ
49. Ⓐ Ⓑ Ⓒ Ⓓ
50. Ⓐ Ⓑ Ⓒ Ⓓ

51. Ⓐ Ⓑ Ⓒ Ⓓ
52. Ⓐ Ⓑ Ⓒ Ⓓ
53. Ⓐ Ⓑ Ⓒ Ⓓ
54. Ⓐ Ⓑ Ⓒ Ⓓ
55. Ⓐ Ⓑ Ⓒ Ⓓ
56. Ⓐ Ⓑ Ⓒ Ⓓ
57. Ⓐ Ⓑ Ⓒ Ⓓ
58. Ⓐ Ⓑ Ⓒ Ⓓ
59. Ⓐ Ⓑ Ⓒ Ⓓ
60. Ⓐ Ⓑ Ⓒ Ⓓ
61. Ⓐ Ⓑ Ⓒ Ⓓ
62. Ⓐ Ⓑ Ⓒ Ⓓ
63. Ⓐ Ⓑ Ⓒ Ⓓ
64. Ⓐ Ⓑ Ⓒ Ⓓ
65. Ⓐ Ⓑ Ⓒ Ⓓ
66. Ⓐ Ⓑ Ⓒ Ⓓ
67. Ⓐ Ⓑ Ⓒ Ⓓ
68. Ⓐ Ⓑ Ⓒ Ⓓ
69. Ⓐ Ⓑ Ⓒ Ⓓ
70. Ⓐ Ⓑ Ⓒ Ⓓ
71. Ⓐ Ⓑ Ⓒ Ⓓ
72. Ⓐ Ⓑ Ⓒ Ⓓ
73. Ⓐ Ⓑ Ⓒ Ⓓ
74. Ⓐ Ⓑ Ⓒ Ⓓ
75. Ⓐ Ⓑ Ⓒ Ⓓ

76. Ⓐ Ⓑ Ⓒ Ⓓ
77. Ⓐ Ⓑ Ⓒ Ⓓ
78. Ⓐ Ⓑ Ⓒ Ⓓ
79. Ⓐ Ⓑ Ⓒ Ⓓ
80. Ⓐ Ⓑ Ⓒ Ⓓ
81. Ⓐ Ⓑ Ⓒ Ⓓ
82. Ⓐ Ⓑ Ⓒ Ⓓ
83. Ⓐ Ⓑ Ⓒ Ⓓ
84. Ⓐ Ⓑ Ⓒ Ⓓ
85. Ⓐ Ⓑ Ⓒ Ⓓ
86. Ⓐ Ⓑ Ⓒ Ⓓ
87. Ⓐ Ⓑ Ⓒ Ⓓ
88. Ⓐ Ⓑ Ⓒ Ⓓ
39. Ⓐ Ⓑ Ⓒ Ⓓ
90. Ⓐ Ⓑ Ⓒ Ⓓ
91. Ⓐ Ⓑ Ⓒ Ⓓ
92. Ⓐ Ⓑ Ⓒ Ⓓ
93. Ⓐ Ⓑ Ⓒ Ⓓ
94. Ⓐ Ⓑ Ⓒ Ⓓ
95. Ⓐ Ⓑ Ⓒ Ⓓ
96. Ⓐ Ⓑ Ⓒ Ⓓ
97. Ⓐ Ⓑ Ⓒ Ⓓ
98. Ⓐ Ⓑ Ⓒ Ⓓ
99. Ⓐ Ⓑ Ⓒ Ⓓ
100. Ⓐ Ⓑ Ⓒ Ⓓ

THE TEST

Time: 3½ hours
100 questions

> **Directions:** Before answering questions 1–8 take 5 minutes to examine the following four wanted posters with the information that accompanies each poster.

WANTED — ESCAPED PRISONER

Joseph Kelly

Age:	19	Race:	White
Height:	5' 6"	Weight:	140 pounds
Eyes:	Blue	Hair:	Reddish Brown
Scars:	Pockmarked Face	Tattoos:	None

Subject, who was serving a life sentence for murder, is believed to be armed and should be considered extremely dangerous. Is known to carry firearms.

WANTED — ESCAPED PRISONER

Josephine Aponte

Age:	58	Race:	Hispanic
Height:	5' 3"	Weight:	125 pounds
Eyes:	Brown	Hair:	Dark Brown
Scars:	None	Tattoos:	None

Subject, who was serving a 5-year sentence for forgery, escaped while on a work release assignment.

WANTED — ESCAPED PRISONER

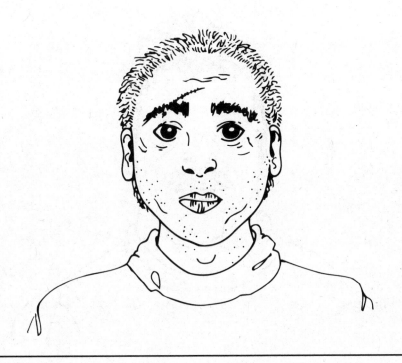

Rob Monchall

Age:	39	Race:	White
Height:	5' 10"	Weight:	175 pounds
Eyes:	Brown	Hair:	Brown
Scars:	6" scar above right eye	Tattoos:	None

Subject, who was serving a 20-year sentence for manslaughter, is an international terrorist who is known to carry explosives on his person. Must be approached with caution.

WANTED — ESCAPED PRISONER

Fred Kruger

Age:	43	Race:	Black
Height:	6'4"	Weight:	250 pounds
Eyes:	Brown	Hair:	Black
Scars:	None	Tattoos:	None

Subject, who was serving a 20-year sentence for felonious assault, must be approached with caution. Is an expert knife fighter and is usually armed with a switchblade knife.

DO NOT PROCEED UNTIL 5 MINUTES HAVE PASSED.

TURN TO NEXT PAGE

Directions: Answer questions 1–8 solely on the basis of the wanted posters on the preceding pages. Do NOT refer back to the posters when answering these questions.

1. Which of the escaped inmates illustrated in the following posters is NOT usually armed with a weapon or explosives?

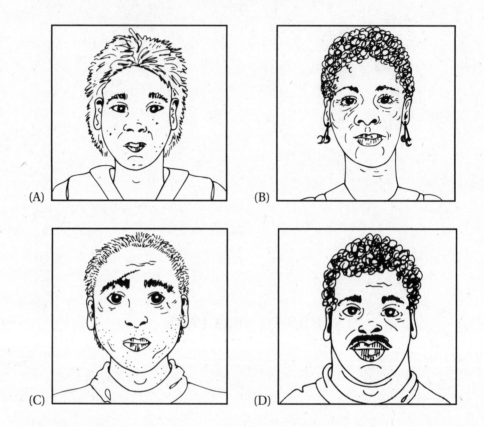

(A)   (B)

(C)   (D)

2. Which of the escaped inmates illustrated in the following posters was serving a life sentence?

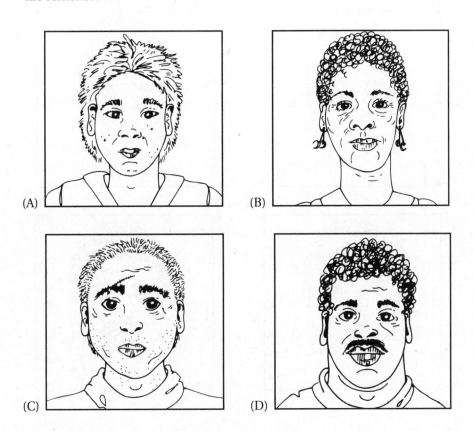

(A)

(B)

(C)

(D)

3. Which of the escaped inmates illustrated in the following posters is the heaviest?

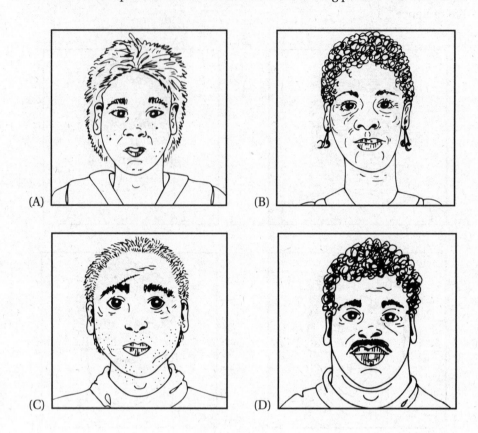

(A)

(B)

(C)

(D)

4. Which of the escaped inmates illustrated in the following posters is the oldest?

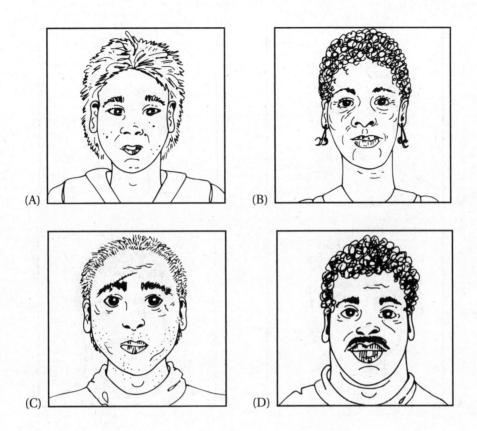

(A)

(B)

(C)

(D)

5. Which of the escaped inmates illustrated in the following posters has blue eyes?

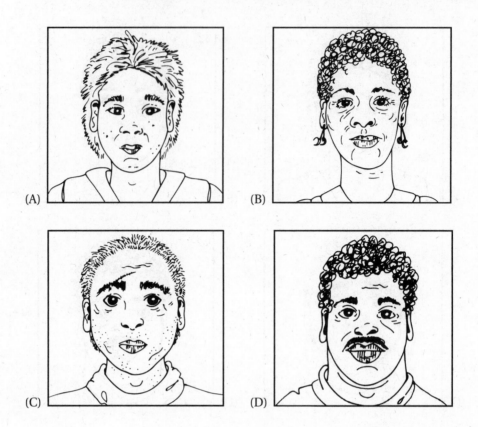

(A)

(B)

(C)

(D)

6. The subject illustrated in the wanted poster directly above

(A) is an expert knife fighter.

(B) is a forger.

(C) is a child abuser.

(D) is a murderer.

7. The subject illustrated in the wanted poster directly above

    (A)   is an expert knife fighter.
    (B)   is an international terrorist.
    (C)   is a child abuser.
    (D)   is a murderer.

8. The subject illustrated in the wanted poster directly above

    (A)   is an expert knife fighter.
    (B)   is an international terrorist.
    (C)   is a forger.
    (D)   is a murderer.

Directions: Answer questions 9–13 based solely on the following passage.

A certain prison has a rule that prohibits employees from entering into any business transaction with an inmate. This rule is officially designated as Rule Number 36. The same rule makes it a violation for prison employees to give an inmate within the prison any medication, any intoxicant, controlled substance, marijuana, or any other contraband article. Any employee of the prison found guilty of violating this rule shall be dismissed and, if appropriate, criminal charges will be instituted. An inmate who requests or solicits a prison employee to violate this rule must also be disciplined. The penalty for the inmate is loss of privileges for 30 days if the solicited employee refuses to cooperate, and for 60 days if the rule is actually broken and the solicited employee cooperates.

On June 13th, Inmate Green approaches Don Wood, a newly hired prison counselor, and asks the counselor to do him a favor by bringing him some marijuana. The counselor agrees and promises the inmate to do as he asks on the following day. Instead he notifies Correction Officer Ginty about the inmate's request. Correction Officer Ginty, in an attempt to gather proof of the violation against the inmate, arranges to have a tape recorder hidden on the counselor the following day to record his conversation with the inmate.

On June 14th, at the prearranged time, the counselor meets Inmate Green and hands him a package containing cigarette tobacco. As he hands the inmate the package, the counselor says, "Here is the marijuana you asked me to bring you," and the inmate replies, "Thanks, man, you're a real cool guy." At that time Officer Ginty appears and tells the inmate he is going to be charged with violating prison rules. Exactly 2 weeks later the inmate was convicted of violating Rule Number 36.

9. Which of the following could a prison employee do and not violate Rule Number 36?

   (A) Sell a car to a prison inmate.
   (B) Give an inmate a bottle of cough medicine.
   (C) Deliver a message to a family member for an inmate.
   (D) Give an inmate some barbiturates.

10. Criminal charges against a prison employee who violates Rule Number 36

   (A) will always be instituted.
   (B) are not a possibility.
   (C) can be instituted in some cases.
   (D) are unconstitutional.

11. Why did Officer Ginty arrange to have a tape recorder hidden on the counselor?

    (A) to make sure that the counselor was telling the truth
    (B) to gather evidence to use against the inmate
    (C) to comply with prison regulations
    (D) to satisfy the directions of the warden

12. What penalty should Inmate Green receive as a result of his conviction?

    (A) loss of privileges for 30 days
    (B) loss of privileges for 60 days
    (C) an additional 30 days of prison time
    (D) an additional 60 days of prison time

13. Inmate Green was convicted on

    (A) June 13th
    (B) June 14th
    (C) June 28th
    (D) not given

Directions: Answer questions 14–16 based solely on the following passage.

The correctional process begins in local institutions. Jails, holding pens, and workhouses are the main types of local institutions. Jails have the authority to detain suspects for periods of 24 hours to 14 days; they also hold convicted inmates who are serving short-term sentences of 1 year or less. Jails are usually administered by the county marshall, but they are sometimes managed by the state government. Holding pens are generally found in city police stations or precinct houses, and they hold suspects for periods of less than 24 hours. The primary function of workhouses, which are operated by cities and counties, is to hold convicted inmates sentenced to short terms of less than 3 months.

14. Which of the following is NOT a local institution?

    (A) a prison
    (B) a jail
    (C) a holding pen
    (D) a workhouse

15. The state government

    (A) does not get involved in local institutions.
    (B) sometimes manages jails.
    (C) sometimes manages holding pens.
    (D) sometimes manages workhouses.

16. A person who is convicted of a crime and who is serving a sentence of 9 months would be confined in a

(A) jail.
(B) holding pen.
(C) workhouse.
(D) prison.

Directions: Answer question 17 based solely on the following information.

Most federal and state court decisions have rejected the claim that incarcerated inmates should be able to freely express their personal views. The courts have refused to grant prisoners the First Amendment right of free speech because such a right could easily create demonstrations and riots in correctional institutions.

17. The courts have not granted the right of free speech to prisoners because

(A) citizens lose this right when they are convicted of a crime.
(B) of the need to maintain order in correctional institutions.
(C) of the feeling that prisoners are not entitled to constitutional protection.
(D) of existing laws.

Directions: Answer question 18 based solely on the following information.

The extent to which wardens and other prison officials can censor the writings of inmates has been the subject of many lawsuits. Prisoner advocates claim that censorship is unconstitutional in the United States. Despite this claim, the courts have consistently upheld the right of prison officials to engage in censorship.

18. Censorship of inmate correspondence

(A) is unconstitutional.
(B) has never been considered by the courts.
(C) has the approval of the courts.
(D) can be engaged in only when necessary.

Directions: Answer question 19 based solely on the basis of the following information.

The courts have generally refused to interfere with prison regulations concerning the physical appearance of inmates. Spokespersons for the inmate community claim that the regulation of physical appearance is a constitutional issue. The courts, however, have consistently held that rules such as those governing facial hair and hair length are not constitutional issues. Instead, the courts have ruled that physical appearance regulations are necessary in a prison setting, primarily for reasons of hygiene, although such regulations can also be supported for reasons of discipline and identification.

19. The main reason why the courts have decided that regulating the appearance of inmates is a necessary function involves

    (A) the health of the prison community.
    (B) the need to maintain discipline in prison.
    (C) the need to quickly identify inmates.
    (D) the need to prevent the concealment of weapons.

Directions: Answer questions 20 and 21 solely on the basis of the following information.

Prisoners do not have an unrestricted right to form prisoner unions and to hold union meetings. This was the decision of the United States Supreme Court when it overruled a state court decision that granted prisoners the right to form a union and hold union meetings. The Supreme Court gave prison officials the right to disallow prisoner unions, if necessary, on the grounds that such unions could be a threat to institutional security. The loss of the unrestricted right to form unions has made it extremely difficult for prisoners to engage in collective bargaining.

20. The right of prisoners to form unions is

    (A) nonexistent.
    (B) completely unrestricted.
    (C) restricted.
    (D) unclear.

21. The opportunity for prisoners to engage in collective bargaining

    (A) is nonexistent.
    (B) has been significantly reduced by court decisions.
    (C) is readily available.
    (D) depends on the status of the prisoners.

Directions: Answer question 22 based on the following information.

The courts have consistently ruled that the protection of the Fourth Amendment of the United States Constitution against unreasonable search and seizures does not apply to incarcerated prisoners.

22. The Fourth Amendment right that guarantees citizens protection against unreasonable searches

    (A) is permanently taken away from people who are convicted of crimes.
    (B) does not apply to inmates while they are in prison.
    (C) has been extended by the courts to cover inmates while they are in prison.
    (D) may or may not apply to inmates who are in prison.

Directions: Answer question 23 based on the following information.

The courts have ruled that in general the use of deadly force is permissible to prevent the infliction of serious injury or death. Therefore, the use of deadly force to prevent an inmate from inflicting serious injury or death on another is lawful but only if the use of such force is a last resort.

23. A correction officer may use deadly force against an inmate

    (A) anytime an inmate attempts to escape.
    (B) anytime an inmate attempts to kill another person.
    (C) only if the inmate is committing some form of a felony.
    (D) only as a last resort to prevent an inmate from seriously injuring or killing another person.

Directions: Answer question 24 based solely on the following information.

There appears to be three factors that account for most of the violent behavior in prisons. They are age, attitudes, and a prior history of violent behavior. Of these, the major cause of violent behavior in prison is related to age. Younger inmates are more apt to engage in violence than older inmates.

24. Younger inmates

    (A) always engage in violent behavior.

    (B) are more likely than older inmates to engage in violence.

    (C) account for all prison violence.

    (D) are as likely as older ones to engage in violent acts.

Directions: Answer question 25 based solely on the following information.

Disturbances by inmates can be either violent or nonviolent. Violent inmate disturbances include assaults, prison takeovers, sabotage, and hostage taking. Nonviolent disturbances include work stoppage, hunger strikes, passive resistance, and rule violations.

25. Which of the following is not an example of a violent inmate disturbance?

    (A) passive resistance

    (B) assaults

    (C) sabotage

    (D) hostage taking

Directions: Answer question 26 based solely on the following information.

The violence and cruelty of inmates toward their fellow inmates is manifested far more often by sexual assaults than by stabbings, killings, or even beatings not involving weapons. And, by far those inmates who are most often sexually assaulted are those who do not exhibit a willingness to fight when challenged.

26. Inmates who seem to be unwilling to fight when challenged

    (A) are often stabbed.

    (B) are often the victims of sexual assaults.

    (C) are the only victims of sexual assaults in prison.

    (D) are always sexually assaulted.

Directions: Answer question 27 based solely on the following information.

Most correction officers are peace officers. A peace officer does not usually make arrests, but they do have special legal authority to do so. When they are working in a prison, a peace officer may make an arrest when they have reasonable grounds to believe that a crime has been committed and that the person being arrested committed that crime. This means that peace officers are legally entitled to make mistakes when they arrest someone provided that their mistakes are reasonable. When correction officers make arrests, it is possible that they will be called upon to testify about that arrest during a criminal trial.

27. Correction officers

(A) are all peace officers.
(B) make numerous arrests.
(C) are legally required to be certain when they make arrests.
(D) may sometimes have to testify in criminal court.

Directions: Answer question 28 based solely on the following information.

There is perhaps no unresolved problem in the correctional field as complex as determining the ability of the death penalty to deter the commission of violent crimes.

28. The use of the death penalty

(A) clearly prevents the commission of violent crimes.
(B) is clearly favored by the majority of law-abiding people.
(C) may or may not prevent the commission of violent crimes.
(D) definitely does not prevent the commission of violent crimes.

Directions: Answer question 29 based solely on the following information.

The typical chronic criminal is neither a hero nor a villain. He is a person who has lost in the game of life. He is an unsuccessful person who has failed in one venture after another. And, he is usually no better at committing crimes than he is at anything else.

29. The typical chronic criminal

(A) is like everyone else.
(B) usually fails in his criminal endeavors.
(C) usually avoids detection.
(D) is very often successful.

Joe Ford was a new inmate in State Prison. He was terrified and confused. He did not know how he should act and what he should or should not do.

At about 1:30 P.M., Joe was in the prison yard when he was approached by an older inmate who introduced himself as Frank White. Frank explained that his belief in the teachings of his church required him to assist new inmates. Frank goes on to advise Joe to never show signs of weakness to anybody, and he described that rule as having the highest priority. He then suggested that Joe refuse to accept small gifts from other inmates. He stated to Joe that "when you take something from another inmate, it won't be long until that inmate will come around and want the gift back. If you can't repay it, you will be asked for some other payment, and that usually involves some sort of sex." Frank then told Joe that he should get hold of a "shank," which is what the inmates call a homemade knife. He further explained to Joe that the best place to get a shank is in the dining room, and the best way to hide it is to tape it to your chest.

30. Frank tried to help Joe because

    (A) he was assigned to do so.
    (B) of his religious beliefs.
    (C) he wanted a favor in return.
    (D) Joe looked terrified and confused.

31. Frank felt that the most important rule for Joe to follow was the one involving

    (A) showing signs of weakness.
    (B) accepting gifts from other inmates.
    (C) obtaining a knife.
    (D) having sex with other inmates.

32. A shank is

    (A) a word used by inmates to describe any knife.
    (B) a piece of meat.
    (C) a prison term for a homemade knife.
    (D) a weak inmate.

Directions: Answer questions 33–36 based solely on the information which follows:

ROSTER OF CORRECTION OFFICERS
ASSIGNED TO CELL BLOCK 94

Correction Officer	Age	Time With Department
Barks	47	15
Dome	32	10
Bell	29	9
Tabs	27	2
Hope	46	20
Lest	35	11
Doe	39	7
Bin	30	6

33. A correction officer is eligible to retire from the department when the officer has at least 25 years of service and is at least 55 years old. Which of the following officers upon reaching 55 years of age will not be eligible for retirement?

(A) Dome
(B) Lest
(C) Doe
(D) Bin

34. The average age of the officers assigned to Cell Block 94 is

(A) between 40 and 41 years old.
(B) exactly 34 years old.
(C) between 35 and 36 years old.
(D) exactly 37 years old.

35. The average length of service or time with the department of the officers assigned to cell block 94 is

(A) 9.5 years.
(B) 10 years.
(C) 10.5 years.
(D) 11 years.

36. The youngest and oldest correction officer have a combined time with the department of

(A) 17 years.
(B) 20 years.
(C) 21 years.
(D) 22 years.

Directions: In each of questions 37–40 you will be given four choices. Each of the choices, A, B, and C, contains a written statement. You are to evaluate the statement in each choice and select the statement that is most accurately and clearly written. If all or none of the three written statements is accurately and clearly written, you are to select choice D.

---

37. According to the directions, evaluate the following statements.

(A) The inmates went to far this time.
(B) The correction officers wanted to be seated altogether.
(C) Do you know who stole the keys?
(D) All or none of the choices are accurate.

38. According to the directions, evaluate the following statements.

(A) Are you trying to infer by your hints that I am lazy?
(B) This time your off base.
(C) Their tired of trying so hard.
(D) All or none of the choices are accurate.

39. According to the directions, evaluate the following statements.

(A) The number of exits are small.
(B) A number of plans is available.
(C) He was found in the woods hiding between two trees.
(D) All or none of the choices are accurate.

40. According to the directions, evaluate the following statements.

(A) After emigrating from France, I immigrated to the United States.
(B) I tried to apprise the information before taking action.
(C) I want to appraise the warden of the facts.
(D) All or none of the choices are accurate.

Directions: Answer questions 41–50 based solely on the following narrative and the Report of Inmate Violation form. Some of the captions on the form may be numbered; some may not be numbered. The boxes are not necessarily consecutively numbered.

On January 19, 20xx, at 1100 hours, Inmate Ray Taps, Inmate Number 3105, assigned to the kitchen detail of the Down Town Correctional Facility, refused to obey an appropriate and direct order from Correction Officer Tab Helper, shield number 5109. The incident resulted in an injury to Inmate Taps' right wrist. The details are as follows:

On January 19, 20xx, Officer Helper, working tour 0900–1700, was assigned to security at the facility's kitchen. At about 1055 hours, Officer Helper observed that the gas pilot light of the kitchen's stove was not lit. Next to the stove was a window looking out onto the facility's recreational area. The window was opened at the bottom about 3 inches to allow air to circulate. The window had been opened during the preparation of the morning meal. However, a breeze entering through the window was preventing the stove's pilot light from staying lit.

Officer Helper directed Inmate Taps to close the window. Taps refused stating to Helper, "Do it yourself." Officer Helper again restated his order. Inmate Taps now moved toward the window and struck the windowpane causing it to break and also cutting his right wrist. Officer Helper called for assistance and Correction Officer Mark Friendly, shield number 17068, responded. The two officers restrained Inmate Taps, wrapped his wrist in a towel, and removed Taps to the infirmary where Taps was treated by Dr. Healer. Taps received ten stitches in the area of his right wrist and was returned to his work detail.

Officer Helper reported the incident to his supervisor Captain Marcia Trials and recommended that Taps suffer a loss of wages to pay for the cost of fixing the window. The incident is recorded as Case Number 10540.

REPORT OF INMATE VIOLATION

Name of Inmate _____(1)_____ Inmate #____(2)____

Case Number_____(3)_____ Cell Block #__(4)__

Details of Violation _____(5)_____

_____

_____

_____

- -

Resulting Injuries _____(6)_____

Medical Attention Received_____

Name of Injured_____(7)_____

Check One

        Inmate [ ] 8

        Facility Employee [ ] 9

        Visitor [ ] 10

Type of Treatment _____(11)_____

Disposition of Injured _____(12)_____

Recommendation of Correction Officer (Check One)

( ) Return to Residential Cell Block }____13_____

( ) Loss of Privileges   }____13_____

( ) Loss of Wages   }____13_____

( ) Criminal Charges   }____13_____

Reporting Officer_____(14)_____ Shield #____(14A)____

Supervisor_____(15)_____ Shield #____(15A)____

Dr. Treating Injury_____(16)_____

Tour Commander_____(17)_____

41. Which of the following should be entered in caption number 1?

(A) Marcia Trials
(B) Ray Taps
(C) Dr. Healer
(D) Mark Friendly

42. In which of the following captions should the name of Tab Helper be entered?

(A) 14
(B) 15
(C) 16
(D) 17

43. It would be most appropriate to enter "Cut on right wrist" in which of the following captions?

(A) 4
(B) 6
(C) 8
(D) 10

44. It would be most appropriate to indicate the recommendation of "loss of wages" in caption

(A) 11.
(B) 12.
(C) 13.
(D) 14.

45. In caption 2 should appear

(A) 10540.
(B) 17068.
(C) 5109.
(D) 3105.

46. The words "returned to work detail" would most appropriately be entered in caption

   (A) 11.
   (B) 12.
   (C) 13.
   (D) 14.

47. The details concerning the pilot light would most appropriately be entered in caption

   (A) 5.
   (B) 6.
   (C) 7.
   (D) 8.

48. Which of the following captions cannot be completed based on the information provided?

   (A) 14
   (B) 15
   (C) 16
   (D) 17

49. Based on the details of the incident, which of the following captions should be checked?

   (A) 8
   (B) 9
   (C) 10
   (D) none of the above

50. Which of the following should appear in caption 15A?

   (A) 17068
   (B) 10540
   (C) 5109
   (D) It cannot be determined.

Directions: Answer questions 51–58 based on the following data.

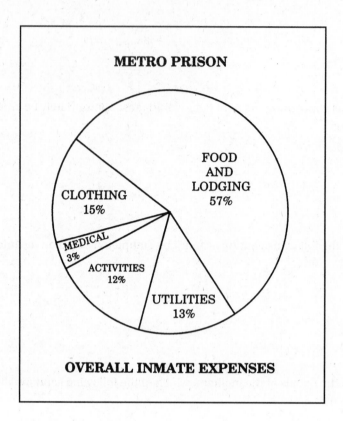

METRO PRISON

FOOD AND LODGING 57%

CLOTHING 15%

MEDICAL 3%

ACTIVITIES 12%

UTILITIES 13%

OVERALL INMATE EXPENSES

51. If the cost for inmate food and lodging at Metro was $1,140,000, what were the overall Metro Prison Inmate Expenses?

(A) $5,000,000
(B) $5,700,000
(C) $2,000,000
(D) $1,750,000

52. Which of the following was the least costly inmate expense?

(A) utilities
(B) clothing
(C) activities
(D) medical

53. According to the graph, it would be most correct to state that

(A) the money spent on inmate clothing was 15% of the food and lodging expenses.
(B) four times as much was spent on activities as was spent on medical expenses.
(C) exactly the same amounts were spent on utilities and activities.
(D) food and lodging comprised less than one half of the entire inmate expenses.

54. If the budget for next year is $3,000,000 and the percentage of expenses remains exactly the same, how much will be spent on medical expenses?

   (A) $900,000
   (B) $90,000
   (C) $9,000
   (D) It cannot be determined from the information provided.

55. If the percentages of the expenses of utilities and clothing were combined, they would represent what percent of the overall Metro Prison Inmate Expenses?

   (A) 28%
   (B) 25%
   (C) 15%
   (D) 13%

56. The total percentage of the overall Metro Prison Inmate Expenses spent on utilities, clothing, activities, and food and lodging represents

   (A) 77%.
   (B) 87%.
   (C) 97%.
   (D) 100%.

57. Which of the following choices represents the greatest expenditure?

   (A) utilities and clothing
   (B) food and lodging
   (C) clothing, activities, medical, and utilities
   (D) medical

58. If next year the warden decides to have food and lodging reduced so that it equals exactly one half of the overall Metro Prison Inmate Expenses, then what percentage of the overall Metro Prison Inmate Expenses will be allotted to clothing?

   (A) 7%
   (B) 22%
   (C) 29%
   (D) It cannot be determined based on the information provided.

Force shall be defined as deliberate physical contact made by a correction officer with an inmate during a confrontation to control the behavior of the inmate or enforce a lawful order.

Force may be used against an inmate to

1.   defend oneself or another correction employee, inmate or visitor from a physical attack;

2.   prevent the commission of an offense, escapes or inmate disturbances;

3.   overcome resistance to an arrest;

4.   prevent serious damage to property;

5.   prevent an inmate from committing suicide or other self harm;

6.   generally enforce Department of Correction rules and court orders but only as a last resort.

In general, force may not be used to punish an inmate. Thus the following are prohibited:

1.   Striking an inmate to discipline the inmate for not obeying an order.

2.   Striking an inmate when pushing the inmate would have achieved the desired result.

3.   Continuing to use force after the inmate ceases to offer resistance or to engage in prohibited conduct.

4.   Hitting an inmate with an unauthorized object such as flashlights, keys, or handcuffs.

5.   Striking an inmate who is already restrained by mechanical restraints. Except that a restrained inmate can be struck if such inmate continues to pose a threat to an employee, a visitor, or other inmate. Such an incident should be immediately reported to the tour commander who shall make a written report to the warden.

6.   Using a choke hold or a blackjack. Note that a regulation baton club may be used but only as a last resort.

59. During a night tour in a cell block, Correction Officer Rems enters the cell of Tom White an inmate to prevent White from destroying the plumbing fixtures inside the cell. Officer Rems strikes White several times with a flashlight to prevent White from further seriously damaging the fixtures. In this instance, the officer acted

(A) properly, mainly because the officer probably prevented more serious damage to the fixtures.
(B) improperly, mainly because flashlights should not be used to hit inmates.
(C) properly, mainly because the situation might spread to other cell blocks.
(D) improperly, mainly because force may never be used to merely prevent serious damage to property.

60. Which of the following actions would be least appropriate in connection with the use of force by correction officers?

(A) using force against an inmate to defend oneself
(B) using force against an inmate in the form of a choke hold
(C) using force against an inmate who is attempting to escape
(D) using force against an inmate who is attempting to strike her husband who is visiting her

61. Jay is an inmate who is being subdued by a correction officer after attempting to strike another inmate. After a brief struggle, the officer is able to restrain Jay with mechanical restraints. In this situation, the officer

(A) is prohibited from ever striking the inmate once the inmate is mechanically restrained.
(B) could strike the inmate even though the inmate is restrained.
(C) is prohibited from striking the inmate unless authorized by the tour commander.
(D) could strike the inmate but only if directed by the warden.

62. Correction officers are generally to use the least amount of force as possible. Nonetheless, however, as a last resort which of the following items would be most appropriate for a correction officer to use against an inmate who is attempting to injure another inmate?

(A) a blackjack
(B) a set of keys
(C) a set of handcuffs
(D) a regulation baton club

63. According to Department of Correction regulations, which of the following least accurately describes a characteristic of force that may be used by a correction officer against an inmate?

(A) The force must be physical.
(B) The force must be deliberate.
(C) The force may be used to control the behavior of an inmate.
(D) The force may be used to enforce any order.

Directions: Answer questions 64–68 based solely on the following information.

A correction officer is prohibited from engaging in any of the following conduct.

1. Using discourteous or disrespectful remarks regarding another person's ethnicity, race, religion, gender, or sexual orientation.

2. Consuming intoxicants while in uniform, whether on or off duty.

3. Bringing or permitting an intoxicant to be brought into a department building, facility, or vehicle, except in performance of duty.

4. Steering business, professional, or commercial persons to a prospective client requiring such services except when transacting personal affairs.

5. Riding in any vehicle, other than a department vehicle to which assigned, while in uniform, except when authorized or in an emergency. (Does not apply to captains and above.)

6. Using department logo unless authorized by the commanding officer of the personnel bureau.

7. Making false official statement.

8. Engaging in card games or other games of chance in a department facility.

9. Engaging in illegal gambling anywhere.

10. Soliciting money for a political club or committee.

64. After an overtime tour of duty, Correction Officer Mary Downs comes directly home. Her husband greets her at the door and, while she is still wearing her uniform, offers her a glass of wine to relax her. Mary accepts and sits down to discuss her day. In this situation, Mary's actions were

   (A) proper, mainly because she is now off duty.
   (B) improper, mainly because she is still in uniform.
   (C) proper, mainly because, even though she is a correction officer, she can do as she pleases in her own home.
   (D) improper, mainly because a correction officer may never consume any intoxicants.

65. Correction Officer John Baker and his boss, Captain Mary Best, are driving to work one day in Officer Baker's personal car. They are both in uniform. According to department regulations,

   (A) both Baker and Best are in violation of department regulations.
   (B) neither Baker nor Best is in violation of department regulations.
   (C) only Baker is in violation of department regulations.
   (D) only Best is in violation of department regulations.

66. A group of correction officers from a certain facility are seeking to form a softball team to play against other city agencies while off duty. Although they are off duty and do not represent the department, their plan is to wear a uniform that displays the department logo. In such an instance, it would be most appropriate if

   (A) the permission of the commanding officer of the personnel bureau was sought.
   (B) the officers sought the permission of the warden of their facility.
   (C) the officers went ahead with their plan since no permission would be required for any such off-duty activity.
   (D) the permission of a captain or above was sought.

67. Correction Officer Barks joins a political club within the confines of the city where the officer is employed. While a member of the club, the officer decides to contribute money to the club. Such actions of the officer are

   (A) appropriate because there is no prohibition against joining and contributing to a political club.
   (B) inappropriate because, even though there is no prohibition against joining a political club, contributing money to a political club is prohibited.
   (C) appropriate because correction officers are even allowed to solicit funds for a political club.
   (D) inappropriate because it is prohibited to join a political club within the city.

68. Evaluate the following statements:

   1. A correction officer is prohibited from engaging in illegal gambling while out of state on vacation.
   2. A correction officer is permitted to play cards in a facility's lunch room with another officer as long as they are both on a meal break and not playing for money.

   Which of the following is most accurate concerning these two statements?

   (A) Only statement 1 is correct.
   (B) Only statement 2 is correct.
   (C) Both statements 1 and 2 are correct.
   (D) Neither statement 1 nor 2 is correct.

Directions: Answer questions 69–73 based solely on the following information describing Department of Correction regulations.

A correction officer shall:

1. Obey lawful orders and instructions of supervising officer.

2. Be punctual when reporting for duty.

3. Maintain a current state driver's license and notify commanding officer, with pertinent details, when license is suspended, revoked, or not renewed.

4. Keep department locker neat, clean, and secured with combination lock (without an identifying serial number displayed on it) that conforms to specifications established by the commanding officer of the quartermaster section. The identifying serial number should not be displayed anywhere on the locker nor should a record of such number be kept by the department.

5. Affix a locker sticker to assigned locker with rank, name, shield, and squad number captions filled in.

6. Be fit for duty at all times, except when on sick report.

7. Refrain from consuming intoxicants to the extent that the member becomes unfit for duty.

8. Give name and shield number to anyone requesting them.

9. Be courteous and respectful.

10. Avoid conflict with department policy when lecturing, giving speeches, or submitting articles for publication. Questions concerning fees offered will be resolved by commanding officer, press relations division before the member accepts the fee.

11. Not smoke in public view outside a department building while in uniform.

12. Not patronize unlicensed premises such as an unlicensed bar except in the performance of duty.

69. Evaluate the following statements concerning Department of Correction regulations.

   1. A correction officer must obey all orders and instructions of supervising officer.

   2. A correction officer must be punctual when reporting for duty.

   Which of the following is most accurate concerning these two statements?

   (A) Only statement 1 is correct.
   (B) Only statement 2 is correct.
   (C) Both statements 1 and 2 are correct.
   (D) Neither statement 1 nor 2 is correct.

70. At the Western Correctional Facility, Joe Lewis is a correction officer. One day Lewis receives a notification that his state driver's license has been revoked. In such a situation, Lewis is required to notify

   (A) his commanding officer.
   (B) the commanding officer of the motor transport division.
   (C) the commanding officer of the press relations section.
   (D) no one in the department because it is his own personal business.

71. One afternoon Probationary Correction Officer Singer arrives at the Stone Correctional Facility for assignment. The captain on duty assigns a locker to Officer Singer, who then proceeds to the locker to secure it with a lock. In this situation, Officer Singer should secure the locker by using a combination lock that conforms to specifications established by the commanding officer of the quartermaster section. According to department regulations the lock should

   (A) not have a serial number displayed on it.
   (B) have a serial number displayed on it.
   (C) not have a serial number displayed on it, but the serial number should be entered on the locker sticker.
   (D) not have a serial number displayed on it, but the serial number should be kept on file with the commanding officer of the quartermaster section.

72. John Jay College of Criminal Justice has asked Correction Officer Bard to address a seminar on penal institutions. The college has offered Correction Officer Bard a modest fee for his services. In this situation Correction Officer Bard should

   (A) refuse to make the speech.
   (B) accept the fee and not notify anyone because the fee is modest.
   (C) notify the commanding officer, press relations division, before accepting any fee.
   (D) notify the commanding officer personnel bureau before accepting any fee.

73. Evaluate the following statements:

1. A correction officer in uniform is never permitted to smoke in uniform outside a department building.

2. A correction officer shall never patronize unlicensed premises such as an unlicensed bar.

Which of the following is most accurate concerning these two statements?

(A) Only statement 1 is correct.

(B) Only statement 2 is correct.

(C) Both statements 1 and 2 are correct.

(D) Neither statement 1 nor 2 is correct.

Directions: Use the information in the following reference table to answer questions 74–78. In the table each number has been associated with a letter. For each question you are to select the choice that contains the letters that, when associated with the numbers in the reference table, can be added together to equal the sum required by the question.

B	**O**	**G**	**U**	**S**	**Z**
1	**2**	**3**	**4**	**5**	**0**

EXAMPLE

Which of the following choices contains the letters that add up to 8 after they are converted to numbers?

(A) B, O, G

(B) B, O, S

(C) G, U, S

(D) O, U, S

Choice B, contains letters B, O, and S, which, according to the reference table are associated with 1, 2, and 5. When added together, they equal 8.

---

74. Which of the following choices contains the letters that add up to 12 after they are converted to numbers?

(A) O, G, U, G

(B) B, U, G, S

(C) G, O, B, S

(D) U, S, Z, U

75. Which of the following choices contains the letters that add up to 9 after they are converted to numbers?

(A) G, Z, U, G
(B) U, B, O, B
(C) S, B, Z, B
(D) O, B, S, B

76. Which of the following choices contains the letters that add up to the greatest sum after they are converted to numbers?

(A) S, Z, S, B
(B) U, U, S, O
(C) G, U, B, O
(D) B, O, B, S

77. Which of the following choices contains the letters that add up to the lowest sum after they are converted to numbers?

(A) G, Z, U, B
(B) S, Z, Z, S
(C) B, O, U, Z
(D) U, G, U, G

78. Which of the following choices contains the letters that add up to an odd number after they are converted to numbers?

(A) S, U, Z, G
(B) Z, U, G, B
(C) B, U, G, O
(D) G, S, B, O

79. There is a standard prison rule that states that correction officers are not allowed to decide on the punishment to give to prisoners who violate a regulation. Instead, it is the job of correction officers to report such violations to their supervisors who, in turn, decide on appropriate punishments. This standard rule is justified by the fact that

(A) deciding on the appropriate punishment is beyond the capability of correction officers.
(B) punishment must be administered somewhat uniformly in accordance with established policy and should not be left to the judgment of many individual officers.
(C) correction officers would always decide on severe punishment that would not fit the violation.
(D) correction officers would always decide on overly lenient punishment in order to win the favor of the inmates they supervise.

80. A correction officer sometimes encounters an inmate who the officer believes has admirable qualities and who, for some reason, wins the sympathy and/or respect of the officer. When this occurs, the officer involved should

   (A) treat that prisoner in the same manner as all other prisoners are treated.
   (B) make an immediate request to have that prisoner transferred.
   (C) treat that prisoner more severely than the other prisoners to avoid claims of favoritism.
   (D) give that prisoner special treatment after first explaining your feelings to the other inmates.

81. The amount of supervision and the degree of security needed for the confinement of each inmate in a correctional facility depends primarily on the

   (A) crime that was committed by the inmate.
   (B) quality of the correctional staff involved.
   (C) basic character and background of the inmate.
   (D) design of the correctional institution involved.

82. Correction officers will often be guarding prisoners who must take prescribed medication. Concerning prescribed medication, a correction officer should understand such prescribed medications

   (A) present no special problems.
   (B) are often used for wrongful purposes.
   (C) are never used for abusive purposes.
   (D) may be possessed without the authorization of a doctor.

83. Whenever a correction officer becomes responsible for a new prisoner, the officer should always

   (A) make sure to instill fear in that prisoner.
   (B) check all available background information about that prisoner.
   (C) ignore that prisoner's previous record.
   (D) treat that prisoner in a very harsh manner to prevent problems from developing.

84. When a correction officer finds that a certain inmate is very cooperative and extremely helpful, the officer should

   (A) find unofficial ways to reward that inmate.
   (B) always praise that inmate to all other inmates.
   (C) pursue officially sanctioned ways to reward that prisoner.
   (D) tell that inmate to stop being helpful and to act like all the other inmates.

85. At the first sign of inmate violence, a correction officer who is alone on duty must always

    (A) make an immediate call for backup assistance.
    (B) immediately intervene.
    (C) use force.
    (D) retreat.

86. Assume that you are a correction officer and are approached by an inmate who you know is a troublemaker and a liar. The inmate informs you that a group of other inmates are planning to execute the warden and that he knows the identity of those involved and the details of their plan and is willing to reveal what he knows. Under these circumstances it would be most correct for you to

    (A) tell him to stop wasting your time because you are not going to give him a chance to cause more trouble.
    (B) make arrangements for him to see your supervisor as soon as possible.
    (C) attempt to corroborate the inmate's story by asking other inmates about it.
    (D) ask the inmate to give you the name of the conspirators and then interview them immediately.

87. Assume that you are a correction officer in charge of a workshop where inmates use tools. In recognition of the fact that tools are often adapted by inmates to serve as weapons, it is essential that you develop a practical way of accounting for the tools at the end of each work day. But, you also want a system that is not overly demeaning to the inmates. The best system to use is to

    (A) search every prisoner every time they leave the workshop for any reason.
    (B) make each inmate sign a sworn statement each day attesting to the fact that no tools have been stolen.
    (C) install closed circuit television coverage of the entire workshop and then monitor it constantly.
    (D) designate a specific location for each tool and make sure that all tools are accounted for prior to allowing the inmates to leave.

88. Consider the following statements of fact:

    Some inmates in cell block 14 are troublemakers.

    Inmate Smith is housed in cell block 14.

    Inmate Green is a troublemaker.

    Which of the following is the most accurate conclusion to reach based on the above statements?

    (A) Cell block 14 is the most violent prone in the entire prison.
    (B) Inmate Green must be housed in cell block 14.
    (C) Inmate Smith may be a troublemaker.
    (D) All inmates who occupy cell block 14 are serving sentences for violent crimes.

Felonies are classified, for the purpose of sentence, into five categories, as follows:

- Class A felonies;
- Class B felonies;
- Class C felonies;
- Class D felonies; and
- Class E felonies.

The penalty for a Class A felony is more severe than a Class B felony, and so on, with Class E felonies having the least severe penalties.

Although, as a general rule, the age when a child can be legally treated as an adult is at age 16, some 13-, 14-, and 15-year-olds are classified as juvenile offenders and treated as adults if the youth involved committed certain specific serious crimes such as:

Murder in the second degree—a Class A felony

Arson in the first degree—a Class A felony

Kidnapping in the first degree—a Class A felony

Robbery in the first degree—a Class B felony

Assault in the first degree—a Class C felony

A juvenile delinquent is a person who is at least 7 years old but less than 16 years old and commits an act that, if committed by an adult, would be a crime. Such a child is considered a juvenile delinquent as long as the child is not 13, 14, or 15 and commits one of the previously mentioned serious crimes, which would then classify the child as a juvenile offender.

A parent can bring a child to a court and formally request that a child be considered a juvenile delinquent for serious acts of disobedience. A parent is a legal mother or father of a child or is a person in *loco parentis. Loco parentis* means someone who acts in the place of a parent.

A youthful offender is a person who is charged with committing a crime when such person was at least 16 but less than 19 years of age. Such youths treated as youthful offenders receive more lenient sentences. However, a person charged with any of following cannot be considered a youthful offender:

- a Class A felony
- an armed felony
- rape in the first degree
- sodomy in the first degree
- any degree of aggravated sexual abuse

89. Evaluate the following statements:

1. There are five categories of felonies.
2. The penalty for a class C felony is more severe than a class B felony.

Which of the following is most accurate concerning these two statements?

(A) Only statement 1 is correct.
(B) Only statement 2 is correct.
(C) Both statements 1 and 2 are correct.
(D) Neither statement 1 nor 2 is correct.

90. For a person who is not a juvenile offender to be charged as an adult, such person must be at least

(A) 14 years old.
(B) 16 years old.
(C) 18 years old.
(D) 21 years old.

91. Which of the following persons would be most appropriately classified as a juvenile delinquent?

(A) a 6-year-old who strikes and assaults another child
(B) a 12-year-old who commits the crime of robbery
(C) a 16-year-old who commits the crime of auto larceny
(D) a 17-year-old who commits the crime of robbery

92. While assigned to the detention pens in juvenile court, Correction Officer Springs overhears an attorney make the following statement. "I am here today in *loco parentis* for John Carter." Such an expression most likely means that the attorney is

(A) the biological parent of John Carter.
(B) acting in the place of a parent of John Carter.
(C) in this location seeking the parents of John Carter.
(D) present to represent John Carter as a result of a local warrant.

93. Which of the following is least likely to be considered a youthful offender?

(A) a 16-year-old
(B) a 17-year-old
(C) an 18-year-old
(D) a 19-year-old

94. Which of the following is most likely to be considered a youthful offender?

(A) a 16-year-old charged with committing a felony while armed
(B) a 16-year-old charged with rape in the third degree
(C) a 16-year-old charged with kidnapping, which is a class A felony
(D) a 16-year-old charged with aggravated sexual abuse

A verdict of guilty convicts a defendant. A person can be convicted or found guilty of an offense by a jury, or in cases without a jury, the judge can find a person guilty.

When any person is convicted of a crime, the judge of the court will either pronounce the sentence on the date of the conviction or postpone the pronouncing of sentence by selecting a future date for the sentencing.

A grand jury is a body of persons called together by a judge of a superior court. The role of a grand jury is to indict or accuse a person of a felony after hearing evidence presented by the prosecutor. There can be no more than 23 persons on a grand jury and at least 16 must be present for a grand jury to meet and decide on issues. In order for a grand jury to indict or find what is known as a true bill, 12 of the grand jurors must agree. An agreement of 12 of the grand jurors is also required for a grand jury to decide not to indict or find what is known as no true bill.

95. A person is convicted when such person is found guilty of an offense. Which of the following can find a person guilty?

(A) only a judge
(B) only a jury
(C) either a judge or a jury
(D) a grand jury

96. When a person is convicted of an offense, who can sentence the person?

(A) the judge
(B) the jury
(C) the grand jury
(D) the prosecutor

97. The minimum number of persons who must be present before a grand jury can meet and decide on issues is

(A) 6.
(B) 12.
(C) 16.
(D) 23.

98. Evaluate the following statements:

1. An indictment is the same as a conviction for an offense.
2. In order for a grand jury to return a true bill, all the grand jurors must agree.

Which of the following is most accurate concerning the statements above?

(A) Only statement 1 is correct.
(B) Only statement 2 is correct.
(C) Both statements 1 and 2 are correct.
(D) Neither statement 1 nor 2 is correct.

Directions: Answer questions 99 and 100 based solely on the following information.

Manslaughter is committed by a person who, intending to cause a serious physical injury to another person, causes the death of such person or another, or when a person, while committing an illegal abortion on a female, causes the death of that female, or when a person, while acting under extreme emotional disturbance, intentionally causes the death of that person.

99. Judy is an inmate at a correctional facility. Irene was recently sentenced to serve a term of imprisonment at the facility. Irene was convicted of scalding her infant son with boiling water. This upsets Judy who sets out to beat Irene by hitting her with a baseball bat in the exercise yard. However, Judy misses Irene and strikes Meg, who happened to be in the area, and kills Meg instantly. In this instance, Judy has

(A) committed manslaughter.
(B) not committed manslaughter because she did not kill the person she intended to injure.
(C) committed no crime.
(D) committed only the crime of assault.

100. Dr. Whacky, the doctor assigned to the facility known as the Women's House of Detention, performs an illegal abortion on one of the inmates, Sue Larks, who had asked the doctor to perform the abortion. As a result of the abortion, the unborn child Sue Larks was carrying dies. In such a situation, Dr. Whacky is

(A) immune from prosecution for any crime.
(B) guilty of manslaughter because the unborn child died.
(C) not guilty of manslaughter because Sue Larks did not die.
(D) guilty of assault.

END OF TEST

ANSWER KEY
Practice Test 3

1. **B**	26. **B**	51. **C**	76. **B**
2. **A**	27. **D**	52. **D**	77. **C**
3. **D**	28. **C**	53. **B**	78. **D**
4. **B**	29. **B**	54. **B**	79. **B**
5. **A**	30. **B**	55. **A**	80. **A**
6. **A**	31. **A**	56. **C**	81. **C**
7. **B**	32. **C**	57. **B**	82. **B**
8. **C**	33. **C**	58. **D**	83. **B**
9. **C**	34. **C**	59. **B**	84. **C**
10. **C**	35. **A**	60. **B**	85. **A**
11. **B**	36. **A**	61. **B**	86. **B**
12. **A**	37. **C**	62. **D**	87. **D**
13. **C**	38. **D**	63. **D**	88. **C**
14. **A**	39. **C**	64. **B**	89. **A**
15. **B**	40. **A**	65. **C**	90. **B**
16. **A**	41. **B**	66. **A**	91. **B**
17. **B**	42. **A**	67. **A**	92. **B**
18. **C**	43. **B**	68. **A**	93. **D**
19. **A**	44. **C**	69. **B**	94. **B**
20. **C**	45. **D**	70. **A**	95. **C**
21. **B**	46. **B**	71. **A**	96. **A**
22. **B**	47. **A**	72. **C**	97. **C**
23. **D**	48. **D**	73. **D**	98. **D**
24. **B**	49. **A**	74. **A**	99. **A**
25. **A**	50. **D**	75. **D**	100. **C**

DIAGNOSTIC CHART

Instructions: After you score your test, complete the following chart by inserting in the column entitled "Your Number Correct" the number of correct questions you answered in each of the eight sections of the test. Then compare your score in each section with the ratings in the column entitled "Scale." Finally, to correct your weaknesses, follow the instructions found at the end of the chart.

Section	Question Numbers	Area	Your Number Correct	Scale
1	1–8	Memory (8 questions)		8 Right—Excellent 6–7 Right—Good 5 Right—Fair Under 5 Right—Poor
2	9–32	Reading Comprehension (24 questions)		24 Right—Excellent 20–23 Right—Good 16–19 Right—Fair Under 16 Right—Poor
3	33–40	Verbal and Math (8 questions)		8 Right—Excellent 6–7 Right—Good 5 Right—Fair Under 5 Right—Poor
4	41–50	Correction Forms (10 questions)		10 Right—Excellent 8–9 Right—Good 7 Right—Fair Under 7 Right—Poor
5	51–58	Graphs (8 questions)		8 Right—Excellent 6–7 Right—Good 5 Right—Fair Under 5 Right—Poor
6	59–78	Applying Correction Procedures (20 questions)		20 Right—Excellent 18–19 Right—Good 16–17 Right—Fair Under 16 Right—Poor
7	79–88	Judgment and Reasoning (10 questions)		10 Right—Excellent 8–9 Right—Good 7 Right—Fair Under 7 Right—Poor
8	89–100	Legal Definitions (12 questions)		12 Right—Excellent 10–11 Right—Good 8–9 Right—Fair Under 8 Right—Poor

How to correct weaknesses:

1. If you are weak in Section 1, concentrate on Chapter 3.
2. If you are weak in Section 2, concentrate on Chapter 1.
3. If you are weak in Section 3, concentrate on Chapter 2.
4. If you are weak in Section 4, concentrate on Chapter 4.
5. If you are weak in Section 5, concentrate on Chapter 5.
6. If you are weak in Section 6, concentrate on Chapter 6.
7. If you are weak in Section 7, concentrate on Chapter 7.
8. If you are weak in Section 8, concentrate on Chapter 8.

Note: Consider yourself weak in an area if you receive anything other than an excellent rating in it.

ANSWERS EXPLAINED

1. **(B)** Kelly carries firearms, Monchall carries explosives, and Kruger carries a switchblade knife. Please note that many of the questions involving wanted posters involve comparisons among the various wanted persons.

2. **(A)** Aponte was doing 5 years, Monchall and Kruger were doing 20 years. Only Kelly was serving a life sentence.

3. **(D)** Kruger is 250 pounds. None of the others are over 175 pounds. Please note that once again the answer involved a comparison among the four inmates.

4. **(B)** Aponte is 58 years old. None of the others are over 50.

5. **(A)** Kelly has blue eyes. The other three have brown eyes.

6. **(A)** Kruger is an expert knife fighter who is usually armed with a switchblade knife.

7. **(B)** Monchall is a terrorist who carries explosives on his person.

8. **(C)** Josephine Aponte was serving a 5-year sentence for forgery when she escaped.

9. **(C)** Choice B is a violation because cough medicine is medication. Selling a car is a business transaction, and barbiturates are controlled substances so choices A and D are also violations of Rule Number 36.

10. **(C)** Criminal charges will be instituted if appropriate. They can, therefore, be instituted. Learn that there is a great difference between *can* and *must*.

11. **(B)** Correction Officer Ginty, in an attempt to gather proof (evidence) of the violation against the inmate, arranges to have a tape recorder hidden on the counselor the following day to record his conversation with the inmate.

12. **(A)** The penalty for the inmate is loss of privileges for 30 days if the solicited employee refuses to cooperate, and for 60 days if the rule is actually broken by the solicited employee. In this case, the solicited employee refused to cooperate.

13. **(C)** The first meeting between the counselor and the inmate took place on June 13th. On June 14th the second meeting was held. Exactly 2 weeks later (14 days), on June 28th, the inmate was convicted.

14. **(A)** Prisons are not mentioned in the entire passage.

15. **(B)** Jails are usually administered by the county marshall but are sometimes managed by the state government.

16. **(A)** Jails have the authority to detain suspects for periods of 24 hours to 14 days; they also hold convicted inmates who are serving short-term sentences of 1 year or less.

17. **(B)** Demonstrations and riots need to be prevented to maintain order in correctional institutions.

18. **(C)** Despite the claims of prisoner advocates, the courts have consistently upheld the right of prison officials to engage in censorship.

19. **(A)** The courts have ruled that physical appearance regulations are necessary in a prison setting, primarily for reasons of hygiene (health reasons).

20. **(C)** Prisoners do not have an unrestricted right to form prisoner unions and to hold union meetings. The Supreme Court gave prison officials the right to disallow prisoner unions, if necessary, on the grounds that such unions could be a threat to institutional security.

21. **(B)** The loss of the unrestricted right to form unions has made it extremely difficult for prisoners to engage in collective bargaining.

22. **(B)** Incarcerated prisoners are those who are imprisoned. Such prisoners are not protected by the Fourth Amendment.

23. **(D)** The key to this answer is the statement from the passage that "the use of deadly force to prevent an inmate from inflicting serious injury or death on another is lawful but only if the use of such force is a last resort." The use of the word *anytime* in choice B makes that choice incorrect.

24. **(B)** The word *apt* is a synonym for *likely*. Note that test writers often rely on the use of synonyms when writing reading comprehension questions. This is yet another reason why you should constantly strive to increase your vocabulary.

25. **(A)** Passive resistance is clearly identified as being a nonviolent disturbance.

26. **(B)** By far those inmates who are most often sexually assaulted are those who do not exhibit a willingness to fight when challenged.

27. **(D)** When correction officers make arrests, it is possible that they will be called upon to testify about that arrest during a criminal trial.

28. **(C)** This question demonstrates quite clearly the danger of introducing personal knowledge into the answering of reading comprehension questions. It is common knowledge that choice B is in fact true, but it is not mentioned in the paragraph so it cannot be the answer. The instructions clearly state that the answer must be based solely on the information contained in the passage.

29. **(B)** The typical chronic criminal is usually no better at committing crimes than he is at anything else, and he is usually a failure in all he does.

30. **(B)** Frank explained that his belief in the teachings of his church requires him to assist new inmates.

31. **(A)** Frank advised Joe to never show signs of weakness to anybody, and he described that rule as having the highest priority, which, of course, means that it is the most important.

32. **(C)** If you picked choice A without looking at the other choices, you learned something from this question. Always read all the choices. The word *any* in choice A makes it wrong.

33. **(C)** Correction Officer Doe may reach age 55 first but will have only 23 years of service at that time.

Correction Officer	Age now	Years to 55	Time With Department at age 55
Dome	32	23	23 + 10 = 33
Lest	35	20	20 + 11 = 31
Doe	39	16	16 + 7 = 23
Bin	30	25	25 + 6 = 31

34. **(C)** First add up all the ages to arrive at the sum of 285; then divide that sum by 8, the number of officers assigned to the cell block; and the result is 35.63, or somewhere between 35 and 36 years.

35. **(A)** The sum of the time with the department of all the correction officers is 80, divided by the number of officers, which is 8, results in an average of 10.

36. **(A)** The youngest is Officer Tabs, who is 27 and has 2 years with the department. The oldest is Barks, who is 47 and has 15 years with the department. Adding 2 + 15 = 17, or choice A.

37. **(C)** Choice A is incorrect because the word *too* should be used in place of *to*. Choice B is incorrect because the correction officers obviously wanted to be seated as a group in which case *all together* should have been used. Choice C is stated correctly.

38. **(D)** All the statements are incorrect. In choice A the word *imply* should be used in place of *infer*. In choice B the word *you're* should have been used in place of *your*, and in choice C the word *They're* should have been used in place of *Their*.

39. **(C)** When *the number* is used as the subject of a verb (an action word), it should be viewed as being a plural; *a number* should be viewed as being singular. Therefore, in choice A *is* would be correct, and in choice B *are* would be correct. Choice C is correct as stated.

40. **(A)** *Appraise*, which means to estimate the value, should be used in place of *apprise* in choice B. In choice C *apprise*, which means to notify or inform, should be used in place of *appraise*. Choice A is correctly stated.

41. **(B)** The name of the inmate who committed the violation should be entered in caption 1.

42. **(A)** Caption 14 requires the name of the officer reporting the violation.

43. **(B)** Caption 6 calls for the resulting injuries.

44. **(C)** Caption 13 requires one of the recommendations to be checked.

45. **(D)** Ray Taps' inmate number should be entered in caption 2.

46. **(B)** Caption 12 asks for the disposition of the injured, which is "returned to work detail."

47. **(A)** The details of the incident such as the information regarding the pilot light should be entered in caption 5.

48. **(D)** The name of the tour commander was not provided.

49. **(A)** Caption 8 should be checked because an inmate was injured.

50. **(D)** Caption 15A asks for the shield number of the supervisor. Such information was not provided by the narrative.

51. **(C)** If $1,140,000 represents 57% of the overall inmate expenses, that means 57% of some unknown quantity or x is equal to $1,140,000. Or expressed as an equation

$$0.57 \times x = \$1,140,000$$

Dividing both sides by 0.57, we get

$$\frac{0.57x}{0.57} = \frac{\$1,140,000}{0.57}$$

and that gives us $x = \$2,000,000$.

52. **(D)** Medical costs were only 3% of the total inmate expenses.

53. **(B)** Choice A is incorrect because clothing expenses were 15% of the overall inmate expenses and not of the food and lodging expenses. Choice C is incorrect because the expense for utilities was 1% more than that of the activities. Choice D is incorrect because food and lodging comprised more than one half of the entire inmate expenses. However four times as much was spent on activities (12%) as was spent on medical (3%). Four times 3% equals 12%. The answer is B.

54. **(B)** Simply multiply 3% or .03 times $3,000,000, which equals $90,000.

55. **(A)** Utilities represents 13%, and clothing represents 15%. Combining them yields 28%.

56. **(C)** The importance of examining the chart and being familiar with it is evident in answering this question. If you recognized that the only expense not mentioned was medical or 3% of the overall Metro Prison Inmate Expenses, then that 3% could have been simply subtracted from 100% to give you the answer of 97%. This would be quicker than adding up the four other percentages to arrive at 97%.

57. **(B)** Once again being familiar with the chart enables you to answer this question quickly and easily. Food and lodging represents 57% of the overall Metro Prison Inmate Expenses. That leaves 43% for all other expenses. Obviously the answer is choice B, food and lodging.

58. **(D)** The only information that was provided was that food and lodging would be reduced from 57% to one half, which is 50%. However, there was no further information to indicate to which expense the 7% would be added. Choice D is the answer.

59. **(B)** Choice D is incorrect because force could be used to prevent serious damage to property, but, according to the procedure, a flashlight should not be used to strike a prisoner.

60. **(B)** Choke holds are prohibited by the regulations.

61. **(B)** Striking an inmate who is already restrained by mechanical restraints is usually prohibited. But if such an inmate continued to pose a threat, a correction officer could justifiably strike such an inmate. The incident should be immediately reported to the tour commander who shall make a written report to the warden.

62. **(D)** Choices A, B, and C suggest items whose use is prohibited.

63. **(D)** Choices A, B, and C represent characteristics but choice D is not accurate. The force may be used to enforce a *lawful* order, not any order.

64. **(B)** The correction officer is in uniform, and intoxicants cannot be consumed in uniform regardless of being on or off duty.

65. **(C)** Captains are excluded from the prohibition against riding in uniform in a private vehicle.

66. **(A)** To use the department logo, the permission of the commanding officer of the personnel bureau would be required.

67. **(A)** The regulation prohibits soliciting funds for a political club. Choice D is incorrect because no such prohibition was included in the regulations.

68. **(A)** Statement 1 is correct, but statement 2 is incorrect because engaging in card games or other games of chance in a department facility is prohibited.

69. **(B)** Statement 1 is incorrect because a correction officer must obey all *lawful* orders and instructions of a supervisor.

70. **(A)** It is the business of the department and his commanding officer must be notified.

71. **(A)** The identifying serial number should not be displayed anywhere on the locker nor should a record of such a number be kept by the department.

72. **(C)** Any fee for a speech should be first cleared by the commanding officer, press relations division.

73. **(D)** A correction officer shall not smoke in public view outside a department building while in uniform. Also a correction officer could patronize an unlicensed bar in the performance of duty.

74. **(A)** According to the reference table, the letters *O, G, U,* and *G* are associated with the numbers 2, 3, 4, and 3, which when added together yield the sum of 12, the number sought by the question.

75. **(D)** This is as indicated by use of the reference table. This kind of question can be time-consuming because each choice must be examined.

76. **(B)** This is as indicated by use of the reference table. Here each choice had to be examined in order to determine which choice yielded the greatest sum.

77. **(C)** Choice A yields a sum of 8; choice B yields a sum of 10; choice D yields a sum of 14; but choice C yields the lowest sum of 7.

78. **(D)** Choice D yields 11, whereas choices A, B, and C yield the even-numbered sums of 12, 8, and 10, respectively.

79. **(B)** Punishment must fit the offense, and it must be administered in a uniform fashion. This means that, when two inmates commit the same violation under approximately equal circumstances, their punishments should be approximately equal. This is very difficult to accomplish when the fixing of punishments is highly decentralized (in the hands of many).

80. **(A)** Equality of treatment is the cardinal rule of correction work. Playing favorites is never appropriate.

81. **(C)** It is well known in correctional science that the amount of supervision and degree of security needed for any given inmate depends mostly on the individual makeup of each inmate.

82. **(B)** Prescribed medicine is medicine that can be possessed only with written authorization from a doctor. In many instances prisoners hoard certain prescribed medication to take or sell in mass dosages because taking mass dosages often creates feelings of euphoria. In other words, prescribed medicines can be used for wrong or abusive purposes.

83. **(B)** The more officers know about the prisoners under their supervision, the better able they are to tailor the correct approach to deal with each individual prisoner. Regarding choice D, it is in conflict with the cardinal rule regarding equal treatment.

84. **(C)** There is nothing wrong with recognizing the efforts of inmates who are helpful and cooperative, but such recognition must be in the form of officially sanctioned rewards, such as being designated as a model prisoner or the making of a positive parole board report.

85. **(A)** Whenever an officer who is alone sees that violence is about to occur, the first step that officer should take is to request backup assistance, even if only one inmate is involved initially. One never can predict if and when violence will spread.

86. **(B)** The matter is entirely too serious for you to put off. It is a situation that demands immediate action and requires immediate intervention by you and your supervisor. It would be a great mistake, however, to immediately interview other inmates based solely on the information of the inmate described in the question.

87. **(D)** Choice C is not practical. Choices A and B are too demeaning. Choice D is practical and less demeaning.

88. **(C)** Because Inmate Smith is housed in cell block 14 and because some of the inmates in cell block 14 are troublemakers, Inmate Smith may be a troublemaker. All the other choices are based on assumptions. The key to doing well on these question types is to differentiate between limiting and absolute words. Absolute words are all encompassing. Examples are *all, every, never, must,* and *none.* Limiting words leave room for exceptions. Examples are *some, many, may, sometimes,* and *often.*

89. **(A)** According to the information provided, the penalty for a Class A felony is more severe than a Class B felony, and so on, with Class E felonies having the least severe penalties. Thus the penalty for a class C felony is not more severe than that of a class B felony.

90. **(B)** A 13-, 14-, or 15-year-old could be charged as an adult only if they committed those very serious crimes that would then classify them as juvenile offenders.

91. **(B)** The age restrictions for a juvenile delinquent are at least 7 but not yet 16. So choices A, C, and D can be eliminated.

92. **(B)** A parent is the legal mother or father of a child. *Loco parentis* means someone who acts in the place of a parent.

93. **(D)** The age range for a youthful offender is at least 16 but less than 19.

94. **(B)** To not be considered a youthful offender, the 16-year-old would have had to commit rape in the first degree. Because the charge is rape in the third degree, the youth could be considered a youthful offender.

95. **(C)** Either a judge or a jury can find a person guilty. Grand juries only accuse or indict a person.

96. **(A)** A judge or jury can convict, but it is the judge who sentences.

97. **(C)** This is as stated in the information.

98. **(D)** An indictment is not a conviction; it is an accusation. Also, only 12 of the grand jurors must agree.

99. **(A)** An examination of choices A and B indicates that the choices are directly opposite. Whenever a candidate discovers that two of the choices in a multiple-choice question are directly opposite, there is a good chance that the answer will be one of those two choices. According to the information given, the death occurring in manslaughter does not have to be the death of the person who was intended to receive the injury. All that is required is that it be the death of any other person.

100. **(C)** Although the doctor could have committed some crime such as abortion, no manslaughter was committed because the death of the female, Sue Larks, did not occur.

Practice Test 4

This is the fourth of five practice tests that you will be taking. Don't forget to

1. take the test in one sitting. You have 3½ hours to answer all 100 questions.

2. use the test-taking strategies outlined in the Introduction. Make certain to develop and use a time management plan.

3. complete the diagnostic chart that appears at the end of this test after you score this practice examination.

4. use the answer sheet we have provided to record your answers.

ANSWER SHEET
Practice Test 4

Follow the instructions given in the test. Mark only your answers in the circles below.

WARNING: Be sure that the circle you fill is in the same row as the question you are answering. Use a No. 2 pencil (soft pencil).

BE SURE YOUR PENCIL MARKS ARE HEAVY AND BLACK. ERASE COMPLETELY ANY ANSWER YOU WISH TO CHANGE.

DO NOT make stray pencil dots, dashes, or marks.

1. Ⓐ Ⓑ Ⓒ Ⓓ   26. Ⓐ Ⓑ Ⓒ Ⓓ   51. Ⓐ Ⓑ Ⓒ Ⓓ   76. Ⓐ Ⓑ Ⓒ Ⓓ
2. Ⓐ Ⓑ Ⓒ Ⓓ   27. Ⓐ Ⓑ Ⓒ Ⓓ   52. Ⓐ Ⓑ Ⓒ Ⓓ   77. Ⓐ Ⓑ Ⓒ Ⓓ
3. Ⓐ Ⓑ Ⓒ Ⓓ   28. Ⓐ Ⓑ Ⓒ Ⓓ   53. Ⓐ Ⓑ Ⓒ Ⓓ   78. Ⓐ Ⓑ Ⓒ Ⓓ
4. Ⓐ Ⓑ Ⓒ Ⓓ   29. Ⓐ Ⓑ Ⓒ Ⓓ   54. Ⓐ Ⓑ Ⓒ Ⓓ   79. Ⓐ Ⓑ Ⓒ Ⓓ
5. Ⓐ Ⓑ Ⓒ Ⓓ   30. Ⓐ Ⓑ Ⓒ Ⓓ   55. Ⓐ Ⓑ Ⓒ Ⓓ   80. Ⓐ Ⓑ Ⓒ Ⓓ
6. Ⓐ Ⓑ Ⓒ Ⓓ   31. Ⓐ Ⓑ Ⓒ Ⓓ   56. Ⓐ Ⓑ Ⓒ Ⓓ   81. Ⓐ Ⓑ Ⓒ Ⓓ
7. Ⓐ Ⓑ Ⓒ Ⓓ   32. Ⓐ Ⓑ Ⓒ Ⓓ   57. Ⓐ Ⓑ Ⓒ Ⓓ   82. Ⓐ Ⓑ Ⓒ Ⓓ
8. Ⓐ Ⓑ Ⓒ Ⓓ   33. Ⓐ Ⓑ Ⓒ Ⓓ   58. Ⓐ Ⓑ Ⓒ Ⓓ   83. Ⓐ Ⓑ Ⓒ Ⓓ
9. Ⓐ Ⓑ Ⓒ Ⓓ   34. Ⓐ Ⓑ Ⓒ Ⓓ   59. Ⓐ Ⓑ Ⓒ Ⓓ   84. Ⓐ Ⓑ Ⓒ Ⓓ
10. Ⓐ Ⓑ Ⓒ Ⓓ   35. Ⓐ Ⓑ Ⓒ Ⓓ   60. Ⓐ Ⓑ Ⓒ Ⓓ   85. Ⓐ Ⓑ Ⓒ Ⓓ
11. Ⓐ Ⓑ Ⓒ Ⓓ   36. Ⓐ Ⓑ Ⓒ Ⓓ   61. Ⓐ Ⓑ Ⓒ Ⓓ   86. Ⓐ Ⓑ Ⓒ Ⓓ
12. Ⓐ Ⓑ Ⓒ Ⓓ   37. Ⓐ Ⓑ Ⓒ Ⓓ   62. Ⓐ Ⓑ Ⓒ Ⓓ   87. Ⓐ Ⓑ Ⓒ Ⓓ
13. Ⓐ Ⓑ Ⓒ Ⓓ   38. Ⓐ Ⓑ Ⓒ Ⓓ   63. Ⓐ Ⓑ Ⓒ Ⓓ   88. Ⓐ Ⓑ Ⓒ Ⓓ
14. Ⓐ Ⓑ Ⓒ Ⓓ   39. Ⓐ Ⓑ Ⓒ Ⓓ   64. Ⓐ Ⓑ Ⓒ Ⓓ   39. Ⓐ Ⓑ Ⓒ Ⓓ
15. Ⓐ Ⓑ Ⓒ Ⓓ   40. Ⓐ Ⓑ Ⓒ Ⓓ   65. Ⓐ Ⓑ Ⓒ Ⓓ   90. Ⓐ Ⓑ Ⓒ Ⓓ
16. Ⓐ Ⓑ Ⓒ Ⓓ   41. Ⓐ Ⓑ Ⓒ Ⓓ   66. Ⓐ Ⓑ Ⓒ Ⓓ   91. Ⓐ Ⓑ Ⓒ Ⓓ
17. Ⓐ Ⓑ Ⓒ Ⓓ   42. Ⓐ Ⓑ Ⓒ Ⓓ   67. Ⓐ Ⓑ Ⓒ Ⓓ   92. Ⓐ Ⓑ Ⓒ Ⓓ
18. Ⓐ Ⓑ Ⓒ Ⓓ   43. Ⓐ Ⓑ Ⓒ Ⓓ   68. Ⓐ Ⓑ Ⓒ Ⓓ   93. Ⓐ Ⓑ Ⓒ Ⓓ
19. Ⓐ Ⓑ Ⓒ Ⓓ   44. Ⓐ Ⓑ Ⓒ Ⓓ   69. Ⓐ Ⓑ Ⓒ Ⓓ   94. Ⓐ Ⓑ Ⓒ Ⓓ
20. Ⓐ Ⓑ Ⓒ Ⓓ   45. Ⓐ Ⓑ Ⓒ Ⓓ   70. Ⓐ Ⓑ Ⓒ Ⓓ   95. Ⓐ Ⓑ Ⓒ Ⓓ
21. Ⓐ Ⓑ Ⓒ Ⓓ   46. Ⓐ Ⓑ Ⓒ Ⓓ   71. Ⓐ Ⓑ Ⓒ Ⓓ   96. Ⓐ Ⓑ Ⓒ Ⓓ
22. Ⓐ Ⓑ Ⓒ Ⓓ   47. Ⓐ Ⓑ Ⓒ Ⓓ   72. Ⓐ Ⓑ Ⓒ Ⓓ   97. Ⓐ Ⓑ Ⓒ Ⓓ
23. Ⓐ Ⓑ Ⓒ Ⓓ   48. Ⓐ Ⓑ Ⓒ Ⓓ   73. Ⓐ Ⓑ Ⓒ Ⓓ   98. Ⓐ Ⓑ Ⓒ Ⓓ
24. Ⓐ Ⓑ Ⓒ Ⓓ   49. Ⓐ Ⓑ Ⓒ Ⓓ   74. Ⓐ Ⓑ Ⓒ Ⓓ   99. Ⓐ Ⓑ Ⓒ Ⓓ
25. Ⓐ Ⓑ Ⓒ Ⓓ   50. Ⓐ Ⓑ Ⓒ Ⓓ   75. Ⓐ Ⓑ Ⓒ Ⓓ   100. Ⓐ Ⓑ Ⓒ Ⓓ

THE TEST

Time: 3½ hours
100 questions

> **Directions:** Answer questions 1–8 based on the following story about an occurrence involving a correction officer. You are allowed 10 minutes to read it and commit to memory as much about it as you can. You are NOT allowed to make any written notes during the time you are reading. At the end of 10 minutes you are to stop reading the material and answer the questions about the story without referring back to the story.

MEMORY STORY—10-MINUTE TIME LIMIT

Correction officers are often required to make recommendations to the parole board based on the conduct of inmates under their supervision. The following is a summary of the conduct of four inmates under the supervision of Correction Officer Don Ginty.

Inmate Number 1—Bill Street. Inmate Street has been a model prisoner. He has earned his college degree during the 6 years he has been under the supervision of Officer Ginty. He is an expert hockey player and has been a starter on the prison hockey team for the past 5 years. He has not been involved in any acts of violence and it is well known that he acts as the prison peacekeeper.

Inmate Number 2—Ernie Banks. Inmate Banks is also a model prisoner. He has become a self-made legal expert. He specializes in assisting other inmates file appeals of their convictions. This is a significant accomplishment considering the fact that Inmate Banks does not have a high school diploma. Inmate Banks has been involved in two acts of violence in the past 3 years.

Inmate Number 3—Dale Mize. Inmate Mize is a problem prisoner. He refuses to participate in any voluntary self-improvement programs. He does participate in mandated programs but never excels. He is constantly arguing with other inmates. He has been involved in several major incidents involving the use of force, and in one such occurrence he was responsible for the hospitalization of two inmates. This despite the fact that Inmate Mize holds a Master's Degree in History from Yale University.

Inmate Number 4—Morty Hertz. Inmate Hertz is the prison's best musician. He plays at least four instruments, but he excels at the piano. He is a high school graduate. He has the reputation of being willing and able to help new inmates adjust to prison life. He is a veteran of the Gulf War having served with the Marines as a tank commander. He has been involved in one act of violence in the past 2 years.

After considering the preceding information, Officer Ginty decides to give Inmates Street, Banks, and Hertz a positive parole board recommendation, but he feels that he has to give Inmate Mize a negative recommendation.

DO NOT PROCEED UNTIL 10 MINUTES HAVE PASSED.

1. Which inmate is an expert piano player?

    (A) Inmate Street
    (B) Inmate Banks
    (C) Inmate Mize
    (D) Inmate Hertz

2. Which of the inmates has a degree from Yale University?

    (A) Inmate Street
    (B) Inmate Banks
    (C) Inmate Mize
    (D) Inmate Hertz

3. Which inmate is an avid hockey player?

    (A) Inmate Street
    (B) Inmate Banks
    (C) Inmate Mize
    (D) Inmate Hertz

4. Which inmate is a veteran of the Gulf War?

    (A) Inmate Street
    (B) Inmate Banks
    (C) Inmate Mize
    (D) Inmate Hertz

5. Inmate Banks is

    (A) a legal expert.
    (B) a prison peacemaker.
    (C) an accomplished musician.
    (D) a tank commander.

6. Which inmate did not graduate from high school?

   (A) Inmate Street
   (B) Inmate Banks
   (C) Inmate Mize
   (D) Inmate Hertz

7. Which inmate has no acts of violence on his prison record?

   (A) Inmate Street
   (B) Inmate Banks
   (C) Inmate Mize
   (D) Inmate Hertz

8. Which inmate is not going to get a positive parole board recommendation from the correction officer?

   (A) Inmate Street
   (B) Inmate Banks
   (C) Inmate Mize
   (D) Inmate Hertz

Directions: Answer question 9 solely on the basis of the following information.

Crime is not a problem that can be easily solved by using the same strategies and methods that allowed man to split the atom or to put an astronaut on the moon. Nor can the problems created by crime be prevented by passing law after law. In fact, it is probably true that the crime problem in this country will never be truly solved.

9. The crime problem

   (A) is easily solved.
   (B) can be solved through technology.
   (C) can be solved through legislation.
   (D) is probably beyond solution.

The purpose of rehabilitation of criminals is to change their behavior. The supporters of rehabilitation as a basic goal of corrections suggest that inmates can leave prisons as better people than when they entered. Those who argue against the concept of rehabilitation argue that it rarely occurs and these people usually favor the concept of reparation. While the truth of the matter is unknown at this time, what is known is that reparation is being used more and more and rehabilitation is used less and less.

10. Rehabilitation

   (A) is definitely working.
   (B) is better than reparation.
   (C) rarely works.
   (D) is being used less and less.

Directions: Answer question 11 based solely on the following rule.

A correction officer shall not carry any weapon while on duty except when specifically authorized by the warden.

11. Correction officers

   (A) are not allowed to carry firearms.
   (B) are not allowed to carry weapons.
   (C) can never carry weapons while working.
   (D) can sometimes be armed when they are working.

Directions: Answer question 12 based solely on the following rule.

All correction officers will unload their revolvers or other firearms prior to entering any area in the psychiatric unit of any prison or hospital. Upon departure from such areas, they shall reload revolvers and other firearms.

12. While in a psychiatric unit of a hospital, a correction officer

   (A) can be armed if off duty.
   (B) can be armed if on duty.
   (C) can obtain special permission to be armed.
   (D) can never be armed.

Directions: Answer question 13 based solely on the following rule.

Carelessness by a correction officer in the carrying, handling, or safekeeping of personal or department firearms, while on or off duty, shall be deemed neglect of duty.

13. An off-duty correction officer who carelessly handles his own handgun

   (A) does not violate any department rule.
   (B) may face disciplinary charges.
   (C) is guilty of neglect of duty.
   (D) might be considered negligent.

Directions: Answer question 14 based solely on the following rule.

A correction officer assigned to yard duty in a prison shall supervise the opening and closing of entrance gates and shall not allow any person who is not an on-duty employee of the prison to enter or leave except those with proper written authority. And, with no exceptions, such officer must examine and search for contraband in all packages coming into or leaving the yard.

14. A correction officer assigned to yard duty

   (A) may let all employees of the prison freely enter or leave the yard.
   (B) must require all persons who enter or leave the yard to have written authorization.
   (C) must search all packages as they come into or leave the yard.
   (D) must personally open the gates for those entering or leaving the yard.

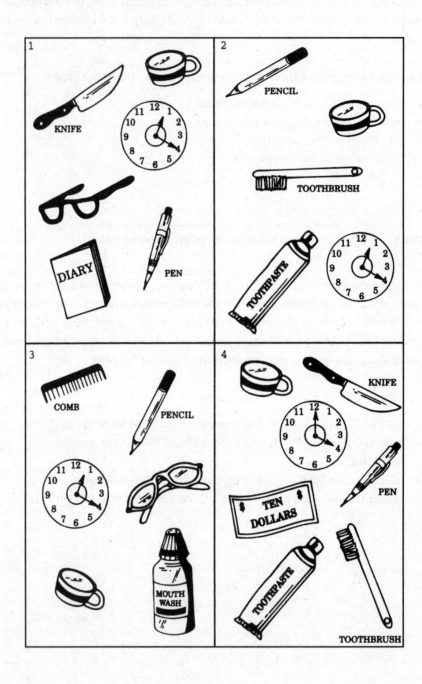

PRACTICE TEST 4

15. There is a prison rule that prohibits inmates from keeping cutting implements in their cells. This rule is being violated by

    (A) one inmate.
    (B) two inmates.
    (C) three inmates.
    (D) four inmates.

16. The inmate who probably keeps a written record of daily events occupies

    (A) cell 1.
    (B) cell 2.
    (C) cell 3.
    (D) cell 4.

17. The clock in which cell is probably not working correctly?

    (A) cell 1.
    (B) cell 2.
    (C) cell 3.
    (D) cell 4.

18. The cell with the most objects is

    (A) cell 1.
    (B) cell 2.
    (C) cell 3.
    (D) cell 4.

19. The cell with the least number of objects is

    (A) cell 1.
    (B) cell 2.
    (C) cell 3.
    (D) cell 4.

20. There is a writing implement in

    (A) only one cell.
    (B) only two cells.
    (C) only three cells.
    (D) all four cells.

Relatives or friends over 16 may visit an inmate in prison provided that the inmate consents to the visit. These visits must be held during normal visiting hours which are from Monday to Friday, from 10:00 A.M. to 4:00 P.M. Children between the ages of 10 and 16 may visit inmates but only on those days that are specifically designated as family visiting days. At least three family visiting days per month will be held. Children under the age of 10 are not allowed on prison grounds. Clergy persons are allowed to visit inmates on any day of the week at any hour between 8:00 A.M. and 11:00 P.M. Such visits require the consent of the inmate. Attorneys are allowed to visit inmates but require written authorization from the inmate. Attorney visits can be held on any day of the week between the hours of 10:00 A.M. and 10:00 P.M. Police officers investigating crimes may also visit prisoners on the same day and during the same times that attorneys are allowed to visit. Visits from the police require written authorization from the inmate or a court order.

21. A 9-year-old child

   (A) could visit a parent in prison on family visiting days.
   (B) is never allowed to visit an inmate in prison.
   (C) could visit a parent in prison on weekdays.
   (D) must be accompanied on to prison grounds by an adult.

22. Which of the following categories of visitors has the greatest number of possible visiting hours each week?

   (A) relatives or friends
   (B) clergy persons
   (C) attorneys
   (D) police personnel

23. Which of the following categories of visitors could possibly visit an inmate without the inmate's consent?

   (A) relatives or friends
   (B) clergy persons
   (C) attorneys
   (D) police personnel

24. A 12-year-old boy whose father is serving a life sentence can visit his father

   (A) as often as he pleases.
   (B) once a week.
   (C) at least 36 times a year.
   (D) four times a month.

Correction officers are legally entitled to use physical force upon another person when and to the extent they reasonably believe to be necessary to defend themselves or a third person from what they reasonably believe to be the use or imminent use of unlawful physical force by such other person. Correction officers may not use deadly physical force upon another person unless they reasonably believe that such other person is using or about to use deadly physical force against them or another.

25. Correction officers

    (A) can use force only to defend themselves.
    (B) can always use an unlimited amount of force to defend themselves.
    (C) can sometimes use force to defend others.
    (D) are not entitled to use physical force upon another person.

26. The use of deadly physical force by correction officers

    (A) is legally permitted only in a prison setting.
    (B) is sometimes legally permissible.
    (C) is never legally authorized.
    (D) is always lawful to prevent escapes.

Directions: Answer question 27 based solely on the following information.

A correction officer may make an arrest of a person for a felony when she has reasonable cause to believe such person has committed a felony. But, a correction officer may make an arrest of a person for a misdemeanor or for a violation only when she has reasonable cause to believe such person has committed the misdemeanor or violation in her presence.

27. A criminal offense is either a felony, a misdemeanor, or a violation. A correction officer

    (A) can arrest for a felony even if the officer was not present when the felony was committed.
    (B) can arrest for a misdemeanor even if the officer was not present when the misdemeanor was committed.
    (C) can arrest for a violation even if the officer was not present when the violation was committed.
    (D) is prohibited from making an arrest for any criminal offense unless the offense is committed in the presence of the officer.

The courts have ruled that a juvenile, someone under the age of 16, who has been accused of a crime, has the right to counsel. The counsel may be of the juvenile's own choosing or appointed by the court for financial or other reasons. Therefore, a correction officer who finds it necessary to arrest a juvenile must give notice of the juvenile's right to counsel. This notice must be clearly understood by both the juvenile and at least one of the juvenile's parents or legal guardians. In addition, such notice must be given both verbally and in writing. Although a waiver of the right to counsel may be made, it is not effective unless the waiver is made in writing by both the juvenile and at least one of his parents or legal guardians.

28.   A lawyer who represents a juvenile who has been accused of a crime

(A)   must be one who is chosen by the juvenile.
(B)   must be one who is chosen by the parents or legal guardians of the juvenile.
(C)   must be one who is appointed by the courts.
(D)   may be chosen by the juvenile or appointed by the court.

29.   A juvenile who is accused of a crime

(A)   must be represented by a lawyer.
(B)   can decide on his own not to have a lawyer.
(C)   can state orally that he does not want a lawyer as long as one parent or guardian also agrees.
(D)   can waive the right to a lawyer if at least one of the juvenile's parents or guardians agrees provided that their waiver is put in writing.

Rehabilitation occurs when a criminal reforms and gives up his criminal life. The most important rehabilitative tool is the impact of one person upon another. Thus a primary objective for the correctional system is the recruitment of quality employees who have good interpersonal skills.

30.   Which of the following is the most important characteristic of a correctional facility that is designed to promote the rehabilitation of inmates?

(A)   the security of the facility
(B)   the skill of its personnel
(C)   the quality of its job-training programs
(D)   the administrative ability of its warden

One of the earliest programs for releasing inmates before their full sentences expired was the first work release legislation. The work release philosophy permits inmates to work on their own outside of the correctional facility. Work release programs present an opportunity for inmates to test their work skills and self-control while on their own in the community, and they allow them to spend most of the day away from the institution where they are incarcerated. Work release programs have benefits other than allowing inmates to be on their own in the community for a period of time each day. One such benefit is an economic one. The salary earned by the inmates allows them to do such things as support their families, reimburse their victims, or build their personal savings. Unfortunately, the general public tends to look unfavorably upon work release programs due to the publicity that occurs in the rare instance when an inmate out on work release commits a crime of violence.

31. Work release programs

    (A) are favored by the general public.
    (B) have only one benefit.
    (C) were the first attempt at early release of inmates.
    (D) are not the cause of many violent crimes.

Recreation is popular with most inmates in correctional institutions because it alleviates the monotony of prison life and serves as a safety valve for pent-up emotions. Recreation varies from formal programs to free-time activities. Some recreational activities involve groups of inmates whereas others are aimed at individuals. It can take place in the prison yard, the recreation room, the prison auditorium, or the cell block. And, for those inmates eligible for security clearance, recreational activities can take place in the outside community.

32. Recreation for inmates

    (A) is limited to formal activities.
    (B) is popular with all inmates.
    (C) can never take place in the outside community.
    (D) can take many forms.

At the receiving station for the Mountain View Correctional Facility, a group of seven (7) newly arrived inmates was being processed. Each of the inmates was found to be in possession of money in bill and coin form. The money was removed from each inmate and was put into individual envelopes bearing the name of the inmate from whom the money was removed. The individual sums were $53.72, $92.76, $9.26, $5.73, $16.41, $11.38, and $11.22.

33. What was the total of all the monies removed from the newly arrived inmates?

(A) under $200
(B) between $200 and $205
(C) between $206 and $210
(D) over $210

34. The average amount of money found on a newly arrived inmate was

(A) under $28.57.
(B) exactly $28.64.
(C) exactly $29.71.
(D) over $30.

35. In a certain correctional facility, the ratio of correction officer to inmates is 2 to 11. If one of the residential cell blocks houses 55 inmates then the number of correction officers assigned should be

(A) 9.
(B) 10.
(C) 11.
(D) 12.

36. In a certain county correctional system 2500 inmates were released one year. Of these released inmates, 10% were rearrested for new offenses within the first 6 months of their release. Within the following 12 months thereafter, an additional 20% of the remaining inmates who remained free were now rearrested for new offenses. Of all the inmates released that year, how many inmates were not rearrested for new offenses within 18 months of their release?

(A) 1625
(B) 1700
(C) 1800
(D) 1925

37. According to the directions, evaluate the following statements.

    (A) The warden's warning was so direct it was implicit.
    (B) He has been behaving very well lately.
    (C) I had to read between the lines of the inmates' demands to understand their hidden explicit warning.
    (D) All or none of the choices are accurate.

38. According to the directions, evaluate the following statements.

    (A) I can't wait to sink my teeth in a steak.
    (B) Latter in the tour, the inmates became noisy.
    (C) Its too time-consuming to visit him.
    (D) All or none of the choices are accurate.

39. According to the directions, evaluate the following statements.

    (A) The inmates' scheme to escape was secretive and ingenuous.
    (B) The inmate was considered ingenious because he answered the questions so honestly.
    (C) The aim of this facility is to foster moral conduct among the residents.
    (D) All or none of the choices are accurate.

40. According to the directions, evaluate the following statements.

    (A) The new institution adopted the motto of the old institution.
    (B) No one beside the captain would listen to me.
    (C) Usually I will take whatever is served, but there are some dishes I just will not except.
    (D) All or none of the choices are accurate.

On December 16, 20xx, at 1410 hours, June Flowers, a white female, 37 years, residing at 666 Court Avenue, telephone number 555-3029, appeared at the Fair Way Correctional Facility to lodge a civilian complaint alleging rudeness against Correction Officer Frank Lee, shield number 947, assigned to the Visitors Screening Unit of the Fair Way Correctional Facility. Said complaint was taken by Correction Officer Early Dubs, shield number 1492. Central Complaint number 6988 assigned. The details are as follows:

On December 15, 20xx, at about 1000 hours, Ms. Flowers arrived at the Fair Way Correctional Facility to visit her brother, Ray Ash, Inmate number 2491. Ms. Flowers was accompanied by her cousin, May Bell, white female, 35 years, of 668 Court Avenue, telephone number 555-3209. While in the waiting room, Ms. Flowers approached Officer Lee and asked why there was a delay in the issuance of visitor passes. Ms. Flowers alleges that Officer Lee responded by saying, "Why don't you relax or you might find yourself waiting for visitors as an inmate." Ms. Bell stated that she overheard most of the conversation between Officer Lee and Ms. Flowers, and although Ms. Bell was not sure of every word that was spoken, she did hear Officer Lee tell Ms. Flowers to relax.

The case is open and the investigation is ongoing. Officer Lee is to be interviewed in the presence of counsel provided by the Correction Officer Benevolent Association.

CIVILIAN COMPLAINT AGAINST CORRECTION EMPLOYEE

time   and date reported   central complaint number

(1)_____(2)_____   (3)_____

- -

how was complaint made?   facility received at

(4) [ ] in person [ ] mail [ ] phone   (5)_____

- -

complainant information

first name (6)_____ last name (6A)_____

address (7)_____

telephone number (8)_____

occupation (9)_____

work address (10)_____

- -

employee complained of

last name (11)_____ first (12)_____

rank (13)_____ assignment (14)_____

shield number (15)_____

- -

time and date of alleged conduct complained of

_____ (16)_____

- -

witness information

name and address_____ (17)_____

telephone number _____(18)_____relationship_____(19)_____

- -

complaint details _____(20)_____

_____

_____

- -

correction employee receiving complaint

name_____(21)_____rank___(22)____shield no.___(23)____

41. Which of the following should be entered in caption 5?

    (A) 666 Court Avenue
    (B) Fair Way Correctional Facility
    (C) Central Command
    (D) 668 Court Avenue

42. Which of the following would be most appropriate to enter in caption 16?

    (A) December 16
    (B) December 15
    (C) the same day it was reported
    (D) cannot be determined

43. The telephone number 555-3029 should be entered in caption

    (A) 18.
    (B) 8.
    (C) 10.
    (D) 15.

44. The name Dubs should be entered in caption

    (A) 6A.
    (B) 11.
    (C) 17.
    (D) 21.

45. The most appropriate entry for caption 12 is

    (A) Frank.
    (B) Early.
    (C) May.
    (D) June.

46. The statement, "Why don't you relax or you might find yourself waiting for visitors as an inmate," would be most appropriately entered in caption

(A) 8.
(B) 16.
(C) 20.
(D) 22.

47. The number 6988 should be entered in caption

(A) 3.
(B) 7.
(C) 15.
(D) 23.

48. The fact that the complainant and the witness are related should be entered in caption

(A) 17.
(B) 18.
(C) 19.
(D) 22.

49. The fact that the complainant appeared in person to make the complaint should be recorded in caption

(A) 4.
(B) 5.
(C) 8.
(D) 9.

50. Which of the following should appear in caption 6A?

(A) Bell
(B) Dubs
(C) Flowers
(D) Lee

MONDAY TO FRIDAY INMATE WORK SCHEDULE
FOR THE MONTH OF MAY

Inmate	Assignment	Meal Time
*Frank Day	Library	Noon
Joe Brown	Motor Pool	Noon
Fred White	Motor Pool	1:00 P.M.
*Don Smith	Hospital	Noon
Charles Beach	Hospital	1:00 P.M.
*George May	Library	1:00 P.M.
*Jack Fine	Machine Shop	Noon
Mike Branch	Machine Shop	1:00 P.M.
Sam Sweet	Reserve	Noon
Leon Waters	Reserve	1:00 P.M.

* Denotes inmate with high school diploma.

ASSIGNMENT INFORMATION

1. The time for all assignments is from 10:00 A.M. to 11:30 A.M., and from 2:00 P.M. to 5:00 P.M., except for Hospital Duty which begins at 9:00 A.M.

2. The inmates assigned to Reserve Duty are to be used to fill in any assignment on an as needed basis, except that only inmates with a high school diploma will be assigned to the library.

3. A new work schedule will be prepared each month. In no case shall the same inmate be assigned to Reserve Duty for two consecutive months.

4. Every effort must be made to keep two inmates on all assignments.

5. When not on assignment, inmates shall be in their cells, except those on Reserve Duty.

6. Inmates on Reserve Duty must stay in the recreation room.

7. Meals must be finished in 1 hour.

51. Which of the following is the most accurate statement concerning the weekday work schedule for the month of June?

(A) Inmate Branch should be given a different assignment.
(B) Inmate Brown should be given a different assignment.
(C) Inmate White should be given a different assignment.
(D) Inmate Waters should be given a different assignment.

52. Which of the following inmates will probably work the most hours in the month of May?

(A) Day
(B) Smith
(C) Fine
(D) Branch

53. Assume that you are the correction officer on duty in the library at 10:30 A.M. when it becomes necessary for Inmate May to report to the prison dentist for treatment of a toothache. You should

(A) assign Inmate Waters to Library Duty.
(B) assign Inmate Branch to Library Duty.
(C) assign Inmate Day to Library Duty.
(D) assign Inmate Sweet to Hospital Duty and assign Inmate Smith to Library Duty.

54. Assume that you are a correction officer and that it is 1:30 P.M. You need to talk to Inmate Brown. To find him you should look

(A) in the inmate dining room.
(B) at the motor pool.
(C) at the hospital.
(D) in his cell.

55. It is 4:00 P.M. Inmate Waters has a visitor. Inmate Waters can be found

(A) in his cell.
(B) in the library.
(C) in the recreation room.
(D) in the hospital.

56. It is 3:00 P.M. on Sunday, May 22. Where can Inmate White be found?

(A) at the motor pool
(B) in the hospital
(C) in the library
(D) cannot be determined

57. Which of the following is probably the most accurate statement about the "Monday to Friday" Work Schedule?

(A) All assignments are of equal duration.
(B) No special qualifications are needed for any of the assignments.
(C) Inmates with the same assignment get different meal times.
(D) An inmate can always get the same assignment two months in a row.

58. Which inmates have high school diplomas?

(A) Day, Smith, May, and Fine
(B) Smith, Fine, Sweet, and Waters
(C) Day, May, Beach, and Branch
(D) cannot be determined

Directions: Answer questions 59–63 based solely on the following procedure.

The purpose of random drug testing of members of the correction department is to establish a credible deterrent to illegal drug usage. As such the following steps shall be taken when such testing is required.

1. Members shall be notified at least twenty-four (24) hours prior to scheduled testing.

2. Members selected shall appear at the Health Section in civilian clothes at the designated date and time.

3. Members must report to Health Section when notified except if said member is on

   a. sick report
   b. regularly scheduled day off
   c. military leave
   d. annual vacation
   e. bereavement leave

   Members missing a scheduled test for any reason will be rescheduled for testing as soon as possible irrespective of any random sampling selection.

4. Members must submit to drug screening. Refusal to submit to test will result in mandatory suspension and may be grounds for dismissal from the department.

59. The main purpose of random drug testing for members of the department of correction is

    (A) to establish a credible deterrent to illegal drug usage among the inmates.
    (B) deter drug use among the employees.
    (C) gain information on who is selling drugs.
    (D) encourage inmates to model themselves after the department's employees and remain drug free.

60. According to the procedure governing random drug testing, which of the following statements is most appropriate?

    (A) The random selection must be conducted no more than 24 hours prior to the actual drug testing.
    (B) Members must be notified 24 hours after the test of the results.
    (C) The test must be given within 24 hours of the member being notified.
    (D) Members must be notified at least 24 hours prior to scheduled testing.

61. Tab is a correction officer. He is ordered to appear for drug testing as a result of being selected randomly. According to the procedure, Tab should appear

    (A) in either uniform or civilian clothes, whichever he chooses.
    (B) in uniform.
    (C) in civilian clothes.
    (D) in either uniform or civilian clothes, whichever his immediate supervisor directs.

62. Correction Officer Barns misses an appointment to be randomly tested for drugs. Unfortunately the officer could not keep the appointment because the officer was on a regularly scheduled day off. Barns should

    (A) be rescheduled within 24 hours.
    (B) be rescheduled as soon as possible.
    (C) be rescheduled but only if the officer is again randomly selected.
    (D) not be rescheduled because the officer had a valid excuse for missing the appointment.

63. If a member refuses to submit to drug screening, the member will be subject to

    (A) suspension only.
    (B) immediate mandatory dismissal.
    (C) mandatory suspension and possible dismissal.
    (D) possible suspension.

An escape is an unauthorized voluntary departure from official custody. All escapes shall immediately be reported to the officer of the day by the tour commander. An inmate can escape from custody by

1. forging a release document or

2. intentionally assuming the identity of another person or

3. overpowering the guards or

4. overcoming physical barriers intended to restrict and restrain the movements of the inmate.

An erroneous discharge is the release from custody of an inmate by correction authorities based on the mistaken belief by the custodian that the inmate is entitled to be at liberty. Erroneous discharges are not escapes but must immediately be reported to the warden by the discovering officer.

64. Correction Officer Limbo is assigned to Cell Block 13 where he discovered that several inmates are missing. Of the following cases of inmates missing from cell block 13, which should Officer Limbo immediately report to the warden?

(A) Pat has knocked down a correction officer and fled through an opened window in the visiting room.
(B) Don has sawed through some bars and dropped to the outside sidewalk below.
(C) Frank intentionally impersonated a correction officer and walked out the front door.
(D) Ray was let out of the institution when a clerical worker mistakenly mixed up his inmate number with that of another inmate who was due to be released today.

PRACTICE TEST 4

The correction officer assigned to the residential cell block concerned shall report the following information to the command center exactly in this order whenever an inmate disturbance occurs.

1. time of the disturbance

2. exact location of the disturbance

3. cause of the disturbance, if known

4. number of inmates involved, if known

5. current status of the level of security at the facility

6. assistance required

7. description of any injuries

8. number of correction officers at the scene

This information shall be transmitted to the command center immediately and updates shall be made every 30 minutes thereafter. If the disturbance should continue for more than 24 hours, then a recap must be given to command center by the tour commander on duty at the end of each day.

65. Correction Officer Lucy Ball is at the scene of an inmate disturbance as the officer assigned to the residential cell block. Officer Ball properly follows department procedures dealing with inmate disturbances and has just notified the command center of the cause of the disturbance. Officer Ball's next step should be to advise command center of

(A) the number of inmates involved, if she knows.
(B) the exact location of the disturbance.
(C) any assistance that is needed.
(D) any injuries that have occurred.

66. After Officer Ball notifies the command center of the situation and gives all necessary information to the center, updates should be made

(A) as soon as possible.
(B) every 30 minutes.
(C) at the end of each tour.
(D) at the end of each day.

Correction officers within designated areas of the facility are authorized to use a liquid hand-held aerosol known hereafter as mace. Only officers who have been trained in the use of mace will be issued mace and authorized to use it in certain situations. Mace should not be used in outdoor areas of the facility. Prior to using mace, an officer should try to resolve the situation by other means such as conflict resolution techniques. Discretion must always be used in situations where mace will be deployed. The liquid hand-held aerosol dispensing mace may be used by a correction officer in the following situations:

1. in defense of self or another;

2. to prevent escapes, serious disturbances, or crimes;

3. to enforce facility rules;

4. to prevent serious damage to property;

5. to prevent an inmate from self-inflicting harm.

Mace is not recommended for use in large areas or against large numbers of persons. It should not be used against more than two persons at any one time. It has proven useful in small cell areas. Mace shall not be used

1. to interrogate an inmate,

2. to threaten anyone,

3. to stop boisterous shouting among inmates,

4. to punish an inmate.

67. Concerning the facility's procedure regarding the use of mace, which of the following statements is least correct?

(A) Certain correction officers within designated areas of the facility are authorized to use mace.

(B) Mace should not be used in outdoor areas of the facility.

(C) Conflict resolution techniques should not be attempted before mace is used.

(D) Discretion must always be used in situations where mace will be deployed.

68. Which of the following is not a recommended use of mace by a correction officer?

    (A) to defend oneself
    (B) to prevent escape by an inmate
    (C) to enforce a rule of the facility
    (D) to prevent any damage to the property of the facility

69. Evaluate the following statements concerning the use of mace by correction officers.

    1. Mace is not recommended for use in large areas.
    2. Mace should be used against as many as three persons at one time.

    Which of the following is most accurate concerning the statements above?

    (A) Only statement 1 is correct.
    (B) Only statement 2 is correct.
    (C) Both statements 1 and 2 are correct.
    (D) Neither statement 1 nor 2 is correct.

70. Which of the following describes the most appropriate use of mace?

    (A) to interrogate an inmate
    (B) to threaten an inmate
    (C) to punish an inmate
    (D) to prevent an inmate from harming himself/herself

Directions: Answer question 71 based solely on the following information.

    Whenever a fire occurs in the city prison, the correction officer concerned shall prepare an investigation report if the fire is considered suspicious. However, the officer concerned shall notify the operations bureau if a fire occurs where

  1.   injury or death occurs,

  2.   the cause of the fire is suspicious,

  3.   the fire department responded and assisted in a forced entry into the affected area,

  4.   an inmate or inmates had to be relocated due to damage to a residential cell area.

71. In which of the following situations would a correction officer be most likely to prepare an investigation report?

   (A) when an inmate is injured in a fire
   (B) if a fire is suspicious
   (C) when the fire department responds and assists in breaking into an area that had been burned
   (D) if an inmate must be relocated because of fire damage to the inmate's cell

---

Directions: Answer questions 72 and 73 based solely on the following information.

The conduct of off-duty correction officers reflects not only on the individual officer but also on the entire department. Often officers become involved in effecting arrests. In those situations where officers are engaged in making off-duty arrests, the following procedure shall be followed in the order given.

1. Inform the individual of the reason for the arrest and your authority. Note that the reason for the arrest is not required if the suspect resists or flees.

2. Rearcuff the prisoner, if handcuffs are available.

3. Search the prisoner for weapons, evidence, or contraband.

4. Advise the prisoner of Miranda Rights if questioning is to take place.

5. Advise the desk officer of the local police agency.

6. Notify the tour commander of the facility where assigned that an arrest has been made. Requests for overtime by the arresting officer should be directed to the immediate commanding officer of the member making the arrest.

72. An off-duty arrest is made by Correction Officer West. According to correction department regulations, which of the following actions must be taken by correction officers in all off-duty arrest situations?

   (A) inform the individual of the reason for the arrest
   (B) rearcuff the prisoner
   (C) search the prisoner for weapons, evidence, or contraband
   (D) advise the prisoner of Miranda Rights

73. Correction Officer Tanks makes a legal off-duty arrest. If the officer wishes to be paid for working overtime to process the off-duty arrest, the officer should request the overtime from

(A) the desk officer of the police agency involved.
(B) the tour commander of the facility where Officer Tanks works.
(C) Officer Tanks's immediate commanding officer.
(D) the warden of the facility where Officer Tanks works.

Directions: Use the following information to answer questions 74–78. For each question you are to select the choice that correctly represents the article and the price for which it is being offered for sale.

At times some inmates act as merchants illegally selling certain sought-after items to other inmates. In order not to be discovered, these inmate merchants advertise these items to other inmates through a coded price list.

In the following information you will find a number associated with an article that is sold illegally by merchant inmates to other inmates.

1. Cigarettes

2. Whiskey

3. Fresh Fruit

4. Hard Meats (Salami)

5. Porno Magazines

6. Hard Cheeses

7. Hand Knives

8. Heroin

9. Cocaine

0. Marijuana

In addition, another reference chart, which associates a letter with a number, follows. This is to be used to determine the price in dollars of each item that is for sale.

A	P	U	O	Y	W	E	R	C	S
0	9	8	7	6	5	4	3	2	1

74. Using the reference tables, which of the following most accurately represents Hard Salami at $5?

(A) 5WOO
(B) 4W
(C) 5OOW
(D) 4WAA

75. Using the reference tables, which of the following most accurately represents Marijuana at $28?

(A) 0AC
(B) 9CA
(C) 0CU
(D) 9CW

76. Using the reference tables, which of the following most accurately represents Hand Knives at $47?

(A) 6OE
(B) 7EO
(C) 6EO
(D) 7OE

77. Using the reference tables, which of the following most accurately represents Whiskey at $62?

(A) 8CY
(B) 2CY
(C) 8YC
(D) 2YC

78. Using the reference tables, which of the following most accurately represents Cigarettes at $24?

(A) 1SE
(B) 1EO
(C) 1CE
(D) 1EC

79. According to Correction Department policy, the unauthorized use of any firearm while on or off duty is prohibited and will result in disciplinary action being taken. Joe, a correction officer, used his weapon while on duty. Mary, a correction officer, used her weapon while off duty. It is correct to say that

    (A) Joe will definitely receive disciplinary action.
    (B) Mary will definitely receive disciplinary action.
    (C) neither Joe nor Mary could receive disciplinary action.
    (D) both Joe and Mary may or may not receive disciplinary action.

80. Consider the following statements of fact:

    Correction officers who lose keys are fined.
    A key was lost.
    The lost key was found by a correction officer.
    It was found in cell block 14.

    Based on these facts, which of the following is the most accurate statement?

    (A) A key was lost by a correction officer.
    (B) The found key fits a lock in cell block 14.
    (C) A correction officer found the lost key in cell block 14.
    (D) A correction officer will be fined.

81. Correction officers shall not, for any reason whatsoever, take prison keys off the premises of the prison or leave them out of their actual or immediate possession or control. Any loss of prison keys must be reported at once to the head of the prison. Based on this rule, which of the following is the least accurate statement?

    (A) It is a violation for a correction officer to take prison keys home.
    (B) It is always a violation for a correction officer to leave a key in a lock.
    (C) It is always a violation for a correction officer to leave prison keys unattended.
    (D) It is a violation for a correction officer who loses a prison key to intentionally delay making a notification to the head of the prison.

82. When it is deemed necessary at any time to search the person of any on-duty prison employee, such search shall be made by a supervisor. Refusal of any such employee to be searched shall constitute grounds for dismissal. This means that

    (A) prison employees can always be searched.
    (B) any prison employee can search another employee.
    (C) prison employees who refused to be searched may be fired.
    (D) prison employees often bring contraband into prison.

83. A very important task of a correction officer is to maintain order within the confines of the prison facility. Based on this statement, it is probably true that

    (A) correction officers have to be stronger than inmates.
    (B) order maintenance is a necessary ingredient of prison life.
    (C) most inmates tend to be disorderly.
    (D) correction officers perform a number of unimportant tasks.

84. The prevalence of drugs in our society is a major cause of our crime problem. Based on this statement, one could conclude that one of the main causes of crime is the

    (A) widespread availability of drugs.
    (B) cheap cost of drugs.
    (C) role of drugs in the commission of violent crime.
    (D) need for people to obtain money to purchase drugs.

85. Experience has shown that there is no reason why all prisons need to be escapeproof. This most nearly means that

    (A) it is not a bad thing for some prisoners to escape.
    (B) escape should not be a major correctional concern.
    (C) escape attempts almost always fail.
    (D) not all prisoners attempt to escape.

86. One frequent and continuous argument against capital punishment is the disproportionate inflictions of capital punishment against minorities. This means most nearly that

    (A) the death penalty represents cruel and unusual punishment.
    (B) the death penalty discriminates against minorities.
    (C) only minorities receive the death penalty.
    (D) the death penalty does not deter crime.

87. Assume that statistics indicate that persons who are sent to prison have average intelligence but have a below average level of formal education. Based on this statement, it is most reasonable to conclude that

    (A) there seems to be a relationship between criminal convictions and the level of formal education.
    (B) stupid people are responsible for most criminal acts.
    (C) criminals are actually smarter than the average citizen.
    (D) people with above average intelligence do not commit crimes.

88. A correction officer may make an arrest of a person for a felony, such as an escape or an escape attempt, when she has reasonable cause to believe such person has committed a felony. But, a correction officer may make an arrest of a person for a misdemeanor, such as a simple assault or petit larceny, or for a violation, such as harassment, only when she has reasonable cause to believe such person has committed the misdemeanor or violation in her presence. Which of the following does not violate this rule?

    (A) A correction officer arrests an inmate for an escape attempt even though the officer was not present when the attempt was made.
    (B) A correction officer arrests an inmate for a simple assault even though the officer was not present when the assault occurred.
    (C) A correction officer arrests an inmate for a petit larceny even though the officer was not present when the larceny occurred.
    (D) A correction officer arrests an inmate for harassment even though the officer was not present when the harassment occurred.

Directions: Answer questions 89 and 90 based solely on the following information.

A person is guilty of Refusing to Aid a Peace Officer when upon command of a readily identifiable peace officer, such person unreasonably refuses to aid a peace officer in effecting an arrest of another or preventing the commission by another person of any offense.

89. Correction Officer Handy is a peace officer. Officer Handy is attempting to arrest Pat Walker for larceny, but Pat runs away obviously refusing to submit to arrest. In this instance, when Pat Walker is apprehended, Officer Handy

    (A) should charge Walker with Refusing to Aid a Peace Officer immediately.
    (B) should not charge Pat Walker with Refusing to Aid a Peace Officer under these circumstances.
    (C) should charge Walker with Refusing to Aid a Peace Officer but only if it can be shown that Walker recognized that Handy was a peace officer.
    (D) should not charge Pat Walker with Refusing to Aid a Peace Officer unless it can be shown that Walker unreasonably refused to comply with Officer Handy.

90. Late one night while returning from court with an empty correction van, Officer Barley has a flat tire on the van. The officer pulls the van to the curb and asks a neighborhood youth to hold a flashlight on the van while the officer changes the tire. The youth refuses, stating, "I hate screws." In this instance, Officer Barley

(A) should charge the youth with Refusing to Aid a Peace Officer immediately.

(B) should not charge the youth with Refusing to Aid a Peace Officer under these circumstances.

(C) should charge the youth with Refusing to Aid a Peace Officer only if it can be shown that the youth knew Barley was a correction officer.

(D) should not charge the youth with Refusing to Aid a Peace Officer unless it can be shown that the youth was physically able to comply with Officer Barley's request.

Directions: Answer questions 91–93 based solely on the following information.

Larceny or the stealing of tangible property occurs when tangible property is removed from the true owner of the property permanently or for such a long period of time that the value of the property is greatly reduced.

Acts of larceny must be done intentionally. For example intentionally taking the property of another without that person's permission would be larceny. Also considered larceny is failing to return the lost property of another, such as keeping a package that was given to you by mistake or putting the wrong hat on when leaving a club and then when noticing that it is the wrong hat, failing to return it because it is worth more than yours.

Larceny is a misdemeanor and becomes a felony if the value of the property is more than $1000 at the time of the theft, or the property consists of a public record, a credit card, or a firearm. If the value of the property cannot be determined, it is assumed that the value is less than $250.

91. Which of the following prisoners being lodged at the county jail would be least likely to be charged with a felony?

(A) June who stole a credit card

(B) April who stole a firearm worth $488

(C) Don who stole a public record

(D) Pat who stole a gold bracelet that, although valued at only $995 at the time of the theft, was marked down from $1500

92. While off duty, Correction Officer Ray Topper visits a restaurant and leaves his coat on a coat rack. After dining the officer puts on what he mistakenly believes is his coat and leaves the restaurant. Soon the officer realizes that the coat he is wearing belongs to someone else. However, this coat is worth more and in better condition than his, which he left at the restaurant. So Topper decides to keep it. In this instance, Officer Topper

    (A) committed larceny because right from the beginning he intended to take the property of another.
    (B) did not commit larceny because he left his coat as a kind of exchange.
    (C) committed larceny because he failed to return lost property.
    (D) did not commit larceny because his initial action was done mistakenly.

93. Which of the following statements is most correct concerning the property involved with the crime of larceny?

    (A) It may be tangible or intangible.
    (B) It must be permanently taken from the owner.
    (C) It does not include property that someone removes from an owner to hold for so long that the value of the property is greatly reduced.
    (D) If its value cannot be determined, then the property is to be considered worth less than $250.

Robbery requires the use of force. The force can be used to overcome resistance to the taking of property or to compel the owner of the property to engage in conduct that assists in the robbery. However, the use of the force involved must be immediate and intended against a person. Threatening to use force against someone tomorrow or some other future date if the property is not handed over is the felony of grand larceny, but not robbery. Similarly threatening to damage the property of another anytime unless property is handed over is also the felony of grand larceny, but not robbery.

Robbery is always a felony and has three degrees. Third-degree robbery occurs when someone forcibly steals property. Robbery becomes second degree and more serious when there are accomplices present, or when the victim is injured but not seriously. Robbery in the first degree occurs when the victim is seriously injured or the robber is armed with a deadly weapon.

94. Which of the following prisoners being held in the department of correction holding pen and awaiting arraignment is least likely to be arraigned on a robbery charge?

(A) Tom, who punched an elderly female and then took her rings.
(B) Pat, who along with Jack approached a young boy in a school yard and told him to give them his jacket or else they would immediately beat him.
(C) Don, who threatened to burn a neighbor's house down right now unless he gave him money.
(D) June, who used force to overcome a man's resistance to the taking of his property, which amounted to only $4.

95. Correction Officer Dukes is interviewing several inmates concerning what exactly were their criminal convictions. Of the following inmates interviewed, which of them is least likely to have been convicted of robbery?

(A) Ray, who received money from a man by threatening to come back the next day with some friends and beat up the man
(B) Pat, who stabbed a person and then took that person's wallet
(C) April, who received property from a victim by putting her hand in her jacket and showing the victim a gun
(D) Don, who knocked a senior citizen to the floor and took his watch

96. Which of the following statements concerning robbery is least accurate?

   (A) Robbery is stealing with force added.
   (B) Robbery in the third degree is less serious than robbery in the second degree.
   (C) Robbery always requires displaying a gun.
   (D) Robbery does not always require that the victim receive an injury.

97. Regarding the crime of robbery in the second degree, which of the following statements is most correct concerning the use of accomplices?

   (A) The accomplice must be armed.
   (B) The accomplice must injure the victim.
   (C) The accomplice must be present.
   (D) The accomplice must share in the proceeds of the robbery.

98. An escaped convict stops a female driving in an open convertible with her dog. The convict tells the woman that unless she gives him her car to continue his escape in, he will kill her dog. The female gives the convict the car. In addition to any other crime stemming from the escape, the convict should be charged with

   (A) robbery in the first degree.
   (B) robbery in the second degree.
   (C) robbery in the third degree.
   (D) grand larceny.

A crime is a felony or a misdemeanor but not a violation.

A person is guilty of an attempt to commit a crime, (i.e., a felony or misdemeanor), when, with intent to commit a crime, such person engages in conduct that tends to effect the commission of such crime.

A person charged with attempting to commit a crime is charged with one level lower than the crime that is being attempted. For example, someone attempting to commit

a class A felony is charged with a class B felony.

a class B felony is charged with a class C felony.

a class C felony is charged with a class D felony.

a class D felony is charged with a class E felony.

a class E felony is charged with a misdemeanor.

99. Which of the following is least correct concerning an attempt to commit a crime?

(A) A person can attempt to commit a felony.
(B) A person can attempt to commit a misdemeanor.
(C) A person can attempt to commit a violation.
(D) All the above statements are equally incorrect.

100. Robbery is a class D felony. Pat Summers, an inmate, was convicted and incarcerated because of his attempt to commit robbery. Therefore, Summers was most likely convicted of

(A) a class C felony.
(B) a class E felony.
(C) a misdemeanor.
(D) a class D felony.

END OF TEST

ANSWER KEY
Practice Test 4

1. **D**	26. **B**	51. **D**	76. **B**
2. **C**	27. **A**	52. **B**	77. **D**
3. **A**	28. **D**	53. **D**	78. **C**
4. **D**	29. **D**	54. **D**	79. **D**
5. **A**	30. **B**	55. **C**	80. **C**
6. **B**	31. **D**	56. **D**	81. **B**
7. **A**	32. **D**	57. **C**	82. **C**
8. **C**	33. **B**	58. **A**	83. **B**
9. **D**	34. **B**	59. **B**	84. **A**
10. **D**	35. **B**	60. **D**	85. **D**
11. **D**	36. **C**	61. **C**	86. **B**
12. **D**	37. **B**	62. **B**	87. **A**
13. **C**	38. **D**	63. **C**	88. **A**
14. **C**	39. **C**	64. **D**	89. **B**
15. **B**	40. **A**	65. **A**	90. **B**
16. **A**	41. **B**	66. **B**	91. **D**
17. **D**	42. **B**	67. **C**	92. **C**
18. **D**	43. **B**	68. **D**	93. **D**
19. **B**	44. **D**	69. **A**	94. **C**
20. **D**	45. **A**	70. **D**	95. **A**
21. **B**	46. **C**	71. **B**	96. **C**
22. **B**	47. **A**	72. **C**	97. **C**
23. **D**	48. **C**	73. **C**	98. **D**
24. **C**	49. **A**	74. **B**	99. **C**
25. **C**	50. **C**	75. **C**	100. **B**

DIAGNOSTIC CHART

Instructions: After you score your test, complete the following chart by inserting in the column entitled "Your Number Correct" the number of correct questions you answered in each of the eight sections of the test. Then compare your score in each section with the ratings in the column entitled "Scale." Finally, to correct your weaknesses, follow the instructions found at the end of the chart.

Section	Question Numbers	Area	Your Number Correct	Scale
1	1–8	Memory (8 questions)		8 Right—Excellent 6–7 Right—Good 5 Right—Fair Under 5 Right—Poor
2	9–32	Reading Comprehension (24 questions)		24 Right—Excellent 20–23 Right—Good 16–19 Right—Fair Under 16 Right—Poor
3	33–40	Verbal and Math (8 questions)		8 Right—Excellent 6–7 Right—Good 5 Right—Fair Under 5 Right—Poor
4	41–50	Correction Forms (10 questions)		10 Right—Excellent 8–9 Right—Good 7 Right—Fair Under 7 Right—Poor
5	51–58	Graphs (8 questions)		8 Right—Excellent 6–7 Right—Good 5 Right—Fair Under 5 Right—Poor
6	59–78	Applying Correction Procedures (20 questions)		20 Right—Excellent 18–19 Right—Good 16–17 Right—Fair Under 16 Right—Poor
7	79–88	Judgment and Reasoning (10 questions)		10 Right—Excellent 8–9 Right—Good 7 Right—Fair Under 7 Right—Poor
8	89–100	Legal Definitions (12 questions)		12 Right—Excellent 10–11 Right—Good 8–9 Right—Fair Under 8 Right—Poor

How to correct weaknesses:

1. If you are weak in Section 1, concentrate on Chapter 3.
2. If you are weak in Section 2, concentrate on Chapter 1.
3. If you are weak in Section 3, concentrate on Chapter 2.
4. If you are weak in Section 4, concentrate on Chapter 4.
5. If you are weak in Section 5, concentrate on Chapter 5.
6. If you are weak in Section 6, concentrate on Chapter 6.
7. If you are weak in Section 7, concentrate on Chapter 7.
8. If you are weak in Section 8, concentrate on Chapter 8.

Note: Consider yourself weak in an area if you receive anything other than an excellent rating in it.

ANSWERS EXPLAINED

1. **(D)** <u>M</u>orty Hertz is a <u>m</u>usician who excels at playing the piano.

2. **(C)** Dale Mize has a degree from Yale University.

3. **(A)** Inmate Street is the hockey player. To remember this you might have thought that he might have learned to play hockey in the street.

4. **(D)** <u>M</u>orty Hertz is a <u>m</u>usician and an ex-<u>M</u>arine who served in the Gulf War.

5. **(A)** Inmate Banks is a self-made legal expert.

6. **(B)** Surprisingly enough, Inmate Banks is a legal expert even though he does not have a high school diploma.

7. **(A)** Inmate Street is the prison peacekeeper who has not been involved in any violent acts in prison.

8. **(C)** This was stated in the last paragraph of the passage.

9. **(D)** It is probably true that the crime problem in this country will never be truly solved.

10. **(D)** Choices A, B, and C are opinions and not facts. Choice D is factual.

11. **(D)** If specifically authorized by the warden, a correction officer can be armed while on duty.

12. **(D)** This rule is absolute. There are no exceptions.

13. **(C)** The rule covers off-duty incidents and includes personal firearms.

14. **(C)** With no exceptions, all packages must be searched as they come into or leave the yard.

15. **(B)** The knives in cells 1 and 4 are the only objects in all four cells that could be classified as cutting implements.

16. **(A)** Cell 1 contains a diary, which is defined as being a daily journal of activities.

17. **(D)** The clocks in cells 1, 2, and 3 all indicate that it is about the same time. The clock in cell 4 indicates a different time. Note that the word *probably* in the stem of the question allows you to make certain assumptions to arrive at the correct answer. Remember, however, that such assumptions must be based on facts. In this question, it is a fact that the clocks in three cells all indicate the same time.

18. **(D)** Cell 4 has seven objects depicted.

19. **(B)** Cell 2 has five objects depicted.

20. **(D)** There is a pen in cell 1, a pencil in cell 2, a pencil in cell 3, and a pen in cell 4.

21. **(B)** According to the passage, children under 10 are not even allowed on prison grounds.

22. **(B)** Clergy persons can visit 15 hours a day, 7 days a week.

23. **(D)** Police can visit if they have a court order.

24. **(C)** 12-year-olds can visit only on family visiting days, which are held at least 3 times a month, or at least 36 times a year (12 × 3).

25. **(C)** Correction officers are sometimes legally entitled to use force to defend themselves or a third party against unlawful force.

26. **(B)** Correction officers may not use deadly physical force upon another person unless they reasonably believe that such other person is using or about to use deadly physical force against them or another.

27. **(A)** The restriction that arrests can be made only if the offense was committed in the presence of the officer does not apply to felonies. It applies only to misdemeanors and violations. This means that arrests can be made for felonies even if the arresting officer was not present when they occurred.

28. **(D)** Having the right to counsel means having a right to a lawyer. The counsel (lawyer) may be of the juvenile's own choosing or may be appointed by the court for financial or other reasons.

29. **(D)** To waive means to give up or to relinquish. While a waiver (a giving up) of the right to counsel may be made, it is not effective unless the waiver is made in writing by both the juvenile and at least one of the parents or legal guardians.

30. **(B)** The skill level of a prison's personnel determines the impact that the guard has on the inmate. And, because the most important rehabilitative tool is the impact of one person upon another, the answer to this question has to be choice B.

31. **(D)** It is a rare instance when an inmate out on work release commits a crime of violence.

32. **(D)** Recreation varies from formal programs to free-time activities. Some recreational activities involve groups of inmates while others are aimed at individuals.

33. **(B)** The sum equals $200.48. Remember when adding numbers with decimals the first thing to do is to properly align the numbers. For example the numbers given should have been aligned in columns to look like this.

$$\begin{array}{r} \$53.72 \\ \$92.76 \\ \$\ 9.26 \\ \$\ 5.73 \\ \$16.41 \\ \$11.38 \\ +\ \$11.22 \\ \hline \$200.48 \end{array}$$

34. **(B)** Dividing the total sum of $200.48 by 7 (the number of newly arrived inmates), the result is exactly $28.64.

35. **(B)** To find the ratio, we first create two fractions. But we must compare the same items. That means in creating the two fractions, if we put a number of inmates on the bottom of one fraction we must put a number of inmates on the bottom of the other

fraction. The same is true for what we place on the top of each of the two fractions we create. The rule for solving ratio questions is to cross multiply and then divide. For example,

$$\frac{2 \text{ officers}}{11 \text{ inmates}} = \frac{x \text{ officers}}{55 \text{ inmates}}$$

Cross multiplying we get $11x = 110$. In other words, what number times 11 equals 110? The answer is 10, as indicated by choice B.

36. **(C)** Here you had to work carefully and be organized. First find 10% of 2,500, which equals 250. Then subtract that 250 from 2,500, which equals 2,250, the number of inmates still remaining free after 6 months. Then find 20% of these remaining 2,250 inmates who were still free after six months ($0.2 \times 2250 = 450$). Then subtract these 450 inmates from the remaining inmates who were still free after 6 months, or $2250 - 450 = 1800$, which is choice C.

37. **(B)** Implicit means implied or to express something indirectly. Explicit means to express something directly. They should be switched in choices A and C. Choice B is stated correctly.

38. **(D)** All the choices are incorrect. Choice A incorrectly uses *in* in place of *into*. Choice B incorrectly uses *Latter* in place of *Later*, and choice C incorrectly uses *Its* in place of *It's*.

39. **(C)** *Ingenious*, which means clever and resourceful, should have been used in choice A to replace *ingenuous*. And *ingenuous*, which means open and frank, should have been used in choice B to replace *ingenious*. Choice C is correctly stated.

40. **(A)** Choice B is incorrect because *besides*, which means in addition to, should have been used in place of *beside*, which means next to. Choice C is incorrect because *accept*, which means to take what is offered, should have been used in place of *except*, which means to exclude. Choice A is correctly stated.

41. **(B)** Caption 5 asks for the facility where the complaint was received, which is the Fair Way Correctional Facility.

42. **(B)** The entry for caption 16 is the date when the alleged misconduct took place, or December 15.

43. **(B)** The telephone number 555-3029 is the complainant's telephone number and should be entered in caption 8.

44. **(D)** Dubs is the name of the officer who received the complaint.

45. **(A)** Frank is the first name of the subject of the complaint.

46. **(C)** Such a statement should be entered under the complaint details in caption 20.

47. **(A)** As indicated by examination of the narrative, 6988 is the central complaint number and should be entered in caption 3.

48. **(C)** Caption 19 would be able to be used to capture such information.

49. **(A)** Caption 4 asks how the complaint was made.

50. **(C)** Caption 6A calls for the last name of the complainant.

51. **(D)** Inmate Waters' May assignment is Reserve Duty. According to the Assignment Information Number 3, in no case shall the same inmate be assigned to Reserve Duty for two consecutive months.

52. **(B)** In May, Inmate Smith is assigned to the hospital. All assignments, other than the hospital, start at 10:00 A.M. The hospital assignment starts at 9:00 A.M.

53. **(D)** Inmates assigned to the library must have a high school diploma, see Assignment Information Number 2. Choice A is wrong because Waters does not have a high school diploma, see the asterisk explanation included as part of the schedule. Choice B is wrong because Branch doesn't have a high school diploma. Choice C is wrong because Inmate Day is already assigned to the library. There is, however, no prohibition against the action described in choice D.

54. **(D)** Brown is not on meal, and he is not due back on assignment until 2:00 P.M. When inmates are not on assignment, they must be in their cells, see Assignment Information Number 5.

55. **(C)** Inmate Waters is on Reserve Duty. Inmates on Reserve Duty must stay in the recreation room, see Assignment Information Number 6.

56. **(D)** If you selected choice A, you neglected the fact that the work schedule that was supplied was a "Monday to Friday" work schedule. The stem of the question tells you that it is Sunday. Choice D is the answer.

57. **(C)** Choice A is incorrect because the hospital assignment is longer. Choice B is incorrect because a high school diploma is needed for assignment to the library. Choice D is incorrect because an inmate cannot receive Reserve Duty for two consecutive months.

58. **(A)** These are the four inmates with asterisks next to their name indicating that they have a high school diploma.

59. **(B)** The aim of this procedure is to deter drug use by employees not inmates.

60. **(D)** The member concerned must be notified at least 24 hours prior to scheduled testing.

61. **(C)** The procedure mandates that the member being tested be in civilian clothes.

62. **(B)** If an employee has a valid reason for missing an appointment, the employee is to be rescheduled as soon as possible.

63. **(C)** Refusing a drug test calls for mandatory suspension and may be grounds for dismissal from the department.

64. **(D)** Erroneous discharges are not escapes but must immediately be reported to the warden by the discovering officer.

65. **(A)** Choice A describes her next step after notifying command center of the cause of the disturbance.

66. **(B)** It is as stated in the procedure.

67. **(C)** Conflict resolution techniques should be attempted before mace is used.

68. **(D)** Choice D is incorrectly stated because it refers to any damage rather than serious damage to property.

69. **(A)** Mace should not be used against more than two persons at any one time.

70. **(D)** Mace is permitted to prevent an inmate from self-inflicting an injury.

71. **(B)** Suspicious fires are the only occurrences that, according to the procedure, require the preparation of an investigation report.

72. **(C)** Choices A, B, and D call for actions that are not done in every situation.

73. **(C)** It is as stated in the procedure.

74. **(B)** Choice B indicates a number 4 for Hard Meats (Salami) at W for $5. Choice D is incorrect because WAA represents $500. Remember that the reference table is expressed in dollars.

75. **(C)** The number 0 represents Marijuana and 28 would be CU, which is indicated by choice C.

76. **(B)** The number 7 represents Hand Knives and 47 would be EO, which is indicated by choice B.

77. **(D)** It is as indicated by the reference tables.

78. **(C)** The number 1 represents Cigarettes and 24 would be CE, which is indicated by choice C.

79. **(D)** Not enough information is given to state definitely one way or the other whether Joe or Mary will receive disciplinary action. The missing information is whether they used their weapons in an authorized or unauthorized manner.

80. **(C)** It is not clear who lost the key. It could have been an inmate. Nor is it clear that the key fits a lock in cell block 14. It is definitely stated that a correction officer found the lost key in cell block 14.

81. **(B)** Note that choices A, C, and D all talk about prison keys, as does the rule. Choice B is too broad to be correct.

82. **(C)** Only on-duty employees can be searched, and only supervisors can do the searching. Choice D may be true, but it cannot be assumed from the rule. Note the use of the soft word *may* in the correct answer. There is a world of difference between saying "employees must be fired" and "employees may be fired."

83. **(B)** If order maintenance was not necessary, then it would not be an important task of a correction officer.

84. **(A)** Prevalence means widespread existence. Note that answering this question correctly depends on the extent of your vocabulary. This is why we stress the importance of increasing your vocabulary by using a dictionary to look up words with which you are unfamiliar.

85. **(D)** If prisons do not all have to be escapeproof, this must mean that some prisoners do not have escape on their mind. To say that escape is not a bad thing or that it is not a major correctional concern is not correct, and there is no justification in the statement for choice C.

86. **(B)** Minorities receive the death penalty not in proportion to their numbers in the overall population. This is what disproportionate means. It is another way of saying that, with respect to the death penalty, minorities are discriminated against.

87. **(A)** People who are sent to prison tend to have a below average level of formal education. One must receive a criminal conviction to be sent to prison. This means that there is probably a relationship between formal education and criminal convictions.

88. **(A)** According to the information given, an escape or an attempted escape is a felony. According to this rule, felonies represent the only crime where an arrest can be made even though the arresting officer was not present at the time of the commission of the felony.

89. **(B)** The charge should not be made because the refusal must involve the arrest of another.

90. **(B)** The refusal must concern either helping to arrest another or helping to stop the commission of an offense by another.

91. **(D)** The larceny of credit cards, firearms, and public records all qualify as felonies. However, a bracelet that is stolen and is presently valued at $995 is not a felony even though it was worth over $1000 in the past. The issue is the value of the property at the time it was stolen.

92. **(C)** Larceny can be committed in a variety of ways, and choice C points out one of the many ways.

93. **(D)** Property must be tangible and may be permanently taken from an owner or held so long that the value to the owner is reduced.

94. **(C)** A threat to damage property is not robbery. It is grand larceny.

95. **(A)** Receiving property by threatening someone with future injury is not a robbery; it is grand larceny.

96. **(C)** Force can be used without injuring someone. Thus you can have a robbery without a victim being injured.

97. **(C)** According to the material provided, the only requirement regarding accomplices is that the accomplice must be present.

98. **(D)** The force that was threatened to overcome resistance to the taking of the car was not a threat of force against a person; it was against a dog.

99. **(C)** Only crimes that are either felonies or misdemeanors can be attempted. Violations are not crimes and therefore cannot be attempted.

100. **(B)** Remember that, in an attempt, the charge is lowered one level.

Practice Test 5

This is the last of the five practice tests that you will be taking. Don't forget to

1. take the test in one sitting. You have 3½ hours to answer 100 questions.

2. use the test-taking strategies outlined in the Introduction. Make certain to develop and use a time management plan.

3. complete the diagnostic chart that appears at the end of this test after you score this practice examination.

4. use the answer sheet we have provided to record your answers.

ANSWER SHEET
Practice Test 5

Follow the instructions given in the test. Mark only your answers in the circles below.

WARNING: Be sure that the circle you fill is in the same row as the question you are answering. Use a No. 2 pencil (soft pencil).

BE SURE YOUR PENCIL MARKS ARE HEAVY AND BLACK. ERASE COMPLETELY ANY ANSWER YOU WISH TO CHANGE.

DO NOT make stray pencil dots, dashes, or marks.

1. Ⓐ Ⓑ Ⓒ Ⓓ	26. Ⓐ Ⓑ Ⓒ Ⓓ	51. Ⓐ Ⓑ Ⓒ Ⓓ	76. Ⓐ Ⓑ Ⓒ Ⓓ
2. Ⓐ Ⓑ Ⓒ Ⓓ	27. Ⓐ Ⓑ Ⓒ Ⓓ	52. Ⓐ Ⓑ Ⓒ Ⓓ	77. Ⓐ Ⓑ Ⓒ Ⓓ
3. Ⓐ Ⓑ Ⓒ Ⓓ	28. Ⓐ Ⓑ Ⓒ Ⓓ	53. Ⓐ Ⓑ Ⓒ Ⓓ	78. Ⓐ Ⓑ Ⓒ Ⓓ
4. Ⓐ Ⓑ Ⓒ Ⓓ	29. Ⓐ Ⓑ Ⓒ Ⓓ	54. Ⓐ Ⓑ Ⓒ Ⓓ	79. Ⓐ Ⓑ Ⓒ Ⓓ
5. Ⓐ Ⓑ Ⓒ Ⓓ	30. Ⓐ Ⓑ Ⓒ Ⓓ	55. Ⓐ Ⓑ Ⓒ Ⓓ	80. Ⓐ Ⓑ Ⓒ Ⓓ
6. Ⓐ Ⓑ Ⓒ Ⓓ	31. Ⓐ Ⓑ Ⓒ Ⓓ	56. Ⓐ Ⓑ Ⓒ Ⓓ	81. Ⓐ Ⓑ Ⓒ Ⓓ
7. Ⓐ Ⓑ Ⓒ Ⓓ	32. Ⓐ Ⓑ Ⓒ Ⓓ	57. Ⓐ Ⓑ Ⓒ Ⓓ	82. Ⓐ Ⓑ Ⓒ Ⓓ
8. Ⓐ Ⓑ Ⓒ Ⓓ	33. Ⓐ Ⓑ Ⓒ Ⓓ	58. Ⓐ Ⓑ Ⓒ Ⓓ	83. Ⓐ Ⓑ Ⓒ Ⓓ
9. Ⓐ Ⓑ Ⓒ Ⓓ	34. Ⓐ Ⓑ Ⓒ Ⓓ	59. Ⓐ Ⓑ Ⓒ Ⓓ	84. Ⓐ Ⓑ Ⓒ Ⓓ
10. Ⓐ Ⓑ Ⓒ Ⓓ	35. Ⓐ Ⓑ Ⓒ Ⓓ	60. Ⓐ Ⓑ Ⓒ Ⓓ	85. Ⓐ Ⓑ Ⓒ Ⓓ
11. Ⓐ Ⓑ Ⓒ Ⓓ	36. Ⓐ Ⓑ Ⓒ Ⓓ	61. Ⓐ Ⓑ Ⓒ Ⓓ	86. Ⓐ Ⓑ Ⓒ Ⓓ
12. Ⓐ Ⓑ Ⓒ Ⓓ	37. Ⓐ Ⓑ Ⓒ Ⓓ	62. Ⓐ Ⓑ Ⓒ Ⓓ	87. Ⓐ Ⓑ Ⓒ Ⓓ
13. Ⓐ Ⓑ Ⓒ Ⓓ	38. Ⓐ Ⓑ Ⓒ Ⓓ	63. Ⓐ Ⓑ Ⓒ Ⓓ	88. Ⓐ Ⓑ Ⓒ Ⓓ
14. Ⓐ Ⓑ Ⓒ Ⓓ	39. Ⓐ Ⓑ Ⓒ Ⓓ	64. Ⓐ Ⓑ Ⓒ Ⓓ	39. Ⓐ Ⓑ Ⓒ Ⓓ
15. Ⓐ Ⓑ Ⓒ Ⓓ	40. Ⓐ Ⓑ Ⓒ Ⓓ	65. Ⓐ Ⓑ Ⓒ Ⓓ	90. Ⓐ Ⓑ Ⓒ Ⓓ
16. Ⓐ Ⓑ Ⓒ Ⓓ	41. Ⓐ Ⓑ Ⓒ Ⓓ	66. Ⓐ Ⓑ Ⓒ Ⓓ	91. Ⓐ Ⓑ Ⓒ Ⓓ
17. Ⓐ Ⓑ Ⓒ Ⓓ	42. Ⓐ Ⓑ Ⓒ Ⓓ	67. Ⓐ Ⓑ Ⓒ Ⓓ	92. Ⓐ Ⓑ Ⓒ Ⓓ
18. Ⓐ Ⓑ Ⓒ Ⓓ	43. Ⓐ Ⓑ Ⓒ Ⓓ	68. Ⓐ Ⓑ Ⓒ Ⓓ	93. Ⓐ Ⓑ Ⓒ Ⓓ
19. Ⓐ Ⓑ Ⓒ Ⓓ	44. Ⓐ Ⓑ Ⓒ Ⓓ	69. Ⓐ Ⓑ Ⓒ Ⓓ	94. Ⓐ Ⓑ Ⓒ Ⓓ
20. Ⓐ Ⓑ Ⓒ Ⓓ	45. Ⓐ Ⓑ Ⓒ Ⓓ	70. Ⓐ Ⓑ Ⓒ Ⓓ	95. Ⓐ Ⓑ Ⓒ Ⓓ
21. Ⓐ Ⓑ Ⓒ Ⓓ	46. Ⓐ Ⓑ Ⓒ Ⓓ	71. Ⓐ Ⓑ Ⓒ Ⓓ	96. Ⓐ Ⓑ Ⓒ Ⓓ
22. Ⓐ Ⓑ Ⓒ Ⓓ	47. Ⓐ Ⓑ Ⓒ Ⓓ	72. Ⓐ Ⓑ Ⓒ Ⓓ	97. Ⓐ Ⓑ Ⓒ Ⓓ
23. Ⓐ Ⓑ Ⓒ Ⓓ	48. Ⓐ Ⓑ Ⓒ Ⓓ	73. Ⓐ Ⓑ Ⓒ Ⓓ	98. Ⓐ Ⓑ Ⓒ Ⓓ
24. Ⓐ Ⓑ Ⓒ Ⓓ	49. Ⓐ Ⓑ Ⓒ Ⓓ	74. Ⓐ Ⓑ Ⓒ Ⓓ	99. Ⓐ Ⓑ Ⓒ Ⓓ
25. Ⓐ Ⓑ Ⓒ Ⓓ	50. Ⓐ Ⓑ Ⓒ Ⓓ	75. Ⓐ Ⓑ Ⓒ Ⓓ	100. Ⓐ Ⓑ Ⓒ Ⓓ

THE TEST

Time: 3½ hours

100 questions

> **Directions:** Before answering questions 1–8 take 5 minutes to examine the following four wanted posters with the information that accompanies each poster.

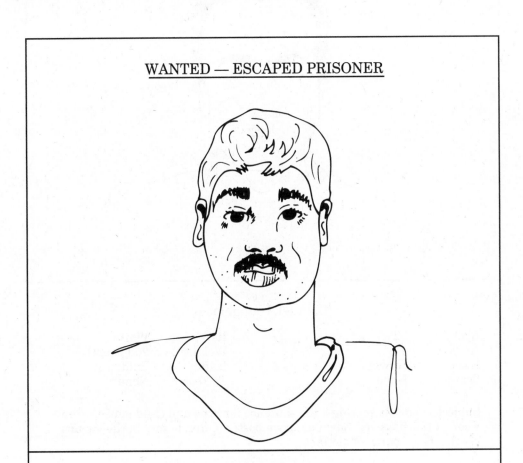

WANTED — ESCAPED PRISONER

Chuckie Gifford

Age:	28	Race:	White
Height:	5' 9"	Weight:	225 pounds
Eyes:	Blue	Hair:	Brown
Scars:	None	Tattoos:	None

Subject, who was serving a 5-year sentence for extortion, is a lifelong con artist who preys on older women. Often represents himself as a law enforcement officer.

WANTED — ESCAPED PRISONER

Samuel Youngblood

Age:	32		Race:	White
Height:	5' 9"		Weight:	200 pounds
Eyes:	Brown		Hair:	Bald
Scars:	None		Tattoos:	None

Subject, who was serving a life sentence for rape and child abuse, often wears a hairpiece as shown in above poster. Often loiters in the vicinity of schools in search of victims.

WANTED — ESCAPED PRISONER

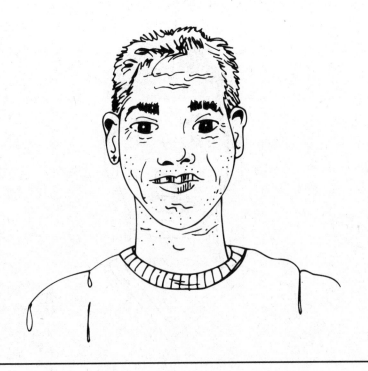

Jack Hunt

Age:	62		Race:	White
Height:	5' 10"		Weight:	210 pounds
Eyes:	Blue		Hair:	Brown
Scars:	None		Tattoos:	None

Subject, who was serving a 10-year sentence for tax evasion, often uses the alias Ben Hogan. He is a chronic drug user.

WANTED — ESCAPED PRISONER

James Short

Age:	45	Race:	White
Height:	5' 9"	Weight:	160 pounds
Eyes:	Brown	Hair:	Brown
Scars:	None	Tattoos:	None

Subject, who was serving a 20-year sentence for armed robbery, is considered armed and dangerous. His weapon of preference is a sawed-off shotgun, which he almost always carries on his person. Speaks five languages, including Chinese and Spanish.

DO NOT PROCEED UNTIL 5 MINUTES HAVE PASSED

TURN TO NEXT PAGE

1. Which of the escaped inmates illustrated in the following posters often loiters in the vicinity of schools?

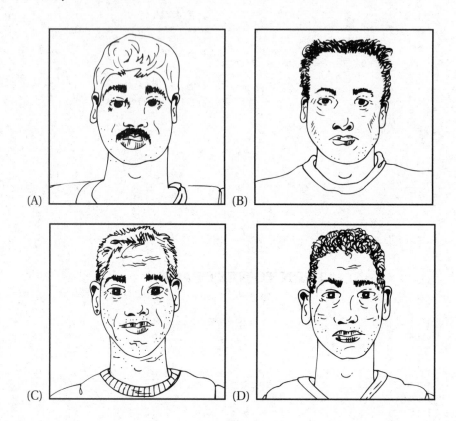

(A)

(B)

(C)

(D)

2. Which of the escaped inmates illustrated in the following posters often carries a sawed-off shotgun?

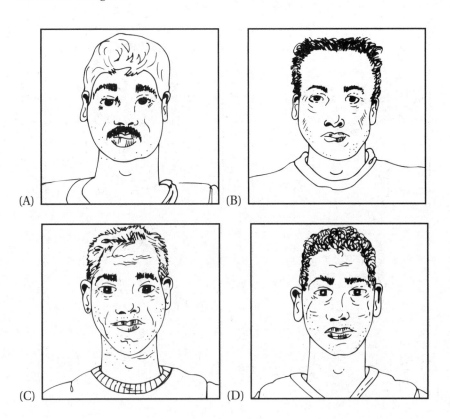

(A)

(B)

(C)

(D)

3. Which of the escaped inmates illustrated in the following posters uses the alias Ben Hogan?

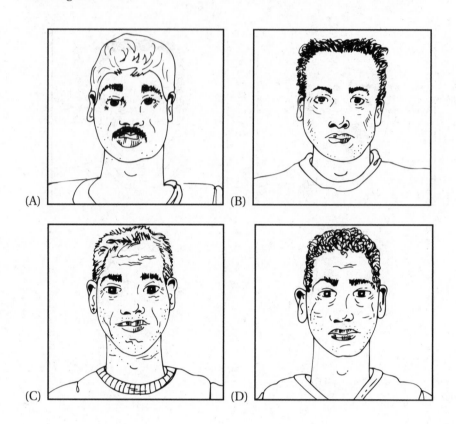

(A) (B)

(C) (D)

4. Which of the escaped inmates illustrated in the following posters often wears a hairpiece?

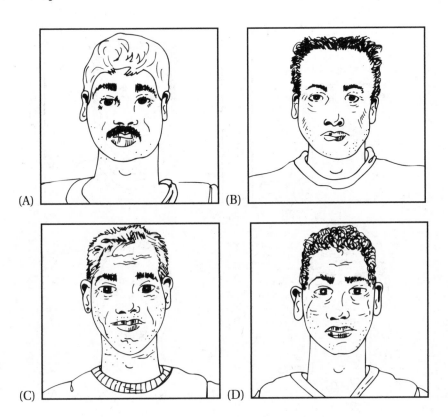

(A)

(B)

(C)

(D)

5. Which of the escaped inmates illustrated in the following posters was serving a life sentence when he escaped?

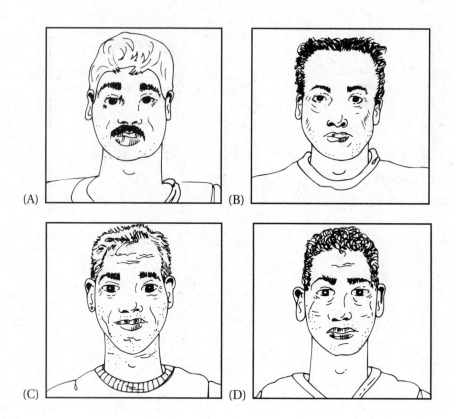

(A)   (B)

(C)   (D)

6. The subject illustrated in the wanted poster directly above

(A) often poses as a law enforcement officer.
(B) is considered armed and dangerous.
(C) is a tax evader.
(D) is a murderer.

7. The subject illustrated in the wanted poster directly above

   (A) often poses as a law enforcement officer.
   (B) is considered armed and dangerous.
   (C) is a chronic drug user.
   (D) is a murderer.

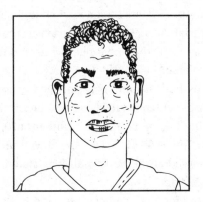

8. The subject illustrated in the wanted poster directly above

   (A) often poses as a law enforcement officer.
   (B) is considered armed and dangerous.
   (C) is a chronic drug user.
   (D) speaks five languages.

Directions: Answer questions 9–16 solely on the basis of the information contained in the following passage.

May North was adopted by her parents, Pat and June North, when she was 1 month old. May was recently appointed as a correction officer and assigned to the Spring Hill Detention Facility for women. Officer North, shield number 8607, has been in contact with "Find Them," a volunteer group whose sole purpose is to assist men and women who have been adopted to find and contact their birth parents.

As a result of Officer North's efforts, she has been able to determine that her birth mother once served a sentence for involuntary manslaughter in Speck Botch Prison. It seems that the officer's birth mother, now identified as April Waters, was once married to Frank Waters, who was in fact Officer North's birth father. During April Waters's pregnancy, a violent quarrel took place late one night between Frank and April Waters. The quarrel centered around Frank Waters's drinking, losses at the racetrack, and affairs with other women. The quarrel moved from verbal to physical, and the police were called. The police who responded, Officers Stem, shield number 8094, and Sterns, shield number 8706, merely separated Frank and April Waters for a brief period, warned them that they both could be arrested, and then left. During the early morning hours following the night of the argument, April Waters took a kitchen knife and repeatedly stabbed Frank to death. At her trial, April Waters's defense was that she had been abused throughout her marriage and could no longer withstand the beatings she claims she was constantly receiving.

The alleged abuse by her husband was not seen as a proper defense by the jury, and April Waters was sentenced to 25 years to life. At the age of 25, she began her sentence at the Sing Prison as Inmate Number 8670. After 5 years she was transferred to the Sun Town Prison where she stayed until the last year of her sentence, which she served at the Parks Half Way Detention House. Altogether she was confined for 25 years.

When April began serving her sentence, she was in the fourth month of her pregnancy and 5 months later she gave birth to Officer North. Widowed and incarcerated, with no family members to turn to, April Waters gave her daughter up for adoption. The only stipulation to the adoption was that her daughter be named May after April's grandmother. The adoption authorities agreed and guaranteed that this would be done.

Officer North was able to ascertain from Detective Walker, shield number 8077, of the Rock Town Police Department, that last year, one year after her mother's release from prison, her mother died of a heart attack. Officer North was never able to meet her mother.

9. Approximately how old was Officer North at the time of her mother's death?

    (A) 26 years old
    (B) 21 years old
    (C) 30 years old
    (D) cannot be determined from the information provided

10. What were the shield numbers of the officers who responded to a family dispute between Frank and April Waters?

    (A) 8607 and 8094
    (B) 8094 and 8706
    (C) 8706 and 8670
    (D) 8670 and 8077

11. Where was May North born?

    (A) in the home of Pat and June North
    (B) in the Spring Hill Detention Facility for women
    (C) in Sing Prison
    (D) in the Parks Half Way Detention House

12. The reason for the quarrel between April and Frank Waters was that Frank was

    (A) drinking.
    (B) gambling.
    (C) unfaithful.
    (D) all of the above.

13. The weapon used to kill Frank Waters was

    (A) poison.
    (B) a kitchen knife.
    (C) a revolver.
    (D) a blunt instrument.

14. May North was most likely named after her

    (A) mother.
    (B) grandmother.
    (C) great grandmother.
    (D) aunt.

15. How old was April Waters when she was let out of prison?

(A) 40 years old

(B) 45 years old

(C) 50 years old

(D) cannot be determined from the information provided

16. April Waters's inmate number at Sing Prison was

(A) 8077.

(B) 8670.

(C) 8607.

(D) 8706.

Directions: Answer questions 17–21 solely on the basis of the information contained in the following passage.

At about 7:30 P.M., on April 28, this year, four inmates attempted a prison break at the Big Pass Correctional Facility. As a result of the prison break, two inmates are still at large and one inmate was killed by the state police. One correction officer was killed, and one was seriously injured as a result of the prison break. The details are as follows:

At the time and place of occurrence, Pat Skipper, Inmate Number 3105; Ray Shine, Inmate Number 5609; and Don Poster, Inmate Number 4569, were being returned to their cells from a late afternoon work detail while accompanied by Correction Officer Frank Gales, shield number 4398. As the group approached D gate, which leads to the residential cell area, Inmate Shine fell to the ground pretending to have severe stomach pains. As Officer Gales went to Shine's aid, the officer was struck on the head with a blunt instrument, which was not recovered. The officer was rendered unconscious and his keys were removed. With said keys, the three inmates were able to exit from the facility, but not before removing two handguns from a locked gun cabinet.

Correction Officer Tom White, shield number 7497, assigned to the front gate, saw the trio escaping and gave chase on foot. Inmate Poster fired six shots at the officer from one of the stolen handguns, striking the officer in the head, killing him instantly. Bob Empire, shield number 4098, is a state trooper assigned to the investigation division. He had been visiting Big Pass Correctional Facility and had just finished interviewing inmate Mat Ballads, Inmate Number 4122, on an unrelated matter. Trooper Empire saw the shooting of Officer White and immediately shot and killed the inmate responsible for shooting Officer White.

The two remaining inmates made their escape by fleeing in a late model sedan driven by a white female in her middle 20s, with red hair. The investigation is continuing.

17. According to the passage, which of the following inmates was killed?

    (A) Inmate Number 3105
    (B) Inmate Number 5609
    (C) Inmate Number 4569
    (D) Inmate Number 4122

18. According to the passage, how was the correction officer in the vicinity of gate D injured?

    (A) The officer was struck with a set of keys.
    (B) The officer was struck with a blunt instrument.
    (C) The officer was shot.
    (D) The officer was stabbed.

19. Who feigned stomach pains?

    (A) Inmate Shine
    (B) Inmate Number 3105
    (C) Inmate Ballads
    (D) Inmate Number 4569

20. The officer who killed the inmate was

    (A) assigned to D gate.
    (B) assigned to the front gate.
    (C) assigned to a late afternoon work detail.
    (D) not assigned to the facility.

21. According to the passage, which of the following statements is most correct?

    (A) Three inmates escaped in a sedan.
    (B) One of the inmates drove the late model vehicle that was used as an escape vehicle.
    (C) The inmates who escaped were assisted by a white female.
    (D) The inmates escaped on foot.

A prison riot began on July 4th, this year, at Reel Time Prison, the state's only maximum security prison. Inmates took over the prison and controlled it for 48 hours. During this time there were 27 injuries, of which 19 were life-threatening. Six of the life-threatening injuries resulted in death. Four of the dead were inmates; the two others were correctional employees. The details are as follows.

At about 4:30 P.M. on the day of occurrence, in the rear of the equipment storage room of the exercise yard, Correction Officer Will Passer, shield number 7068, observed three inmates drinking homemade liquor from a plastic soda pop bottle. The officer entered the room and directed the inmates to hand over the liquor. The inmates identified as Ray Malice, Inmate Number 4576; Don Catcher, Inmate Number 4765; and Pat Grant, Inmate Number 4567, all refused and overpowered the officer. Other inmates observed what had taken place and took as hostages Correction Officers Tom Walker, shield number 7292; Frank Halls, shield number 7680; and Jay Marks, shield number 7229. The inmates took these officers along with Officer Passer to the dining room and barricaded themselves inside the dining room. After approximately 1 hour and 15 minutes from the start of the initial confrontation in the equipment storage room, the entire prison was being controlled by the inmates and all correction employees, except the four officers being held hostage, were now safe and outside the walls of the prison. It was at that time that a list of demands was drawn up by the inmates.

The list of demands included such things as more television sets for the recreation areas, food selections to recognize the religion of certain inmates, and the extension of visiting hours. The number one demand was the reduction of overcrowding. Strangely no formal request was ever made for amnesty for inmates who rioted. The list of demands were personally communicated to Warden Stows by Officer Halls, who was released by the inmates because of a medical condition.

The takeover resulted in extensive damage to the institution. The actual extent of the damage is still being evaluated. The inmates agreed to return to their cells after a representative from the governor's office agreed to form a panel with representation from the inmates to look into the list of demands. The investigation into the criminal acts that took place during the riot and takeover is continuing.

22. How long did the takeover of the prison last?

   (A) 24 hours
   (B) 2 days
   (C) . 72 hours
   (D) 1 week

23. What is the name of the correction officer who was overpowered in the equipment storage room?

   (A) Officer Passer
   (B) Officer Walker
   (C) Officer Marks
   (D) Officer Halls

24. At what time of the day were the demands drawn up by the inmates?

   (A) 4:30 P.M.
   (B) 5:30 P.M.
   (C) 5:45 P.M.
   (D) immediately after the takeover began

25. Which of the following most accurately represents Officer Jay Marks's shield number?

   (A) 7292
   (B) 7680
   (C) 7068
   (D) 7229

26. The main demand of the inmates dealt with

   (A) entertainment.
   (B) food.
   (C) visitation hours.
   (D) overcrowding.

27. Based on the passage, evaluate the following statements.

   1. The inmates demanded amnesty for all inmates involved in the takeover.
   2. Reel Time Prison is the state's only minimum security prison.

   Which of the following is most accurate concerning these two statements?

   (A) Only statement 1 is correct.
   (B) Only statement 2 is correct.
   (C) Both statements 1 and 2 are correct.
   (D) Neither statement 1 nor 2 is correct.

28. What was the exact illness or injury suffered by Officer Halls?

   (A) a broken nose
   (B) a heart attack
   (C) a stab wound
   (D) It cannot be determined based on the information provided.

29. What percent of the dead resulting from the riot were correction employees?

   (A) 2%
   (B) $33\frac{1}{3}$%
   (C) 11%
   (D) $66\frac{2}{3}$%

> **Directions:** Answer questions 30–32 solely on the basis of the information contained in the following passage.

Most ordinary citizens believe that juvenile inmates are not any different from adult inmates. The only difference is age. Nothing could be further from the truth. Although both groups of criminals can be held to know the difference between right and wrong, juvenile offenders often lack an appreciation of the effects of their crimes on the rest of the community.

To a lesser degree, juveniles do not see the risks of punishment to themselves as a result of their actions. They see themselves as eternal and indestructible. Even though juveniles see on television how criminals are punished and are also told about prison life by ex-convicts returning to the neighborhood, they remain unaware of the punishments able to be dealt out by the state mainly because of a lack of personally experiencing adult incarceration.

To try to bridge this gap of inexperience with the realities of prison life, programs such as "Scared Stiff" have been developed. These programs take juveniles identified by the local police as headed in the wrong direction and have them live a day in the life of an adult inmate in an adult correctional facility. The day is complete with the feeling of being locked away in a tiny cell and even limited supervised interaction with volunteer adult inmates who pull no punches and treat the juveniles as they would any new inmate. The hope is that, by seeing what prison life is really like, some change in attitude will occur in the juvenile. Although such programs are not seen as the cure-all for rising juvenile crime nor as a replacement for the role of parents or educational institutions, some progress has been realized.

30. Based on the passage, which of the following statements is most correct?

   (A) The ordinary citizen sees great differences between an adult inmate and a juvenile inmate.
   (B) The only difference between an adult inmate and a juvenile inmate is age.
   (C) Juvenile criminals are not expected to know the difference between right and wrong.
   (D) Juvenile offenders often lack an understanding of the results of their criminal activity on the rest of the community.

31. Juveniles do not see the risks of punishment to themselves as a result of their actions mainly because

   (A) they see themselves as eternal and indestructible.
   (B) they do not see on television how criminals are punished.
   (C) ex-convicts returning to the neighborhood do not talk about their prison life.
   (D) of a juvenile's lack of personally experiencing adult incarceration.

32. "Scared Stiff" programs

   (A) hope that a change in attitude will occur in certain juveniles.
   (B) are seen as the cure-all for rising juvenile crime.
   (C) can be a replacement for the role of parents.
   (D) are structured to take the place of educational institutions.

33. Correction Officer Jones works the following overtime on the following days: 1 hour and 30 minutes on Monday, 1 hour and 15 minutes on Wednesday, 3 hours on Thursday, and 2 hours and 45 minutes on Friday. The amount of overtime worked by Officer Jones is

   (A) 7 hours and 30 minutes.
   (B) 7 hours and 45 minutes.
   (C) 8 hours and 15 minutes.
   (D) 8 hours and 30 minutes.

34. If a certain prison housed 1309 inmates this current year and 1190 inmates the previous year, there has been

   (A) approximately a 9% increase in inmates.
   (B) exactly a 10% increase in inmates.
   (C) approximately a 9% decrease in inmates.
   (D) exactly a 10% decrease in inmates.

The following mileage was recorded on a correction department form indicating vehicle usage for van Number 23:

Day of Week	Mileage at Start of Tour	Mileage at End of Tour
Monday	31110	31175
Tuesday	31175	31243
Wednesday	31243	31268
Thursday	31268	31343
Friday	31343	31413
Saturday	31413	31513
Sunday	31513	31592

35. Of the following days, the day with the greatest vehicle mileage usage for van Number 23 is

   (A) Monday.
   (B) Wednesday.
   (C) Thursday.
   (D) Saturday.

36. If van Number 23 gets 18 miles per gallon of gasoline, how many gallons of gasoline were used during the week?

   (A) between 26 and 27 gallons
   (B) between 28 and 29 gallons
   (C) exactly 30 gallons
   (D) over 31 gallons

Directions: In each of questions 37–40 you will be given four choices. Each of the choices A, B, and C contains a written statement. You are to evaluate the statement in each choice and select the statement that is most accurately and clearly written. If all or none of the three written statements is accurately and clearly written, you are to select choice D.

37. According to the directions, evaluate the following statements.

    (A) I couldn't hardly breathe.
    (B) He taught me a lesson which took me a long time to learn.
    (C) The inmate left without scarcely beingnoticed.
    (D) All or none of the choices are accurate.

38. According to the directions, evaluate the following statements.

    (A) They were sure of their facts.
    (B) The tower of the facility was a stationery post.
    (C) Someone wrote a note on department stationary threatening the warden.
    (D) All or none of the choices are accurate.

39. According to the directions, evaluate the following statements.

    (A) The continuous noise in the prison created a never-ending disturbance.
    (B) I learned to do that quite good.
    (C) In prison you learn to do you're own time.
    (D) All or none of the choices are accurate.

40. According to the directions, evaluate the following statements.

    (A) Don is the inmate who was convicted of shooting at several passer-bys from his office.
    (B) Ray was married twice and killed both his mother-in-laws.
    (C) If anyone wants a job, they can get one here.
    (D) All or none of the choices are accurate.

On August 4, 20xx, at 1120 hours, Correction Officer Cliff Short, shield number 682, of the Big Point Correctional Facility was injured in the line of duty. The details recorded as Department Injury Case Number 207 are as follows.

At about 1120 hours on August 4, 20xx, Officer Short, performing tour 0800 to 1600 hours and assigned to the outdoor recreation field of Big Point Correctional Facility, observed two inmates fighting. As Officer Short approached the two inmates, he observed Inmate Dawn Knight, Inmate Number 8269, and Inmate June Bogs, Inmate Number 8814, involved in an altercation. Officer Short got between the inmates to separate them and was bitten several times in both arms by both inmates who attempted to continue the altercation. Correction Officer April Taps, shield number 1493, responded to the scene and assisted in subduing both inmates and restoring order to the area.

Officer Short was removed to St. Mary's hospital by ambulance 4309 and treated by Dr. Angles who diagnosed the injury as lacerations of both arms. Officer Short returned to the facility and remained on duty for the rest of his tour. The incident was investigated by Officer Short's supervisor, Captain Sue Taller, shield number 609, who was also the tour commander. Captain Taller interviewed a witness, Mr. Pat Oils, a private civilian painting contractor who was working on the east tower at the time of the incident. As a result of the interview of the witness and other investigative efforts, Captain Taller found no misconduct on the part of any correction officers. Inmates Knight and Bogs will be the subject of a disciplinary hearing to be held on September 15, 20xx.

CORRECTION EMPLOYEE INJURY REPORT

Injured Employee Information
Rank____(1)__ Name_____(3)_____
                (Last)   (First)
Shield#____(2)___ Soc/Sec #____(4)_____ Assignment____(5)___
Date of Birth ____(6)____ Ht.___(7)____ Wt.___(8)____
Check One: [ ] On____(9)___ [ ] Off ____(10)____ Duty

- -

When Injury Occurred
Date:_____(11)_____ Time:____(12)_____

- -

Where Injury Occurred
Facility_____(13)_____Address_____(14)_____
Check One [ ] Indoors____(15)____ [ ] Outdoors____(15A)_____

- -

Description Of Injury
Dept. Injury Case Number_____(16)____
Member Remained On Duty? Circle One:____(17)___Yes / No___
Treated By_____(18)_____ Diagnosis_____(19)_____
Injury Was To: Check one_____(20) _____
[ ] Head   [ ] Arms   [ ] Legs   [ ] Torso   [ ] Eyes   [ ] Feet
[ ] Hands   [ ] Other
Was Employee Assaulted? Circle One:____(21)____Yes / No_____
Type Of Assault____Circle One ___(22)_____
Cut / Stab / Shot / Bite / Kick / Struck by object/ Other/

- -

Injured Employee's Account Of Incident:
_____(23)_____
_____
_____
_____

- -

Witness (if any) Account Of Incident:
_____(24)_____
_____
_____
_____

- -

Details Of Supervisor's Investigation Of Incident
_____(25)_____
_____
_____
_____

- -

Signature of:
Supervisor_____(26)_____ Shield #_____(27)____
Dr. Treating Injury_____(28)_____
Tour Commander_____(29)_____Shield #_____(30)_____

41. Which of the following should be entered in caption number 1?

    (A) Doctor
    (B) Captain
    (C) Supervisor
    (D) Correction Officer

42. In which of the following captions should the name of Angles be entered?

    (A) 3
    (B) 28
    (C) 29
    (D) 5

43. It would be most appropriate to enter information about being injured in both arms in which of the following captions?

    (A) 11
    (B) 13
    (C) 16
    (D) 20

44. The entries in which of the following would be identical?

    (A) 27 and 30
    (B) 28 and 29
    (C) 27 and 29
    (D) 26 and 30

45. The fact that the employee who was injured remained on duty should be entered in which of the following captions?

    (A) 16
    (B) 17
    (C) 18
    (D) 19

46. There is not enough information given to complete any of the following questions except caption

    (A) 4.
    (B) 5.
    (C) 6.
    (D) 7.

47. It would be most appropriate to enter the account of the incident given by Pat Oils in caption

    (A) 23.
    (B) 24.
    (C) 25.
    (D) 26.

48. It would be most appropriate to enter the number 207 in which of the following captions?

    (A) 23
    (B) 27
    (C) 2
    (D) 16

49. Based on the details of the incident, which of the following captions should be checked?

    (A) 9 only
    (B) 10 only
    (C) either 9 or 10
    (D) both 9 and 10

50. It would be most appropriate to enter the number 1493 in which of the following captions?

    (A) 2
    (B) 27
    (C) 30
    (D) none of the above

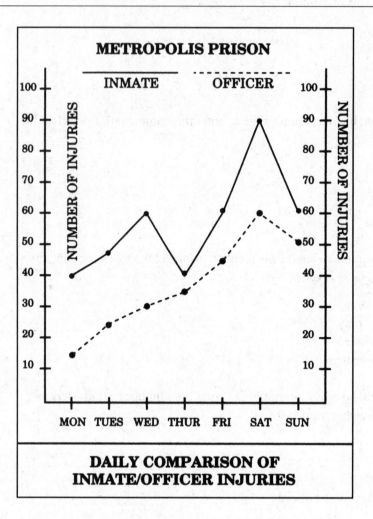

51. The day of the week that accounted for the most injuries to inmates

    (A) was Wednesday.
    (B) was Friday.
    (C) was Saturday.
    (D) cannot be determined.

52. On the average, injuries to correction officers

    (A) were lower than injuries to inmates on every day of the week.
    (B) were higher than injuries to inmates on Thursdays.
    (C) were higher than injuries to inmates on Saturdays.
    (D) were higher than injuries to inmates on Sundays.

53. The percentage of all injuries to inmates that occurred on Saturday

    (A) was approximately 15%.
    (B) was approximately 23%.
    (C) was approximately 41%.
    (D) cannot be determined.

54. The least number of injuries to correction officers

    (A) occurred on Monday.
    (B) occurred on Wednesday.
    (C) occurred on Friday.
    (D) cannot be determined.

55. The greatest number of injuries to correction officers

    (A) happened on Wednesday.
    (B) happened on Friday.
    (C) happened on Saturday.
    (D) cannot be determined.

56. The number of injuries that happened to inmates on Wednesdays was approximately equal to the number of injuries that happened to inmates on

    (A) Fridays.
    (B) Saturdays.
    (C) Mondays.
    (D) It cannot be determined.

57. The ratio of inmate injuries to officer injuries on Wednesdays

    (A) was about 2 to 1.
    (B) was about 3 to 1.
    (C) was about 4 to 1.
    (D) cannot be determined.

58. On what day of the week was the number of injuries to inmates closest to the number of injuries to officers?

    (A) Monday
    (B) Wednesday
    (C) Thursday
    (D) cannot be determined

When a member of the department of correction is to be tested as a result of the department's random drug testing program, the following procedure shall apply:

1. Prior to testing, the individual member being tested shall prepare a form listing all foods, alcohol, mixes, and medicine ingested in the past seventy-two (72) hours.

2. At the testing location, the member being tested shall present the shield and identification card to ensure that the proper individual has reported for testing.

3. Privacy and dignity will be protected. Urine samples will be given in maximum feasible privacy. Only one (1) person of the same sex will be present with the member being tested when urine is collected.

4. No more than two (2) samples will be taken, each in a separate vial.

5. Prior to testing, a code number assigned to the member and the date of the testing will be affixed to each vial. The code number will be logged separately with the member's name.

6. Immediately after giving the urine sample, the member being tested will then initial the vial sticker. The vials will be sealed in the member's presence after the sample has been given. Appropriate procedures to create and follow a strict accounting of custody will be followed at all times.

7. Negative test results will not be maintained but will be destroyed.

8. Positive test samples will be maintained by the laboratory involved and will remain confidential unless and until department disciplinary action is taken.

9. A member whose test is positive may, within sixty (60) days of notification of such result, submit a written request to the department attorney's office for further independent retesting of the original sample.

10. Testing will be done only for illegal drugs and controlled substances. No other substances will be screened.

59. Prior to testing, Correction Officer Nick Bianco, who is being randomly tested for drugs, should prepare a form listing all foods, alcohol, mixes, and medicine ingested

   (A) in the past 7 days.
   (B) in the past 5 days.
   (C) in the past 72 hours.
   (D) in the past 24 hours.

60. When urine samples are given in connection with random drug testing, the maximum number of people present while the urine is being collected is

   (A) one, just the person being tested.
   (B) two, and both persons must be of the same sex.
   (C) three, with at least one of the persons the same sex as the employee.
   (D) four, with two persons of each sex present.

61. Regarding the actual giving of urine, which of the following statements is most appropriate according to the procedure concerning random testing for drugs?

   (A) A minimum of two samples will be taken.
   (B) A maximum of two samples will be taken.
   (C) Exactly two samples must be taken.
   (D) If multiple samples are taken, they shall not be put in separate vials.

62. Correction Officer Don Watts is undergoing random drug testing and, therefore, is giving a urine sample. Don has just completed giving the urine sample. What should Don do next?

   (A) seal the vials
   (B) initial the vial sticker
   (C) write his name on the vial sticker
   (D) write the date on the vial sticker

63. May is a correction officer who has tested positive during a random drug test. She strongly denies the use of drugs. If May wishes to protest, she should do which of the following?

   (A) Immediately make a phone call to the department attorney's office protesting the results of the test.
   (B) Submit a written request to the laboratory that conducted the test asking for further independent retesting of the original sample.
   (C) Immediately make a phone call to the laboratory that conducted the test protesting the results of the test and asking that a new sample be tested by them.
   (D) Submit a written request to the department attorney's office for further independent retesting of the original sample.

Directions: Answer question 64 based solely on the following.

Whenever three or more complaints regarding illnesses stemming from food served in the dining hall are received within a 24-hour period, the officer in charge of the dining hall shall treat the situation as an unusual incident and notify the command center within 1 hour of receiving such information.

64. Bill Mast, the correction officer in charge of the dining hall, receives three complaints regarding food illness at the following close intervals: one at 1930 hours, the next one at 1945 hours, and the last one at 2000 hours. The earliest that Officer Mast should notify the command center is no later than

(A) 2030 hours.
(B) 2045 hours.
(C) 2100 hours.
(D) within a 24-hour period.

Directions: Answer questions 65 and 66 based on the following information.

Small fires occurring within the institution may be classified as still fires or contained fires.

Still fires include burning of bedding, trash paper, and clothing and attempts at cooking in residential cells.

Contained fires are those that are confined to one residential cell and do not result in damage to the structure of the building, or physical injury to anyone, and that do not require assistance from outside the cell block to put out the fire.

The officer discovering a still fire shall notify the tour commander who shall notify the command center. Contained fires shall be immediately brought to the attention of the command center by the officer discovering a contained fire.

65. Bob Matches is a knowledgeable veteran correction officer. One day a newly hired officer, Don Hooks, approaches Officer Matches and asks him for practical examples of the kind of fires known as still fires. In his response, Officer Matches would be least correct if he gave which of the following examples?

(A) a burning mattress
(B) smoldering waste papers
(C) shirts that have been singed
(D) fires confined to a residential cell with no damage and not requiring outside assistance to put it out

66. In which of the following situations involving fires would the correction officer discovering the fire be most correct to notify the tour commander?

(A) an attempt to cook a meal in a residential cell
(B) a small fire in a residential cell where no one is hurt and the fire is put out by the officer assigned to the cell block
(C) a fire where no damage results and the fire is put out by the inmate in the cell where the fire occurred
(D) all of the above

Directions: Answer questions 67–70 based solely on the following information.

The use of tear gas may be authorized only by the highest-ranking senior supervisor on duty in the correctional facility. Tear gas may be used to restore order, break up unruly gatherings, or as a deterrent to violence, but never as punishment. Before using tear gas in the facility, the best possible information available shall be utilized to determine if any of the inmates who will be contaminated by the tear gas

1. have serious medical problems such as respiratory ailments or

2. have any history of mental illness or

3. are currently under the influence of alcohol or drugs.

This is done to determine if the use of tear gas will aggravate any existing condition of an inmate.

When tear gas is administered, the officer designated by the supervisor in charge will record the following information in this exact order:

1. the time and date of the use of the tear gas,

2. the location within the facility where it was used,

3. the name(s) of the person(s) against whom the tear gas was intended,

4. the name of all persons contaminated,

5. the dosage of the tear gas that was used,

6. the length of time inmates were exposed to the tear gas,

7. any reported adverse physical effects on inmates,

8. the time the use of tear gas was concluded.

All incidents involving the use of tear gas shall be reported to the state corrections commissioner within 24 hours of such use.

67. Tear gas is being considered for use in the Nearing Correctional Facility to deal with a situation. Correction Officer Barks is asked for an opinion concerning when it would be appropriate to use tear gas. According to the facility's procedures governing the use of tear gas, it would be least correct for the officer to state that tear gas may be used

(A) to restore order.
(B) break up unruly gatherings.
(C) as a deterrent to violence.
(D) as punishment for violating facility rules.

68. While considering the use of tear gas, certain characteristics of the inmates who will be contaminated should be considered. According to the facility's procedure regarding the use of tear gas, which of the following is least appropriate to consider when evaluating whether to use tear gas?

(A) respiratory ailments of any of the inmates
(B) history of mental illness of any inmates
(C) the past criminal records of any inmates
(D) whether any inmates are currently under the influence of alcohol or drugs

69. Officer Barks has been designated to record required information concerning the use of tear gas. After recording the length of time inmates were exposed to the tear gas, what should the officer record next?

(A) any reported adverse physical effects on inmates
(B) the names of all persons contaminated
(C) the time the use of tear gas was concluded
(D) the location within the facility where it was used

70. Evaluate the following statements of Officer Barks concerning the use of tear gas.

1. "All incidents involving the use of tear gas shall be reported to the Federal Bureau of Prisons within 24 hours of such use."
2. "Any supervisor may authorize the use of tear gas."

Which of the following is most accurate concerning these two statements?

(A) Only statement 1 is correct.
(B) Only statement 2 is correct.
(C) Both statements 1 and 2 are correct.
(D) Neither statement 1 nor 2 is correct.

When using mace sprayed from an aerosol can, a correction officer shall:

1. direct the spray at the neck and chin area of the target person.

2. not aim or spray directly into the eyes of the target person.

3. not use the spray at a distance of less than 4 feet (mace sprayed from an aerosol can has an effective range of 12–15 feet).

4. limit application of the spray to a one second blast, which may be repeated if necessary up to three additional applications.

5. identify a controlled exit for the target person prior to applying the spray. This is done to avoid backing the target person into a corner and thereby escalating the confrontation.

After the situation has subsided, in order to decontaminate affected persons, the correction officer concerned shall:

1. remove individuals from the contaminated area. Unprotected individuals should not be allowed to remain in contaminated areas more than 5 minutes after the mace application.

2. advise contaminated persons not to rub their eyes.

3. warn against the use of salves and greases because they tend to trap the mace on the affected area thereby causing irritation and even blistering.

4. attempt to expose contaminated areas of affected persons to the fresh air.

5. wash or destroy contaminated clothing.

6. provide cool water to apply to affected areas.

71. A correction officer intending to use mace from an aerosol can against an inmate would be correct if the officer did which of the following?

(A) aimed the spray at the inmate's eyes
(B) sprayed the inmate from a distance of 3 feet
(C) identified a controlled exit for the inmate after spraying the inmate
(D) limited the initial application of the spray to a one second blast

72. After a correction officer has used mace against an inmate, the officer would be most correct if the officer did which of the following?

   (A) not allow unprotected individuals to remain in contaminated areas more than ten minutes
   (B) encourage affected individuals to rub their eyes
   (C) advise affected individuals to use salves and greases on contaminated areas
   (D) have contaminated clothing washed or destroyed

Directions: Answer question 73 based solely on the following.

In those instances where a correction officer effects an off-duty arrest, the officer shall

1. inform the prisoner of the reason for the arrest unless the prisoner attempts to escape,

2. handcuff the prisoner with the prisoner's hands behind the back,

3. immediately search the prisoner for weapons, evidence or contraband,

4. advise the prisoner of legal rights if the prisoner is to be questioned.

73. One night while off duty, Correction Officer Bailes is given the description by a neighbor of a man who is attempting to steal the neighbor's car. Bailes catches the man near the car and tells him he is under arrest, informs him of the reason for the arrest, and immediately handcuffs the man's hands behind his back. The local police arrive and all parties are taken to the local station house where the man is identified by Bailes's neighbor as the person who attempted to steal the auto. The actions taken by Officer Bailes were

   (A) appropriate mainly because the prisoner was positively identified at the police station house.
   (B) inappropriate mainly because the prisoner was not searched.
   (C) appropriate mainly because the prisoner was handcuffed with his hands behind his back.
   (D) inappropriate mainly because the prisoner was not given his rights.

Directions: Use the information in the following reference table to answer questions 74–78. In the table each number has been associated with a letter. For each question you are to select the choice that contains the letters that, when associated with the numbers in the reference table, accurately depict the numerical calendar date required by the question.

I	H	A	T	E	D	C	O	P	S
1	2	3	4	5	6	7	8	9	0

EXAMPLE

Which of the following choices represents February 09?

Explanation: First convert the month into a numerical date. February would be 02 or, using the reference table, *SH*. The date of 09 would be represented by the letters *SP*. Therefore, February 09 would be represented as the letters *SH-SP*.

74. Which of the following choices represents January 05?

   (A) IS-ES
   (B) ES-SI
   (C) SI-SE
   (D) SI-ES

75. Which of the following choices represents August 30?

   (A) OA-SS
   (B) SO-AS
   (C) SO-ES
   (D) OS-SA

76. Which of the following choices represents October 15?

   (A) IS-IE
   (B) SI-EI
   (C) IO-IE
   (D) IE-IS

77. Which of the following choices represents December 16?

   (A) HI-DI
   (B) ID-IH
   (C) HI-DI
   (D) IH-ID

78. Which of the following choices represents July 14?

(A) SI-TC
(B) SC-IT
(C) SC-TI
(D) SI-CT

Directions: Answer questions 79 and 80 based on the following legal rule.

Correction officers are legally entitled to use physical force upon another person when and to the extent they reasonably believe it to be necessary to defend themselves or a third person from what they reasonably believe to be the use or imminent use of unlawful physical force by such other person. Correction officers may not use deadly physical force upon another person unless they reasonably believe that such other person is using or about to use deadly physical force against them or another.

79. Which of the following represents a violation of this rule?

(A) A correction officer uses physical force against an inmate who was assaulting another guard.
(B) A correction officer uses physical force against an inmate who is assaulting him.
(C) A correction officer uses physical force against an inmate who threatens to "get him one day."
(D) A correction officer uses physical force against an inmate who is about to assault him.

80. Which of the following is NOT a violation of this rule?

(A) A correction officer shoots at an inmate who is using his fists to beat another inmate.
(B) A correction officer shoots an inmate who is about to attack him with a homemade knife.
(C) A correction officer shoots an unarmed inmate who is threatening to have another inmate shot.
(D) A correction officer shoots an unarmed inmate who is attempting to escape.

81. The argument that the death penalty is more financially economical than life imprisonment does not stand up under close examination. The most reasonable conclusion that can be drawn from this statement is that

(A) it is cheaper to execute prisoners than to incarcerate them for life.
(B) the death penalty is not an effective deterrent.
(C) the administration of the death penalty is not as financially economical as some people say it is.
(D) the cost of administering the death penalty is equal to the cost of financing a life sentence.

82. The courts have ruled that a juvenile, someone under the age of 16, who has been accused of a crime, has the right to a lawyer. In turn, the juvenile can decide to waive the right to a lawyer providing the parents/guardians of the juvenile concur with that decision. The lawyer may be of the juvenile's own choosing or appointed by the court for financial or other reasons. Therefore, a correction officer who finds it necessary to arrest a juvenile must give notice of the juvenile's right to a lawyer. Based on the statement, the most reasonable conclusion to reach is that

(A) a lawyer must be assigned to represent a juvenile.
(B) a 16-year-old can waive his right to a lawyer without obtaining concurrences from a parent or guardian.
(C) a correction officer who arrests a juvenile must secure a lawyer for that juvenile.
(D) the only time the court can appoint a lawyer for a juvenile is when there are financial considerations involved.

83. Notification shall be made, as soon as practicable, by telegraph to the nearest relative or friend of any inmate who unsuccessfully attempts to commit suicide. The notification shall include an invitation to visit the institution. The main purpose of this rule is most probably to

(A) explore ways to prevent further suicide attempts.
(B) prepare loved ones for a possible tragedy.
(C) avoid civil liability.
(D) comply with the law.

84. A correction officer assigned to a post requiring the supervision of inmates shall immediately take a count of the inmates on said post. The main reason for this rule is most probably to

(A) make sure enough officers are assigned.
(B) make sure no escape attempts are in progress.
(C) promote prison discipline.
(D) emphasize the authority of the officer.

85. No inmate under 19 years of age shall be transferred together with adult prisoners in any correctional vehicle. The main purpose of this rule is probably to prevent

    (A) disputes and confrontations.
    (B) escape attempts.
    (C) exposure of younger prisoners to the views of adult criminals.
    (D) possible assaults on younger prisoners by adult prisoners.

86. Inmates confined in punitive segregation shall be observed by the assigned correction officer at least once every half hour on each tour of duty. This rule is most probably a result of

    (A) the need to prevent contraband from coming into the hands of inmates confined in punitive segregation.
    (B) the strong possibility of suicide that tends to develop among inmates confined to punitive segregation.
    (C) the necessity to prevent violent confrontations from taking place between inmates confined in punitive segregation.
    (D) the desire to escape that is developed by inmates who are confined in punitive segregation.

87. A correction officer shall not authorize the use of a photograph of himself in uniform in connection with any commercial enterprise. The purpose of this rule is most probably to

    (A) protect the identity of correction officers.
    (B) prevent officers from enjoying unethical commercial gain.
    (C) maintain the image of the correctional uniform.
    (D) prevent the endorsement of substandard products.

88. When a correction officer has been assigned to conduct visitors through an institution, she shall not allow them to give anything to inmates. This rule is most probably a result of the

    (A) ever-present need to protect and maintain the security of the correctional institution.
    (B) need to prevent inmates from sending and receiving messages to the outside world.
    (C) pressing need to keep confidential all business of the correctional institution.
    (D) violent nature of the entire general prison population.

A firearm means any pistol, or revolver, or shotgun having one or more barrels less than 18 inches in length, or a rifle having one or more barrels less than 16 inches in length. An antique firearm is not considered a firearm as long as it is unloaded.

A person is guilty of criminal possession of a weapon when such person possesses:

1. a deadly weapon or a cane sword or a Kung Fu Star or

2. an ax, razor, imitation pistol, or hunting knife and has an intent to use the same unlawfully against another or

3. any weapon and is not a citizen of the United States.

A deadly weapon is a gun that is loaded and operable and that can cause a serious physical injury, or a gravity knife, dagger, switchblade knife, billy, blackjack, or metal knuckles.

Law enforcement officers, state militia, and federal armed services members, and other persons licensed to legally possess firearms, when trained and qualified, are exempt from any legal restrictions concerning the possession of weapons.

Criminal possession of a weapon is a misdemeanor but becomes a felony if the defendant has been previously convicted of the same crime within the last 10 years.

89. A rifle is considered a firearm if its barrel is

    (A) less than 16 inches in length.
    (B) less than 18 inches in length.
    (C) more than 16 inches in length.
    (D) more than 18 inches in length.

90. Pat possesses an antique firearm. In order for the antique firearm to be considered a firearm, which of the following must occur?

    (A) The antique firearm must be carried in public.
    (B) The antique firearm must have a barrel length less than 16 inches in length.
    (C) The antique firearm must have a barrel length less than 18 inches in length.
    (D) The antique firearm must be loaded.

91. Which of the following actions violates the statute concerning criminal possession of a weapon?

   (A) Don is carrying an ax to kill a turkey for Thanksgiving.
   (B) Pat has a hunting knife strapped to her leg under her skirt.
   (C) Ray puts an imitation pistol in his belt intending to frighten a neighbor into giving him money.
   (D) June has in her coat pocket a razor that she intends to use to harm herself.

92. Which of the following is least likely to be considered guilty of criminal possession of a weapon?

   (A) Pat, who is carrying a Kung Fu Star
   (B) Don, who is carrying a cane sword
   (C) Ray, who is carrying an operable gun
   (D) April, who is carrying metal knuckles

93. Against which of the following would a charge of criminal possession of a weapon be most correct?

   (A) Don, who is in the United States temporarily on a student's visa, buys a rifle to protect himself.
   (B) Tab is carrying an imitation pistol in a shoulder holster to impress a new girl friend.
   (C) Ray has an inoperable but loaded firearm in his pocket.
   (D) June is carrying a razor on her way to work as a hairdresser.

94. The following inmates were recently convicted. Which of them should have been convicted of a felony?

   (A) Don, who illegally possessed a blackjack and was never arrested before
   (B) Tab, who illegally possessed a dagger and was convicted of the same crime 12 years ago
   (C) Ray, who illegally possessed a Kung Fu Star and was arrested for the same crime 2 years ago
   (D) Pat, who illegally possessed a switchblade knife and was convicted of the same crime 9 years ago

95. Which of the following may legally possess firearms, when trained and qualified, and are exempt from any legal restrictions concerning the possession of such weapons?

(A) law enforcement officers
(B) state militia members
(C) federal armed services members
(D) all of the above

Directions: Answer questions 96–98 based solely on the following information.

A person acts in a reckless manner when he perceives the risk of his actions but pursues that course of action anyway.

Reckless endangerment of property occurs when a person recklessly engages in conduct that causes a substantial risk of damage to the property of another.

Reckless endangerment occurs when a person recklessly engages in conduct that causes a substantial risk of injury to another.

Assault occurs when a person intentionally causes physical injury to another person or recklessly causes physical injury to another person.

96. Which of the following persons would most likely be acting in a reckless manner?

(A) a man who is told not to leave his windows open because it may rain but leaves them open anyway
(B) a woman who puts around her swimming pool a gate, which falls down during a winter storm
(C) a correction officer who is told repeatedly to lock his locker but fails to do so and as a result an inmate steals his revolver
(D) a correction officer who forgets to lock her car in the employee's parking lot of the prison and as a result has her car stolen

97. Correction Officer Brown is warned about the faulty brakes on the facility's van and is told to get the brakes fixed. Instead Brown disregards the warning because the officer does not want to work overtime waiting for the brake repairs. The next day while driving the van, Brown is unable to stop at an intersection and almost knocks an old man down. Brown has committed

(A) reckless endangerment of property.
(B) reckless endangerment.
(C) assault.
(D) no crime.

98. While off duty, Correction Officer Parks is practicing her golf game in an open field. A nearby home owner warns the officer that the golf balls she is hitting are coming dangerously close to his roof, which has several large expensive skylights. Parks apologizes and tells the home owner that she was unaware of the danger and stops her golf practice. In this situation, Parks has committed

(A) assault.
(B) reckless endangerment of property because the skylights were expensive.
(C) reckless endangerment.
(D) no crime.

Directions: Answer questions 99 and 100 based solely on the following information.

Violent felony offenders are often assigned to maximum security facilities with increased sentences. One way a defendant is categorized a violent felony offender is if the defendant is convicted of an armed felony.

A person commits an armed felony when such person during the commission of a felony

1. is armed with a deadly weapon or

2. causes a serious physical injury to a nonparticipant by means of a deadly weapon or

3. displays what appears to be a gun.

The amount of time that can be added to the sentence of a felony offender is one-half the original sentence called for by the original felony but an addition of more than 4 years is never permissible.

99. Which of the following should not be considered a violent felony offender because of having committed an armed felony?

(A) Joe who, prior to committing a felony, arms himself with a deadly weapon, which he carries in his pocket while committing the felony
(B) Tom who, while committing a felony, arms himself with a deadly weapon
(C) Jay who, during the commission of a felony, stabs and seriously injures one his coparticipants during an argument about the escape route
(D) Hal who, during the commission of a felony, waves what appears to be a gun at the victim of the felony

100. It would be least appropriate if a violent felony offender who received an original sentence of

   (A) 2 years received 3 years as a violent felony offender.
   (B) 4 years received 6 years as a violent felony offender.
   (C) 8 years received 12 years as a violent felony offender.
   (D) 10 years received 15 years as a violent felony offender.

STOP

END OF TEST

ANSWER KEY
Practice Test 5

1. **B**	26. **D**	51. **C**	76. **A**
2. **D**	27. **D**	52. **A**	77. **D**
3. **C**	28. **D**	53. **B**	78. **B**
4. **B**	29. **B**	54. **A**	79. **C**
5. **B**	30. **D**	55. **C**	80. **B**
6. **A**	31. **D**	56. **A**	81. **C**
7. **C**	32. **A**	57. **A**	82. **B**
8. **D**	33. **D**	58. **C**	83. **A**
9. **A**	34. **B**	59. **C**	84. **B**
10. **B**	35. **D**	60. **B**	85. **C**
11. **C**	36. **A**	61. **B**	86. **B**
12. **D**	37. **B**	62. **B**	87. **B**
13. **B**	38. **A**	63. **D**	88. **A**
14. **C**	39. **A**	64. **C**	89. **A**
15. **C**	40. **D**	65. **D**	90. **D**
16. **B**	41. **D**	66. **A**	91. **C**
17. **C**	42. **B**	67. **D**	92. **C**
18. **B**	43. **D**	68. **C**	93. **A**
19. **A**	44. **A**	69. **A**	94. **D**
20. **D**	45. **B**	70. **D**	95. **D**
21. **C**	46. **B**	71. **D**	96. **C**
22. **B**	47. **B**	72. **D**	97. **B**
23. **A**	48. **D**	73. **B**	98. **D**
24. **C**	49. **A**	74. **C**	99. **C**
25. **D**	50. **D**	75. **B**	100. **D**

DIAGNOSTIC CHART

Instructions: After you score your test, complete the following chart by inserting in the column entitled "Your Number Correct" the number of correct questions you answered in each of the eight sections of the test. Then compare your score in each section with the ratings in the column entitled "Scale." Finally, to correct your weaknesses, follow the instructions found at the end of the chart.

Section	Question Numbers	Area	Your Number Correct	Scale
1	1–8	Memory (8 questions)		8 Right—Excellent 6–7 Right—Good 5 Right—Fair Under 5 Right—Poor
2	9–32	Reading Comprehension (24 questions)		24 Right—Excellent 20–23 Right—Good 16–19 Right—Fair Under 16 Right—Poor
3	33–40	Verbal and Math (8 questions)		8 Right—Excellent 6–7 Right—Good 5 Right—Fair Under 5 Right—Poor
4	41–50	Correction Forms (10 questions)		10 Right—Excellent 8–9 Right—Good 7 Right—Fair Under 7 Right—Poor
5	51–58	Graphs (8 questions)		8 Right—Excellent 6–7 Right—Good 5 Right—Fair Under 5 Right—Poor
6	59–78	Applying Correction Procedures (20 questions)		20 Right—Excellent 18–19 Right—Good 16–17 Right—Fair Under 16 Right—Poor
7	79–88	Judgment and Reasoning (10 questions)		10 Right—Excellent 8–9 Right—Good 7 Right—Fair Under 7 Right—Poor
8	89–100	Legal Definitions (12 questions)		12 Right—Excellent 10–11 Right—Good 8–9 Right—Fair Under 8 Right—Poor

How to correct weaknesses:

1. If you are weak in Section 1, concentrate on Chapter 3.
2. If you are weak in Section 2, concentrate on Chapter 1.
3. If you are weak in Section 3, concentrate on Chapter 2.
4. If you are weak in Section 4, concentrate on Chapter 4.
5. If you are weak in Section 5, concentrate on Chapter 5.
6. If you are weak in Section 6, concentrate on Chapter 6.
7. If you are weak in Section 7, concentrate on Chapter 7.
8. If you are weak in Section 8, concentrate on Chapter 8.

Note: Consider yourself weak in an area if you receive anything other than an excellent rating in it.

ANSWERS EXPLAINED

1. **(B)** Hopefully, you haven't forgotten to use associations to deal with memory questions. It doesn't matter what specific type of memory question you are given—the association technique is always applicable. In this question the word *young* in the inmate's name would be a good way to remember that he loiters near schools (where young people attend).

2. **(D)** Sawed-off shotguns are shorter than regular shotguns. This inmate's name is Short. A perfect association.

3. **(C)** An alphabetical association suits this question just fine. Jack Hunt uses the alias Ben Hogan.

4. **(B)** Once again the *young* in this inmate's name could have helped you remember the information needed to answer the question (e.g., young people don't often wear hairpieces).

5. **(B)** Youngblood was serving a life sentence. An association like Youngblood will get old in prison would have been perfect for this association.

6. **(A)** Chuckie Gifford is a con artist who poses as a cop.

7. **(C)** According to the posters, it is Jack Hunt who is a chronic drug user.

8. **(D)** Hopefully you had an association to help you remember that it is James Short who speaks five languages.

9. **(A)** April Waters gave birth to her daughter, May North, in the first year of April's incarceration. Twenty-five years later, April was released from prison. One year later, April died. This would make May approximately 26 years old at the time of her mother's death.

10. **(B)** Examiners often ask questions requiring attention to detail.

11. **(C)** April Waters began her sentence in Sing Prison. At that time she was in the fourth month of her pregnancy and five months later gave birth to Officer North.

12. **(D)** The quarrel centered around Frank Waters's drinking, losses at the racetrack, and affairs with other women.

13. **(B)** April Waters took a kitchen knife and repeatedly stabbed Frank Waters to death.

14. **(C)** The only stipulation to the adoption was that April Waters's daughter, who is May North, be named after April's grandmother, who would, of course, be May's great grandmother.

15. **(C)** At the age of 25, she began her sentence at the Sing Prison and altogether at various institutions she served 25 years of her sentence. Thus 25 + 25 = 50. Please note that it is not unusual to use information found in different parts of a passage in order to answer a question.

16. **(B)** As stated in the passage April Waters's inmate number at Sing Prison was 8670. Note the similarity between this number and the shield number of Officer Sterns, which is 8706. You must be careful with numbers.

17. **(C)** Inmate Don Poster, Inmate Number 4569, shot Correction Officer Tom White. To answer this question, the candidate was required to find the name of the inmate who shot the officer and then find that inmate's number in a different part of the passage.

18. **(B)** Officer Gales was struck on the head with a blunt instrument, which was not recovered.

19. **(A)** Inmate Shine fell to the ground pretending to have severe stomach pains. The inmates referred to in choices B and D were Skipper and Poster, respectively.

20. **(D)** State Trooper Empire is assigned to the investigation division and was visiting the facility on an unrelated matter. Trooper Empire saw the shooting of Correction Officer White and immediately shot and killed the inmate responsible for shooting Officer White.

21. **(C)** The two remaining inmates Skipper and Shine (Poster was killed) made their escape by fleeing in a late-model sedan driven by a white female.

22. **(B)** Inmates took over the prison and controlled it for 48 hours, which is, of course, 2 days.

23. **(A)** Correction Officer Passer entered the room and directed the inmates to hand over the liquor. The inmates overpowered the officer. In reading passages with many names, you should be reading with your pencil and underlining or circling those which your advance scanning of the questions has revealed will be the basis of questions.

24. **(C)** Approximately 1 hour and 15 minutes after the start of the initial confrontation, which began at 4:30 P.M., the entire prison was being controlled by the inmates. It was at that time that a list of demands were drawn up by the inmates.

25. **(D)** Examiners consistently ask questions concerning details such as numbers.

26. **(D)** The number one demand was the reduction of overcrowding.

27. **(D)** Strangely enough, no formal request was ever made for amnesty for inmates who rioted. Reel Time Prison is the state's only maximum security prison. It is important for a candidate not to tire when reading and to continue to concentrate for long periods of time. That is why taking these practice examinations is so important.

28. **(D)** Officer Halls was released as a hostage because of a medical condition. No further information about this condition was given. Therefore, no assumptions should be made because the questions are to be answered based solely on the information provided.

29. **(B)** During the riot six of the life-threatening injuries resulted in death. Four of the dead were inmates, the two remaining were correctional employees. Therefore, 2 divided by 6 = $\frac{1}{3}$ or $33\frac{1}{3}$%.

30. **(D)** Most ordinary citizens believe that juvenile inmates are not any different from adult inmates except for age. Nothing could be further from the truth. Although both groups of criminals can be held to know the difference between right and wrong, juvenile offenders often lack an appreciation (understanding) of the effects (results) of their crimes on the

rest of the community. At times, an examiner may change the words in an answer choice slightly, but the choice still reflects the meaning or intent of the passage.

31. **(D)** Choices B and C are incorrect statements in that juveniles do see how criminals are treated in prison on television and are told some things about prison life by neighborhood ex-convicts. Choice A is correct, but the main reason that juveniles do not see the risks of punishment to themselves is as stated in choice D.

32. **(A)** The hope of such programs is that, by seeing what prison life is really like, some change in attitude will occur in the juvenile. Although such programs are not seen as the cure-all for rising juvenile crime nor as a replacement for the role of parents or educational institutions, progress is being made.

33. **(D)** The first step is to convert all the fractions of hours into minutes and align the figures. For example:

Monday	1 hour	30 minutes
Wednesday	1 hour	15 minutes
Thursday	3 hours	
Friday	+ 2 hours	+ 45 minutes
Add them to get	7 hours	90 minutes

But 90 minutes = 1 hour and 30 minutes, so adding 1 hour and 30 minutes to 7 hours yields 8 hours and 30 minutes.

34. **(B)** Because the numbers went up from last year to the current year, there was obviously a percentage increase. Therefore, eliminate choices C and D. Now find the "distance" between the two numbers which were given, 1190 and 1309. That is 119. Then divide 119 by 1190 by placing 119 over 1190 (the old number). So we get 119/1190; that yields 0.10, which is the same as 10%. If you placed 119 over 1309 (the new number from the current year), you would get 0.09 or 9%. Remember that, when dealing with percentage increases or decreases, it's the

$$\frac{\text{distance between the old and new numbers}}{\text{the old number}} \quad \text{(divided by)}$$

35. **(D)**

Monday	31175 − 31110 = 65
Wednesday	31268 − 31243 = 25
Thursday	31343 − 31268 = 75
Saturday	31513 − 31413 = 100

36. **(A)** First, you must calculate the total mileage usage for van Number 23. Simply subtract the mileage started with on Monday from the mileage finished with on the following Sunday or

31592 (end of Sunday) − 31110 (beginning of Monday) = 482

Then divide 482, the amount of miles traveled by van Number 23, by 18, the amount of miles per gallon, and the result is 26.78 gallons.

37. **(B)** In choices A and C the words *hardly* and *scarcely* are unnecessary negatives and not needed. Choice B is correctly stated.

38. **(A)** Stationary means placed in a fixed position, whereas stationery means writing supplies such as envelopes and writing paper. Choices B and C are therefore incorrect. Choice A is stated correctly.

39. **(A)** Choice B should state, "quite well," and choice C should state, "your own time." Choice A is correctly stated.

40. **(D)** All the choices contain incorrect statements. Choices A and B are incorrect because such compound words are not made plural by adding the letter *s* to the end of the word. They are made plural by adding the *s* to the first word making up the compound word. For example passers-by and mothers-in-law would be correct plurals. Choice C is incorrect because *anyone* indicates one person wanting a job but then a switch is incorrectly made and more than one person is indicated by the word *they*.

41. **(D)** The rank of the employee who was injured should be entered in caption 1.

42. **(B)** Angles is the name of the doctor who treated the injury and should be entered in Caption 28.

43. **(D)** Caption 20 records what part of the body was injured.

44. **(A)** Caption 27 asks for the shield number of the supervisor and 30 asks for the shield number of the tour commander. However, they are the same person; thus they have the same shield number.

45. **(B)** Caption 17 requires that either yes or no be circled to indicate if the member (employee) remained on duty. Remember when you are given questions that ask, "Which of the following captions...," it is not necessary to examine the entire form. You should focus on the captions suggested by the choices to make your selection.

46. **(B)** There is information given in the narrative concerning the assignment of Correction Officer Short. But there is no information available concerning the officer's social security number, date of birth, or height (ht.).

47. **(B)** Pat Oils was the witness identified in the narrative and that account of the incident would most appropriately appear in caption 24.

48. **(D)** The number 207 is the Department Injury Case Number, which should be entered in caption 16.

49. **(A)** Caption 9 should be checked because the officer who was injured was on duty at the time of the injury.

50. **(D)** The number 1493 is the shield number of Correction Officer April Taps who responded to assist Correction Officer Cliff Short. It would not be appropriate to enter such information in any of the captions suggested by the choices.

51. **(C)** About 90 injuries occurred to inmates on Saturday.

52. **(A)** There was no day of the week that had a higher average number of injuries to officers than to inmates.

53. **(B)** Concerning injuries to inmates, there were about 40 on Monday, 48 on Tuesday, 60 on Wednesday, 40 on Thursday, 60 on Friday, 90 on Saturday, and 60 on Sunday. This is a total of about 398 injuries. Since there were about 90 on Saturdays, by dividing 398 into 90 it is determined that Saturday accounted for about 23% of inmate injuries.

54. **(A)** Only about 15 officers were injured on Mondays.

55. **(C)** Approximately 60 injuries happened to officers on Saturdays.

56. **(A)** There were approximately 60 injuries to inmates on both Wednesdays and Fridays.

57. **(A)** There were about 60 inmate injuries on Wednesdays and about 30 officer injuries, which is a ratio of 60 to 30, or 2 to 1.

58. **(C)** There were about 40 inmate injuries on Thursdays, and about 35 officer injuries on Thursdays.

59. **(C)** It is as stated in the procedure.

60. **(B)** Only two persons will be present, and they shall be of the same sex.

61. **(B)** According to the procedure, "No more than two (2) samples will be taken, each in a separate vial."

62. **(B)** Immediately after giving the urine sample, the member being tested should initial the vial sticker.

63. **(D)** Such a request must be made within 60 days of the notification of such results.

64. **(C)** Officer Mast must notify the command center within 1 hour of receiving such information, but the information must involve three complaints. So actually it is within 1 hour of the third complaint which was received at 2000 hours or by 2100 hours.

65. **(D)** Choices A, B, and C are representative of still fires. Choice D describes a contained fire.

66. **(A)** Choices B and C are examples of contained fires and so an immediate notification should be made to the command center by the officer discovering them. The best choice is choice A, which describes a still fire, which should be brought to the attention of the tour commander. Therefore, choice D is incorrect.

67. **(D)** The procedure clearly states, "not for punishment."

68. **(C)** Criminal records are not mentioned in the procedure.

69. **(A)** Remember that the procedure stated that the information was to be recorded in a certain exact order.

70. **(D)** The use of tear gas may be authorized only by the highest ranking senior supervisor on duty. And it is the state corrections commissioner who must be notified of the use of tear gas.

71. **(D)** Mace spray should be aimed at the neck and chin while no closer than 4 feet from the subject. A controlled exit should be identified before spraying the inmate.

72. **(D)** Eyes should not be rubbed nor salves used. Unprotected individuals should not be allowed to remain in contaminated areas more than 5 minutes.

73. **(B)** The prisoner was not immediately searched by Officer Bailes.

74. **(C)** January 05 is the same as 01-05. Using the reference table, 01 is SI and 05 is SE or, as indicated by choice C, SI-SE.

75. **(B)** August 30th is the same as 08-30. Using the reference table, 08 is SO and 30 is AS or, as indicated by choice B, SO-AS.

76. **(A)** October 15 is the same as 10-15. Using the reference table, 10 is IS and 15 is IE or, as indicated by choice A, IS-IE.

77. **(D)** December 16 is the same as 12-16. Using the reference table, 12 is IH and 16 is ID or, as indicated by choice D, IH-ID.

78. **(B)** July 14 is the same as 07-14. Using the reference table, 07 is SC and 14 is IT or, as indicated by choice B, SC-IT.

79. **(C)** The rule allows correction officers to defend themselves against the use or imminent use of force. It does not allow the use of force to defend against future threats such as, "I will get you one day."

80. **(B)** According to the rule, correction officers may not use deadly physical force upon another person unless they reasonably believe that such other person is using or about to use deadly physical force against them or another. Choice B is the only example that satisfies this rule.

81. **(C)** According to the statement there are those who argue that the death penalty is more financially economical than life imprisonment but that argument does not stand up.

82. **(B)** The passage defines a juvenile as being under 16 years of age. Choice B speaks of a person who is already 16 years of age.

83. **(A)** The thinking behind such a rule is that those closest to a person can shed insight into preventative measures that may be taken to avoid repeat suicide attempts.

84. **(B)** If there are supposed to be 20 inmates and only 18 are counted, an escape attempt is probably already in progress.

85. **(C)** The thinking behind this rule is that younger prisoners have a better chance of rehabilitation if they do not associate with hardened adult criminals.

86. **(B)** Punitive segregation, as the term implies, means being kept alone for purposes of punishment. Suicide attempts often occur under such circumstances.

87. **(B)** It is unethical for an officer to use his uniform or any symbol of his public office for personal gain or profit.

88. **(A)** The security needs of a correctional institution demand that constant attention must be directed towards the prevention of contraband, especially weapons, from entering the facility. Choice B is incorrect because inmates are not prevented

from communicating with the outside world. Choices C and D are incorrect because of the use of the absolute words *all* and *entire*.

89. **(A)** The length of the barrel must be less than 16 inches for a rifle to be considered a firearm.

90. **(D)** An unloaded antique firearm is not considered a firearm according to the information provided.

91. **(C)** Neither the ax nor hunting knife nor razor was possessed with an intent to harm another, but the imitation pistol was so possessed.

92. **(C)** Choices A and B are specifically mentioned in the information provided as being in violation of the statute. Possessing deadly weapons also violates the criminal possession of a weapon law. Choice D represents one of the deadly weapons. Choice C mentions an operable revolver that would also have to be loaded to qualify as a deadly weapon.

93. **(A)** Neither choice B nor D indicates an intent to use the item against another. Choice C does not describe a deadly weapon because a firearm must be loaded and operable. Choice A is the answer because a noncitizen of the United States cannot possess any weapon.

94. **(D)** Choices A and B indicate persons who illegally possessed deadly weapons but neither was convicted of the same crime within the last 10 years. Choice C can also be eliminated because there is no evidence of a conviction within the last 10 years. Choice D represents the only offense which should be a felony; it is a felony because there is a previous conviction within the last 10 years.

95. **(D)** It is as stated in the information provided.

96. **(C)** Choice C is the only choice that indicates that someone was aware of a risk and disregarded it.

97. **(B)** It cannot be an assault because no one was actually injured.

98. **(D)** No crime was committed because Correction Officer Parks did not perceive the risk in that she was unaware of the danger involved.

99. **(C)** The serious injury must be to a nonparticipant of the felony, such as a victim.

100. **(D)** The additional sentence cannot be more than 4 additional years. The sentence should be 14 years.

A Final
Word

The Final Countdown

Students have often asked us, "What should we do in the days right before the exam?"

If you have prepared for the exam, you should do well. If you have made an honest effort and practiced answering the various types of questions, especially those that give you difficulty, your score on the exam should reflect how hard you have worked. Every time candidates sit down and prepare with this text, they are actually helping themselves pass the actual exam. In other words, when the actual test is imminent, we tell our students, "Even though you will take your actual exam in a few days, you have already begun passing the exam by studying hard, learning test-taking strategies, and answering practice questions." Think of taking the correction officer examination in terms of appearing at the exam site to collect what is owed you for the hard work you have already done. The real work is over. When you take the exam, you are actually collecting a reward for what you have already done.

Nonetheless, the question is still asked, "What should be done in the days right before the exam and even on the day of the exam?" Here are our recommendations.

SEVEN DAYS BEFORE THE EXAM

About a week before the exam, you should wind down your study efforts and focus on certain areas. By reviewing the Diagnostic Examination you took in the beginning of this text, you should be able to identify those question types that are hardest for you and seem to give you the most difficulty. Devote your preparation time in the days immediately preceding the exam to reviewing these question types along with the chapters dedicated to them, and practicing questions in these areas.

In addition, sometime during the week you should take a trip to the examination site. If you plan to use public transportation, then actually go to the site using public transportation. Find out what stop to get off at, how best to go from the bus or train stop to the site, and what the transportation schedule will be on the day of the examination. Very often the examination will be given on weekends when a reduced transportation schedule is in effect. On examination day do not be left waiting for a train or bus that never comes. All the preparation in the world is of no use if you don't get to the examination site and take the exam.

If you decide to use private auto, drive there during the week that precedes the examination. Make sure you know what parking will be available on the day of the examination. Make sure that your car is in good mechanical order. Many students have someone drive them to the site. If car trouble should then develop, the car can be left with the driver and the candidate can proceed on to the site alone. The bottom line is that you should know where the site is, how to get there, and, if driving, where to park your car safely and legally. A candidate once reported to us that after hurriedly parking his car and entering the examination site, he began the examination. A little while later, he looked up and saw through a window his brand new car being towed away. Apparently because he was unfamiliar with the area and somewhat in a hurry, he had neglected to notice that he had parked his car in a No Parking area. He now had to continue taking the examination with the stress of knowing that, when he finished, he then had to undergo the unpleasant and expensive experience of getting his car back. Taking an examination while you are unnecessarily preoccupied about your car certainly is not a good idea. You should give yourself every advantage and be able to concentrate exclusively on your examination.

SIX AND FIVE DAYS BEFORE THE EXAM

Reread the chapter(s) that deal(s) with what you have found to be difficult. Do not waste your time with areas that are easy for you. For example, if reading comprehension is difficult for you but memory questions seem easy for you, then you should concentrate on the chapter and any questions that deal with reading comprehension. Continuing to study the chapter and practice questions on memory would not be most effective for you in the time remaining before the examination.

FOUR, THREE, AND TWO DAYS BEFORE THE EXAM

During these 3 days review the practice examinations that appear in the text. However, you should make everything as close as possible to actual examination conditions. For example, you should sit in a chair at a desk or table, just like you will be called upon to do when you take your examination. Time yourself and make sure you can finish the practice examinations in the time allotted. Use the same kind of writing implement that you will be required to use on the day of the examination. Usually you will be required to bring and use a No. 2 pencil. If on each of these 3 days, you review the practice examinations under simulated examination conditions, when you finally do take your examination, you will be used to sitting in one place for a fairly long period of time without tiring.

ONE DAY BEFORE THE EXAM

Study the chapter in the text dealing with test taking and how to maximize your test score, especially the part that gives you strategies for handling multiple-choice questions. It is not a good idea to try to cram. Your study efforts are over. You should begin to relax and mentally prepare to take the examination tomorrow.

The night before the exam, you should eat your usual dinner and lay out what you will need the next day including any admission cards, pencils, and other equipment you may want to take the examination. Regarding test-taking equipment, you should have ready anything that the testing agency requires you to bring such as pencils or an identification card. In addition, we recommend bringing a sweater. If the room is too cool, you can wear it. If it becomes too warm you can remove it and sit on it. A sweater can serve to soften a desk seat that can become quite hard and uncomfortable after several hours.

Anything else? We recommend a reliable watch to help you keep track of your time, extra pencils with erasers, and if required a pen to sign your name. If you wear glasses, bring a spare pair and something to clean them with. Some candidates have found it helpful to bring a few packets of alcohol wipes to refresh themselves while remaining in their seats thus saving time by not having to leave their seats. If allowed and it does not present dietary problems, you might want to bring along a candy bar as a quick source of energy during the examination.

Get what is for you a good night's sleep. Some candidates have asked if they should take sedatives to help them get to sleep. It is not recommended unless there is some medical reason and such sedatives have been recommended by a physician. Otherwise, it might be harmful to you the next day, examination day.

The idea is to treat yourself as you would any other day. Remember that you have already taken the steps necessary to help you pass the examination. Exam day is just the day when you demonstrate what you have learned during your many weeks of preparation.

EXAMINATION DAY

Wake up with enough time to dress. It is not a bad idea to have a friend call you to make sure that you are up. Have your normal breakfast and check over whatever test-taking equipment you have decided to take with you.

Upon arriving at the examination site, follow the instructions you receive from the monitors. When directed, proceed to your assigned room and seat. Now is the time to look over your seat. If there are any problems with your seat, report them immediately to the test monitor. Follow all instructions exactly. Relax and get ready to demonstrate what you have learned as a result of your many hours of study and preparation. If you follow what has been outlined for you in this text, you should be successful. Be confident as you open your test booklet. Although there may be slight variations in the question item types from state to state, if you follow what has been outlined for you in this text, you will be successful. Believe in your preparation effort and ability.

Good luck!